HOW TO BE YOUR OWN DETECTIVE

A Step-By-Step, No-Nonsense Guide To Conducting Your Own Investigations

KEVIN SHERLOCK

J. FLORES
PUBLICATIONS

P.O. BOX 830131
MIAMI, FL 33283-0131
1-800-472-2388

HOW TO BE YOUR OWN DETECTIVE by Kevin Sherlock

Copyright © 1993 by Kevin Sherlock

Published by:
J. Flores Publications
P.O. Box 830131
Miami, FL 33283-0131

Direct inquires and/or order to the above address.

This publication is designed to provide accurate and authoritative information in regard to the subject matter covered. It is sold with the understanding that the author and the publisher are not engaged in rendering legal or other professional service. If legal advice or other expert assistance is required, the services of a competent professional person should be sought.

Neither the author nor the publisher assumes any responsibility for the use or misuse of the information contained in this book. The author and publisher specifically disclaim any personal liability, loss, or risk incurred as a consequence of the use and application, either directly or indirectly, of any advice or information presented herein.

ISBN 0-918751-27-6

Library of Congress Catalog Card Number: 92-72150

Printed in the United States of America

Notice

This publication is designed to provide accurate and authoritative information in regard to the subject matter covered. It is sold with the understanding that the author or the publisher are not engaged in rendering legal or other professional service. If legal advice or other expert assistance is required, the services of a competent professional person should be sought.

Neither the author nor the publisher assumes any responsibility for the use or misuse of the information contained in this book. The author and publisher specifically disclaim any personal liability, loss, or risk incurred as a consequence of the use and application, either directly or indirectly, of any advice or information presented herein.

Contents

Introduction

When you were young, you had to take civics courses in school. Teachers taught you the framework of American government. And if your parents cared enough, you also had to take some sort of religious instruction. The nuns or the Sunday School teachers or the rabbis taught you the basics of your faith.

As you grew older, you realized the teachers and the religious people glossed over a lot of rotten things people have done and continue to do. You realized there are a lot of evil people in your neighborhood, in your school, in your work place, and in your hometown. You found out that members of the opposite sex try to manipulate you to get you to do what they want you to do. You learned that while many people are usually fair, they aren't the ones holding down the most powerful jobs in society. A high percentage of those in positions where they can hurt your grades, your wallet, your career, your safety, your freedom, or your life are abusive, jerkish, or both.

You found out advertisements are often lies, and consumer goods are often junk. You found out that co-workers goof off and bosses act like little Hitlers. You found out that back-stabbers and ass-kissers usually go farther than decent folks. You found out that politicians grab for power and money, while the working people are taxed to death to pay for the politicians' promises to loafers, fat cats, and special interests. You found out school officials soak up your tax dollars to graduate functional illiterates. You found out the judges let criminal scum go free while the system hammers the victims. In short, you discovered how real life works.

Now that I've made you feel good about the world around you, I'm going to help you improve it a little bit. I've written this book to help you find out whether the people you have to deal with are good, no good, or somewhere in between. I'm going to show you how to check up on almost anyone you can imagine. And when you've found out good, bad, or indifferent information on the people you want to check on, you can trust them, avoid them, or attack them.

There are many good reasons for you to know how to check people's backgrounds. If you're going to spend money on property, a car, or medical treatment, for example, you'd certainly like to know if the providers are honest and capable. Or what if you want to invest money or go into a business with a partner? You'd like to reassure yourself the guy is reasonably honest and didn't make his money on dope pushing, pimping, or insider trading!

Knowing how to check on someone is good for personal affairs as well. Would you like to know if your lover is hiding an unsavory past (or present) from you? Or what if you suspect your daughter's fiance is a lowlife? Would you like to know his criminal record?

Don't laugh! LBJ used FBI agents to check on one of the young bloods who was sniffing around after his girls; and they found out the guy DID have an undisclosed perversion! And the parents of Maria Barker Tanner—a young Ohio woman whose husband cut off her head with a butcher knife on Valentine's Day 1990—told me Maria found out a lot of negative things about Raymond Tanner after their wedding. They told me they advise parents to check fiances from one end to the other!

But what if someone has *already* done you wrong? Wouldn't you like to find out how often a businessman who has cheated you has been prosecuted or sued for unethical business practices, and then use that information to hurt his business? Or, better yet, wouldn't you like to check on his assets so you'll know what to attach when you go to court against him? Wouldn't you like to trash some shyster lawyer or hack artist doctor by spreading the word about how often former clients have sued him or her for malpractice?

Or what if you're zealous for a cause or angry at a public official? Would you like to find out a politician's voting record? Would you like to know who's giving money to his campaigns, or would you like to know his financial interests? How would you like to be able to track waste, fraud, or abuses in government-funded projects? How would you like to find out what corporations get pinched for health, safety, labor, and/or environmental code violations? Would you like to know who the high-income tax deadbeats are in your area? How would you like to determine how many killers, white-collar criminals, and sex offenders your judges are turning loose on the public through technicalities?

Knowing how to use public records and related data will help you find out information in all of the above listed examples. You can use the info to inform and protect yourself and your loved ones, punish the bad, and maybe fight City Hall and force positive change. The good word on this is that it's not too hard to find out any of the things I just mentioned. The bad word on this is that you're probably going to have to become a competent citizen investigator sooner or later, because the System won't help you, and the media won't, either.

That's why I wrote this book for you. We the people need to know how to find out about those who can affect us. I'm a former newspaper reporter whose entire journalistic training consisted of only three classes at night school. But I routinely beat my competition and wrote good ugly stories about government officials and other lowlifes. And I truly believe the average American, armed with a little intelligence, some righteous anger, and a set of good instructions, can likewise become a competent citizen investigator.

This book will show you how to find out the following things:

- personal data and personal "dirt".
- criminal records.
- lawsuits and other legal entanglements.
- real estate and land use information.
- corporate records and wrongdoing.
- labor, environmental, and health code violators.
- politicians' track records, holdings, and financial backers.
- government taxing, spending, and use of power.
- school spending and quality of education data.
- who's getting money from Uncle Sam, and why.
- coroner records, public health records, and malpractice records.

The book will also show you how to put this information to good use. It will show you how to use this information for business reasons, for personal reasons, or for "good citizenship" (muckraking) reasons. It will show you how to use this information to influence or expose government officials and business people. It will show you how to fight crimes of dishonesty and attack sex offenders. In short, this book can help you become better informed, it can help you protect yourself and your loved ones from the unscrupulous, it can help you expose and punish such people, and it can help you force positive change.

As you might expect, and maybe even HOPE for, I've thrown in a number of war stories about the dirt-digging I did as a reporter and as a researcher. I've also thrown in a lot of other people's investigation war stories, so you won't think I'm on a total ego trip! And I've referred to some well-known political and historical and crime events in which someone like you did some digging and made a difference. I promise you'll find the stories and examples entertaining, but you'll also find them instructive. Since I'm trying to teach you how to research, I've got to show you how it's done. Also, a good prof stimulates the imagination and creativity of his students, and maybe these accounts will do it for you. And finally, I want to give you hope; it IS possible for anyone who tries this to achieve something.

So that's this book in a nutshell. It's a book with a sarcastic humor all its own, and a mission to continue the American muckraking tradition of exposing evil to promote change for good. If you're serious about making changes in your area, or even if you only want to become better informed, I'm sure you'll consider this book one of the best investments you ever made. And if you like the book, tell your friends and acquaintances about how good it is so they'll buy it, tell their friends and acquaintances to do likewise, and help continue another tradition I like... financial reward for me for honest labor!

God bless you all—even you atheists!
— KEVIN SHERLOCK

How To Use This Book

"Let's look at the record."—Al Smith.

The purpose of this book is to show you how to find out information on people and organizations from the public record and from other sources. The purpose of this chapter is to show you what parts of the book cover the public records and other information that exists on those you want to investigate.

This chapter contains a "user-friendly" guide to each of the other chapters of the book. It also contains a word or two on muckraking (documenting evil and exposing it). And it explains some terms that will appear in the book repeatedly, because I wrote this book as a "one size fits all" guide to the public record for the federal, state, and local governments. In practice, most laws and government structures are similar around the country at all levels of government. Only the names have been changed to protect the guilty!

PEACEFUL AND WARLIKE USES FOR THIS BOOK

The Pentagon spenders like to say certain items they want have "civilian" uses as well as "military" uses. That doesn't mean the brass hats will rent out B-52 squadrons to crop-dust the entire Corn Belt in one fell swoop. It means many military items can be used for purposes other than for killing enemy servicemen and civilians.

Likewise, this book has "military" and "civilian" uses. A "civilian" use, by my definition, is research you do to become better informed without hurting anyone else—even if they deserve it! For example, you can use the information you find with this book's help to make health care decisions, figure out where to send your kids to school, buy property and make investments with more confidence, and even do a "background check" on a member of the opposite sex before or after you've gotten involved with this person.

And the "military uses?" A "military" use, by my definition, is any investigating you do to advance your own causes, attack other people's causes, or expose a wrongdoer's deeds to punish him or her in some way. For example, you can use the information you find with this book's help to uncover people's wrongdoing in business, politics, labor, education, health care, and the environment, for starters.

You can find out and expose people's criminal records, you can announce how often they've been sued, and you can drop ugly little tidbits about their personal lives if you're interested in punishing them for what they've done to you or your loved ones. And you can use the information to fight for change in society, from stopping bad development projects to forcing school administrators to do their jobs better to getting bad public officials thrown out of office. And you can use the information to protect society from white-collar criminals and protect women and children from sex offenders.

If you want to use this book for muckraking purposes, use its instructions to find out and publicize negative info on people. However, if you only want to check into someone's background for business or personal reasons and you don't want to trash him or her, follow the instructions in the book anyway, but do so with a "kinder and gentler" approach. Try to overlook my accusatory and suspicious tone of voice if you can.

A USER-FRIENDLY GUIDE TO THIS BOOK

This section describes the information in each of the other chapters of the book. This will help you "lock on" who and what you want to check out.

Attitude Adjustment. This chapter gives you instructions on knowing what records are public records, how to deal with the government employees and others who are the custodians of these records, and the best mindset for "doing research" or "digging dirt."

"THE BASICS" CHAPTERS

These chapters focus on information that applies to everyone, from your lowlife neighbors to the lowlifes in Washington and on Wall Street. Topics include:

Personal Affairs. The chapter titled *Pry Into Personal Affairs* contains a number of sources to check for determining a person's background. Divorce and marriage records, voter registration records, military records, school records, birth and death records, car and driver records, and other info sources all get explanations in this chapter. The chapter also gives advice on how to approach people, who know your target, for information. This information will help you determine the subject's character and credentials; it will also help you accept, avoid, or discredit the subject of your research. As a bonus, this chapter contains public record info on the divorces, dalliances, and dishonest behavior of a number of politicians and other famous Americans.

Criminal Records. The chapter titled *Investigate Criminal Records* shows you how to look up a person's criminal record in state and federal courts. This chapter will help you make decisions about a person's character, and alert folks to him if he's a threat. This chapter also includes an explanation of how the criminal court system works. For training, I included the stories of a couple of murderers whose cases I covered with the help of public records. One of the killers got a stiffer sentence for possessing firearms than he did for killing a man; the other killer beheaded his wife on Valentine's Day and escaped criminal prosecution!

Lawsuit Records. The chapter titled *Civil Courts Hold Uncivil Information* shows you how to find out how often a person or an organization has been involved in lawsuits. This chapter will also help you make decisions about a person's character, and alert folks to him if he's unethical. This chapter also includes an explanation of how the civil court system works. For training, I included the story of an abortion facility I checked on using lawsuit records; I found the place retained the services of a child molester and two often-sued doctors who had evidently killed women.

Real Estate Records. The chapter titled *Excavate Real Estate Information* shows you how to find out who owns property, and who they bought it from. It shows how to perform a title search, how to determine property lines, and how to check for problems like easements and liens and mortgages and mineral rights. Further, it contains information on zoning and land-use planning, and info on building codes. You can use this chapter as a guide to help yourself buy real estate, or uncover shady activity involving land.

"PRIVATE SECTOR" CHAPTERS

These chapters focus on finding out information involving corporate wrongdoing in a number of areas. Topics include:

Private Sector Data. The chapter titled *Public Information on the Private Sector* shows you how to figure out who owns and who operates a corporation, check out the corporation's taxes and licenses, check into professional licenses, and check on other common public records (such as criminal complaints, lawsuits, and agency citations) on businesses. The chapter titled *Cleanup Work on the Private Sector* shows you how to get information from the government agencies which monitor specific types of businesses, and how to monitor public utilities for rate hike plans and lawbreaking. You can use these chapters to decide whether to do business with certain companies; you can also use them to expose the misconduct of your favorite robber barons. As a bonus, these chapters contain information on major corporate wrongdoing, such as the *Exxon Valdez* oil spill, Ford's "exploding" Pintos, and a couple of spectacular defense contract thieveries.

Labor Issues. The chapter titled *This One's for the Working Man* shows you how to check if companies violate worker safety laws, wage laws, or anti-discrimination laws. It also shows you how to find out if companies are union-busters or foot-draggers with worker compensation claims. Further, this chapter covers investigating union corruption and discrimination practices. Finally, this chapter addresses checking on farm worker conditions. You can use the info you find to decide on whether to work for or do business with a company. You can also use the info you find to expose a robber baron employer or a racketeer union boss.

Environmental Issues. The chapter titled *Pure as the Driven Sludge* shows you how to check for whether any business pollutes the environment or misuses land. It also shows you how to find out if government agents are too strict or too lax in enforcing antipollution and land reclamation laws. Further, it shows you how to check on records relating to the nuclear industry's behavior. Finally, it shows you how to fight those who want to close down job-producing industries or put an environmental hazard in your area because they don't want it in their area. You can use the info you find in this chapter as dirt on a polluter or as ammunition in your fight for or against a manufacturer, a utility, or any other land user.

GOVERNMENT CHAPTERS

These chapters focus on finding out information involving government wrongdoing in a number of areas. Topics include:

Politicians. The chapter titled *Dig Dirt on Politicians* covers how to check on politicians' and bureaucrats' financial interests, how to find out who's making campaign contributions to politicians, and how to document politicians' ethics problems. You can use this info to decide on who to vote for or against, or you can use the info to help your favorite politicians and special-interest groups sling mud. As a bonus, this chapter includes a "trip down memory lane" ... a summary of some of the most notorious recent scandals involving presidents, congressmen, and judges.

Public Officials. The chapter titled *Check on How Government Officials Use Power* covers how to use public records to figure out what official actions your local, state, and federal executives, legislators, and judges have been taking. It discusses how to check officials' voting records, executive orders and administrative decisions, judge rulings, and actions of government bodies. The chapter titled *Check on How Government Officials Spend Your Money* shows you how use public records to track government spending, how to check on government officials' behavior in relation to government contracts, and how to uncover various tricks the bureaucrats play with the budget. You can use the info in these chapters to inform yourself on how your public officials operate, monitor their performances, or expose the wrongful behavior of these officials.

Government Grant And Contract Records. The chapter titled *Contracts and Grants* covers how to find out who's getting government grants and contracts. It also shows you how to analyze public records on grants and contracts. Further, it shows you how to check if the grant-getters and contract-winners are defrauding the public, breaching the contracts, or breaking the law in any other way. You can use the info to track down waste and fraud, or document how well or how poorly the contractors are serving the taxpayers. For training, I included the story of how a newswoman broke open the Wedtech scandal by simply doing a little public records research on the company's government contracts. I also wrote about the *Challenger* disaster to show problems NASA and its contractors had in doing business.

PUBLIC HEALTH, EDUCATION, AND SAFETY CHAPTERS

These chapters focus on finding out information on wrongdoing in the education, law enforcement, and health fields. A related chapter on coroner records and other death records focuses on wrongful death cases. Topics include:

Schools. The chapter titled *Flunk Failing Educators* shows you how to use public records and other indicators to grade the performance of teachers and administrators. The first half covers checking on your local school system; it includes instructions on how to find out what kind of education your kids are getting. It also includes instructions on how to figure out tax levies and check into harmful social programs.

The second half focuses on studying problems in colleges, such as quality of education, unethical and wasteful research, student loan mooching, and educator money fraud. You can use the info you find to pick schools for your kids, or simply to monitor your local school's performance. You could also use the info to expose educator wrongdoing, or use it to pressure school authorities to end harmful programs. You can also use the info you find on colleges to get the trustees, the alumni, or government officials to apply a little paddling to the college officials. The chapter includes a story from the public record on the Ivy League price-fixing scandal. It also includes a story on how a citizen's group caught educators in hundreds of school districts across the country misrepresenting achievement test scores to the public.

Police And Prosecutors. The chapter titled *Bust Bad Cops and Shyster Prosecutors* shows you how to find out if police are guilty of excessive ticketing, brutality, wrongful shootings, lawbreaking, perjury, or simple incompetence. This chapter also shows you how to find out if prosecutors abuse plea-bargaining, handle cases poorly, or engage in other forms of unjust conduct. You can use the info to monitor police and prosecutor performance, or you could use it as dirt to demand punishment of police and removal of prosecutors. As examples of problems, I included accounts of how police brutality helped cause the Miami rioting in 1980, how L.A. police mistakes allowed Manson Family members to commit more crimes, how Ohio lawyers wrongly sent a teenager to prison for rape so the real rapist could kill some young women, and how the L.A. prosecutors tried to let one of the Hillside Strangler murderers escape prosecution for his murders.

Health Issues. The chapter titled *Who's Hazardous to Your Health?* covers how to check doctors, clinics, hospitals, and nursing homes for evidence of malpractice, health code violations, and other problems. It also covers checking health care providers for theft of public health care money. Further, it contains instructions for checking on other potential public health problems in the community. You can use this info to help make up your mind on whether to do business with a particular doctor, clinic, hospital, nursing home, eatery, market, or any other outfit regulated by public health people. You can also use it to expose an unsavory doctor, facility operator, or food merchant for the public health menace or thief that he is. For training, I included stories on how a newswoman uncovered women's deaths and massive health code violations at an L.A. abortion facility, and how a newsman figured out how many people serial killer Donald Harvey murdered in a Cincinnati hospital.

Coroner And Death Records. The chapter titled *Grave Digging* covers instructions on how to find and check autopsies, coroner inquests, and death certificates. It also provides information on tying wrongful death cases to people who cause them. Further, it covers checking and interpreting death certificates. And it has a disturbing section on using autopsies and death certificates to give young people and others the ugly truth about suicide and substance abuse; it is here to help responsible folks level with young people and help them avoid these acts. For training, I included an account of how two writers used public documents on the death of Mary Jo Kopechne in Teddy Kennedy's car to write a hard-hitting book about him, and a story on how a United Mine Workers staffer used coroner records and other records to show evidence of a corporate cover-up of a miner's death.

SPECIAL PROJECTS CHAPTERS

These chapters cover special research projects and special citizen action projects. Topics include:

Real Estate Mudslinging. This chapter shows you how to uncover real estate scams, find out hidden owners of property, look up building code violations, figure out tax assessing and appraising, and figure out who's skating on paying property taxes. It also shows you how to marshal your facts to fight zoning and planning battles.

Organized Digging on Organizations . This chapter covers general research tactics you can use on all groups. You'll receive instructions on how to check for an organization's purpose, its leaders' records, which politicians they back, and how they handle money. You can use this info to check on the relative cleanness or dirtiness of an organization for your own information, or you can use it for dirt if you want to fight the organization.

Tap Other Information Sources. This chapter is a "mop-up" chapter that tells you about more information sources you can use.

Fight Crimes Of Dishonesty. This chapter shows you how to use records and observations to determine if people are committing white-collar crimes, bribery, probation violation, perjury, or tax evasion. It also tells you how to take your evidence to the authorities. I included the story of how a Florida accountant used public records to show crime lord money was probably behind a large number of Miami real estate deals. As a bonus, I included the story of how IRS agents used public records and observations to help prove Al Capone was guilty of income tax evasion.

Fight Sex Offenders. This ugly chapter shows you how to use records and observations to determine whether certain individuals pose sexual abuse risks to women and children. It also shows you how to check if government officials are to blame for not protecting the innocent from such abuse. Further, it contains a frightening section on how government employees further sex abuses. And it contains a section which shows you how to fight any commercial sex business. To illustrate my points, I included information from the McMartin Preschool case, the Hillside Strangler case, and the case of homosexual serial killer John Wayne Gacy.

Spread The Dirt. This chapter contains some solid suggestions and proven ideas on how to use the information you've found to make serious trouble for those who deserve it.

ALL YOU WANTED TO KNOW ABOUT MUCKRAKING BUT WERE AFRAID TO ASK

Why Don't Media People Expose More Wrongdoing? The answer is simple. They don't have the time, the money, or—in many cases—the know-how.

As an example of the media's know-how deficiency, I present the media's coverage of the war against Iraq. You were probably as angry as I was hearing the cast of idiots in the media pool ask stupid or life-endangering questions of the military briefers. You saw Peter Arnett sink almost to the level of Hanoi Jane Fonda. Do you want another example? Nationwide scandals in the banking industry showed the newspeople were asleep at the switch, because they were just as surprised about it as everyone else was. Then add in routine news media lack of coverage of our tax-grabbing elected officials, our loafing bureaucrats, and our senile judges, and you get the picture about how little they really do to keep the public informed about wrongdoing!

And the watchdog role of the media will decline even further. Newspapers have been folding like crazy, so even fewer reporters will be available to keep track of government corruption, power abuse, and incompetence at the local level. TV newspeople, limited in the time they have to look at any news items, will continue to give slanted stories and fluffy little features to the public because it's easier than doing real investigative work. And radio news has never been a yard for watchdogs, anyway.

Am I Allowed To Do All This Research? Yep. "Sunshine" laws and "freedom of information" laws have opened up many government records to public access. Courthouse records have been open to the public for ages. Other forms of information this book shows you how to dig for are also either public information or are not greatly protected. Remember, we the people OWN the government's information, because we PAID for it in taxes! The government only stores it for us!

Do The Methods Taught In This Book Work? You bet! I've given these instructions to many "average folks" who had never received any formal journalism or investigation training before, and they've discovered quite a few unsavory things about the people they were investigating. Using the information they found, they were able to save themselves a lot of trouble in buying land, in dealing with shifty businessmen partners, and dealing with other criminal types. They were also able to cause bad politicians, bad businessmen, and bad people in their communities a whole lot of trouble.

Why Should I Do This Kind Of Spadework? There are two good reasons. One is that it will cost less for you to do your own research on many items than it will for you to hire someone else. The more important reason is if you want a job done well, do it yourself. If a bad situation needs changing, you can bitch all you want and watch it continue, or you can put on your digging clothes, dig up the info you need to prove why the situation needs changing, then contact the right people to get the changes accomplished. What other motivation do you need than making the world a better place for your loved ones?

What If I Don't Want To Mess With It? Then, brother ...or sister, you deserve to get dumped on!

THE RULES OF THE ROAD

Al Smith, who I quoted at the start of the introduction, was the reform governor of New York and the first Catholic to win a major party's presidential nomination. Smith, who grew up in poverty, built on his humble beginnings to rise to high office. Smith, who was known as the "Happy Warrior", owed much of his success to his anger at those who picked on his kind—the working poor. And he owed much of his success to his ability to harness his anger. He researched the public record well so he always seemed to have the information he needed to convince others to go along with his way of thinking. Follow Al's example. "Look at the record" using the methods in this book, find info, then put it to use.

This book is meant to be a "one size fits all" guide for people in all 50 states. State laws often parallel federal laws. Most states have the same kinds of laws, but different names for government officials and agencies. For example, some of you readers may know your county (or parish) elected officials as supervisors, or commissioners, or freeholders, or fiscal court members. And you may know your felony court judges as superior court judges, or common pleas court judges, or circuit judges, or county supreme court judges.

So it follows that—even though all states tend to make the same kinds of records available to the public—each state has its own unique set of statutes concerning criminal records, lawsuit records, regulation of businesses, labor laws, environmental laws, property records, tax records, personal records, and the like. This means you will have to find out the names of the appropriate government agencies in your county and state. It won't be hard; just follow the instructions in this book. I may not be able to nail down every special situation that applies to your research needs, but I will at least point you in the right direction. You'll get one break—laws concerning federal officials and agencies are the same in all 50 states.

Throughout this book, I wrote the instructions as if you were only doing research in your area. Actually, you can get information from officials, agencies and courthouses across this country with a letter or a phone call. Keep that in mind when you do research.

I've said enough about what this book is going to say. It's now time to let you tear into it. Happy hunting!

Attitude Adjustment

This chapter comes before all of the other chapters in the book because attitude is such an important part of research. Knowing what kinds of public records are available to you as a private citizen will help you focus your investigating and help you overcome government employees and others who try to withhold such information from you. Knowing how to deal with government employees and others when you are searching for information is very important; it means you can find what you need with a minimum of hassle. Developing the proper mindset for digging will help you do it properly and keep you from losing heart.

KNOW WHAT RECORDS ARE PUBLIC

A very important ground rule in the research field is FORMAL ACTION EQUALS PUBLIC RECORD. This means if a government agent or a law enforcement official has filed criminal or civil charges against your target, the charge and the outcome of the action are public record. YOU HAVE THE RIGHT TO SEE THOSE RECORDS.

Likewise, any time someone applies for a license, a permit, a government contract, a grant, or certain types of tax breaks, the paperwork the person files is a public record. Anyone whose business comes under some sort of government regulation has to file paperwork that is public record. And many organizations whose activities are monitored somewhat by the government, like labor unions, foreign agents, special interest groups, and nonprofit organizations, are the subjects of many kinds of public records.

Further, when someone is born, marries, divorces, buys a car, buys property, registers to vote, joins the military, dies, or does any number of other things, the government has some sort of record on it. And most often, the record is open to the public.

However, many government records are confidential and are not open to the public. For example, if lawmen investigated a person, but didn't take any formal action against him (such as filing a criminal charge or a lawsuit, seeking a restraining order or an injunction, or issuing a citation), then the record of the investigation is not public. One reason for this is to protect the rights of the suspect. Another reason is to

keep secret what info the government has on the suspect. A third reason is to protect witnesses and informers.

Industry records in government custody that are usually confidential are proprietary information companies have to submit to compete for government contracts, prices companies quote the government when submitting bids (before—but not after—the contract is awarded), some paperwork on federally-regulated banks, certain data relating to mineral exploration, and other industry trade secrets. Most tax returns are confidential. Certain government personnel files and other personnel data, and some memos related to agency policy discussions are confidential.

Records pertaining to national security matters and some questions of personal privacy are also confidential. As you can imagine, government officials routinely abuse the law when refusing to disclose information on these grounds. Government officials are notorious for wrapping personal misconduct in the cloak of "national security." And many doctors and public health officials withhold information or issue false medical information, or hide behind privacy laws in other ways... especially when AIDS or medical malpractice is involved.

Then there are some records that are available to some people, but not to others. These are called "need to know" records, because the average person doesn't have the need to see them, but a person whose job (like a defense attorney, reporter, bail bondsman, or doctor) or circumstance (crime victim, crime suspect, party in a lawsuit) puts him or her in a position to need access to these records.

The chapters of this book will cover many types of public records. There will be some differences in public records keeping and disclosure from state to state and from agency to agency. For detailed information on what is and isn't public information in your state, you can contact your state's press association (get its phone number from your local paper) and order its handbook on laws concerning public records and news reporting. The press handbook will explain your state's public records codes in a lot more detail. On the federal level, the Freedom of Information Act (5 *U.S.C.* 552 in the federal law books) regulates what federal records are public. Your state's press association can give you more detailed information about this federal government public records law.

Knowing the law will help you get records you are entitled to if some clerk or agent tries to deny you access to them. Knowing how to get what you need without getting snotty about it will keep your working relationships with the clerks and agents in good working order.

Once you've gained access to the records you need, YOU'LL NEED TO MAKE PHOTOCOPIES OF THOSE DOCUMENTS THAT WILL SHOW THE TRUTH ABOUT YOUR TARGET. You'll be able to do it yourself, or the clerks will have to do it for you, depending on the agency. Getting public records copied can be inexpensive to very expensive. I've paid anywhere from a dime a page to a dollar a page, depending on where I've done digging. But having copies of these records is the only way you can have your own concrete evidence on someone's track record. So grin and bear it when the clerks hand you the bill ...anything worth having is worth paying for.

BEHAVE YOURSELF WHEN IN PUBLIC

When you were a kid, you learned the Golden Rule. And if everyone lived by the Golden Rule—do unto others as you would have them do unto you—I wouldn't have needed to write this book. But the Golden Rule is still a good rule for you to live by when you're doing research. Why? Because being nice to government employees and others who are in a position to help you makes your job as a citizen investigator a lot easier.

Many government employees are quite capable, but others are not so good at their jobs. Also, despite public opinion, many clerks and agents are overworked. Further, some bureaucrats are sticklers about policy, while others will routinely (and often incorrectly) deny you access to public records because they want to cover their backsides, or because they don't know the law and are too lazy to look it up. In my own experiences, most government employees have given me the help I've needed, and some have gone out of their way to help me.

At any rate, the key ground rule in behavior toward others is TREAT PEOPLE, ESPECIALLY THE LOW-LEVEL CLERKS, WITH AT LEAST AS MUCH RESPECT AS YOU WOULD WANT. Comply with their agency's procedures, and be calm about their mistakes. Always assume (or at least act like you feel) the clerks are doing their best. Remember, your fight is with your target, not with the clerks or their bosses.

If you run into trouble with a clerk, resolve the problem as calmly and as pleasantly as you can. If the clerk is a total jerk or a fool, ask to see the clerk's supervisor. Don't hesitate to ask to see a clerk's supervisor, but be sure you're right, and don't get huffy about it when you ask. Complain *reasonably* and *quietly* to the clerk's supervisor, not to the clerk. And don't ridicule the clerk when the supervisor handles things your way. Your poise and self-control will help keep the clerk's resentment to a minimum.

On the other hand, if a clerk really puts out for you, make sure you let her know you appreciate how well she served you. Also, make sure you let her supervisor know what a good job she did for you. Doing good for those who help you will help you down the road. Besides, giving a good person a boost is good in itself!

Another ground rule is DON'T TIP YOUR HAND. YOUR BUSINESS ISN'T ANYONE ELSE'S. So act as if the bureaucrats are friends of your target or are enemies of your cause. Why? Some of them *ARE*, and they don't wear badges saying so! Don't spill your guts to the clerks about why you're looking up all kinds of bizarre information on people. Since you have a right to those records, all you have to do is ask for them. If a clerk gets nosy about your intentions and tries to put you on the spot, say only that you're doing research for "school" or for "the boss" or give some other nonspecific answer. Likewise, when you ask an agent for help in obtaining or deciphering a certain kind of record, say as little about your project as possible.

It goes without saying these rules also apply to you when you deal with people who aren't government employees. But I thought I'd say so anyway.

THE BEST MINDSET FOR RESEARCH

Since I'm by nature and experience a suspicious guy, I've always assumed people were up to no good. And I know a lot of you out there are naturally suspicious, too. Why else would you want a book like this? And since you people are already with the program, you know there's dirt on many people.

But I know some of you who are reading this book are good guys and sweetheart gals—good, wholesome, God-fearing people who have always played fair and have treated others with charity. If there were more like you out there, I wouldn't have had to write this book! You're trusting people who have tended to avoid trouble. However, something has come up in your life... like an injustice done to you or your loved ones, or a cause you care deeply about, or the need to know the facts about people, businesses, or organizations. You are going to have to adopt a mindset that is probably foreign to your thought process—PEOPLE ARE NO GOOD UNLESS YOU CAN PROVE OTHERWISE.

Now that I've said that, I'll lay down another mindset ground rule that may seem contradictory to my first mindset ground rule. DON'T MAKE UP YOUR MIND UNTIL YOU'VE GOT ALL THE FACTS. You may KNOW the people you're checking on are scum, but you need all the documentation before you publicly say so. The documents you find may confirm or disprove your suspicions. If you're able to let your common sense overrule your emotions when you don't find exactly what you want, you'll resist the temptation to smear someone without having the facts to back it up. (Defamation, libel, and slander suits are ugly things you don't want.) You'll also be able to evaluate if you need to do follow-up digging to really nail your target to the wall, wait awhile until your target makes a mistake, back away from the investigation on grounds you can't prove a specific item of wrongdoing, or end an investigation on grounds your target really isn't the unethical law-breaking jerk you thought he was. (Do I hear sarcastic laughter out there?) In short, having an open mind will maintain or build your credibility and keep you out of trouble.

A mindset ground rule that goes hand-in-hand with the above ground rule is DEVELOP THE PATIENCE OF A VULTURE ALONG WITH THE AGGRESSIVENESS OF A SHARK. You might not have all the dirt you need on your target yet. Work aggressively to get it. But in the meantime, consider a person who is bad will probably continue to do rotten things... and if you're patient, you'll get solid evidence of it once it surfaces.

Another related mindset ground rule is DEVELOP A SENSE FOR WHAT IS LEGAL AND WHAT IS ILLEGAL. Usually, unethical behavior is also illegal behavior, and this holds true in business and government circles. But there are exceptions— known as loopholes—in which unethical behavior enjoys political protection, so it's legal. Having a sense of what the law allows and what it won't allow will help you focus on proving whether your target has violated some law. (You can still use info on someone's legal but unethical behavior as far as questioning his character is concerned.) Having this feel can also save you problems caused by incorrectly reporting someone for lawbreaking when he didn't do anything illegal!

Yet another mindset ground rule is HAVE OR DEVELOP STREET SMARTS. Reporter M. Harry said it best when he said street sense included the ability to fabricate stories as needed without being self-conscious, the ability to sense when others are lying, a nose for trouble, and a sense for what is a scam and what is legitimate. I'd add that street smarts also involves sensing how people will try to take advantage of others without getting into trouble.

I know some of you might have problems with telling a fib or two now and then. I look at it this way: Putting out the truth about bad people or protecting yourself and others doesn't mean you can't use strategy and street smarts. You God-fearing folks out there—consider the rich tradition of the Scriptures. God's servants often used craft to defeat the enemies of His chosen people and do His will. This applied to women heroes such as Jael, Judith, and Miriam just as much as it did to the men! Also recall that Pope John XXIII, when he was a Vatican envoy, baptized thousands of Jews to save them from the Nazis even though he had no intention of making them stay in the Catholic Church!

A key mindset ground rule is HARNESS YOUR ANGER. There are times when you will have to cover your true feelings when you do investigating. Stifle your ego and do what you have to do. Imagine yourself as a guerrilla warrior who uses cunning and iron discipline to attack the enemy while his guard is down, then sneaks away before the enemy can fight back. Not only will this mindset make your digging more interesting, but it will keep you on your toes when you are searching through records, dealing with government employees or other possibly hostile sources, or performing surveillance.

On the subject of anger, don't be ashamed you've got it. Anger proves your conscience is still alive. In fact, you have to RELY on your anger at the wrongdoing of your targets to do your digging properly. A healthy sense of anger gives you the courage and persistence to do the digging, even the tedious, hard, and risky digging. It is NOT wrong to use the dirt you've dug to punish and suppress evil. Consider this: Jesus Christ didn't like crooked businessmen any better than you or I, and He had the guts to run the money worshipers out of the Temple!

The last mindset ground rule is this: YOU CAN DO GOOD RESEARCH WORK, IF ONLY YOU TRY. With this book's instructions, and with your own drive and common sense, you will be able to accomplish something. Don't make lame excuses for yourself; there are a lot of people out there with more imperfections than you who are *doing* instead of wishing.

The Basics

Pry Into Personal Affairs

Once upon a time, I did a favor for a lovely lady who worked as a clerk for one of my clients. I dug into my stockpile of 1950s and early 1960s rock'n'roll records and made for her a tape of an album I had of some girl-group singers who were popular in that era. I mentioned this small act of kindness to my mom and dad when I called them a couple of days later. Instead of saying, "How nice!" like most other moms, MY mom responded, "I think one of those girls was a mobster's mistress!"

I had to laugh. If there's dirt on anyone, Mom and Dad know about it. I inherited my nose for dirt from them.

Then there's the story of a lady friend of mine (whom I'll call Carmen Cienfuegos) who lived what many would call a double life. Her church and charity group friends knew her only as an enthusiastic witness to God and a caring friend to unwed mothers, poor people, and the elderly. But I also knew this lovely Latina as a high-energy exotic dancer. Every now and then, I served as her escort when she had a gig to work. She didn't strip or do anything immoral in her act, but I can testify she was an uninhibited showwoman who could really turn on the men in an audience, and make the women in the audience more than a little jealous!

Now I understood Carmen was an honest entertainer making an honest living with her God-given talent, but some of her churchgoing friends might have been scandalized to hear about her career as a dancer. On the other hand, many of her enthusiastic male admirers would be disappointed to find out she was a woman of good character!

What's the point of this little anecdote? Simply this—dirt is in the eye of the beholder!

This book contains all kinds of ways to find information on the powerful, such as government officials, business and labor figures, high-income professional people, and cause group leaders. Other chapters will cover the specifics of digging dirt on those kinds of people. This chapter's focus is on using public records and other sources to dig up the personal dirt that exists on many people in their private lives, whether they are co-workers of yours, or they are rich and powerful people like Teddy Kennedy.

For "civilian" purposes, you can use the techniques in this chapter to check on someone's background before you or a friend or a loved one gets involved with that person for business or social reasons. After all, your savings, your reputation, your safety, and your heart are terrible things to entrust to the wrong person. The "military" uses for these techniques are obvious; they all revolve around finding and exposing a person's rotten behavior.

PERSONAL INFORMATION BASICS

Private detectives, investigative reporters, and G-men follow the same process in checking on other people. THEY LEARN THE BASICS ABOUT THEIR TARGETS. And believe it or not, such information isn't really all that hard to find. The public record and people who know your target can give you these basics. Let's cover a few, for starters.

How would you find out where the person was born? Birth certificates and voting registration records contain this info; this chapter will cover checking these documents. Also, people who know your target might tell you.

How would you find out where the person went to school? School yearbooks and school registrars are good sources for this info. If your target works for someone else, the company's personnel officer might give you this info. If your target needs a license or some other certificate for his profession, the state board which regulates his profession will have information on his schooling.

How would you find out the person's work history? Personnel officers of companies and government agencies will have this info on their employees; they sometimes give it out to people who call to say they're verifying the target's loan application. If your target is a union member, his union will have this info on him. Also, those who say they're "headhunters"— people who find good white-collar workers and highly-skilled blue-collar workers for business clients for a living—can get many people to tell them their job histories. After all, the people might think the "headhunter" could get them much better jobs!

How would you find out if the person needs a license or a certificate for his profession, or if he needs a security clearance? State boards which regulate professions have such info on your target if he needs a license or certificate from them. Also, the personnel people of the person's company or the appropriate government agency's people can tell you if he holds a government clearance.

How would you find out about the person's property and business holdings? Chapters on real estate and the private sector go into detail on tracking down owners of land and companies. Those who hold government positions have to disclose their holdings; the chapter on politicians and government officials covers how to gain access to this info. Personnel officers and bankers have been known to reveal such info to those who call to say they're verifying the target's loan application or business proposal.

How would you find out about the person's marital status, his/her divorce record, dependents, and other family obligations? The sections on marriage and divorce records will cover this info. Also, voter registration records have some info. A target's friends and associates are good sources of this info. And people who say they're political pollsters or phone solicitors sometimes get such info from the target when they call to ask questions or peddle certain types of goods and services.

How would you find out if the person is active in an organization, or if he broke with the organization? Calling the organization should provide you with the answer. Also, people tend to talk about their organizational activities to those who say they're political pollsters if the so-called pollsters ask the right questions about people's backgrounds. Further, friends and associates of the target would know.

How would you find out if the person is active in a religion or a cult, or if he broke with the religion or cult? The process for finding this out is similar to the process for finding out your target's status in an organization.

How would you find out if the person is active in politics, and find out what his views are? A chapter in the book on politicians and a chapter in the book on government officials' use of power will cover finding out much of this info. Also, calling local political parties and groups will turn up much of this info. Also, those who say they're political pollsters can often find out the target's political views and political ties simply by calling and asking!

How would you find out if the person ever served in the Armed Forces? Service records contain this information. A section in this chapter will cover gaining access to these documents.

How would you find out the person's driver and vehicle registration info? Driver and car records kept by a state's motor vehicle bureau contain this info. A section of this chapter will cover gaining access to these documents.

How would you find out if the person has a criminal history? The chapter on criminal records will tell you how to find out this info.

How would you find out if the person gets sued or sues others in court? The chapter on lawsuits will tell you how to find out this info.

How would you find out other interesting or sleazy details on the person...like if they're dopers, alcoholics, homosexuals, lechers, wife-beaters, child abusers, sex offenders, dead beats, drug pushers, fences, welfare cheats, or some other kind of dirtbag, for example? Or how would you find out if someone has "entanglements" like an ex-wife or a current lover? Detective manuals and "lover's spying" books can give you further pointers on finding out such info. (The scope of this book is far wider than just snooping on people's personal lives, and snooping has been covered by many authors, so I'm making reference to such books as other resources for you.) Also, people who know your target, like family members, friends, co-workers, ex-spouses, ex-lovers, and nosy neighbors, can also tell you what you need to know if you use the right approach on them. Other sections of this chapter will talk more about these topics.

INTERVIEWING PEOPLE FOR DIRT ON THEMSELVES AND OTHERS

People like Kitty Kelley get dirt on celebrities by interviewing (or by having other people interview) friends, associates, co-workers, enemies, and other people in a position to know about the celebrity. You can do this, too and put together your own unauthorized biography on your target!

Muckraker M. Harry agrees wholeheartedly. In his underground classic *The Muckraker's Manual*, he recommends talking to targets' business associates, organization associates, neighbors, and others to get info on the target. And we agree on contacting the person's enemies for dirt on him or her. Harry also dropped one last dime; he said, "Knowledge of what the subject is doing in his or her life will enable you to develop a feel for what opportunities he/she has to get money illegally and what set of laws regulate the subject's life." I couldn't have said it any better myself.

Dirt-digging heavyweight Louis Rose also agrees. In his book *How to Investigate Your Friends and Enemies*, he quoted an article which Bob Olmstead wrote for the *Chicago Sun-Times* about how a 17-year-old high school kid was able to dig up a lot of information on an ACLU official. He did this because the ACLU official wanted to see how much info the kid could gather on him to test privacy provisions of certain institutions.

The youth found out from ACLU employees what the official's salary, address, and phone number were, and an ACLU secretary also told him where the official banked. Posing as a prospective employer, the kid called the ACLU official's landlady and she gave him a lot of answers about the official's financial and personal situations. She also got the trendy complex's doorman to give the youth more info on the official. He got the official's checking account balance from his bank by having a friend at a brokerage house make a bogus credit check on him.

The teen could have gotten other information from ACLU personnel sources, but since he already knew a little of the official's past, he contacted the man's previous employers and got information on him from these people. He then suckered the official by sending him a questionnaire on a radio station's letterhead under the ruse of getting some information for a news show. The questionnaire, with some well-chosen open-ended questions, and many personal questions worked in, caught the ACLU official like a fly on flypaper. He volunteered a ton of info about his past, as well as his personal views on a number of topics.

The ACLU official said he was flabbergasted and angry when he found out how thorough a job the kid had done on him. He said he felt dumb for falling for the kid's sucker questionnaire, but he was angry that other people would have volunteered so much info on him without verifying who was asking for it, and why.

In my own experiences, I have played a prospective employer, a private eye, a creditor, a banker who was involved in making business loans and home loans, a landlord, a businessman who wanted to give people prizes I said they'd won in a promotion, a former boyfriend, a newspaper reporter, a freelance writer, a political pollster, a "headhunter", an appliance delivery man, and a potential client in order to get personal info on targets. There's nothing that says you can't do this, either. One word of caution—I don't recommend you try to impersonate a police officer or other government law-enforcement agent. You could wind up in jail if you get caught.

DIVORCE DIRT

Some of the meanest dirt available on your target will be in divorce records. Why? Because husband and wife have to justify why they are divorcing, and why they should keep as much property from the marriage as possible. Remember the Roxanne Pulitzer divorce? Her ex-husband Peter claimed she cheated on him, had sex with lesbians, used drugs like crazy, had sex with race car driver Jackie Ickx on the beach in front of her toddlers, and took part in group-grope bed seances with a psychic, a dozen or so friends, and a trumpet! Roxanne, for her part, accused Peter Pulitzer of the comparatively minor offenses of drug dealing and having incestuous sex with his 26-year-old daughter.

You may write off such cases to the crazy behavior of the rich and famous, who think they're above the law. But everyday people engage in bizarre behavior, too. Husband and wife both accuse each other of sexual infidelity, sexual frigidity or impotence, molesting or beating the hell out of the kids, drug or alcohol addiction, and physical or mental cruelty. Every now and then, one of the parties (the peabrained one) gets sucked into a religious cult or a witches' coven, and the non-pea-brained spouse wants out of the marriage for himself/herself and for the protection of their children.

Divorce cases cause the release of other types of ugly information. For example, in his book *Citizen Jane*, Christopher Andersen noted when Jane Fonda and Tom Hayden were divorcing, Hayden reportedly threatened to expose Fonda as a female Scrooge if she didn't come up with more money in the settlement. Supposedly, Andersen wrote, Ms. Jane paid performers in her workout videos minimum wages and was a tightwad when it came to giving out pay raises to her workout studio employees. (Andersen, earlier in the book, wrote that three women sued Lady Jane in 1983 on sexual discrimination grounds for reportedly paying them $2.50 an hour less than men who did the same work at her workout studio. They won roughly $1000 apiece from her, he reported.) Andersen also said the publicizing of Ms. Jane's multimillion dollar stock portfolio would embarrass her as an anticapitalist activist.

In some states, divorce records are private, but in many states they are public records. And the information you can find on a target in a divorce file could kill his or her reputation. Mean divorce proceedings sometimes hurt even the powerful. For example:

- Edward Brooke, a former senator from Massachusetts, lost a re-election bid in 1978 amid allegations he lied about his assets to keep his ex-wife from getting them.
- Julian Bond's estranged wife said he was a doper after he lost a 1986 primary race for a Georgia Congressional seat. (During the race, his opponent and fellow civil rights activist John Lewis dared him to take a urine test for drugs, and he wouldn't.) But Alice Bond didn't stop at naming

Julian as a coke freak; she also claimed Julian's longtime friend Andrew Young—the mayor of Atlanta—liked to snort a little white powder every now and then as well. Young soon found himself in front of a grand jury. Even though Alice Bond later recanted, Julian Bond, the one-time aide to Dr. Martin Luther King, has not had the influence he once held.

- Sooner or later, someone is going to pry into the 1978 divorce of Virginia governor Douglas Wilder.

Unfortunately, racism is alive and well in politics, because many white politicians have retained power despite being involved in far uglier domestic problems than these men, who are black. Teddy Kennedy comes to mind immediately. So does Gerry Studds; he admitted to having sex repeatedly with a teenage boy page, and to propositioning two other boy pages, and nothing substantial happened to him.

Gary Hart doesn't count; he had to quit the presidential race in 1987 for stupidity, not poor morals. Hart's infidelities were known to many, but he was still dumb enough to dare the media to catch him cheating on his wife. Nelson Rockefeller doesn't count, either; he was out of office at the time of his fatal heart attack, which some speculate happened while he was reportedly having a tryst with his gal Friday.

Or consider this: Marion Barry, the black mayor of Washington, was set up in a sting operation in which he reportedly used a little crack with a shady lady, then was prosecuted. Meanwhile, Barney Frank, a white Congressman whose place of work is Washington, admitted to paying a male prostitute for sex, then letting him become a more or less live-in lover. The male prostitute started running his call-boy service for homosexuals out of Frank's apartment, and Frank (of whom brassy Brooklyn Dodger manager Leo Durocher might sneer, lives "the 'chaste' life of a politician") claimed he was unaware of it for 18 months. But BF was not made a target by any law-enforcement types. Are federal law enforcement officials racists? Or are they limpwrists? Or are they just stupid? You be the judge.

If your target has ever gone through a divorce in your county, you'll usually find the case file in the court clerk's office of your county courthouse. Since a divorce is basically a high-dollar lawsuit, the clerks treat it the same as the other high-dollar cases. Look through the case paperwork just like you would check a civil lawsuit file per the instructions in the chapter on lawsuits. Check the documents for why the divorce took place, note any bizarre and hateful charges that will make your target look like a jerk or a tyrant or a lowlife or worse, and check what property is involved. Even if the divorce was an "it's been swell" divorce instead of a "thank God and Greyhound you're gone" divorce, you can always use the info on what real estate or businesses or bank accounts or other property your target owns. Make photocopies of the documents that contain this information.

You may find out (by searching marriage records, voter registration records, court records, or by hearing from someone who knows) that your target was divorced outside your county. In this case, contact the court clerk of the county in question, and find out the procedure for getting photocopies of the divorce records.

VOTER REGISTRATION VITALS

My grandpa Charlie, who came to Chicago from Ireland in the early 1900s, was a big Mayor Daley man. Yeah, Richard Daley SENIOR, probably the last real man to hold public office in America. Some people kidded Grandpa Charlie about voting "early and often" and about packing the voter rolls with names from the tombstones in the graveyards. But Grandpa Charlie laughed back and said, "A crooked stick has dealt many a blow." He served as a precinct captain, and when I was a kid, I'd help him get out the vote.

Grandpa Charlie, who had been a police detective before he suffered a car wreck that ruined his health, cost him his police career, and nearly took his life, was like the Good Shepherd. He knew his voters and they knew him. Why? Because he had taken the time to case his precinct. He had gotten voter registration rolls for his precinct, and from these, he got a lot of information he needed to know about the people in the precinct. I learned from Grandpa Charlie that there was a lot of good info on people in voter registration records.

Voter registration records contain a large amount of personal information on people, and they are public information in most states. Most people are registered to vote, even though they don't always do so. Hey, with the current herd of misfits running for public office, can you *blame* 'em?

If your target is registered to vote, his voter registration record will contain his residence and his previous residence, unless he has lived at his present residence for many years. It may also note his birthday and age, his birthplace, his political party, his Social Security number, his personal appearance (height, weight, race), and the names of his spouse and children.

Here's how to use the voter registration records in your county:

First find out the name of the voter registration agency in your county by checking the county government listings in your phone book. Then call the agency. Ask the clerk where the voter registration records are kept and how you would go about looking at them.

Then, go to the voter registration agency office. Ask to see the voter registration records. These documents, which are in the form of a computer printout or a series of microfilm cards or a handwritten sheaf of papers, will usually contain the names of all registered voters in the county by name, address, precinct, party, and voter registration number.

Look up your target on the voter registration records. Write down his name, address, precinct, date of birth, and voter registration number. This information is good to have, and can also serve to distinguish him from other people with the same name. Then scan the voter registration records; try to locate other people with the same last name who live at the same address as he does. These people will usually be his wife, older children, or older relatives who are living at his house. Note ages of these people; for example, checking a woman's age will probably tell you if she's your target's wife or his daughter. (But if you're checking on someone like Ari Onassis or Strom Thurmond, the older woman might be his daughter!)

Often the record will show the target's moves within the area, and where he came from if he's not a native. In the case of a woman, her name changes will show up on her registration form. In the case of a man, the changing names of women who live at his residence could indicate wife deaths or divorces or new marriages. Make notes of all these items and of any other info that could come in handy.

BIRTH, DEATH AND MARRIAGE RECORDS

Marriage Records. Marriage licenses are public records. They are usually kept at the county clerk's office in each county. Your target's marriage license should be there if he got married in the county. Marriage licenses include some useful information about a target's personal life. Often, for both husband and wife, a marriage record will include the date of birth, place of birth, names of parents, some form of identification, residence, occupation, number of minor children, and previous marriages and divorces. In some states, the court(s) where previous marriage(s) and divorce(s) took place and the record or case numbers of these previous affairs will also appear on the marriage record. I bet Liz Taylor's marriage record by now probably reads like *War and Peace!*

I've got one little piece of historical dirt on a marriage record and a related divorce case involving one of our Presidents. In 1790, a rich man named Lewis Robards filed divorce papers against his wife Rachel Donelson Robards with the Virginia legislature, which was the law in those days. But the legislators sent him word to file the case in a Kentucky court. Why? Because Kentucky, where he and Rachel lived, was due to break off from Virginia and become a new state. However, Robards decided to tell everyone he got his divorce, and he sent Rachel on her way.

Within a year Rachel Donelson would marry again. Her new husband was a hot-blooded young Irish-American adventurer from the Carolinas named Andrew Jackson. People would eventually celebrate Jackson's victory over British invaders in the battle of New Orleans, and would later elect him to be President. But at this time in his life, he was just a young man in love with a young woman. (And believe it or not, a Catholic priest married the couple even though neither was Catholic and Rachel was a divorcee. Why? Andrew and Rachel married in Mississippi, which was then under the rule of the Catholic Spanish. And maybe the priest thought that Rachel, an unwilling teenage bride in her first marriage, would have probably been qualified for an annulment anyway. But I digress.)

Jackson, though a lawyer, didn't check to see whether Rachel's divorce had become final. Two years later, Lewis Robards finally did file for divorce in a Kentucky court. Since Rachel wasn't informed of the suit, and the divorce suit notice was never published even in a Kentucky newspaper, she didn't answer the suit, so he won it. The paperwork in the lawsuit was ugly; Robards accused Rachel of deserting him and of living adulterously with Andrew Jackson.

Andrew and Rachel went through a civil marriage ceremony a couple of months later to clear up the court paperwork. But people seeking to tar Jackson throughout his long public life often accused him of being a wife-stealer and accused Rachel of being a shameless hussy. These false and malicious accusations crushed poor Rachel's spirit; people said the strain of bearing up under these lies for more than 30 years caused her to die of sorrow in 1828, the year Andrew first won the Presidency. Andrew, from the day he learned of Robards' trickery until the day he was too old and feeble to fight, would feel the need to use his fists, his cane, his sword, and his handguns to punish these slanderers who kept hurting his wife. Jackson injured many men, and killed at least one man for his wife's honor.

Even back then, lawyer incompetence, divorce proceeding conniving, and mudslinging were part of the American scene. So you see, dirt-digging and revenge are as American as the Flag!

Birth And Death Records. Birth and death certificates are public records in most states. Check in with the vital statistics people of any county's public health department to find out how to gain access to these records.

A person's birth certificate will contain his or her date of birth, place of birth (city or township), and location of birth (hospital or home, for example). The birth certificate will also contain info on his parents, such as their names, addresses, birthplaces, dates of birth, marital status, and ethnic backgrounds. Some birth certificates also list the parents' occupations and education levels, and will list some medical info on the mother.

A word to the wise: Usually, these records are good, but sometimes they have bad information on them. Sometimes a baby is born in one state but the parents record the birth certificate in another state for insurance reasons, for establishing residency for government entitlements, to protect the mother, or for some other reason. Sometimes the parents are illegal aliens whose only crime is wanting to come to the U.S., work hard, live in freedom, and further the American dream. If they can claim one of their children was born in the U.S., they can stay, so a child born in Asia or Africa or Latin America or Ireland or Eastern Europe suddenly gets a birth certificate listing him as American-born. Adoptive parents who adopt privately from a relative or from a young woman or girl who can't raise the child sometimes present newborns as their own to avoid bureaucratic red tape.

Sometimes a birth record is altered to protect a prominent person. In his book *It Didn't Start With Watergate*, Victor Lasky recalled a George McGovern supporter may have clumsily eradicated the South Dakota Democrat's name from a birth certificate during the 1972 election campaign because it showed he may have been the illegitimate father of a child. The mother, reached for comment, said she knew McGovern, but denied he was the father of the child. The editor of the newspaper in the city where the child was born tried to have the matter investigated, Lasky said, because he was angry someone had tampered with a public record.

As for death records, this book has a whole chapter full of things to tell you about how to research them. But for now, I'll say this: Sometimes the cause of death is incorrect or is intentionally false. In such cases, an official might just list the very last thing that killed the person. Or a doctor could be covering up his own malpractice, a doctor could be covering up to spare loved ones grief, or a doctor could be trying to help survivors get benefits they would otherwise lose. Or a company's officials might pressure the death certificate preparer to cover the real cause of death so they could save lawsuit, insurance, and death benefit money.

Sometimes a birth certificate or a death certificate is entered by someone deliberately trying to create a new identity for himself to escape creditors, ex-wives, Mob hitmen, IRS agents, or other people who don't wish him well. So use the information the certificates show, but double-check the info when you can.

Also, decide wisely on how to use birth and death records. You may hurt innocent people needlessly, or you may look stupid if you don't think before you trash. Or you may make people feel sorry for your target, or he may show some character and turn it around on you. As an example, I'll tell the following true story about another one of our Presidents.

In the old days, it was common mudslinging practice to find out whether a prominent man had fathered a child out of wedlock, then publicize the hell out of it if he did. This tactic worked well against those men too cowardly to face up to the problems they caused their lady loves. (Failure to pay child support still would be legitimate dirt today.) Republicans found such dirt on Grover Cleveland when he ran for President in 1884. Much to their chagrin, Cleveland—a bachelor—was a real man. Grover, who was as big as a football lineman, admitted he had fathered the child, and showed he was paying his former lover child support for the little one.

Meanwhile, some bigoted clergyman said Democrats were the party of "rum, Romanism, and rebellion." James Blaine, Cleveland's opponent, was present when the minister made this meatheaded remark. Blaine was not man enough to disavow the bigotry, and virtually all Catholics, Southerners, and drinkers voted against Blaine. Cleveland's manhood beat Blaine's wimphood, and Cleveland became president. Cleveland then got married while he occupied the White House.

CHECKING OTHER RECORDS

Military Service Records. Sometimes former servicemen file their discharge papers at the county courthouse. You can check these for data on a target. The Defense Department has a locator service for active-duty military people (people who are still in the service); call the Pentagon for details. Each service keeps a register of officers; you can write to the

Pentagon for info on your target if he is an officer, or maybe gain access to the registers if they are in any library in your area.

An excellent source of info on former military types is the National Personnel Records Center in St. Louis. At this writing, the clerks of this agency can send you the following info on your target's military career:

- Period of service.
- Military and civilian education.
- Military training.
- Decorations and awards.
- Military rank.
- Duty stations (where he served).
- Entitlements (pay and allowances).
- Court-martials and other major disciplinary actions.

Believe it or not, the law won't allow these clerks to say whether or not your target got an honorable discharge. A less-than-honorable discharge is proof a target has gotten into major-league trouble or was somehow judged unsuitable for military service, so the clerks say lawmakers wouldn't let them make discharge disclosures. But the law says they can still tell you if your target got into serious trouble in the first place. Go figure. However, some records you get may contain this info anyway, because bureaucrats sometimes make mistakes and fail to purge such info from the records they will send you.

High School And College Records. Policies at schools vary, but you can usually verify if a target went to a certain school by calling the school's registrar office and asking someone to check. If they ask why you need to know, tell them you're doing an employment check or a loan check on the target. Usually, the clerks will try to help you, thinking they're helping your target. Yearbooks from schools can also give you insights into a person's academic background and personal interests. Some schools' staffers might give out information on courses a target took if they think you're an employer trying to verify the target's credentials for a job.

There's another use for such info: finding out whether someone has the credentials he claims to have. Joe Biden, a senator from Delaware who ran for the 1988 Democratic nomination, had to drop out of the race in 1987 when information surfaced that he claimed he did better in school than he actually did. Biden was already bleeding from accounts of his plagiarizing while in law school and evidence he or his staffers were stealing speeches from other public figures. So the sharks had already circled, and they went in for the kill when word leaked out that some-

one had researched Biden's academic record and determined he was lying about how good a student he had been.

Car And Driver Information. In many states, vehicle registration information is a public record, and vehicle registration records are tied to license plate numbers. Contact your state motor vehicles bureau for instructions on how to get a copy of your target's vehicle registration. Likewise, in many states, driver license information and driving records are public records. Again, contact your state motor vehicles bureau for instructions on how to get your target's driver license information and driving record abstract.

Also, in many states, vehicle title information is filed at the county clerk's office for tax or public records purposes. Check with your county clerk to see if this is the case with your state.

Probate Court Records. Probate courts are for deciding how to divide a dead person's property. If you need to find out how a dead person's estate was divided up, here's where to look. Also, there may be some information pertaining to your target as an inheritor of property (or as someone who is nastily contesting the will) in this court's records.

Medical Records. These are usually impossible to get. However, there are those who will call insurance companies or hospitals on the pretext of being a health care professional (or the target himself) to obtain these records. Also, some people use a hospital's staffers to obtain these for them. (This is also illegal, but the shady doctor, nurse, or clerk who's willing to "borrow" records is at risk, not you.) A legitimate way to get some info on a person's medical condition is to call the hospital's PR person, identify yourself as a writer, and ask if a target is now in the hospital or has ever been in the hospital. Information disclosure policies vary from hospital to hospital.

Traditionally, medical records have been confidential. But in an age when AIDS-infected doctors infect innocent young women like Kim Bergalis, and AIDS-tainted blood infects medical people and transfusion patients, the public outcry will eventually force some sort of public disclosure. And when the rules change, a target's medical information will be easier to get.

Library And Media Sources. Two resources investigators often overlook are libraries and media outfits. Both sources contain a lot of good information you can use. At almost any library, for example, is the *Reader's Guide to Periodical Literature*, a set of reference books that can tell you which major magazines carried articles about your target in the last several decades. Your library (or one in your area) will carry back issues of these magazines so you can copy the articles. Your library may also carry back issues of local newspapers, and index them for you so you can find articles about your target. If your target is prominent enough, maybe someone has written a book about him, or has mentioned him in a book on another subject. (For info on authors that may point to possible biases, check the reference books known as *Contemporary Authors.*) And your library should have several sets of *Who's Who* reference books for a number of fields.

And media outlets have some goodies for you, too. Newspapers keep copies of articles their reporters have written. You may be able to get a newspaper employee (usually a reporter if the paper is small, or a librarian if the paper is big) to make photocopies of articles on the target for you. TV and radio newspeople have less documentation lying around, but sometimes they can send you transcripts or other helpful info. It won't hurt to identify yourself as a writer when you call media people, because many of them treat John and Joan Public like lepers. But like sharks and lawyers, the media people will treat others in their trade with professional courtesy.

Social Security And Welfare Rolls. One of the most blood-boiling things for many of us to hear is an account of someone dishonestly collecting public assistance or other government handouts. We've all heard stories of people who rip off Social Security money by cashing Granny's checks long after she's cashed in her chips. Or we'll see luxury-car drivers pay for groceries with food stamps. Or we'll hear of slugs who fraudulently collect disability payments for alleged workplace back injuries, which leaves them plenty of time to play golf, take up karate, or help buddies swap engines in their pickup trucks.

You can find out if your target is taking government handouts simply by calling the agencies in question. Some agents might tell you if your target is on the dole. Others won't, so you'll have to scam them by telling them you're a prospective employer or a moneylender or a landlord who gives rent discounts to poor people or a charity group representative, and you want to verify the target's participation in the agency's handout program for job or financial reasons. Or you could ask for a forwarding address so you can send a package to the person (or do something else that's nice). How you handle this is up to you.

Match your target's assets (property, cars, business interests, salary) against his presence on the handout list. If you find out your target receives some sort of public assistance and you know he doesn't belong there, turn him in; he's a leech who needs to be prosecuted! And your target might suffer if word gets out he's a claimant of benefits—nobody likes a freeloader who fattens up at the public trough at taxpayer expense. Some will think he's a lazy slob even if he technically meets the criteria of a certain handout program.

Many people sue government agencies for failure to pay claims like Social Security. This also holds true for other government entitlements and handouts. Check lawsuit records per the info in the chapter on lawsuits for evidence your target is suing the government to collect government benefits. Likewise, check civil and criminal records per those chapters in the book for evidence the Feds or the state authorities have gone after your target for taking money he shouldn't have gotten. Further, check in with the enforcement officials and the inspector general of all of these agencies to see if they've gone after your target in some other way for taking handout money illegally.

On a related topic, I once caught a restaurant operator in a freeloading scam. He used his mother to collect all kinds of free food from a local church, then he evidently used some of it for his family and sold the rest. I had his mother cut off of the recipient list of the church, but I couldn't get the nuns who ran the food pantry program to press criminal charges against her and her son. I did, however, have the health inspectors show up at her apartment. It seems her restaurateur son was having many of his precooked entrees cooked at her place!

TAPPING OTHER PERSONAL SOURCES

The underground presses put out many detective manuals, specialized crime and security and missing persons books. Scan such books for info and ideas. Likewise, some private eyes offer books for women who want to check on whether their lovers have the kinds of careers they claim, or if they have prior social engagements (like wives and children) they don't claim, or if they are sleazy in other areas. Scan their offerings for ideas also. I've used digging tips I've learned from these kinds of sources, and you can, too.

WHEN YOUR ENEMY'S ENEMY IS YOUR FRIEND

If your target is as big a jerk as you think he is, odds are other people think so, too. Once you know where your target lives and works, who he associates with, and who his family and friends are, you can contact people who might be unfriendly to him. Neighbors, certain co-workers called for job references, ex-spouses, members of rival organizations, and those who have sued him or accused him of criminal activity are usually good people to talk to about your target.

Before you contact such people, come up with a plausible story as to why you're calling about the target. Sometimes telling a target's vicious enemy you're looking for dirt on him is an excellent approach; sometimes the "detached" approach of a reporter or a reference checker is more appropriate. For further ideas on who to contact, and for advice on how to act when you find someone who will talk about your target in a negative way, check the chapter on checking organizations.

A FINAL PERSONAL NOTE

To show you how important personal records can be, I'm going to close with the tale of Alger Hiss, a sleazy Communist agent who was the State Department official who conned FDR into signing Eastern Europe away to the Soviets at Yalta in 1945. Hiss helped sentence millions of innocent people to up to 45 years of Communist enslavement with this swinish act. A few years later, ex-Communist agent Whittaker Chambers, who was now an editor at *Time* magazine, accused Hiss of being a Communist agent also. Hiss denied it, and claimed he didn't know or barely knew Chambers. The matter went before a Congressional committee.

One area where Hiss really screwed up was lying about items of his personal life that public records existed on. He lied about cars he owned, for example, and the congressmen (especially young Richard Nixon) were able to trap him when they had the public record checked. Chambers' account of Hiss' cars jibed with the public record, so the congressmen implied Hiss was lying when he claimed he didn't know Chambers well. Hiss' poor showing caused media people to pressure him to sue Chambers for defamation if Chambers' charges weren't true. Hiss did, and then Chambers cut Hiss' throat by releasing a stack of State Department memos, cable messages, and other important documents which Hiss had given to Chambers to turn over to their Communist spymasters. In short order, Hiss was indicted on two counts of perjury for lying under oath to the congressmen. (The statute of limitations on any espionage or treason Hiss may have committed in connection with sending secret documents to the Communists had run out.)

During Hiss' trials, his wife Priscilla inadvertently hurt his case by contradicting the public record herself. She denied taking typing classes and applying for a chemistry course; Chambers' wife and another witness said she had done both. She also denied being a Socialist Party member. The prosecutor produced college records showing Mrs. Hiss took the typing course and applied for the chemistry course. He also produced her voter registration, which showed she registered as a Socialist. Her denial she knew Chambers and his wife well carried little weight as a result.

Hiss was eventually convicted on both counts of perjury and drew a five-year prison sentence. Remember, the first crack in Hiss' credibility with many came when he lied about details of his personal life that could be checked on the public record.

You will probably never look into a case as huge as the case of Alger Hiss. But the dirt you dig on the seemingly trivial details of a bad person's personal life may damage him to a great extent. And don't feel bad about doing it. If your target is as bad as you think he is, you're doing the public a service. As my Uncle Don says, "Those who get nailed usually have it coming."

END NOTES

1. Information on the Pulitzer divorce case comes from an article in the October 11, 1982 issue of *Time*.
2. Information on Jane Fonda's divorce, fortune, and reportedly questionable employment practices comes from Christopher Andersen's book *Citizen Jane*. The discrimination suit that three of her former employees filed against her is Case 807215, filed in San Francisco City/County Superior Court.
3. Information on Edward Brooke's divorce case comes from an article in the June 19, 1978 issue of *Newsweek*.
4. Information on Julian Bond's difficulties comes from an article in the September 22, 1986 issue of *Jet*, and an article in the June 1, 1987 issue of *Newsweek*.
5. Information on Douglas Wilder's divorce comes from an article about Pat Kluge, a British porn starlet-turned-Virginia society dame. The article, which appeared in the July 23, 1990 issue of *People*, implied the two were romantically linked.
6. Information on Gerry Studds' homosexual use of a Congressional page comes from an article in the July 25, 1983 issue of *Newsweek*.
7. Information on Gary Hart's dalliances and daring the media comes from articles in the May 18, 1987 issue of *Newsweek*.
8. Information on Nelson Rockefeller comes from articles in the February 19, 1979 issue of *Newsweek* and the February 12, 1979 issue of *Time*.
9. Information on Marion Barry's case comes from an article in the August 20, 1990 issue of *Newsweek*.
10. Information on Barney Frank and his call boy comes from an article in the September 25, 1989 issue of *Time* and a 1990 article written by Michael Wines of the *New York Times*.
11. The story on Andrew Jackson comes from Marquis James' book *Andrew Jackson, Border Captain*.
12. The allegation that George McGovern fathered a child out of wedlock comes from Victor Lasky's book *It Didn't Start With Watergate*.
13. The story on Grover Cleveland comes from Edmund Morris' book *The Rise of Theodore Roosevelt* and from Michael Schwartz's book *The Persistent Prejudice*.
14. Information on Joe Biden's lying and plagiarism affair comes from articles in the September 28, 1987 and October 5, 1987 issues of *Newsweek*.
15. The story on Alger Hiss comes from Ralph De Toledano's book *Seeds of Treason*.

Investigate Criminal Records—Help Justice Beat The System

Criminals come in all colors, but Hollywood and the media have the average American thinking only minority youths commit crimes. As a reporter, I saw wealthy white males, little old ladies, he-man farmers and tradesmen, matronly women, and yuppie types of both sexes in the defendant's chair in criminal court. If you do a little digging, you may find your target has sat in that seat himself from time to time.

The "military" use of knowing how to check a person's criminal record is obvious. Finding out and publicizing someone's criminal record will do serious damage to his reputation. It could cost him employment and credit opportunities, and will make a lot of people think he is a lowlife. And it may get him in further trouble with the law, because he might have illegally covered up his criminal past in order to take advantage of certain opportunities.

For "civilian" purposes, knowing how to check a person's criminal record will enable you or a friend or loved one to check a target's character before getting involved with the target on a business or personal basis. And if you find out the person is a thief, a sex offender, or a serious threat to physically harm people, you can protect other people by warning them about him.

The public's need to know who is violent, perverted, or crooked enough to commit crimes so they can protect themselves from these people is so obvious that I shouldn't even have to defend it in this book. But since there are a few people out there who need to wake up and smell the coffee, I'll say it here for your benefit. THE PUBLIC'S RIGHT TO PROTECTION IS MORE IMPORTANT THAN THE CRIMINAL'S RIGHT TO ANONYMITY. And I'll take it one step further. I believe so strongly in your right to know about criminal swine in your community that I'm going to show you how to do your own criminal record checking.

In fact, let me tell you a war story or three about why it is good for the average person to know how to research criminal records.

A buddy of mine who's known on the streets as Greg the Sicilian called me one day and asked me how to look up a certain guy's criminal record. He said he had an uneasy feeling about this guy, who he was planning to do business with. I told Greg how to check the guy's criminal record, and he checked it. That night, he was back on the phone with me; he said he found out his would-be business partner had been convicted of a string of felonies over a 10-year period. Need I say Greg the Sicilian told this guy to stick his business proposition where the sun doesn't shine?

Or consider a case I knew about which concerned a professed bisexual who wanted to become a foster parent for young boys. I checked on this guy with local lawmen, and they told me at least two different mothers had complained about the pervert's advances toward their young sons. Unfortunately for justice, the mothers never pressed charges after they had made their original complaints. One of the mothers told me she was afraid her little boy would be scarred by the court experience. While my heart went out to her, I know her failure and the other woman's failure to do the right thing (if what they charged was true) left this scumbag free and capable of targeting other little boys. (Yeah, I DID judge him. From seeing his mannerisms, from hearing about his alleged advances toward the young boys, and from listening to what he told me about his lifestyle and about the homosexual advocacy groups he said he was in touch with, I saw in him the profile of a potential child molester.)

In my book, what's good for the children is more important than some deviate's right to gain access to children. So I looked up the bisexual's criminal record. I found out the self-proclaimed switch hitter had an arrest record for a serious drug charge (manufacturing marijuana). In a plea-bargain arrangement, he had pleaded guilty to a reduced charge; the more serious offense was dropped. I made sure this information about the more serious charge that was dropped reached the paper. The social workers shredded the maggot's application. And when he sued the social workers for discrimination, a judge drop-kicked his case out of court and told him in so many words never to show his face in his courtroom again.

Or consider the case of Raymond Tanner.

Raymond, a meat cutter by trade, chased his wife Maria around the parking lot of their Cincinnati area apartment complex with a foot-long butcher knife on the morning of Valentine's Day, 1990. He caught Maria, dragged her into the foyer of their building, and cut off her head in front of a terrified neighbor woman. I interviewed Maria's parents after Raymond was found not guilty by reason of insanity for beheading their daughter. They showed me a picture of the attractive young blonde, and they told me Maria found out a lot of negative things about Raymond after they got married...he was apparently discharged from the service with a less-than-honorable discharge, he had been married and divorced before, he had financial problems, and he had fathered children by his ex-wife and a previous girlfriend. Maria learned she would have to help him pay child support for these children. Maria's parents told me, "Parents should delve into the fiance's background...and check him from one end to the other."

Have I revved you up enough? Good. Then let's talk about how the judicial system functions (or fails to) for criminal cases. We'll discuss how criminal cases work, how plea-bargaining works, how to find out if your target has a criminal record, and how to review your target's criminal cases in various courts.

HOW A CRIMINAL CASE WORKS

Since the criminal court process has many twists and turns, we'll first walk through what happens to someone accused of a felony (a serious crime which can bring down a sentence ranging from a year in a penitentiary to execution). Then we'll walk through what happens to someone accused of a misdemeanor (a less serious crime for which the maximum sentence is a year in a county jail).

The Felony Process. A person accused of a felony will be arrested or will be summoned to appear in court later. After being arrested, or after being summoned to appear in court for allegedly committing a felony, a defendant will be arraigned (formally notified of the charges against him) in front of a judge. He can then plead GUILTY or NO CONTEST and receive his sentence from the judge, or he can plead NOT GUILTY and demand a trial. If the defendant pleads GUILTY, it means he is admitting he did what he is charged with doing. If the defendant pleads NO CONTEST, it means he is not denying the charge, but is not admitting it, either. (In criminal law, a NO CONTEST plea is basically the same as a GUILTY plea. However, if a person pleads NO CONTEST, the plea can't be used as conclusive evidence against him in any lawsuit involving the criminal incident in question.)

If the accused felon pleads NOT GUILTY, he will then undergo a pretrial hearing. At a pretrial hearing, the judge can dismiss the charge against the defendant because he's clearly innocent, or because of lack of evidence, or on some technicality. Or the judge can decide there is enough evidence to warrant a trial for a misdemeanor offense, but not a felony offense; he would send this type of case to a trial court that handles misdemeanor cases. (See the paragraphs below which cover the misdemeanor process.).

But what if the pretrial hearing judge thinks there's enough evidence the defendant has committed a felony to warrant a criminal trial? In states where the grand jury's use is required for felony cases (and in federal courts), the pretrial hearing judge sends the accused felon's case to a grand jury. (Or a prosecutor can submit a case to the grand jury—like a racketeering case—for investigative reasons. Or the prosecutor can submit a case to the grand jury even if the pretrial hearing judge decided there wasn't a good reason to try the defendant.)

In a grand jury session, the grand jury members usually see only evidence on a defendant that the prosecutor shows them. They can decide there isn't enough evidence to indict the defendant, which means the charges are usually dropped. Or the grand jury members can indict the accused felon, and send his case to a criminal trial. (A grand jury's members, in indicting someone, are not convicting him; they are saying there is enough evidence against him to justify a criminal trial.)

Not every state uses the grand jury for felony cases. In these states, the defendant will undergo a trial if the pretrial hearing judge determines there's enough evidence he committed a felony to warrant a criminal trial.

When the accused felon undergoes his trial, a judge or jury will hear his case and find him GUILTY or NOT GUILTY, and then the judge will sentence the defendant if he is found guilty. Or the judge will dismiss the case during the trial on a technicality, or he will dismiss the charge on the wishes of the defense attorney or the prosecuting attorney. It takes the agreement of all jurors to find the defendant guilty or not guilty. If the jurors can't agree unanimously, they are called a hung jury. When the jury is hung, or if an unusual or improper event happens during the trial, the judge can declare a mistrial so the defendant can get another trial. Often, a prosecutor will decide not to retry a felony case that is declared a mistrial, and the defendant goes free.

The Misdemeanor Process. A person accused of a misdemeanor will be arrested, or will be summoned to appear in court later. After being arrested, or after being summoned to appear in court for allegedly committing a misdemeanor, a defendant will be arraigned in front of a judge. He can then plead GUILTY or NO CONTEST and receive his sentence from the judge, or he can plead NOT GUILTY and demand a trial.

If the defendant pleads NOT GUILTY, he will then undergo a pretrial hearing. At a pretrial hearing, the judge can dismiss the charge against the defendant because he's clearly innocent, or because of lack of evidence, or on some technicality. Or the judge can decide there is enough evidence against the defendant to justify a misdemeanor trial; he will send the defendant's case to a trial court that handles misdemeanor cases. (Also bear in mind a pretrial judge in the felony system can send a defendant to a misdemeanor trial if he rules there is enough evidence to indicate the defendant may have committed a misdemeanor, but not enough to indicate he may have committed a felony.)

When the defendant undergoes his trial, a judge or jury will hear his case and find him GUILTY or NOT GUILTY, and then the judge will sentence the defendant if he is found guilty. Or the judge will dismiss the case during the trial on a technicality, or he will dismiss the charge on the wishes of the defense attorney or the prosecuting attorney. It takes the agreement of all jurors to find the defendant guilty or not guilty. If the jurors can't agree unanimously, they are called a hung jury. When the jury is hung, or if an unusual or improper event happens during the trial, the judge can declare a mistrial so the defendant can get another trial. Usually, a prosecutor will decide not to retry a misdemeanor case that is declared a mistrial, and the defendant goes free.

HOW PLEA-BARGAINING WORKS

Despite what the media and Hollywood lead people to believe, most criminal cases end in plea-bargaining. Criminal justice surveyors report that anywhere from 65 percent to 95 percent of all criminal cases in various jurisdictions around the country end in guilty pleas. The reasons for plea-bargaining are obvious. From the court's side, there is a backlog in the court system due to convoluted legal procedures (which were written by lawyers), due to increases in crimes, and due to increases in arrests. From the defendant's side, most accused criminals are in fact guilty of something, so they look to plea-bargaining to get lighter sentences.

Plea-bargaining works like this: At any time after arrest or summons, the prosecutor or the defense attorney can propose that the prosecutor reduce the original criminal charge to a less serious charge in exchange for the defendant pleading GUILTY or NO CONTEST to the lesser charge. If there is an agreement between the prosecutor and the defense attorney on this deal, the defendant will then plead GUILTY or NO CONTEST to the lesser charge so he can receive a lighter sentence. There will be no trial; a judge will usually formally note the agreement and sentence the defendant to the pre-arranged punishment. (Sometimes, but not often, a judge will reject a plea-bargain deal.)

There are some good aspects to plea-bargaining. It clears much of the backlog in court, it ensures the guilty receive at least some punishment for their offenses, and it allows judges and lawyers to handle "dispute" cases like brawls and domestic problems on a more rational level.

But there are many more negative aspects to plea-bargaining. It allows police to ridiculously overcharge suspects for crimes so they can pad their arrest statistics. It gives prosecutors far too much power. Many prosecutors are building track records for political gain; a plea-bargained conviction counts just as much for them as a conviction won in a trial. So they're tempted to underpunish truly dangerous criminals just to get the easy guilty pleas. And they're also tempted to bully innocent people into plea-bargaining instead of trying to determine whether they really committed the crimes, or if the real culprits are still on the loose and free to commit more crimes. Many defense lawyers also sell out their clients, especially if the clients are paying them fixed amounts. Trying a case will cost the defense lawyer some of his profit, so he is tempted to con his client into pleading guilty to lesser offenses just so he can make more money.

From the public's standpoint, plea-bargaining releases too many truly evil and dangerous people into society so they can prey upon more victims. Bullying a defendant into a guilty plea costs the public money to imprison him. From the public safety angle, bullying the wrong person into a guilty plea means the real culprit is still roaming free and can victimize more people. Many consider the plea-bargaining process a perversion of justice.

Are you ready to hear about a couple of plea-bargains I covered or investigated? Good, because I'll use them as examples when I teach you how to examine criminal files.

I covered the trial of a guy in the hills who was being charged with a number of assaults and firearms offenses. He allegedly had gotten into an argument with his girlfriend in front of her parents' house, where they shacked up. He allegedly beat her with a shotgun, then pumped a couple of shotgun shells into the house to let off a little steam. Sheriff's deputies arrived on the scene, and they arrested the guy after a brief scuffle.

It may sound to most folks that this guy was in a heap of trouble, but he had been in much hotter water before. (We'll call him Ricky Slaughterhouse in this book, because he's the kind of guy who would probably feel proud over getting this kind of attention if I used his real name. I know, because I talked with him several times. He also called my paper one night from the jail and toyed with the fool copy editors by saying they printed an inaccurate story about him. He and I chuckled about it the next day in court.) Rumor had it that Ricky had apparently been a suspect in the early 1970s in connection with the rape and dismemberment of a young woman. No case against Ricky was proven.

Ricky ran into serious trouble in the mid-1970s; he shot a man to death in Kentucky. He was convicted of murder, and received a life sentence. However, Ricky didn't find prison life to his liking, so he escaped from the pen and fled north. He stabbed another man to death in an Ohio tavern, and received a 7-25 year sentence for voluntary manslaughter to run concurrently (at the same time) as his Kentucky murder sentence. He appealed his Kentucky conviction, a federal judge threw it out on a technicality a couple of years later, and prosecutors plea-bargained the Kentucky shooting down to a five-year sentence for a "hindering prosecution" charge. (In other words, Ricky "hindered prosecution" of a felony assault-with-a-gun charge by fatally shooting the man he assaulted with a gun.) When he served the reduced sentence, he was freed on the Ohio charge, too, because he had served at least seven years total.

In short, the plea-bargain made it possible for Ricky Slaughterhouse to walk free and have the chance to beat up his girlfriend, ventilate her parents' house, and duke it out with the lawmen. The local jury, by the way, saw fit to give Ricky only a few months in the county jail. There are two bright points about this ugly story, however. One was that Ricky served as his own attorney, so the public didn't have to pay for a public defender. The other was that the local federal prosecutor—a hulking bearded mountain man who could freeze you with a stare or crack you up with a quip—found it interesting that a convicted felon had such easy access to firearms. Since such an act is a felony in itself, the federal prosecutor got him convicted on six counts of felony firearm possession. The judge hit Ricky with a 46-year sentence, and then told

me he figured the punishment he handed out would "keep the boy locked up for 15 years, at least until he reached his fifties and slowed down a bit."

The other two stories ended less happily. In one case, a child molester in the Cumberland Gap area (Lee County, Virginia) named Carson Payne cut a deal with a local prosecutor, and pleaded guilty to the charge of sodomy in order to stay out of prison. A judge gave Payne a 10-year suspended sentence and five years of probation and ordered him to undergo treatment. I was so enraged, I printed the judge's name, the prosecutor's name, the defense attorney's name, and Carson Payne's name and address in the article I wrote. I felt people needed to know the identity of this menace to their children. (Also, folks in the hills have been known to resort to vigilante methods—which I prefer to call "participatory democracy" or "citizen's law enforcement"— when their justice system lets them down.)

And then there was the case of Laurence Reich. This Southern California abortion provider was accused of multiple counts of sexual assault, sexual battery, sexual abuse of patients, and trying to coerce or persuade his female victims into refusing to testify against him. Five women accused Reich of assaulting them sexually before or after he treated them; a sixth accused Reich of forcing her to perform oral sex on him as she lay helpless on the table just after the abortion. Reich's lawyer and Santa Monica prosecutors cut a plea-bargain deal in June 1984; Reich was allowed to plead NO CONTEST to two counts of battery and pay an $800 fine for each count. Reich, I understand, is still operating on women in Southern California at this writing.

GETTING OFF ON THE RIGHT FOOT

Now that I've shown you a few instances in which the lawyers gang-raped Ms. Justice, I'm going to show you how to check criminal records.

There are five ways to check a target's criminal record. The easiest way is to have a policeman friend of yours run the target's name through the police computer network. (The National Criminal Information Center runs this network, and the police refer to its data as an "NCIC printout" or an "NCIC readout".) The plus side of this method is that it's easy and fairly complete. (Some jurisdictions don't participate in the network, but most do.) Your friendly cop can find out by computer your target's police record in all 50 states. The down side of this method is that it's probably illegal for your lawman buddy to do this. Strictly speaking, it's not police business for him to use the taxpayer-financed system to help a friend with a vendetta. Also, there are privacy (criminal rights) considerations; that could be why so many government types and antigun people don't want to allow gunshop owners access to the police computer network so they can verify if a would-be gun buyer is a convicted felon forbidden to own any guns.

Another way that's almost as easy is to have a private investigator do this for you. He will charge you a few bucks, and he'll get you the same kind of info as any policeman could. How? Most private investigators are ex-cops or have friends who are cops. The P.I.s have their policeman buddies use the police computer network for them to check out targets for their clients. Of course, this might be illegal for the policemen involved, but they are probably getting favors from the private investigators for their trouble. And anyway, that's none of your concern. At least you aren't putting any strain on your friendship with a lawman. And you're getting the dirt anyway.

A third method is to find out who your target's parole officer is, then ask him about your target's criminal record. The parole officer will have access to your target's nationwide criminal record, and he may or may not divulge it to you. If you have some info on your target indicating he may be violating parole, or if it's understood you're a writer who is doing some investigative research on the target, the parole officer may be willing to help you. I've gotten this kind of help from these fine civil servants several times.

A fourth method that applies in some states involves gaining access to the state's central criminal register or criminal index. In some states, the state court system administrator in the state capital keeps this record; in other states, the attorney general's people keep it. Although the state people maintain this kind of record as a law enforcement tool, there's nothing that says you can't use it as a research tool if it is a public record in your state; some states' lawmakers have been democratic enough to make these records available to the public. Check with your state's court system administrator or with the attorney general's agents to determine if you can gain access to your state's central criminal register or criminal index.

The hardest way is doing it yourself. It's not hard to research records at a courthouse, but it's possible your target could have arrests all over the state (and the country), so you'll really have to know where your target has been in order to perform a thorough (yet legal) check. Also, each city and township in any county usually has its own lower court, so you'll have to check the records of every single one of these courts to get a complete look at your target's misdemeanor

record in that county. It might be a good idea to pay a private investigator to have a police buddy check on WHERE your target has been arrested, then contact each of these places' courthouses—which is clearly legal—to obtain information on the criminal cases of your target.

Let's assume you want to check your target's criminal record in your county. You'll first need to know which courts in your county handle felony cases and which courts handle misdemeanor cases.

All states have lower courts and upper courts. Criminal prosecutions for misdemeanors—minor crimes in which the maximum penalty is 12 months in a county jail—take place in the criminal portion of lower courts. (Lawsuits for small amounts of money take place in the civil portion of lower courts.) Criminal prosecutions for felonies—serious crimes in which the sentence can go from a year in a state prison to life imprisonment or execution—take place in the criminal portion of upper courts. (Lawsuits for large amounts of money take place in the civil portion of upper courts.) Figure out what they call the upper and lower courts in your county by checking the county government listings in a phone book for your county.

Once you know the names of the courts, you can start checking. Start checking in the upper court of the county for felony cases, then go to each of the lower courts in the county to check for misdemeanor cases. There are two steps to checking a target's criminal record in your county. These are:

- Find out the case numbers of all cases involving your target.
- Using the case numbers, have court clerks pull the case files for you so you can look at the legal paper in them. Then copy all important or damaging info from each case file!

We'll now go through each step in detail, using your county's upper court as an example.

FINDING OUT CASE NUMBERS

The list of all the felony criminal cases filed in the upper court in your county is called a "criminal index" (or docket, or something close to it). This list will be on microfilm, in a computer, in drawers full of index cards, or handwritten into a very heavy set of books. You will have to check this list to get case numbers for all cases involving your target.

In each county, there is one office where an upper court criminal index or a docket for all upper courts in that county will be available to the public. (In almost all counties, this place is the upper criminal court clerk's office; in a handful of huge counties which have more than one upper courthouse, this place will be the central courthouse's upper criminal court clerk's office.) To find out where it is, call the court clerk of the upper court whose records you want to check. The clerk's number will be in the phone book under the upper court portion of the county government listings.

Then, go to the courthouse where the court's criminal index or docket is, and look up all felony cases involving your target. Write down the target's name, and each charge, each case number, and each case date. A couple of notes follow:

- The most recent cases (those filed in the last couple of months or so) might not be in the criminal index. They'll be on a separate list the court clerks keep. Ask to see this list, too.
- Some "ancient" cases (those that are more than 10 or so years old) might not be readily available in the clerk's office. Ask the clerks where these older records are kept, then make arrangements to view them.

CHECK THE FILES

Once you get the case numbers of felony cases involving your target that have been filed in the upper court of your county, you'll be able to look at the actual case files. Here's how to do it properly.

First, ask the court clerk in your county's upper court how to have clerks pull criminal case files for you. Follow the clerk's instructions; use the target's name and each case number.

Once the clerks pull the cases for you, go through each case file to see what the case is about. This information will be in a document called a "charge document" or a "complaint sheet" or something similar. This document contains the felony charges the county's prosecuting attorney has made against the target. Mark these pages.

Next, check all exhibit sheets, affidavits, police reports, and other supporting evidence. These documents explain exactly why your target was (or is) in hot water. They contain details of alleged crimes, schemes, conspiracies, and the like. They also contain victim testimony, witness testimony, and police testimony. Besides being loaded with information, these documents make for some entertaining reading, if you're not squeamish. For example, the victims' affidavits on abortion provider Laurence Reich read like bondage letters from a porno magazine. And the file on Appalachian killer Ricky Slaughterhouse reads like a special edition of *True Detective*.

Also, these documents might contain nice-to-know information like the target's Social Security number, property holdings, business ventures, insurance policy numbers, home address, facts on his life and career, and other such items. Mark any page that contains information that will come in handy.

Next, figure out the outcome of the case. Some criminal cases will be active (not decided yet), but most will have already ended in a GUILTY or a NOT GUILTY verdict, a plea-bargained sentence, a hung jury, a mistrial, or some other form of dismissal (or directed verdict) based on a technicality. Check documents for proof the prosecutor and the target's lawyer worked out a plea-bargain agreement. Check for proof a judge threw out charges against the target on a technicality, or threw out charges at the request (motion) of the prosecutor or defense attorney. Check the verdict document for a outcome (GUILTY, NOT GUILTY, dismissed case, or hung jury) if the target went to trial. Check the sentencing document to see what kind of punishment the target received for his crime(s) if he was found guilty. Check if the defendant appealed the case if he was found guilty. Mark the pages which show the outcome of the case, and show why the case turned out the way it did.

In a pinch, if documents are missing from the file, you can check the clerk's record books to see what motions or orders or other actions took place, the outcome of the case, and the names of the judge, the prosecutor, and the defense lawyer. Ask her how she files such information, and follow her instructions on how to find it.

THEN HAVE PHOTOCOPIES MADE OF ALL PAGES YOU'VE MARKED. YOU'LL NOW HAVE HARD-COPY PROOF OF YOUR TARGET'S LOWLIFING.

WHAT TO DO IF YOUR TARGET BEATS THE RAP

It's important to know the outcome of a case, but it's almost as important to know your target was accused in the first place. Why? Because people make up their own minds about whether a person is guilty or innocent, no matter what the outcome is in court. And, like it or not, most people assume an accused person is a guilty person.

People know defendants walk free all the time due to judge incompetence, due to defense lawyer skill being better than prosecutor skill, or due to the defendant's standing in the community as opposed to the victim's standing. People are skeptical of lawyers in the first place. After all, if prosecutors couldn't convict John Hinckley after he shot Ronald Reagan, or if Teddy Kennedy never spent a day in jail for Mary Jo Kopechne's death, why *SHOULD* people blindly trust the justice system?

If charges against your target were dismissed, check the record closely for WHY the charges were dismissed. A dismissal at the request of the defense attorney or by the judge himself sometimes means the defendant was innocent. (Good lawyers will try to get charges against innocent clients dismissed by all legal means to avoid subjecting them to the hassles and risks of trials.) Or it means the defendant was guilty but the police and/or prosecutor handled his case unjustly or incompetently. It could also mean the judge himself is no good. (You can use any evidence of substandard prosecutor, police, or judge performance against responsible parties at budget time or at election time.)

A dismissal at the request of the prosecutor indicates either the target was innocent and the police were wrong to arrest him, or the target was guilty but the prosecutor decided he would be unable to win a conviction. Either instance could be evidence of defective police and/or prosecutor performance in your county.

You could present information on your target's case in such a way that people to see things your way on the target's guilt or lack of character. But here's a word to the wise: DON'T MAKE ANY STATEMENT REGARDING A PERSON'S CRIMINAL ACTIVITIES UNLESS IT IS TRUE. Sometimes the police arrest innocent people. Sometimes prosecutors go after innocent people, and manage to get them indicted on false pretenses. If you trash the reputation of a person who was clearly unjustly accused just because you don't like him, you'll deserve any trouble that will come your way because of your immoral vindictiveness.

However, if the case paperwork indicates your target beat the rap on a technicality, or because the judge was a bleeding heart, or because the cops who handled the case were incompetent Nazis, or because the prosecutor who handled the case botched the job, or because the jury was full of dummies or because they had to decide guilt or innocence on the basis of a narrowly-interpreted law, you can certainly say so as long as you cite the documents and don't say anything that isn't untrue. (See the chapter on putting negative information to positive use for details.) Reporters write such articles all the time which imply that allegedly guilty-as-sin people beat raps. Witness the accusatory articles written about people like Oliver North or Teddy Kennedy!

We hear often of police errors that screw up cases. But prosecutors also screw up cases badly enough that judges or juries have to acquit the defendants. Many people have made that accusation, for example,

against Moira Lasch, who prosecuted William Kennedy Smith for allegedly raping Patricia Bowman. In fact, a published report says law students are buying videotapes of Ms. Lasch's cross-examination of Smith to see how *not* to cross-examine a defendant!

As my own example of prosecutor error, I submit the following exhibit:

In the Raymond Tanner case, prosecutor Robert N. Piper III told me he decided not to prosecute Tanner for cutting off his wife's head on Valentine's Day. Why? Because, he said, two state-retained psychologists who interviewed Tanner many weeks after he beheaded his wife believed Tanner thought his wife and the Masons were involved in a plot to kill him. (By the way, Roger Fisher, one of the shrinks in question, bitched at me over the phone when I tried to set up an interview with him about his analysis. He also told me he was forbidding his staffers from talking to me about the Tanner case. Would such behavior on his part be evidence of clinical paranoia?)

I asked prosecutor Piper why he hadn't checked with the two psychologists who examined Tanner in the Butler County jail the day after he killed his wife and concluded he was faking insanity. The prosecutor replied with some astonishment that he wasn't aware of any other evaluation. When I told Piper the sheriff had reported to the media he had gotten these two psychologists to examine Tanner, the prosecutor confessed he was unaware of their findings. In short, the prosecutor overlooked a huge piece of evidence in the murder case of a man who cut off his wife's head.

Was Raymond Tanner insane? Maybe so. Most rational men don't decapitate their wives on Valentine's Day ...or on any other day, for that matter. But jury members who received all the evidence should have made that decision, not a prosecutor who may very well have mishandled the case.

By the way, Tanner was found not guilty by reason of insanity in June 1990. He can walk free from the state nuthouse when a shrink like Fisher convinces a judge he is sane.

CHECKING LOWER COURTS

The procedure for checking a misdemeanor record is much the same as the procedure for checking a felony record. The only major difference is that you have to look up your target's name at each lower court in your county to figure out his complete misdemeanor record in your county, while you only have to check the main upper court in your county to determine your target's countywide felony record.

With all the hassles involved, why is checking your

target's misdemeanor record worth the bother? I can think of three good reasons.

The first reason is that many misdemeanor convictions are felonies that were plea-bargained downward. Still others are cases that should have been tried as felonies. Laurence Reich, the abortion provider I mentioned earlier, could have been tried for rape. However, the way local authorities handled his case, his seemingly felony-weight offenses didn't make the Superior (felony) Court criminal docket. Instead, his case landed in Municipal (misdemeanor) Court in Santa Monica, California.

Another good reason for checking misdemeanor records is that many serious health, labor, environmental, and safety code violations are only considered misdemeanors by the state authorities. In many jurisdictions, it's a felony to carry a handgun, but only a misdemeanor to discharge poison from a factory into drinking water, to maintain a place of business unsafely enough so that workers die from the hazardous conditions, or to allow non-doctors to work on women at an abortion facility so that women are at even more risk. These serious crimes, although only misdemeanors in the blind eyes of Ms. Justice, classify as serious dirt to most normal people.

A third good reason is that for some people, any conviction (or even accusation) on any crime will hurt. A person convicted of shoplifting or passing bad checks is probably untrustworthy. A person convicted of sex crimes, even if they are "only" misdemeanors, is probably a safe bet to keep committing such crimes until he dies or loses his genitalia. A person convicted of a drug or alcohol-related offense will probably struggle against addiction and foul up many more times until he or she either kicks the habit or becomes an incurable junkie or drunk. Any such conviction (or valid accusation) will trash a person's reputation in the eyes of people in a position to help or hurt him or her.

If your target lives in a heavily-populated county which has a lot of cities and townships that run their own lower criminal courts, definitely consider having your policeman friend (or get a private investigator to have his policeman friend) run a criminal record check on your target.

Once you have case numbers, either through the help of your "friends" or by your own efforts, you're home free. The procedure for researching misdemeanor cases is the same as for researching felony cases.

CHECKING TRAFFIC COURT

Traffic violations are usually very small potatoes unless the traffic violations are serious or are those of public officials. The driving problems of two senators immediately come to mind. Teddy Kennedy is nationally known for driving off a bridge and killing Mary Jo Kopechne in what many people believe was a blatant case of drunk driving. (There are some wild and crazy folks out there who'd pay Teddy's bar tab if only he'd drive Jane Fonda to Key West; with 110 miles of bridges, they figure he'd miss one sooner or later!)

Roger Jepsen, a senator from Iowa in the 1980s, made news when he arrogantly beat a traffic ticket by claiming he had congressional immunity from prosecution. This display of un-American lordliness angered down-to-earth folks in the Hawkeye State. And it may very well have been a factor in Jepsen's loss in his bid for re-election in 1984.

Checking a person's driving record is easy to do in many states. Just call the state's motor vehicle bureau for the procedure for obtaining a printout of your target's driving record. In some states, it's impossible to do this, so you'll have to check traffic courts all over your county, or enlist the aid of a policeman or a private investigator to run a check of your target on the police computer network. Once you have citation numbers, you can get copies of tickets at the courts in the areas where the tickets were written, if the tickets are relatively recent ones.

CHECKING FEDERAL COURTS

Federal courts handle special crimes and violations of certain federal laws. For example, a person could wind up as a defendant in a federal criminal case if he is suspected of crimes like income tax evasion, espionage, perjury at a federal proceeding, racketeering, civil rights violations (a sometimes hate group or police crime), obstruction of justice, taking bribes while a federal official or employee (a common crime that is seldom prosecuted), restraint of trade, firearms and explosives violations, smuggling, or interstate pimping (just ask Chuck Berry).

Federal crime convictions can be serious affairs. Look at Julius and Ethel Rosenberg; these Communist spies were caught stealing atomic bomb secrets and sending them to the Stalin regime. They were convicted of treason, and were executed for their crimes in 1953.

Or look at Frank Sturgis and Cuban patriots Virgilio Gonzalez and Eugenio Martinez. They were suckered into carrying out the Watergate break-in, and received long sentences. Victor Lasky, in his classic exposé book *It Didn't Start With Watergate*, recalled the stupidity that helped topple Richard Nixon as follows:

Supposedly, Republican big shots told Sturgis and the Cubans they would help Cuban refugees and exiles from the Castro regime in exchange for their work. James McCord and the other Nixon operatives who planned this fraternity prank-turned-national scandal did such a sorry job of keeping it under wraps that journalist Jack Anderson, prominent Democrats, and many in the "intelligence community" knew about the break-in well in advance; they were appropriately unalarmed. After all, they knew political dirty tricks are as American as apple pie. McCord ran the operation and bungled it so badly that he got Sturgis and the Cubans caught as well as himself. Later, Jack Anderson tried to get Sturgis—an old pal of his—out of jail when he found out Sturgis had been arrested, but U.S. Justice Department agents fought him. McCord later spilled his guts about the operation. Judge John Sirica hit Sturgis and the Cubans with provisional 40-year prison terms in an obvious attempt to get them to squeal, too. (Sirica later sentenced the trio to 1-4 years in prison, and they each served about a year behind bars.)

Or look at Al Capone. An IRS agent sent him to Alcatraz on an income tax evasion conviction after numerous lawmen couldn't pin him down for more serious crimes he committed in Chicago. Or ask my buddy Ricky Slaughterhouse. A federal judge gave him 46 years for possessing firearms as a felon when a county jury gave him only a few months for a lot more violent offenses.

Now that you know the types of criminal cases the federal courts handle, I suppose I should say a thing or two about how to check criminal records in these courts. So here goes.

Check the phone book for the address and phone number of the U.S. District Court that covers your area. There are several of these courts in most states, and virtually every metropolitan area with a couple of hundred thousand or more people has one. Also, there are federal courts in centrally located small towns in rural areas. For instance, there are federal courthouses in Sioux Falls, South Dakota, Big Stone Gap, Virginia, Bango, Maine and Muskogee, Oklahoma, to name some towns off the beaten path that are so chosen.

Once you find the right courthouse, research cases just like you would in your county courthouse. The settings are a little more formal, but the concept is the same. Remember, an accusation of federal lawbreaking, like any other criminal accusation, tends to make most people who hear about it feel less good about the accused.

Here's one last point about federal cases. If your target operates in more than one area, you'll appreciate knowing the general counsel (top lawyer) of almost every federal agency, the inspector general of the agency, or someone else in the agency keeps a file of all criminal cases the agency has ever filed for violations of laws the agency enforces. And since a case is a public record once it is filed, you can write to the freedom of information officer of the agency with a Freedom of Information request, and ask him or her to research which cases the agency has filed against your target. This goes a lot quicker than trying to contact every federal courthouse in the country to find this kind of dirt on your target. You could also try writing the U.S. Justice Department's freedom of information officer for this kind of criminal case listing against your target. And I'm sure state agencies with the same functions probably have the same kind of files for the state you can access.

CLOSING ARGUMENTS

Documents in a courthouse file do not adequately explain the pain and suffering a criminal inflicts on his victims. The victims of a simple burglary get the eerie feeling their home has been invaded and violated and they are no longer safe. The elderly widow who's been swindled out of her life's savings feels dumb, helpless, and hopeless, for what will she live on now? Likewise, the farmer who loses his land because of white-collar criminal manipulations has lost his roots, his sense of manhood, and his way of life.

The man who is robbed or mugged in front of his family feels the shame of being unable to protect himself or his loved ones, while they feel the terror of knowing they could be defenseless in the face of another such attack. A child who has been molested will always consider in fear who the next adult might be who will viciously rape him or her. A woman who's been raped, and then tossed aside like an empty can once the rapist has violated her body, is a victim who's been stripped of her womanly dignity, her privacy, and her sense of self-worth. And the murder victim—who can say what indescribable panic goes through his or her mind in the last moments before he or she dies at the hands of another?

Or what about the anguish, and then lifetimes of helpless grief that beset the loved ones of a murder victim, especially those who have to identify the body in some drawer at the county morgue? Or what about the terrified witnesses to such crimes—like the poor woman who quaked in her boots as she watched Raymond Tanner cut off his wife's head, then turn around and look at her, with the blood-stained blade in his hand? I can't explain it adequately enough on paper, but if any of you out there saw the movie *Batman*, recall the scene in which the young Bruce Wayne watches, horrified, as evil thugs murder his mom and dad before his eyes. His look of abject terror, his look of heart-shattering sorrow, and the welling of tears in that little boy's eyes were enough to break your heart.

That's why I hate criminals. That's why I hate oily defense attorneys who get them off the hook, and that's why I hate judges who let them off the hook. That's why I hate prosecutors who botch cases so criminals escape justice or plea-bargain to the point of letting dangerous criminals get back on the streets. That's why I hate idiots like hard-core ACLU members who aid and abet these vermin; they ought to be made to house the criminals in their own homes with their own loved ones once they manipulate The System enough to spring them from prison. The problem is that all of these people view the criminal justice system as a game of "Beat the Other Lawyer" instead of the serious business it really is.

The most worthless aspect of the criminal justice system is VERY FEW PLAYERS THINK OF THE VICTIM'S RIGHTS. For damn sure the criminal didn't think of the victim's rights when he committed his crime(s) against the victim. Nor does the defense lawyer—who works loopholes and technicalities to get his usually guilty-as-sin client as light a sentence as he can—often think of the victim. Nor, seemingly, does the judge, who all too often is either a criminal rights freak or a state fascist concerned only about the process and not the people it affects. Or maybe the judge is simply worrying about clearing his case load so he can head to the golf course quicker.

Nor is the prosecutor often concerned about victims' rights. Many prosecutors are oilier than defense attorneys. These people view criminal cases like statistics; the more convictions they can show, the better it will look for them when they run for office or get into private law practices.

That's one key reason why they plea-bargain so easily. A knife-wielding thug who pleads guilty to a plea-bargained simple assault charge counts as a conviction just as much as if the prosecutor had to work a little and try him and convict him on much more serious offenses so he could stay locked up for a while. That's why some prosecutors bully innocent people into pleading guilty to reduced charges while the real culprit still roams on the loose. And too many prosecutors act and think as if the State, and not the victim, is the wronged party. To these prosecutors, the victims are only government witnesses, not people whose homes have been invaded, or whose bodies have been attacked or violated, or whose possessions have been taken away, and whose senses of security have been shattered and whose senses of self-worth have been degraded.

To illustrate my point, let me tell you about a crime story I covered in New Jersey. Some creep reportedly jumped a woman in a parking lot. In the process, he allegedly choked her, threw her to the ground, put her in a headlock, then started pawing her private parts. Police later arrested a man in connection with the case.

I was in township (misdemeanor) court the night they were going to try this man on charges of simple assault. In fact, I was sitting right behind the woman victim. (The woman, afraid to testify in a full-blown attempted rape trial, where she probably figured some weasel of a defense attorney would drag her sex life through court and claim she was hot to trot with a lowlife like his client, told prosecutors she would testify only to the fact the assailant beat her up.) The trial was put off that night because a township policeman would not transport the defendant to court from the county jail several miles away. So the judge rescheduled the trial and the woman went home.

Why didn't the policeman transport the defendant? It turned out the officer didn't want to jeopardize the safety of the other people in the courtroom, because the accused criminal had AIDS!

I wrote my story on the case, then went home for the night. When I woke up the next morning, it dawned on me that the attacker had made the woman bleed, and some body fluid exchange may have taken place. Something else dawned on me— maybe nobody told the woman her alleged attacker had AIDS.

I cut short my morning workout and drove to work. Even though I had the woman's address, I figured it would be in poor taste for me to contact her myself. After all, who wants to get that kind of news from a reporter? So I called the policewoman who ran the county's victim assistance program, and she got in contact with the woman right away.

Meanwhile, I called the county jailer, and asked him if he let the victim know about her possible danger. He declined comment. The woman who served as the jail's medical officer was unavailable for comment. I then called the prosecutor to ask him if he had told the woman. The prosecutor, whom I had berated to his face in an earlier confrontation after he bitched about an anti-lawyer column I had written, said he didn't know for sure if the woman had been told. As I was about to ask him if he had told the victim himself, he blurted, "I'd hate to have her find out in the newspaper she was assaulted by someone with

AIDS," then admitted he didn't tell her that her alleged assailant had the fatal disease.

I called the township police chief, and he told me the officer who wouldn't transport the AIDS-infected defendant told the woman himself that night. So of all the law-enforcement people (and me, too), only the policeman who thought of the safety of other people had thought of the victim.

Bear these things in mind when you dig dirt on your targets. If they are bad people, you are doing a public service in making as much trouble for them as you can by exposing their crimes. That's why I think it's so important for you good people in society to know how to investigate; only you have the morals to make the country work fairly and justly. We need more of you.

Remember, we the people built the courthouses with the sweat of our brows. The judges and lawyers have to answer to US! And with our help, Ms. Justice will be served more and gang-raped less.

END NOTES

1. Information on the case of the bisexual with alleged child-molesting tendencies who wanted to become a foster parent comes from my articles in the *Kingsport* (Tennessee) - *Times-News* on August 10, 1986 and on September 26, 1986. Info also comes from a November 1986 article in the *Bristol Virginia-Tennesseean*.
2. Raymond Tanner's murder case is CR 90-02-169, Butler County (Ohio) Common Pleas Court. Besides interviewing prosecutor Robert Piper, I interviewed police officials, Butler County Sheriff Richard Holzberger, two of the psychologists who checked Tanner (neither would comment), the coroner who conducted the autopsy of Maria Barker Tanner, and family members of both Raymond Tanner and Maria Barker Tanner. I also reviewed the autopsy, some psychological evaluations on Tanner, and several newspaper articles on the case, as well as the criminal case file.
3. Statistics on plea-bargaining come from separate studies by Herbert S. Miller and David A. Jones that Robert Bonn referred to in his textbook *Criminology*.
4. My article on child molester Carson Payne appeared in the *Kingsport* (Tennessee) *Times-News* on October 24, 1986. Payne's case is A-0959-01, filed in Lee County (Virginia) Circuit Court.
5. Osteopath abortion provider Laurence Reich's sex offenses case is M107591, Santa Monica (California) Municipal Court. Other allegations concerning Reich's sexual abuse of patients come from the California osteopath examiner board's case against him. This civil case is C407986, and it was filed in Los Angeles County Superior Court in 1982.
6. Information on the "how not to" video starring Moira Lasch and William Kennedy Smith comes from an article in the December 23, 1991 issue of *Time*.
7. Information on Roger Jepsen's traffic ticket comes from an article in the October 8, 1984 issue of *Time*.
8. Information on Chuck Berry's Mann Act conviction (transporting a female across state lines for immoral purposes) comes from an article in the October 26, 1987 issue of *Newsweek*.
9. Information on the Watergate break-in and Jack Anderson's ties to Frank Sturgis comes from Victor Lasky's book *It Didn't Start With Watergate*. Information on James McCord's "squealing" and the sentences comes from Judge Sirica's book *To Set the Record Straight*.
10. My articles on the accused New Jersey sex offender and those of us who didn't tell the victim her reported attacker had AIDS appeared in the Ocean County *Observer* on January 7, 1987, January 9, 1987, and January 21, 1987.

Civil Courts Hold Uncivil Information

If a teenage girl shoplifts from a store and gets caught, she goes to jail. But if the store's owner sets up the computer on his cash register scanner to over-charge and rip off his customers, he escapes scot-free. If a street punk knifes a woman and gets caught, he goes to jail. But if a doctor tears this woman's insides out while performing an abortion on her, he escapes scot-free. If a father beats the hell out of his kids, the neighbors complain and he goes to jail. But if a teacher abuses the father's kids, the school bureaucrats and the teacher's union will try to help the teacher escape scot-free.

The legal system protects too many professional and business types from the criminal consequences of their actions. However, there is one weapon their victims can use against them—the lawsuit. And in lawsuits, people accuse professional and business people (and other people, too) of behavior that make street punks look clean by comparison.

For "civilian" purposes, knowing how to check a person's lawsuit record will enable you to check on his character before getting involved with the target on a business or personal basis. And if you find the person is a crook, an incompetent, or some other type of unethical louse, you can protect other people by warning them about him. For "military" purposes, knowing how to check a person's lawsuit record will enable you to find and publicize evidence of his crookedness, incompetence, or all-around rottenness, and ethically damage his reputation. In either situa-tion, if your target has been involved in a lot of lawsuits (especially as a defendant), these lawsuits may very well document a pattern of questionable behavior on his part.

WHY DO PEOPLE SUE?

Because it's the American way, that's why! And besides, for most people, suing is the best way they can punish those who hurt them without resorting to vigilante tactics. From the justice angle, people sue wrongdoers because it is easier than getting the local prosecutor to file criminal charges against those who hurt them. From the financial angle, it's also more lucrative. After all, very few crime victims get any real compensation, even if the criminal who vic-

timized them goes to prison. But people who win lawsuits win money—sometimes very serious money.

And there is a good reason why federal, state, and local officials sue certain lawbreakers. They stand a much better chance of punishing these lowlifes in civil court than in criminal court. Why? It takes ALL the jurors to return a guilty verdict. One holdout, out of stupidity, bias, or bribery, can hang a jury and maybe kill a criminal prosecution. But a civil trial usually takes only two-thirds to three-quarters of the jurors' votes to win. And the standard of proof of guilt in a civil case is nowhere near as high as it is in a criminal case; lawyers say you have to be 100 percent guilty to lose a criminal trial, but only 51 percent guilty to lose a civil trial. Government prosecutors can't send the criminals to prison if they win civil suits, but they can get the lowlifes fined, revoke their licenses or permits, and set them up for criminal prosecution on contempt-of-court or other grounds if they renege on their fines, or if they break the law again.

COURT SHORTS

Lawsuits are like "Spaghetti Westerns"; some are good, some are bad, and all are ugly. I've seen some lawsuits filed by people who belong in the Nut House for the Insanely Greedy. For example, I watched a civil trial in which the parents of a kid sued the local police force for causing him to lose his job as a stock clerk. How? According to their oily lawyer, the cops arrested the kid for driving through some bushes in the parking lot of a drive-in eatery. The manager of the eatery knew the kid, called his boss, and told him he was employing a young hoodlum with an arrest record. The kid's boss fired him, and all of this would never have happened, the lawyer said, if the arrest hadn't taken place. When I asked the lawyer why he hadn't gone after the fast food place manager for being a character assassin or the kid's boss for being an unreasonable jerk, the lawyer said these men's megabuck corporations would be harder to fight in court than the police force of a little Podunk town. Fortunately for justice, the parents lost the case against the cops.

Let's move on to the rich and famous. *Star Wars* actress Carrie Fisher had some people thinking she truly was a space case when they found out about her 1988 lawsuit against her former business manager. Ms. Carrie, whose best role in my opinion was swooning in the arms of John Belushi, then getting dropped into the sewer in *The Blues Brothers*, claimed her ex-moneyman did basically the same thing to her bankroll, according to a published account of her case. She claimed she was unaware of how badly he was mismanaging her money because her head was in the orbit of a serious drug problem!

Another recent favorite of mine is a case involving Madalyn Murray O'Hair. The nation's best-known atheist showed the god she worships is money. Why? Because in the 1980s it became known that she and other atheists were fighting for control of the multi-million dollar estate of atheist/racist/miser James Harvey Johnson. Armando Acuna, a reporter who covered the case, said O'Hair had tried to wrest Johnson's money away from him even when he was alive. The following passage from a letter which Acuna said Ms. O'Hair wrote to Johnson in 1983 implies the milk of human kindness in her breasts might run sour from time to time.

"You (O'Hair reportedly wrote to Johnson) are a dying, defunct, discredited old man who will grow moldy in an unmarked grave, having squandered atheist funds. In the interests of a movement which you have injured by your presence in it, it appears to me you should be now making arrangements to turn everything over to American Atheists."

According to Acuna, the case unfolded as follows:

Ms. O'Hair and her supporters accused Johnson of amassing his fortune by stealing money left to atheist causes by dead atheists. She then printed her own stock certificates in an atheist publishing company Johnson owned and was planning to will to an atheist group which she and her supporters claimed they were members of. She held a "board meeting," and had her followers vote Johnson out of power. Johnson responded by re-writing his will so the publishing company would be willed to someone else. The wrangling went on after Johnson's death because the old atheist couldn't take his money with him, wherever he went.

For comic relief, few cases beat the hilarious "galimony" lawsuits which pitted tennis stars Billie Jean King and Martina Navratilova against their lesbian lovers. When Billie Jean's ex-lady sued her in 1981, the jockette at first denied she was the woman's lesbian lover. However, the woman's lawyer let it be known he had more than 100 letters Billie Jean sent the woman (and records of a joint credit card account for the two), and Billie Jean knew she was licked. Ms.

King admitted to the tryst. And in Martina's case, you may have gotten a chuckle over reading in the summer of 1991 that the athlete got to keep the dogs she shared with her lady love, but her "ex" would get visitation rights to the pooches.

On the other hand, I've seen some truly ugly civil suits which people filed justly to avenge some very ugly activities. For example, I saw a civil case in which the parents of a statutory rape victim, dissatisfied with the month-long sentence the girl's sexual abuser (a doctor) drew, sued him, and they won the girl a pile of money. I've also investigated or covered lawsuits involving wrongful death, doctors molesting patients, medical malpractice, unsafe workplaces, worker exploitation, major health code violations, massive environmental damage, businessmen's fraud involving goods and services, school systems being unable to educate students, tax evasion, breach of contract, and government employees stealing property. Believe me, NONE of these cases enhanced the reputations of the defendants, once I reported on them!

What does this all mean to you? Simply this: There is a lot of negative info on people in civil case files in the courthouses of this nation. You can use these files to check doctors and lawyers and other professional people for malpractice suits or professional negligence suits or misconduct suits which allege everything from fraud to sexual imposition. You can check business people for really ugly business suits alleging fraud, failure to perform contracted work, or other forms of unethical conduct. You can also check on these people for health and safety violations, pollution control problems, labor law violations, or other forms of unethical behavior.

Have I sold you on the kinds of info you can find in lawsuit records? I hope so. Since America supposedly has more lawyers than the rest of the world put together, it's not unlikely your target has been involved in one or more lawsuits. In this chapter, we'll talk about what happens in a lawsuit, how to find out if your target has ever been involved in a lawsuit, and how to review your target's lawsuit records in various courts.

WHAT HAPPENS IN A LAWSUIT

Anyone who has watched *The People's Court* knows basically how small claims court works. But higher-dollar lawsuits work differently. First, the person suing (the plaintiff) consults with a lawyer before suing. After all, there could be a lot of money involved, and most people aren't competent to represent themselves when thousands or millions of dollars are at stake. (Not all that many lawyers are that competent, either, but that's another story.)

The plaintiff's lawyer then writes up a complaint (in which he lists the reasons why his client is suing the defendant), files the complaint at the courthouse, and has the defendant (the person being sued) served with the complaint. The defendant (also known in some quarters as the respondent), then gets his own lawyer, then the lawyers fight.

For example, the lawyer for a woman who sues a trucker for driving his Peterbilt into her Volvo may demand in interrogatories (out-of-court written questioning) that the truck driver admit he's had a zillion traffic tickets, a drunk driving conviction, a drug problem, and a long-term legal blindness condition. The trucker's lawyer, in response, may demand in deposition (out-of-court verbal testimony) that the woman admit she was applying makeup while driving, exposing herself to other motorists, speeding to elude an irate cheated-on husband, or trying to stunt-drive her way into a sequel movie about lady drag racer Shirley Muldowney.

Before the case is scheduled for trial, both lawyers will also file motions to get the judge to rule in their favor on the case. Some of the tactics they use in filing these motions are legitimate; other tactics are pretty creative at best and unethical as hell at worst.

Finally, one of four things will happen. The plaintiff will drop the case without collecting anything, the defendant will settle out of court with the plaintiff, the case will go to an arbitrator for a decision, or the case will go to trial. If the case goes to an arbitrator or goes to trial, an arbitrator, a judge, or a jury will rule in favor of the plaintiff or the defendant. Most cases, however, end up being dropped or settled out of court.

GETTING OFF ON THE RIGHT FOOT

Let's assume you want to check your target's lawsuit record in your county. You'll first need to know which courts in your county handle high-dollar cases and which courts handle low-dollar cases.

All states have lower courts and upper courts. Lawsuits for small amounts of money are handled in the civil portion of lower courts. (Criminal prosecutions for misdemeanors take place in the criminal portion of lower courts.) Lawsuits for large amounts of money are handled in the civil portion of upper courts. (Criminal prosecutions for felonies take place in the criminal portion of upper courts.) Figure out what they call the upper and lower courts in your county by checking the county government listings in a phone book for your county.

Once you know the names of the courts, you can go after the records. Start checking in the upper court for high-dollar lawsuits involving your target. Then go to each of the lower courts in your county to check on lower-dollar cases involving your target.

There are two steps to checking a target's lawsuit record. These are:

- Find out the case numbers of all cases involving your target.
- Using the case numbers, have court clerks pull the case files for you so you can look at the legal paper in them. Then copy all important or damaging information from each case file!

We'll now go through each step in detail, using the upper court in your county as an example.

FINDING OUT CASE NUMBERS

The list of all the lawsuits filed in an upper court in any county is called a "civil index" (or docket, or something close to it). This list will be on microfilm, in a computer, in drawers full of index cards, or handwritten into a very heavy set of books. You will have to check this list to get case numbers for all cases involving your target.

In each county, there will be at least one place where an upper court civil index or docket for all upper courts in the county is available to the public. (In almost all counties, this place is the upper civil court clerk's office; in a handful of huge counties which have more than one upper courthouse, this place will be the central courthouse's upper civil court clerk's office.) To find out where it is, call the court clerk of the upper court whose records you want to check. The clerk's number will be in the phone book under the upper court portion of the county government listings.

Then, go to the courthouse where the court's civil index or docket is, and look up all cases involving your target. Look him up by name, and look up all his businesses by name. (See the first chapter on the private sector for finding out the names of businesses your target owns.) Some states list cases alphabetically by plaintiff (person suing), then alphabetically by respondent or defendant (person being sued). Other states list alphabetically by name, and lump the plaintiffs and respondents/defendants together. Write down the target's name, the name of the other party in the case, the case number, and the date of the case. A couple of notes follow:

- The most recent cases (those filed in the last couple of months or so) might not be in the civil index. They'll be on a separate list the court clerks keep. Ask to see this list, too.
- Some "ancient" cases (those that are more than

10 or so years old) might not be readily available in the clerk's office. Ask the clerks where these older records are kept, then make arrangements to view them.

Court clerks in some states (like New York) do not list cases by defendant or respondent; the clerks list cases only by plaintiff. This means it's damn near impossible to look up cases against people who have been sued in these states. Either by unethical design or by bureaucratic laziness, these states shield lawsuit defendants from public knowledge because of the clerks' sorry records-keeping process. However, there is a way around this problem. Each New York court carries a list called "Request for Judicial Intervention (RJI)." The court clerks make up these lists for all civil cases they assign to judges. The RJI list will alphabetically name defendants as well as plaintiffs, and you can check the RJI list for your target (or have the clerks do it) without too much effort.

But RJI lists run back only so far. Or maybe your county's court records are so snarled that you might consider having a court services firm, a law review journal publisher, or a lawyer run the check for you. Having these things done will cost you some money, but it might be worth it to you.

The court services firm's people will do their work by poring over the old records. This is time-consuming, and therefore expensive. A law review journal publisher probably has all court cases listed in some computer program, so he might be able to search for all cases naming your target. And lawyers have access to computerized case records, so one of them might be able to find cases involving your target.

There are two other ways—both relatively cheap—to find out about cases involving your target. The first way involves checking a law newspaper in your area. If your county has a law newspaper which lists all cases filed day-by-day, you might be able to go through back issues or the newspaper's index of cases. You can see if your area has such a paper by asking the court clerks or local lawyers.

The other way is to contact the county sheriff's deputies (or applicable police force) and ask to check their process serving log. This log shows the lawmen served papers on defendants (formally notified them they were being sued) as part of their jobs after the plaintiffs paid for them to serve the papers.

(Even though it might cost more to have a lawman serve papers than have a private firm do it, many people realize lawmen are more effective. Why? Because lawmen have a high intimidation factor, and they can make defendants acknowledge the papers they serve on them. Lawmen serve papers in uniform, and they have guns, billy clubs, and the power to make police-style arrests. They also have the disturbing tendency to show up at a target's work place or business during business hours; their presence embarrasses the target in front of a boss or a client. I know of many private process servers who have been beaten up by irate defendants, but no lawsuit defendant in his right mind is going to attack an armed lawman.)

Once I had to check a target's lawsuit record in a county in upstate New York. The county's inept court clerks had failed to record under my target's name any cases in which he was a defendant. Further, they refused me access to the county's RJI list, and I didn't have the time to file a freedom-of-information action against them. But a lady sheriff's deputy bailed me out. As a dedicated and courteous public servant, she ran a check of the sheriff's process serving log over a 10-year period for me to find cases in which her brother officers had served papers on my target. You should be so lucky.

CHECK THE FILES

Once you get the case numbers of all high-dollar cases involving your target (and his businesses) that have been filed in your county, you'll be able to research the actual case files. Here's how to do it properly:

First, ask the court clerk in your county's upper court how to have clerks pull civil case files for you. Follow the clerk's instructions; use the target's name and each case number.

Once the clerks pull the cases for you, go through each case file to see what the case is about. This information will be in a document called a "complaint" or a "petition" or a "pleading." In this document, the plaintiff will accuse the defendant of some sort of misconduct (fraud, malpractice, violation of codes, breach of contract, or the like). The plaintiff's lawyer may amend (update) the complaint every so often, so check all of the complaints. Mark the complaints that contain the most recent and complete information.

Check the target's response. This legal brief, full of legalese, will usually contain a denial, but little valuable information. Skim through it, then mark it only if you find some information you can use.

Scan the rest of the file. Some pages contain interrogatories (questions from one side to the other side) and answers to interrogatories. Other pages contain depositions (a party's statement); still others contain legal motions.

The interrogatories and answers to interrogatories usually contain some interesting stuff. For example, the answers to interrogatories in a fraud case might lay out the details of what the defendant did to make the plaintiff sue him. Or in a code violation case, here's where the details of the wrongful activity that reportedly took place might surface. Or in a malpractice case, many of the details of the damage a victim reportedly suffered at the hands of her doctor will appear here. Also, these documents often contain nice-to-know information like the target's property holdings, business ventures, insurance policy numbers, home address, facts on his life and career, and other such items. Mark any page that contains information that will come in handy.

Likewise, check the depositions with a fine-tooth comb. They will contain many of the same kinds of items the interrogatories and answers to interrogatories contain.

Don't spend too much time on the motions. They're usually not pertinent to what you really want to know. However, some motions will hint at the eventual outcome of a case, so check them.

As you work your way through the file, try to figure out the outcome of the case. Some cases are settled out of court, some cases go to an arbitrator hearing or to a jury or a judge trial, some cases are ended because the plaintiff doesn't want to continue the fight, and some cases are still active (they haven't been decided or settled yet). Mark pages which show the case's outcome. Some hints follow:

- Check judge orders or other prominent pieces of paper in the file. These often indicate action of one sort or another by a judge. These include denying or granting motions, forcing arbitration, or scheduling a trial.

- Check motions. Sometimes the lawyers will spell out an out-of-court settlement proposal in these. Or sometimes they will try to get the judge to impose a settlement or throw out the case.

- Check the dismissal document. This will note that the case is over. It might also hint at whether the defendant settled out of court, if a judge threw out the case, or if the plaintiff merely decided to end his suit without getting anything. Unfortunately, the records aren't always clear on why a case was dismissed.

- Check the verdict sheet if there was a trial. This document will list the outcome.

In a pinch, if documents are missing from the file, you can check the clerk's record books to find other motions or orders or other actions that took place, the outcome of the case, and the names of the judge and the opposing attorneys. Ask her how she files such information, and follow her instructions on how to find it.

THEN HAVE PHOTOCOPIES MADE OF ALL PAGES YOU'VE MARKED. YOU'LL NOW HAVE HARD-COPY PROOF OF YOUR TARGET'S LOWLIFING.

If you HAVE to know more than what's in the files, get a lawyer you trust to contact the attorneys in the case (preferably the winning ones, unless you sense a cover-up) and have the lawyer try to get the paperwork for you out of what they call "professional courtesy"—a lawyer's practice of doing favors for other lawyers (even, sometimes, at the expense of his clients).

One quick note about the outcome of a case—it's nice to know the outcome, but in very many cases, it's more important to know that a victim filed suit against your target in the first place. Why? Because the target might settle quietly out of court. Or he might be able to weasel out of a lawsuit on technicalities, on his lawyer's skill, on the victim's lawyer's ineptness, or on a judge's stupidity. But it won't mean your target caused the victim no harm. For example, journalists routinely damage people's reputations with negligent and/or biased reporting. But they seldom lose libel suits because the people they hurt have to prove their negligence or bias was a deliberate malicious attempt to smear them.

The most swinish of targets fight against lawsuits even if they're DEAD WRONG. They do this to intimidate the plaintiff, wear him or her out, reduce the amount of money they'll eventually have to cough up, and obstruct justice in general. If your target gets sued a lot, it's evidence he might be an unethical louse, even if his lawyers can help him weasel out of trouble. By digging up ugly lawsuits against him, you can show many people have accused him of wrongdoing and you can show he's responsible for a pattern of evident unethical conduct.

ADVICE AND CONSENT—A CASE HISTORY

I once took on a research job for some clients which involved checking on the abortion providers of Akron Center for Reproductive Health. The operators of this Ohio abortion facility were challenging a parental notification law requiring abortion facility operators to notify the parents of teenage girls when their children were undergoing abortions. (Parents, if your girl needs your permission to get her ears pierced, why shouldn't you know about when she undergoes invasive surgery under anesthesia?) The law would definitely hurt the profits of abortion facility operators. My job was to find instances in which girls had reportedly suffered damage at the hands of the staffers of this facility.

By researching lawsuit records in Ohio, Kentucky, and Florida, I found two of the doctors associated with this place—Max Gaujean and Nabil Ghali—had run up roughly 30 malpractice suits between them since abortion on demand became legal. Each of them had been sued by survivors of women who had died after undergoing abortions at their hands. I also found other doctors with ties to this facility and/or its sister abortion facility in Cleveland had high numbers of malpractice cases on their records. I also found a civil case filed by the parents of a young girl whom Ghali had manipulated into having sex with him.

This was a bonanza compared to what state medical authorities had on the facility. Ohio doctor licensing authorities said Gaujean had a clean record (despite being sued for malpractice five times as often as the average Ohio OB-GYN). And all they said they had on Ghali was that he had lost his license over a four-count conviction involving his having sex with an underage girl in Kentucky, then got it back in an appeal. I was able to use this information to confirm the conviction with Kentucky authorities.

After I got through running checks on the doctors associated with Akron Center for Reproductive Health, it made sense to me why the operators were fighting the parental notification law—and why they had fought a previous informed consent law. If you ran an abortion facility, would you want women, girls, and the parents of these girls to know your doctors were constant malpractice risks? Would you want them to know your doctors were sued for wrongful deaths? And would you want young girls (or their parents) to know one of your doctors is a convicted sex offender before they go into a room with him without all their clothes on?

CHECKING LOWER COURTS

Usually, you won't find any really juicy lawsuits in lower courts. Most cases at this level involve unpaid bills. (Local government officials do file against tax deadbeats in the lower courts; sometimes you can verify a target's holdings or estimate his income by reviewing these cases.) Also, the average city or township in each county runs its own lower court, so this means you will have to check every lower court in your county for low-grade civil dirt on your target. To save time, concentrate on the lower court in the city or township in which your target lives or does business. The procedure for researching lower court lawsuits is the same as for researching cases in upper courts.

CHECKING FEDERAL COURTS

Federal courts handle civil matters such as bankruptcy cases and cases involving alleged violations of federal regulations. So if your target has ever declared bankruptcy (or has had one of his businesses declare bankruptcy), you can find the case in a federal bankruptcy court. If the Feds have ever sued your target for violations of federal labor, health, safety, environmental, civil rights or tax laws, you can find the case in a federal district court.

And if your target has sued a government body over some sort of alleged violation of his Constitutional rights, the record will be there in the files, too. In fact, I know of several bizarre federal cases involving prisoners suing for alleged violations of their rights. One such case involved a yoyo who was doing time in a county jail for a string of burglaries. As part of a jail-wide crackdown, the jailer confiscated the burglar's tape deck and a number of Jimmy Swaggart tapes, along with all the other prisoners' electrical appliances. The thief sued the jailer in federal court, claiming his loss of the tapes caused him to backslide and lag behind in his spiritual development. The case was thrown out, praise the Lord!

On a more serious note, another prisoner I knew sued a state government because state law-enforcement authorities evidently welshed on a deal they made with him. He had witnessed a murder inside prison, and his testimony hung the death sentence on the killer. He had asked for anonymity before the trial, a transfer out of the prison he was in, and a reduction of his own armed robbery sentence. State officials broke their word on two of the three promises, he alleged, and somehow the killer's friends got a copy of his sworn statement before the trial. As you could well imagine, frequent beatings he got from these thugs were soon the least of his worries.

Social Security lawsuits also are filed in federal courts. Usually, these kinds of cases involve people suing the Feds for not shelling out Social Security benefits they claim they're owed. Then there are cases the Feds file against people to recover Social Security benefit money these people allegedly shouldn't have gotten. Your target's involvement in such a case could cause him problems if you find out about it and publicize it. After all, who wants people to know the Feds are suing him for what looks like an attempt to freeload on the taxpayers? And your target might suffer even if word gets out he's a claimant of benefits—nobody likes a freeloader who tries to fatten up at the public trough. Some will think he's a lazy slob even if he technically meets the criteria of a certain handout program.

As an aside, the Inspector General of the Department of Health and Human Services goes after those who defraud the Social Security program and other public assistance programs. Contact his office or the freedom of information officer of HHS or the general counsel of HHS to see if the agency has taken any civil (or criminal) action to recover any money your target may have stolen with a fraudulent claim.

There is not enough space in this book to mention all the bankruptcy and federal code violations I reported on after I checked items in the federal courts. But I will add one last note on the types of lawsuits you can find there: The federal courts handle diversity of citizenship cases also. A diversity of citizenship case is one in which the plaintiff lives in one state and the defendant lives in another state, and legal problems would arise in handling the case in the plaintiff's state court or in the defendant's state court.

Now that you know the types of lawsuits the federal courts handle, I suppose I should say a few words on how to check the records in these courts. So here they are.

Check the phone book for the address and phone number of the U.S. District Court or the U.S. Bankruptcy Court that covers your area. There are several of these courts in most states, and virtually every metropolitan area with a couple of hundred thousand or more people has one. Also, there are federal courts in centrally located small towns in rural areas. (Before I forget, I'd like to say the ladies who clerked the federal courthouses in Big Stone Gap, Abingdon, and Roanoke, Virginia, were the nicest and most helpful government employees I ever dealt with. They were courteous, helpful and pleasant; they were gracious Southern ladies in the finest sense of the term.)

Once you find the right courthouse, research cases just like you would in your county courthouse. The settings are a little more formal, but the concept is the same.

One last point about federal cases. If your target operates in more than one area, you'll appreciate knowing the general counsel (top lawyer) of almost every federal agency, the inspector general of the agency, or someone else in the agency keeps a listing of all civil lawsuits the agency has ever filed for violations of codes the agency enforces. And since a case is a public record once it is filed, you can write to the freedom of information officer of the agency with a Freedom of Information request, and ask him or her to research which cases the agency has filed against your target. This goes a lot quicker than trying to contact every federal courthouse in the country to find this kind of dirt on your target. You could also try writing the U.S. Justice Department's freedom of information officer for this kind of lawsuit listing against your target. And I'm sure state agencies with similar functions probably have the same kind of files for the state you can access.

CLOSING STATEMENTS

People didn't know germs spread diseases until after the invention of the microscope. Scientists used this tool to find these harmful microbes in the tissues and fluids of sick people and animals. Lawsuit research ability is much like the microscope. This tool enables you to focus in on your target to see if he's rotten.

Other chapters of this book will discuss specialized dirt-digging on businesses, government employees, land owners, environmental polluters, labor law violators, health care providers, school officials, and government contractors. They will cover certain kinds of dirt-digging unique to the misconduct of each kind of violator's field. Since many of these acts result in civil cases, you can use the research techniques in this chapter to review their civil cases.

Lawyers and judges like to think courthouses are like their country clubs—places to keep the rabble like us at arm's length. But we the people have the right to crash the party, track mud on the carpet, and treat the courthouses the way they should be treated—as places where our interests should be protected and documents that belong to US are kept! If you're merely checking someone's background for peaceful civilian purposes, you may be able to verify your target is either good, evil, or somewhere in between before you or someone you care about gets involved commercially or personally with the target. And for those of you looking to bomb your targets back to the Stone Age, the dirt you find on them in civil case files will enable you to tell them, "Here's mud in your eye!"

END NOTES

1. Carrie Fisher's lawsuit is C675338, Los Angeles County (California) Superior Court. Also, an article on her case appeared in the Hollywood publication *Daily Variety* on February 3, 1988. (Her case file has been unavailable during the writing of this book due to court proceedings, according to the clerks.)
2. Information on Billie Jean King's "galimony" case comes from articles in the May 11, 1981 issues of *Time* and *Newsweek*.
3. Information on Martina Navratilova's "galimony" case comes from a June 1991 article in *USA Today*.
4. Armando Acuna's article on Madalyn Murray O'Hair appeared in the Dayton *Daily News* on July 2, 1989. Acuna wrote the article originally for the *Los Angeles Times*.
5. On the Akron Center for Reproductive Health research project, I found the following malpractice cases which women or their survivors filed against doctors with ties to the operators of this facility and/or its sister facility in Cleveland:

In Summit County (Akron), Ohio Common Pleas Court, I referred to cases CV 76-5-1131, CV 80-2-0566, CV 80-11-3101, CV 81-12-3466, CV 82-4-1036, CV 85-11-3599, CV 86-5-1750, CV 88-4-1280, and CV 88-7-2130.

In Cuyahoga County (Cleveland), Ohio Common Pleas Court, I referred to cases 914470, 916389, 918706, 920030, 924488, 928352, 936175, 937202, 938314, 939123, 940921, 945324, 947388, 970935, 975317, 981776, 988576, 992028, 992176, 012790, 17342, 32571, 34064, 41169, 64227, 74483, 76595, 79182, 82907, 83336, 87715, 91279, 91977, 93883, 100244, 102926, 110247, 124086, 166395, 168183, and 175142.

In Campbell County, Kentucky Circuit Court, I referred to cases 78-CI-730, 79-CI-350, 79-CI-899, 81-CI-438, 81-CI-534, 81-CI-9114, 86-CI-1147, and 87-CI-478. (I also referred to Kentucky v. Ghali, 82-J-431, for Ghali's sex offense conviction.)

In Dade County (Miami), Florida Circuit Court, I referred to cases 85-14112, 86-37853, 88-6307, 89-4859, and 89-49634.

The Ohio medical board file I referred to is State Medical Board of Ohio vs. Ghali. The state medical officials took action against Ghali's license in 1984, and he got the action overturned on appeal in 1986.

Excavate Real Estate Information

When you were in school, you no doubt saw historical maps of the United States. These maps showed how the British stole land from the Indians on the East Coast, then stole land from the Spanish, the Dutch, and the French (who had stolen land from Indians in the South, the East, and the Midwest).

The maps then showed the Patriots liberating the 13 colonies from British tyranny, and showed Jefferson making the Louisiana Purchase from Napoleon. The maps showed the unstoppable growth of the United States, from American agents buying Florida from the Spanish through American settlers grabbing Texas from the Mexicans, through the American Army forcing Mexico to give up California and the Southwest, through American diplomats pressuring the British into giving up their fraudulent claims to the Pacific Northwest. The maps showed the South's secession and defeat in the Civil War, then they showed the continuation of America's growth, from the purchase of Alaska from Russia, to the purchase of the Virgin Islands from Denmark, to the seizure of Hawaii from Queen Liliuokalani and her people, to the takeover of Puerto Rico from Spain. And they showed "how the West was won" at the expense of the Indians and the Eskimos.

"The history lesson was nice, Kev," you're saying, "but what's your point?"

My point is this: In the courthouse of your county are records much like the maps you saw in school. Your county government has maps which show how the land in your county passed from the white people who took it from the Indians to the lawyers, bankers, robber barons and government agents who took it from these people's descendants, to the people to whom they resold the land at inflated prices, and on down to the owners of today. And your county government has records which shows a trail of paper on each piece of land in your county. The records show who owns the land now, who used to own it, and what special circumstances (like mineral rights, easements, mortgages, liens, and the like) apply to the land. And these maps and records are all open to the public.

There are some very good reasons land records are in the hands of the government. The best reason, as far as we the people are concerned, is that it keeps people "honest." Government custody of land records reduces the number of arguments over boundaries, theft or forgery of titles, and other problems that arise when someone tries to take unfair advantage of someone else. It's a public service, because there are fewer land disputes to clog the courts, and fewer shootings and knifings over land disputes to clog the hospitals and cemeteries.

The best reason, as far as the politicians are concerned, is that having access to land records makes it a lot easier to tax the land. The county assessor (in some counties, he is called an auditor) assesses (estimates) the worth of all property registered in the county recorder's office, and the county treasurer bills property owners for the taxes based on the estimated worth of their property. If you're a property owner, you already know this. If you're a renter, your landlord pays the taxes, then takes it out of your pocket in the form of higher rent. So no one escapes.

ALL YOU WANTED TO KNOW ABOUT LAND BUT WERE AFRAID TO ASK

This chapter is basically a crash course in how to research real estate records. And I've written it for you as if you were someone wanting to buy property. I did this just in case you want to use this chapter for a peaceful "civilian" purpose like buying land, but also because if you put yourself in a buyer's mindset, it usually makes it easier for you to check property records thoroughly. This way, you can do land research to find dirt on others as well as do land research to help yourself. At the end of each set of instructions will be a brief blurb on how you can use the information for "military" (muckraking) purposes. (A second chapter on real estate covers specialized muckraking techniques involving real estate records.)

Bear in mind that this chapter's instructions won't cover every little nuance in real estate records from county to county. But it will give you some good general guidance on how to search the most important property records. And it will set you up to handle some special projects covered later in this book—special projects which entail making legitimate trouble for those who are benefiting from shady real estate deals.

FINDING OUT WHO OWNS LAND

Let's say you wanted to buy land in your county. After knowing how much the seller wants for the property, you'd want to know what you're getting, and what hassles you might inherit when you buy the land.

So you go to the county recorder (or whoever it is in your county government who handles property records). Once you get to his office, you see a map room loaded with yellowing maps and a records room with hundreds of very heavy books full of property records. You see a bunch of real estate agents and bank agents busily checking records. And it's just dawned on you that you're going to stick out like a sore thumb because you don't really know where in these huge piles of paper the records you need are.

Don't worry. Be happy.

You do at least know the name of the property owner (or you maybe know who used to own the property) and the general location of the property. That's all you'll need to know to be able to find what you need. Even though county recorders across America use different methods to keep land records, these methods all hinge on using property owners, former property owners, and location to keep track of land.

Let's assume you know only the name of the owner of the property. Find the grantee books in the room. These books contain, alphabetically by year, a list of everyone who ever bought or was given a piece of property in your county as far back as people kept records in your county. (A grantee is legalese for a person, partnership, corporation, or government agency who receives or buys property.) If your county hasn't alphabetized its records on a computer yet, you'll have to check the owner's name in each grantee book from this year on back—year by year—until you find his name and the property you're interested in one of the grantee books. (If you're lucky and your county has computerized or microfilmed records, have the clerks show you the procedure for finding out all the parcel numbers of all the properties the target property owner owns.)

When you find the owner's name, you'll see an entry in the book like this:

GRANTEE	GRANTOR	INST	BOOK/PAGE	DATE	PARCEL	DESCRIPTION
Chump, Don	Capone, Al	DEED	777/1111	2-14-91	666-666	1 Crooked Lane Lot 13, Atl. City

The entry tells you Chump received Parcel 666-666 (Lot 13 at 1 Crooked Lane in Atlantic City) from Capone as the result of a deed filed 2/14/91. You'll now pull Deed Book 777, turn to page 1111, and find the deed. The deed will contain the names of the grantor and the grantee, a description of the surveyed boundaries of the property, and the terms of the land transfer (including price in most cases).

Now let's assume you don't know the current owner of the property, but you do know who owned the property at one time. Find the grantor books in the room. These books contain, alphabetically by year, a list of everyone who ever sold or gave away a piece of property in your county as far back as people kept records in your county. (A grantor is legalese for a person, partnership, corporation, or government agency who sells or gives away property.)

Checking for grantors is like checking for grantees. You may have to check through grantor books year by year or you may be able to check computerized or microfilmed records, depending on how your county keeps land records.

When you find the former owner's name, you'll see an entry in the book like this:

GRANTOR	GRANTEE	INST	BOOK/PAGE	DATE	PARCEL	DESCRIPTION
Capone, Al	Chump, Don	DEED	777/1111	2-14-91	666-666	1 Crooked Lane Lot 13, Atl. City

The entry tells you Capone deeded Parcel 666-666 (Lot 13 at 1 Crooked Lane in Atlantic City) to Chump 2/14/91. You'll now pull Deed Book 777, turn to page 1111, and find the deed. The deed will contain the names of the grantor and the grantee, a description of the surveyed boundaries of the property, and the terms of the land transfer.

Or let's assume you know only the location of the property in question. You'd go to the county recorder's map room and find the property on one of the maps. This works well for property in town and property in the country.

If the piece of property is in a city or town, find the street the property fronts on in the appropriate city or town map. (These maps are usually bound together in map books, like an atlas of your county.) Write down the number or letter code (or name) of the parcel that appears on the map. Then find this code on the page used as a key to the map; often the page is opposite the map for convenience. When you find the code, note the parcel number (and owner or grantee, if your county also includes that information in the map book). In many counties, you can also find the parcel number of a city lot or town lot by matching the address of the property to the parcel number using the records the county recorder's people have made.

If you now have the parcel number of the property, but still need the grantor's name or the grantee's name, check the numerical order list of parcel numbers the county recorder's people have made to match the grantor or grantee to the parcel number. Using the example above, you find the property known as 1 Crooked Lane (Lot 13) on the Atlantic City town map, and find out its parcel number is 666-666. You then consult the records tied to the maps; you find out the grantor is Al Capone and the grantee is Don Chump. Now you can use the grantor books or the grantee books to find out where the deed to the property is, just like in the examples above.

A piece of land out in the country is a little harder to check on, but the principle is the same. You'd know roughly where the property is, and you'd probably know what township or at least what part of the county the property is in. You'd then check a map of that portion of the county where the property is. Once you find the property on the map, write down the number or letter code (or name) of the parcel that appears on the map. Then find this code on the page used as a key to the map; often the page is opposite the map for convenience. When you find the code, note the parcel number (and owner or grantee, if your county also includes that information in the map book). And, just like for city lots or town lots, match the property's parcel number to a grantor or grantee using the numerical order list of parcel numbers the county recorder's people have made. Then use the grantor books or the grantee books to find out where the deed to the property is, just like in the examples above.

What are the "military" applications? You'll be able to find out the owner of a target piece of property, and the most recent previous owner, and so on. This will come in handy for a number of different kinds of investigations. You'll also be able to use the grantee records to see what real estate your target owns, how he got it all, and who he got it all from. You'll further be able to use the grantor records to find out what real estate your target unloaded, to whom, and for what prices. This info will point to your target's business partners and practices. It may indicate whether he takes advantage of people by suckering them out of a fair selling price or suckering them into an exorbitant buying price. It may indicate he's getting rich at taxpayer expense. It will indicate whether zoning changes, planning decisions, or other government actions benefit him.

FINDING OUT WHAT STRINGS ARE ATTACHED TO PROPERTY

Now that you know who owns the property you're interested in, and where the deed to the property is, you're going to need to know what strings are attached to the property. Records in the county recorder's office will let you know the possible problems you'll be inheriting when you buy property. The problems may be great enough that you'll be only too happy to buy elsewhere.

It takes a good title searcher and real estate lawyer (and I recommend getting title insurance, in case they screw up) to determine exactly all the strings that are attached to the property before you buy it. But you can check on most of the potential problems yourself.

PERFORM A TITLE SEARCH

A title search involves tracing how the present owner got his hands on the land, who the previous owner got the land from, and so forth. Usually, the property changed hands legally and correctly, but sometimes previous owners and realtors, in their hurry to close deals, overlooked paying all the people who had some stake in the property. Or there might be an unresolved dispute concerning the property.

You can do your own title search by checking the most recent deed to the property, then noting in the deed the location of the deed for the previous time the property changed hands. Check the previous deed, and trace back as many years as you feel comfortable tracing. (A quick note—WARRANTY DEED means the owner guarantees he is the only owner of the property and will defend the buyer against all claims on the property made by others. QUIT CLAIM means the owner is giving up only his own claim to the property when he sells it, but doesn't guarantee no one else has a claim to the property, and he doesn't offer to defend the buyer against claims on the property made by anyone else. DEED OF TRUST means the grantor (the borrower) will pay back the loan he received from the grantee (the money lender) to buy the property.)

While you're at it, check the boundaries of the property, check on any loans involving the property, check on any liens against the property, and check on any easements, mineral rights, zoning, and planning involving the property. Also check on whether the buildings and utilities on the property conform to the building, fire, electrical, plumbing, and waste codes. Instructions on all of these checks will follow. You may satisfy your worries about the property, or you may decide it isn't worth the hassle to buy the property if it comes with too many built-in problems.

Consider the plight of a man whose case I reported on down in Appalachia. He bought a 60-acre tract from a politically well-connected woman, then he started building houses on the land. His problems began when he started building an access road into the tract across a two-acre segment of the 60 acres he had bought. It turned out that the woman had not paid all the heirs of the people from whose estate she had bought the two acres the access road was on. So naturally the heirs wanted this man to pay them off now that the land was jumping in value because of his home-building.

To avoid problems in case he was to lose the two-acre segment, the man decided to provide an alternate access road for home buyers. He found 300 tons of coal during his road grading, removed it, and sold it for $7000. To add insult to injury, he received a citation from the state for mining without a permit. That's when he called me.

What galled the man was that leading local officials, bankers, and lawyers all said the woman had valid ownership of ALL of the property—including the two-acre segment— before he bought the 60-acre tract from her. They were in a position to know, because they had supposedly checked the titles to the acreage for her, or sold her the land at a county tax sale, or had been trustees for her on dealings concerning the land in question. And once the problems surfaced, none of these people I contacted for an interview would comment on the matter.

At last word, the developer filed for bankruptcy to force the issue in federal court. He did this, he said, to get the ownership issue cleared up and keep the local politicians, bankers, and lawyers out of it. The woman who sold him the property denied all wrongdoing, but she turned around and sued the engineer who mapped the property for alleged negligence.

Title problems usually indicate your target is up to no good somewhere. He may have cheated someone in selling property without a clear title or with improperly-determined boundaries. He may be a tax deadbeat. Or he may be a deadbeat who owes money on other projects, and his creditors have had to go after his property to make him pay up. Or he may be a dishonest businessman who uses lien filings to extort money like mobsters use leg-breakings to enforce shakedowns. Exposing wrongful conduct on your target's part is a valid "military" use of info on title problems.

DETERMINE THE BOUNDARIES

Check the deed to the property for a description of the property. Verify the property lines and buildings really are where they're supposed to be. Bugs Builder and Daffy Developer sometimes make mistakes in this area, and you the property owner suffer if you don't find out in time.

A brief trivia point—George Washington was a surveyor. His surveying field notes are probably still on file in many courthouses in Virginia. I just thought you'd like to know about a politician who actually worked for a living.

Boundary determination might provide evidence your target may have sold someone property knowing he didn't have this major title problem resolved. Or maybe he was just grossly negligent instead of crooked in selling property this way. But then, getting publicly accused of negligence is not what I'd call favorable publicity, either.

CHECK FOR EASEMENTS

Another thing you'll want to know about are easements on the property. An easement is a right-of-way a property owner may have to grant, for example, so someone else can reach his own property by going through the property in question, or so workers of a utility company can perform work on power lines or pipes. Can the local power company run heavy equipment through your back yard all the time to work on electrical cables? Does a private developer have an easement to put an access road through your corn field for a project he is developing—say, a People's Temple for New Age purple Kool-Aid drinkers, or a nudist colony for Roseanne Barr look-alikes? I'm sure you'll want to know about that before you buy.

Check the deed to the property. It will show what kinds of easements are involved. It also wouldn't hurt to check the deeds back a couple of property sales just to verify the present and past owners didn't overlook any of their obligations when the land changed hands.

As an example, a friend of mine considered buying a house in a town in Southwest Ohio. As an ex-military man, he was set to use a Veterans Administration loan. The federal people processing his loan found out the yahoos who developed the subdivision where the house was had given the town and the local power company a utility easement that ran right through the house he wanted. Checking further, they found the same problem with several other pieces of property in the subdivision. And some of the local yokels in that town's government, they determined, had apparently been blissfully ignorant of the situation for years. The VA people had to muscle town officials to resolve the problems.

Easement checking provides evidence of your target's dealings with those he granted easements to or got easements from. Maybe he granted an easement to others for a price bordering on extortion. Or maybe he got an easement through someone else's property that hurt the owner, but the target had enough pull so that the owner had to give in. Exposing wrongful conduct on your target's part is a valid "military" use of info on easements.

LOOK INTO LOANS AND MORTGAGES

Most people don't have the money to plunk down the purchase price for a piece of property, especially if it has a building on it. So they borrow money to get the property, and pay the money back with interest over time. Developers often do business the same way, on a larger scale. They'll borrow money to develop a subdivision, then buy back houses (and their sites) from the lender once they're built so they can sell them. This way, they still have operating money for more construction.

You can see if there are any mortgages or loans involving the property by checking the grantor and grantee books in the county recorder's office under the present owner's name and under the name of people who previously owned the land. If loans or mortgages exist, or if there is proof they have been paid off and the money lender has released his claim on the property, the instrument column of the record will show them and refer you to the books and pages where the loan documents are. You can then review the loan paperwork in the loan books (mortgage books, certificate of release books, or similar records) to see what loans were made for the property and whether the alleged owner has paid off the loans.

The "military" applications here are obvious. You can get information on your target's possibly shady financial dealings, his business partners, and his possible crookedness on a number of fronts. Maybe he gets sweetheart loans at low rates if he's a borrower. Maybe he forces buyers to do business with his banking buddies. Maybe he's overextended, or maybe he's using the same piece of property as collateral in more than one deal. Maybe loan rescheduling or late payments are proof he's in some financial trouble. Maybe he's making loans or getting loans that smell funny. Maybe he's calling in loans or manipulating them in some other way to make money illegally or unethically. Maybe there's conflict of interest. Maybe buddies of his are involved in enforcing the provisions of loans.

LEARN ABOUT LIENS

A lien is a creditor's right to seize and hold or sell property to settle a debt. Creditors, like bankers, con- struction contractors, and local governments, file liens in the county recorder's office all the time to collect debts from property owners. And you might become responsible for liens against property you buy if the former owner hasn't paid his debts and gotten the liens removed. A number of situations can lead to liens, including the following:

- The present owner owes taxes on the land that may cause county officials to claim it.
- The present owner uses the land as collateral for a loan, and the lender has the right to take the land in case the present owner defaults on the loan.
- The present owner had work done on his house, and the contractor filed a mechanic's lien on the property because he got stiffed by the present owner.
- The contractor stiffed a subcontractor, and the subcontractor filed a mechanic's lien against the property as a way of making the property owner force the contractor to pay up.

You can find out what liens people have filed against the property by checking the grantor and grantee books in the county recorder's office under the present owner's name and under the name of people who previously owned the land. If liens exist, the instrument column of the record will show them and refer you to the books and pages where the lien documents are. You can then review the liens in the lien books (tax lien books, mechanic's lien books, or similar records) to see exactly what claims people have against the property.

The "military" applications here are also obvious. Liens against your target are possible evidence he's shady enough to have stiffed creditors or have put off paying his bills. Maybe they're proof he's in financial trouble. If he's a lien-filer, maybe he's a crook for trying to shake down the owners for money he doesn't deserve. Maybe there's conflict of interest involved. Maybe buddies of his are involved in enforcing the liens. Liens involving your target are also evidence of his business dealings and his business ties.

DIG INTO MINERAL RIGHTS

Can a coal company strip-mine your farm or back yard or parking lot if its owners want to? Can Exxon drill for oil on your property? They can if they own the mineral rights to the property. Check all deeds to the property to see whether or not the present owner or someone else holds the mineral rights to the property. If you're buying property in an area known to have coal, oil, or natural gas deposits, then worry a little if a mining company or some other conglomerate has the mineral rights. Verify what rights you will have in case the company wants to drill on or dig up the land.

The "military" application here is that maybe your target knew about mineral reserves, and he conned property owners into giving up their mineral rights. This sort of banditry impoverished and made homeless quite a few people in Appalachia. Years ago, land swindlers conned folks into giving up mineral rights, then coal companies evicted them from their land or tore it up so badly they couldn't make a living farming it.

FIGURE OUT PLANNING AND ZONING

It's not only nice to know what people are allowed to do with their property—it's also nice to know what people or the government are GOING to do with property, especially if it's going to affect you in some way. Let's say, for instance, your state highway department intends to build a highway through property you own, want to own, or live near. Or let's say the county needs a sewage treatment facility, and the officials want to build it near you. Or maybe British Petroleum or Royal Dutch Shell or one of those other greedy multinational oil companies intends to arrogantly treat your town like a colony and run oil pipelines through it. In each case, some government planner for the planning commission in your area will have to work the project into a master plan for the area. And I'm sure you'd want to know about such plans for your own peace of mind.

And then there is zoning for land use. If you're tough or crazy like me, you probably could handle living next door to any site zoned for a nuclear plant, a steel mill, an incinerator, a petrochemical complex, a tank farm, a sewer works, a toxic waste dump, a rock quarry, a strip mine, a landfill, a wrecking yard, or a stockyard and meat packing plant. But if you can't handle the thrill of having these kinds of neighbors, you might want to know if anyone holding land near your neighborhood has the right to use his land for one or more of these activities.

To find out this kind of information, you'll want to check the property you've got your eye on and all property in the area for its planning and zoning. This way, you'll be able to tell what designs the moneyed interests or the government planners have on your area five, ten, or more years from now. Also, you'll be able to tell whether the area will be open to residential, agricultural, commercial rental, business, or industrial uses. And then buy or bail out accordingly.

My advice sounds easier said than done. How do you find out what's planned for an area, and what kinds of uses properties in the area are zoned for?

Let's go through how planning and zoning processes often work. Then I'll tell you what records you can get your hands on.

Planners develop plans for an area's growth and development. Planning commissioners vote whether or not to recommend the planners' plans to the zoning commissioners. Zoning commissioners make zoning decisions on property in their area; they more or less decide whether to adopt the planning commissioners' recommendations on a parcel-by-parcel, neighborhood-by-neighborhood, or section-by-section basis. Of course, the dominant local government group—like the county supervisors or the city council members—could always put an end to any plan or zoning if they don't like it. However, they don't usually do so.

Planning commissioners and zoning commissioners can make recommendations or make zoning changes. Sometimes they make planning recommendations and zoning decisions based on requests (or bribes) from property owners, developers, and big companies, or on requests of the people who oppose them. As examples, let's see how two separate projects fare.

Let's say a planner plans for the area's leaders to allow residential growth in previously rural areas. And he also plans to bring more service industries into the downtown area of a city in his area. The planning commissioners hold a public hearing to check on this plan and take in comments from the public. They will review the plan in a committee meeting, and will then vote on whether to recommend the plan at another public meeting. If they vote to recommend the plan, they send it on to the zoning commissioners for action. The zoning commissioners hold a public hearing on the proposed plan. They will review the plan in a committee meeting, and then at another public meeting will vote on whether to rezone property in the area of the proposed plan so the development can take place. Of course, the county supervisors or city council members could reject or okay the planning.

Or let's say a local businessman wants to build some apartments on vacant lots zoned for single-family houses. He would petition the zoning commissioners to change the zoning of the lots so he could build the apartments. The zoning commissioners hold a public hearing on the businessman's request, and listen to comments from the public. Neighbors who think their property values might drop or traffic and crime would rise might fight the businessman, but some low-income groups might support him if his proposed rents seem reasonable. The zoning commissioners will review the request in committee, and at another public meeting will vote on whether to rezone the vacant lots. Of course, the county supervisors or city council members could reject or okay the rezoning.

(By the way, certain upper-income snobs routinely manipulate zoning and planning officials to keep out the huddled masses like you and me. How? They get the officials to specify anyone wanting to build a house in the area has to have a lot the size of a truck farm to build on. Or they get the officials to impose overblown environmental impact studies and requirements on tract houses. Or they get the officials to pull other stunts that add tens of thousands of dollars to the cost of an average dwelling in their community. The results? Affordable housing for we the people is diminishing, because houses in areas which would be perfect for affordable housing are shooting up in price because of the artificial scarcity created by the zoning bluenoses.

Too many Americans can no longer afford to buy a house. Available housing is skyrocketing in price. Neighborhoods are declining because people who rent, then move constantly, don't have roots in the neighborhood. Landlord/tenant disputes clog the courts. Commuters clog the highways because they have to live so far from work to find affordable housing, and their cars' pollution clouds the skies. And the number of homeless people is on the rise.)

Planning commissioners have their planners maintain maps showing an overall land use plan for their area. Zoning commissioners have their employees maintain a set of map books that show the zoning on all parcels in the area they control. These maps are public records and are a lot easier to use than most other real estate records. Minutes of planning commission and zoning commission public hearings and meetings (including the committee meetings) are also public records. So are plans, special studies, and other paperwork involved in planning and zoning. And of course, so are the laws that govern planning and zoning. You can review these records at your local government's planning commission office and zoning commission office. You can use these records to find out the status of land in your area, and to find out what projects are planned for your area.

A "military" application for this info is figuring out who will gain from zoning and planning decisions, then documenting their business and political ties to those who make such decisions. Another such application is showing patterns of exclusionary zoning and planning to discriminate against lower-income people or job-providing companies.

BONE UP ON BUILDING CODES

Building codes are the government's way of making buildings meet minimum safety and quality standards. If they weren't in place, even more of this country's buildings would be firetraps. (Opponents of some codes argue the law discriminates in favor of snooty rich people and builders and against mobile home owners and do-it-yourselfers. And in a country that was built by homesteaders who wanted to escape mindless government control, this argument still carries valid weight.)

However, the codes on the books aren't always enforced. A classic example is the Kansas City Hyatt Regency Hotel disaster. This building's walkways collapsed in 1981, killing more than 100 people. It turned out that the original plans for the walkways violated the city's building code, but no city inspector voided them. And as a result, all those people died needlessly.

An ignored building code can come up and bite people later on in other ways. A friend of mine tried to buy a house in Southwest Ohio that he and his family had been renting from the seller. The seller had built a garage over his septic tank, and the unit wasn't working properly. However, the local yokels who enforced the building codes hadn't figured out the garage would be a problem when they gave the seller the permit to build it. The garage was a clear code violation, and the owner wanted my friend to pay for the cost of relocating the septic tank as part of the deal. My friend was tempted to move out, but since he wanted to buy via FHA, the FHA agents muscled the seller into correcting the problem his own stupidity (and that of the building inspectors) had caused.

No two local governments are alike in handling building codes. Check with your local government officials for more specific instructions on what codes they use, and what local additions they have made to the state building codes. A nonspecific guide follows; it should point you in the right direction.

- Building codes are usually enacted by states and modified locally. Building codes are enforced by a building department or some similar agency. Electric codes are usually based on the National Electric Code and are enforced by the same local agency.

- Fire codes are usually enforced by the fire marshal or some fire department official.

- Plumbing and wastewater codes are usually enacted by states and modified locally. These codes could be enforced by the building department (or some similar agency) or by the local public health department.

These agencies maintain building plans as they relate to the agency's law enforcement concerns. They also maintain records of all permits and citations they issue. These are public records available to you. You can use these records to check on the property you are interested in, and check on the relative talent the seller has for gaining the negative attention of the building inspectors. After all, if he violates codes on other properties, who's to say everything's hunky-dory with the property he wants to pawn off on you?

The "military" applications here are also self-evident. Building code violations prove your target is a crook, a negligent or incompetent landowner or builder, a robber baron who doesn't care about people's safety, or all of the above. Overlooked building code violations indicate your building code inspectors are overworked, or maybe they're just lazy, incompetent, or on the take.

SECURING THE PROMISED LAND

Land disputes are as old as the dawn of time. And they'll be with us until Hell freezes over. Even the Bible contains accounts about land disputes, such as the one in which Naboth refused to sell a vineyard to King Ahab because it was land his forefathers owned. Ahab didn't seize it because the laws of his kingdom forbade even him as the king from seizing land. How-

ever, Ahab's wife, the evil Queen Jezebel, had her agents trump up charges against Naboth, and Naboth was stoned to death. King Ahab then took possession of the land.

However, Ahab's and Jezebel's land piracy didn't go unpunished. Elijah the prophet told King Ahab that God would kill him, Jezebel, and all their descendants to wipe their bloodline from the face of the earth. And it happened. Ahab was killed in battle, Jezebel was thrown to her death from the palace, and Jehu had their descendants executed. The moral? God doesn't like real estate thieves, either!

Take a lesson from the New Testament as well. Christ spoke of building a house on solid rock so the elements couldn't destroy it easily. Likewise, doing rock-solid research on real estate will keep you sheltered, and it might bring down a legitimate storm on those who deserve it!

END NOTES

1. Information on the 1981 Kansas City Hyatt Regency Hotel tragedy comes from Emily and Per Ola D'Aulaire's article *There Wasn't Time To Scream*. This article appeared in the July 1982 issue of *Reader's Digest*.
2. The story of Ahab and Jezebel comes from the first and the second *Books of Kings*.

Private Sector

Public Information On The Private Sector

Before I give you a whole chapter on how to investigate the captains of industry and commerce, I will say a brief word or two on behalf of the business world. It's the businessmen of this world who provide most of you with your jobs, and all of us with the extravagantly high level of goods and services we as a nation enjoy. I served in Latin America and in Asia with two separate Army outfits, and I got a look at how the other nine-tenths lives. Count your blessings that we have the standard of living we do.

I myself am a businessman; I own and operate a technical publishing business and a research firm. But I normally wear a coat and tie only when I'm in church, and I drive American-made vehicles instead of BMWs. Now that I've distanced myself from the losers who attack the business world because they don't know any better, I'll take my own shots at business people. I'm in favor of making businessmen treat their workers fairly, and making them abide by some basic level of conduct in not poisoning the planet or cheating the public. All too often, businessmen and businesswomen don't show basic morality in dealing with others. But then, they're no different from government employees, or many other people!

This chapter will show you how to find out who owns businesses and corporations, how to check on whether businesses are tax deadbeats, and how to find out what licenses and permits businesses need to operate. This chapter will also steer you toward some of the other chapters of the book that contain instructions for specialized private sector research, such as checking on real estate irregularities, unfair labor practices, environmental pollution, and government contract waste or fraud.

For "civilian" purposes, you can use this chapter's techniques to check on companies to decide whether to do business with them. For "military" purposes, you can use this chapter's techniques to expose the wrongful conduct of crooked business people. This chapter will also give you a few ideas on how to make trouble for your favorite robber barons.

FIND OUT WHO OWNS AND OPERATES THE BUSINESS

If you're targeting a company, you should always know who its owners and key people are. At the very least, you tend to get better response from a company if you can contact its big wheels. At the very most, these are the guys who you'll be digging dirt on. These are the guys who you'll check for crooked dealing, massive lawbreaking, and "ownership" of politicians and bureaucrats.

Most people know the Ford family has something to do with owning Ford Motors. But how many other owners of Fortune 500 companies can you name? Or how many owners of smaller companies in your area whom you would like to target can you name? Damn few, I'd bet.

I'm going to digress a bit here and explain why people incorporate businesses, talk about corporate tax, and then get back to telling you how to determine who a company's owners are.

Most owners form a corporation, then issue stock to make money and spread the risk of running a business. Even the small-time owners who don't issue stock form corporations. Why? Because it's good business. It keeps business people from losing their assets if they get sued, and it keeps their tax bills lower.

The liability angle works this way: If you sue a doctor or an architect or a lawyer or any other proprietor (a businessman who owns his own business and operates it without incorporating) and win a big enough money judgment, you can take all his business equipment, make him work to pay you off, and take his house and cars until you get all the money the court has awarded you (or until he declares bankruptcy to duck out of paying the award). But if you sue any of the same people, and they've incorporated their practice or business, usually you can collect no more than the net worth of the practice or the business, no matter how much the court says you can take. So this is why most professional people and small businessmen, as well as big companies, incorporate.

The tax angle works this way: Rich people can easily ditch big money into a corporation they own and control. Howard Hughes, for example, reportedly ditched his wealth into his corporations, which in turn seemingly owned damn near everything he used. Rich people's assets, placed in a corporation, are really not taxable because corporations pass on taxes to customers. If their corporation thrives, they can make big money in returns or sell out at a big profit. If their corporation bombs, they can write off losses against income elsewhere.

And then they can give expensive perks to themselves and to top people, then write it off as a cost of doing business. Car perks should be allowed, my Uncle Bill once slyly suggested, only if the company officials tastelessly decorate these cars with the company logo, like a pizza delivery car. Mary Kay Ash, the owner of Mary Kay Cosmetics, is probably one of the few honest people in Big Business; the gaudy pink Mary Kay Cadillacs she gives her top saleswomen are proof she shares my Uncle Bill's sense of impish integrity!

Which brings up another point—when the politicians scream, "Tax the big corporations!", they really mean, "Raise the price of goods and services to cost American jobs and cost American pocketbooks so we can look cool on TV." The corporations SHOULD pay some taxes to prevent abuses like I listed above. But "tax the corporations" is usually a political scam; people who own corporations have the corporation officers pay the taxes, then raise prices so we the buying public cover the costs. When you buy a car, for example, you're paying for the car company's property tax, its corporate tax, its inventory tax, utility and fuel and phone taxes, the portion of the Social Security contributions it has to make for its workers, sales taxes on its parts, AND the same taxes for all the little companies that supplied parts to the car maker for your car! I've heard estimates that as much as 50 percent of the cost of some manufactured goods made in this country are the result of taxes imposed on the manufacturers, which they pass on to you. (Some manufacturers take another way out. They export manufacturing jobs to countries with low taxes, few environmental or labor standards, and peon workers.)

Now I'll come back to the issue at hand.

The papers people file to incorporate are known as the articles of incorporation. In some states, these documents include the names of the people in the corporation, the registered agent of the corporation (usually the company's attorney), and other good information. In other states, these documents don't have to contain much information. Corporate officials have to file these documents with the Secretary of State's office in the capital of the state they have incorporated in. They usually also have to notify the Secretary of State's office in other states where they do business.

Some states require corporations to file annual reports. These documents will often include the names of the people in the corporation, the registered agent of the corporation, key officials and major stockholders of the corporation, and other good information to know. Often, such documents will give out information on how big a corporation is, and how it makes money.

Such documents are public records. Contact the Secretary of State in your state capital and ask to get in touch with its bureau whose people regulate corporations. Ask the clerks of the Secretary of State's corporation-monitoring bureau to send you any corporate information on your target company that is a public record. The clerks will send copies of these documents to you, or will refer you to Delaware or any other state in which the corporation is incorporated.

Many companies incorporate in the states their main offices are in. But roughly 300 of the nation's Fortune 500 corporations have incorporated in Delaware, according to Jeff Lewis, that state's assistant secretary of state. In an interview I conducted with him in 1991, Lewis told me the state taxes corporations a maximum of $150,000. (So the automakers might make cars and decisions in Detroit, but they pay their state taxes in Delaware—basically a county with two U.S. senators.) Lewis also told me his state's laws discourage takeover bids (a good idea), limit liability of corporation directors (a so-so idea), allow anonymous corporate ownership (a lousy idea), and promote speedy business lawsuits via a special court which can knock out decisions on complex lawsuits in weeks instead of years (an excellent idea). So you may want to check with the Delaware secretary of state if your target corporation is a biggie.

Even in states which require business people to report very little information about their corporations, you can find out something about any corporation. For example, agents in the state bureau which collects state corporate taxes will usually keep a list of a corporation's key figures so they'll know who to contact when they want the corporation to "render (taxes) unto Caesar." Likewise, county agents who collect property taxes or issue vendor's licenses might have documents on your target corporation. Agents in regulatory agencies which monitor your target corporation may very well have placed info on its owners and key officials into the public record. Further, agents in the U.S. Securities and Exchange Commission make companies which issue stock and are big enough file some sort of annual status report. All these documents are public records.

Corporations get involved in lawsuits. And sometimes government agents pinch them or sue them for their wrongdoing. In these court records, you might find evidence of who owns the corporation. Check the chapters on criminal records and lawsuit records for more detailed instructions.

Many industry guides can shed some light on who runs your target company. The *Thomas Register* and some of its rival industry guides are available at many libraries. These references contain info on company executives. Industry information services contain some info on corporate ownership. Some libraries also have the *Directory of Corporate Affiliations*. This reference—commonly known as "Who Owns Whom"—has listings on thousands of companies and their parent firms. This source also contains info on companies' goods and services, bosses, finances, employees, and corporate charities.

In a pinch, the corporation's public relations person or its registered agent can give you some info on your target company. I've determined corporate ownership many times by posing as a potential client or investor and asking about the target company's owners so "I'd feel comfortable doing business with them." Also, PR people and registered agents will sometimes release info on corporate ownership to people who identify themselves as writers. Also, staffers of trade and industry associations and local Chambers of Commerce often know who the owners of their member businesses are.

What if your target business isn't a corporation?

Maybe the business you are interested in is only a partnership (an unincorporated business owned by two or more people) or a proprietorship. These businesses don't have to have articles of incorporation on record. But most of them do file other paperwork in the counties in which they operate.

One of these items is the fictitious name statement, or the "doing business as (DBA)" statement. Business operators have to file these statements if they run a business under any name other than their own names. For example, Charles Keating and Marvin Warner could operate "Keating's and Warner's Loan Shark Finance" without needing to file a fictitious name statement. But if they wanted to operate a financial institution with a name like "Lincoln Loan" or "Home State Bank" or "Silverado Savings", they would have to file proper paperwork so the public would know they are the two characters behind the business.

At any rate, the fictitious name statement and who operates under a business' fictitious name is a public record. An office at your county courthouse has a log containing the list of fictitious names in your county.

To check on who is operating any unincorporated business, call your county administrator, ask for information on which county agency handles fictitious name filings, and find out how to view the records.

County clerks tend to keep their fictitious name logs indexed by business name and by name of businessman. You should be able to use their logs to find out the operators of a business if you know the business name. Likewise, you should be able to look up a target's name on their logs, and see how many businesses in the county he is involved in.

A QUICK WAR STORY ON CORPORATION OWNERSHIP TRACKING

My knowledge that the owner of a coal company in southwest Virginia was Occidental Petroleum led to a reasonably ugly story I wrote a couple of years ago. At the time, Virginia senator Paul Trible wanted to kill Romania's trading privileges because of Communist dictator Nicolae Caecescu's policy of persecuting Jews and Christians. (Romanians, like Russians, Serbs, Bulgarians, and Greeks, tend to be Orthodox Christians). Rick Boucher, the congressman for far southwest Virginia, said he was going to support Trible's move, but then changed his mind. Trible's attempt failed. Boucher said he found out Island Creek Coal, a major mining company in far southwest Virginia, had recently made a deal to sell the Caecescu regime 14 million tons of coal over 35 years. So Boucher bragged he flip-flopped to save miners' jobs.

Something about the Island Creek incident smelled funny to me. I did some research, and found out Island Creek's parent company was Occidental Petroleum. And I also knew that this oil company was at the time a 25 percent investor in what was supposed to become the world's largest coal mine—a massive pit mine in Red China which every year would produce an amount of coal equal to the output of Virginia's 10 largest coal companies combined. This gargantuan output, an Occidental spokesman told me in an interview, would allow Red China's Communist slavemasters to sell coal at rock-bottom prices to Japan. This of course would cost many American miners their jobs. Why? Because American miners work in much safer mines and earn decent wages, while Chinese miners work as virtual slaves in unsafe mines to produce cheaper coal. And the cost-conscious (some say conscienceless) Japanese would surely buy the cheaper coal.

I called Boucher and laid out Occidental's apparent finagling for him. On the one hand, I noted, Occidental's American subsidiary was pleading for special treatment for Romania to save American jobs. On the other hand, I said, Occidental was going to get megabucks to help China's Red dictators gear up to put American miners out of work. Didn't he feel duped?

No, the congressman replied. He termed Occidental's actions "unfortunate," said the free enterprise system allows companies to mine where they want to, and added he would try to get tax breaks for coal operators who would not mine overseas.

Trible, naturally, bit Occidental's and Boucher's hides when I asked him for a quote. He attacked Occidental Petroleum for making money off the backs of oppressed workers in Communist countries in general and for mining in China while its subsidiary company lobbied Boucher in Virginia. He accused the congressman of changing his mind "because of heat at home."

As a postscript, an Occidental spokeswoman told me in the summer of 1991 that her company sold its interest in the Red Chinese mine in 1991 for undisclosed reasons. The company's press release claimed money losses were behind the sale.

CHECKING ON BUSINESS TAXES AND LICENSES

For tax purposes, the operators of corporations and businesses usually have to have business licenses in the areas they operate. Check with the auditor, assessor, or treasurer in your city, township, or county to see what licenses your target has to hold to do business in the area. Then check these agencies to see if your target has these licenses. He can get in trouble if he's reported for not having a license he should have.

And there are other taxes business operators have to deal with at the local level. For instance, they usually have to pay property taxes on their real estate, and they have to pay a tax on their machinery and on their equipment and on their inventory; this is called personal property tax. The tax records for these kinds of taxes on businesses are public records. You can check the tax rolls in the county treasurer's office to see if your target businessman is paying his fair share of property tax and personal property tax.

I wrote several articles about businesses getting low property assessments or being behind in tax payments. You should be able to find a certain percentage of businesses you check are tax deadbeats or moochers of some sort. One time, I nicked a county treasurer because he wasn't comparing the number of business licenses issued (which generates a tax account for the business in the county) to the number of corporations and "DBAs" listed in the county. He was

probably not getting full compliance in taxpaying from all the local businessmen because of this. If he had found a difference, he could have generated a list of company names, checked off those who paid taxes, and then dunned the deadbeats.

I got the idea for doing this story from Don Bennett, a brother reporter and one-time co-worker of mine who is everything a journalist should be. Don one time was told to write a "fluff" feature on how well businesses were doing in our part of New Jersey. Neither the local officials nor the business people seemed to be able to answer many of his questions on business indicators. So instead of a "fluff" piece, our editor got from Don an ugly little article about how ignorant government and business people were.

On the subject of taxes, operators of businesses usually have to have some sort of vendor's license to collect sales taxes. You can check with the city, township, or county auditor, assessor, or treasurer to see if your target has a vendor's license. He'd better have one if he's collecting sales taxes!

The amount of sales tax money a business sends in to your state treasurer's tax agency is supposed to be confidential. Why? Because if you know the state and local sales tax rates, and if you knew how much sales tax money the business sent the state, you could figure out how much money the business took in (assuming, of course, its businessmen were honest). However, I guess some state taxing agents could be tricked into releasing the information by someone making an inquiry who has done his homework on the company in question.

Business operators have to pay state taxing officials a number of other taxes. In most states, business operators have to pay corporate income tax. Sellers of alcoholic beverages and tobacco have to pay taxes on sales of these items. Fuel sellers have to pay taxes on the amount of fuel they sell. Trucking firms have to pay highway use tax to repave the highways after their trucks help tear them up. Bankers, stockbrokers, and other dealers in financial instruments have to pay taxes on sales of these items.

Gambling operators have to pay special taxes on the amounts bettors wager. Public utilities (power companies, gas companies, water companies, telephone companies, and railroad companies) have to pay utility taxes on receipts. Mining companies and drilling companies have to pay severance taxes on the minerals they remove from the ground. Some of these tax figures will be public records; others won't. Check with the state treasurer's people in your state capital to see what taxes they levy on businesses and to see what tax records you can view.

CHECKING PROFESSIONAL LICENSES

Each state licenses all kinds of workers, from doctors, lawyers, and engineers to barbers, beauticians, and security guards. Each state also licenses certain kinds of businessmen, especially people like contractors and brokers. And in order to do business in a chosen field, individuals and businesses must have the proper licenses or certifications. These licenses are public records.

The government benefits from licensing people and businesses, because the bureaucrats know who is operating what kind of business, and who is working there in positions of responsibility. This translates into tax dollars in general, and translates specifically into money for government agents to investigate the bad apples (or harass the governor's enemies in the business world, some cynics would say).

Licensing usually also benefits the public because government regulators usually regulate the businesses in the public interest. In many cases, a license is a sign the government has imposed some minimum set of standards on a profession, and the license holder at least has shown he or she meets or exceeds these standards. And having passable service providers in society, even by government decree, benefits us all. However, many service providers also benefit from licensing if unrealistic licensing requirements freeze out worthy competitors. In fact, many professional groups lobby to keep the clamps on so they can charge more since they're "already in the club" with their state licenses or certificates.

Licensing also benefits the person with an ax to grind if he can find information on the target's license or if he can find out the target isn't properly licensed or accredited to perform the sort of work he's performing in the state. The trick to finding out whether a person or a business has the proper license for the line of work is figuring out which government agency regulates the field. You can start by checking the state entries in your phone book. You could also contact your state representative's office and put his staffers to work checking this out for you. Or you could contact your Secretary of State's office and order a "Red Book" or a "Blue Book". This book, which gives information on state government, will list the various agencies which regulate the private sector and will give their addresses and phone numbers.

Once you find out what the proper regulatory agency is, give its agents a call and ask for instructions on verifying your target has the proper license. Getting information from a target's license or certificate is good in itself. Licenses and certificates tend to carry info on a holder's training, his address, and several other pieces of information on his business or employment history.

Also, ask the agents if their agency has investigated and cited (or revoked the license of, or otherwise punished) your target, and ask how you can get paperwork on any such incidents. You should be able to get these documents easily, if agents have taken formal negative action against your target. Any dirt you can find in the form of a license revocation or some other sort of disciplinary action by the agency will be nice to have.

Since other people complain, why not you? If a licensed person or business operator hurts you in some way, bypass the Better Business Bureau and take your complaint straight to the agents who can yank or cut corners off of your target's license or certificate.

Ladies, if you go into a beauty salon looking for a Dorothy Hamill cut or a Debi Thomas cut, and the hairdresser deliberately makes you look like Sinead O'Connor or Grace Jones, don't follow up on your desperate urge to ask her to complete the decapitation so at least you can hide your poor head in your handbag. You need your head to drive home. Besides, you may be able to complain to the right state agency and get that Lizzie Borden's license revoked.

Or guys, if some punk security guard goes Nazi on you and threatens you with his gun, you can complain to the right agency and have his gun permit executed. This will knock him out of many security jobs entirely, and castrate his paycheck at other jobs, because unarmed guards make less money than armed guards.

Certain types of skilled workers require certification or licensing through federal agencies. You can get license information on many professions by checking in with the agency most closely related to the occupation for licensing or certification information. For example, the Federal Aviation Administration provides licensing or certification to pilots and aircraft mechanics. The Federal Communications Commission issues radio operator's licenses to many disc jockeys and others at radio stations. And some nameless federal bureaucrat in the U.S. Coast Guard issued a skipper's license to *Exxon Valdez* tanker captain Joseph Hazelwood.

If your target is a doctor, dentist, pharmacist, nurse, paramedic, lawyer, accountant, architect, engineer, teacher, or someone else from what people call "the professional world," your target's licensing requirements are stricter, because people's lives, health, safety, liberty and/or property are in the hands of these people. (Actually, blue-collar and pink-collar workers are professionals, too...they just work in different professions!)

Medical people lose their licenses or get put on some sort of suspension more often than most people realize. In fact, a whole chapter of this book is devoted to checking on health care providers. However, losing massive amounts of malpractice cases or having AIDS does not automatically disqualify the unethical or infected medical person from holding a license and practicing in most places.

Engineers and architects of projects that fail disastrously can suffer actions against their licenses, too. For example, two of the engineers who designed walkways for the Hyatt Regency Hotel in Kansas City lost their licenses after the walkways collapsed in 1981 and killed more than 100 people. Members of the Missouri Board for Architects, Professional Engineers, and Land Surveyors in 1984 accused the engineers of gross negligence, incompetence, misconduct, unprofessional conduct, and vicarious liability (responsibility for the work of people who worked for them—work they were supposed to check). They were found responsible for most of the charges, which revolved around designing walkway components incompetently, failing to give the steelworkers adequate instructions for fabricating them, failing to conduct a design review, failing to make engineering calculations, and lying to people by claiming that they had done the needed review and calculation work.

Lawyers, accountants, and teachers occasionally lose licenses or credentials as well (but not as often as they need to).

The paperwork showing any agency disciplinary act against such white-collar professionals is a public record. Agents with the licensing bureaus covering these occupations are generally quite willing and able to help you, because they are used to handling such inquiries. One other note—a white-collar professional who suffers action against his or her license in one state may also suffer the same kind of restriction in other states if those states' licensing agents find out about his or her professional problems (especially if he or she has lied in order to cover up the problems).

Unfortunately, state agents don't communicate with their colleagues in other states as well as they could. But you could be the human data link who fries your targeted white-collar "professional" if he or she leaves your area and decides to prey on the public in another state. You could also check on your target with licensing agents in other states your target has worked before he or she darkened your area. Then, in the interests of good citizenship, you could notify your local licensing agents of the skeletons in your target's closet from the past.

If your target is a fly-by-night building contractor who does shoddy work, you may be able to put the wrecking ball to his business. How? If you check with the building contractor's licensing bureau in your state and find out he doesn't have the appropriate license for the kind of construction work he gets involved in, he could be in a heap of trouble if you report him. After all, like architects, building contractors are supposed to provide safe and functional structures for fair prices, and an unlicensed contractor probably lacks the expertise needed to perform to this minimum standard.

Or if the contractor does possess the required skill, he may not have the respect for the law you think he needs to have to do right by his customers and the public at large. If he's performing some construction work now, check to see that his building, fire, electrical, plumbing, and other permits for the project are in order. If they aren't, report him.

Every now and then, a person passes himself or herself off as a medical professional, and it turns out he or she is not licensed to practice medicine. Some of these lowlifes are people who have lost licenses; others are people who never had the know-how to get one. Or a doctor allows a non-doctor to practice medicine at his facility because it's cheaper than hiring a real medical professional. I personally know of abortion providers in L.A., Chicago, New York, and Connecticut who evidently allowed unqualified office employees (or in one case, an ex-Navy corpsman) to assist in giving anesthesia, performing surgery, and/or rendering follow-up treatment. Some of these quacks were reportedly tied to women's deaths.

At any rate, the quack who practices medicine in any capacity is a health menace. You can check on any doctor, nurse, dentist, or related medical professional by calling the state medical board in your state capital and asking if the person in question has a license for the profession he or she is operating in. If the person in question is a quack, report him or her.

HOW MY FRIEND NAILED A BUNCH OF REALTOR CROOKS

On the subject of licenses, felons can't hold many licenses —especially the kinds of licenses needed to handle large-dollar transactions. For example, in many states, at least one of the operators of any real estate business must have a real estate broker's license to operate the business legally. And in many states, felons can't hold real estate broker licenses. Remembering this information helped a friend of mine in the real estate business get even with a bunch of thieves who were muscling in on his business.

My friend, an honest guy, sometimes mistakenly assumes other business types are honest, too. He made the mistake of taking on two partners who turned out to be crooks. As an honest guy, my friend wanted to get rid of them, and figured he could do so, because neither of them had a broker's license. But the thieves found another realtor with a broker's license willing to help them muscle my friend out of his business. They also threatened my friend physically. My friend may be naive sometimes, but he is never a coward. He roughed up the pair, but then they filed criminal battery charges against him.

My friend and I talked about these revolting developments, then we both hit on the same idea: run a criminal check on the realtor with the broker's license. A cop buddy of my friend's ran the appropriate check, and he found out the target had a felony burglary conviction when he was a young adult. (This was before he bought a suit and tie and decided to steal from people by going into business.) My friend dropped this little bombshell on his crooked partners, and dissolved his business partnership with them HIS way. He kept the lion's share of the business, and they dropped their trumped-up criminal charges against him.

Justice was evidently served in another way. It turned out that one of the crooked partners was having an affair with the wife of a very jealous and very muscular businessman. He and she would have sex in houses the little weasel was selling (when the occupants weren't home). Somehow, someone familiar with the whole sordid affair contacted the businessman about it. Reports soon surfaced that the low-crawling love bandit suffered a major-league beating at the hands of the enraged big husband or one of his hired thugs.

CHECKING OTHER GOVERNMENT RECORDS

Criminal businessmen will have the same kinds of records as other criminals. Check their criminal histories per instructions in the criminal records chapter of this book. Crooked businessmen also get sued a lot, or sue customers who wouldn't pay them for their crooked or incompetent work. They also go through bankruptcy courts—sometimes honestly, sometimes dishonestly. Check their lawsuit and bankruptcy track records per instructions in the lawsuit records chapter of this book.

Businessmen get in all kinds of trouble with the law with conduct ranging from consumer fraud to price-fixing to antitrust violations to price gouging. And the list keeps on keeping on; labor law violations, environmental law violations, tax evasion, and discrimination continue despite laws against these crimes. So if your target businessman is as crooked as you think he is, you should find a criminal case or several civil lawsuits filed against him.

You can also check the chapter on government grants and contracts for detailed information on how to check for possible private sector wrongdoing in connection with government grants and contracts. Check the chapters on real estate records and personal records of businessmen to find dirt on them in these areas.

You can also check with the regulatory agencies. Several chapters of this book cover specific ways in which labor, health, and environmental agencies regulate businessmen and keep records of their violations. The second chapter on the private sector describes which agencies are most likely to regulate the various kinds of businesses. Whether your target businessman is covered more thoroughly in one of the other chapters or not, the major agencies basically play by the same kinds of rules. The general guidelines for checking state and federal agencies for dirt on your target business are these:

- If federal or state agents inspect a businessman's facility and cite him for violations, the citation and related paperwork will be on file at some specified location. Call the agency in question and ask where records for inspections and citations for your area are kept. Make arrangements to review these files. If a company's officials have problems obeying laws enforced by the agency in question, federal or state agents will file civil cases against them to correct their attitude problems. If a company is a persistent or particularly vicious violator of these laws, agents will file criminal charges against its key officials. Federal agents file criminal cases in federal courts; state agents file charges in state courts. If your target company operates in your area, go to the state and federal courthouses in your area and see what kinds of cases government agents have filed against them.

- If your target company operates in more than one area, you'll appreciate knowing the federal agency's general counsel, the inspector general, or the freedom of information officer can compile a listing of all criminal cases and civil cases the agency has ever filed against companies for violations of laws it enforces. Since a case is public record once it is filed, you can write to the freedom of information officer of the agency with a Freedom of Information request, and ask him or her to research what cases the agency has filed against your target company. This goes a lot quicker than trying to contact every federal courthouse in the country to find this kind of dirt on your target company. You could also try writing to the freedom of information officer of the U.S. Justice Department for criminal and civil case listings against your target company. And I'm sure the similar state agency probably has the same kind of file for the state you can access.

THESE CONVICTS WEAR PINSTRIPES

Just to refresh your memory, here are a few well-known criminal and civil cases involving your favorite corporations:

- Exxon is at this writing still involved in some legal actions over the *Exxon Valdez* oil spill calamity in Alaska in 1989. Apparently, a judge charged, Exxon's top people seemed more concerned about controlling damage to their bottom line than they were about controlling damage to the environment.

- In the wake of the *Challenger* tragedy, a presidential commission found Morton Thiokol officials had ignored engineers' concerns about the safety of the rocket engines that propelled the space shuttles. Government investigators also checked on whether company officials punished the engineers who had raised the safety issue.

- Several years earlier, American Airlines officials paid a $500,000 fine because their company's improper maintenance of airplanes caused one to crash in Chicago and kill nearly 300 people.

- General Electric brings good fraud to life, according to federal prosecutors. The U.S. Justice Department brought suit against the manufacturing giant in 1991 because managers of its aircraft engine division allegedly conspired with a general in the Israeli air force to cheat Uncle Sam out of $32 million in a jet engine deal with Israel. The Israeli general pleaded guilty to 12 counts of criminal activity in connection with the deal, and received a 12-year sentence from Israeli authorities.

- Unisys Corporation, not to be outdone, agreed in 1991 to pay $190 million in fines for the fraud, bribery, theft of information on competitors' defense contract bids, and illegal campaign contributing that corporate officials had committed. The computer manufacturer, to date, paid the most money in fines of any company implicated in the U.S. Justice Department's Operation Ill Wind investigation of defense contractors.

- Westinghouse, Lockheed, Gulf Oil, Phillips Petroleum, and Diamond International officials pleaded guilty at various times to making illegal campaign contributions and bribing foreign officials in the 1970s.

- On the other hand, Wedtech's crooked bosses "bought American" when they bribed Bronx congressmen Mario Biaggi and Robert Garcia during the 1980s. These and other dishonest activities (including possible attempts to bribe Attorney General Ed Meese through one of his best friends) enabled them to steal millions of dollars on defense contracts and minority set-aside projects. It also sent them to prison, cost the two congressmen criminal convictions, and forced Ed Meese to resign from his post after one of his own prosecutors called him "a sleaze" in court.

- And let's not forget that Lincoln Savings boss Charles Keating got five U.S. Senators to muzzle bank regulators who were checking on his failing financial empire. For the record, Alan Cranston, Dennis DeConcini, Donald Riegle, John McCain, and John Glenn were the senators involved. Keating's savings and loan collapse will cost the taxpayers $2.5 billion to clean up.

- Ford executives evidently knew an $8 part would have kept many Pintos from bursting into flames during rear-end collisions. They evidently figured not adding the part would save them enough money to cover medical and death claims arising from their exploding Pintos.

- Likewise, Firestone officials evidently knew their "500" tire was dangerously flawed. Congressional investigators determined the exploding tire caused 41 deaths. For a real thrill, how about putting four of these babies on an exploding Pinto? Now that's a car you could truly call a "bomb"!

- Hooker Chemical bosses allowed toxic waste dumping into New York's Love Canal. They also allowed pesticide dumping that poisoned wells in California and allowed fluoride releases that polluted the air in Florida.

- A.H. Robins officials have had to pay many, many dollars to women who alleged in lawsuits they suffered damage from IUDs that A.H. Robins dumped on the market without adequate testing.

Government agents reportedly started at least one criminal or civil action against 60 percent of the country's largest 600 firms in a two-year period. Many of the corporations were alleged multiple offenders during this same period. So if I missed your favorite corporate criminals, I'm sorry… there are so many sleazes and so little space!

Media companies aren't exempt from allegations of wrongdoing, either. A Pennsylvania editor told me state environmental agents cited his paper for illegal disposal of pressroom chemical wastes.

And the owner of the Cleveland *Plain Dealer*, whose staffers fancy themselves as crusading journalists, was under investigation for antitrust violations in the 1980s. It seems U.S. Justice Department officials were interested to know about the deal in which owner Samuel Newhouse paid $22.5 million for the subscriber list of the rival Cleveland *Press* and a small company the *Press* owned. Newhouse paid $14.5 million for the subscriber list alone—$6.5 million more than what the entire Cleveland *Press* operation sold for a year and a half earlier. On top of that, the *Press* was losing several hundred thousand dollars a month. A week after the sale to Newhouse, the *Press* shut down.

The reason for suspicion revolves around the way a newspaper makes money. The owners of the only paper in town charge what they want for advertising. Grocers, car dealers, and many other advertisers are stuck because they have no valid alternative to newspaper advertising.

The printers of the now-defunct *Press* sued Newhouse, the *Plain Dealer*, and the former owner of the *Press* over the sale as well. They alleged the closing of the *Press* was a breach of the job-security contract their union held with the paper. They also alleged the deal was a conspiracy to give the *Plain Dealer* a monopoly in Cleveland.

But like so many businessmen their paper covers, the *Plain Dealer's* top cats escaped punishment. In March 1985, U.S. District judge Ann Aldrich dismissed the printers' lawsuit. She ruled they couldn't prove the deal was designed to hurt them. She also said there were technicalities in the law that prevented them from suing as individuals. However, she wrote, "The record is replete with facts from which a jury could conclude that the *Plain Dealer*, Press Publishing, and Cole (the ex-owner of the *Press*) conspired together in restraint of trade for the purpose and with the intent of creating a monopoly in the product market for the greater Cleveland area."

In 1987, a federal grand jury refused to indict Newhouse or anyone else connected with the *Plain Dealer*. Meanwhile, a federal prosecutor involved with the case was fired after he blew the whistle on his bosses' alleged repeated attempts to kill the investigation against Newhouse and the newspaper. He said they granted immunity from prosecution to the key defendants, and withheld evidence from Judge Aldrich. U.S. Justice Department officials said the prosecutor was fired for "failing to co-operate in meetings, being disrespectful, and for not following the chain of command in airing his complaints," according to Akron *Beacon-Journal* reporter Ken Myers.

Have I convinced you the dirt is there for the digging? I hope so.

THE BOTTOM LINE

Learn a lesson from my honest businessman friend. There are several ways to dish out a beating even if you're a 97-pound weakling instead of a 230-pound tough guy like him. If you get the right amount of dirt on a targeted businessman, you'll be able to make him eat it and choke on it!

END NOTES

1. My article on Occidental Petroleum and Rick Boucher's flipflop on revoking Romania's most favored nation status appeared in the Kingsport (Tennessee) *Times-News* on September 23, 1986. (As a side note that shows the value of business and union journals, an article in the September 1986 issue of *United Mine Workers Journal* noted Occidental Petroleum was a partner with the Red Chinese government in the giant Chinese coal mine, and an article in this magazine's October 1986 issue noted Occidental Petroleum owned Island Creek Coal.) Further, Oxy's 1989 annual report noted it still held Island Creek Coal. And a press release Oxy officials issued July 1, 1991 announced the sale of the company's interests in the giant Red Chinese coal mine.

2. Information on the Hyatt Regency Hotel disaster comes from the case *Missouri Board for Architects, Professional Engineers, and Land Surveyors vs. Duncan, Gillam, and G.C.E. International, Inc.* This case, numbered AR-84-0239, was heard by the Missouri Administrative Hearing Commission.

3. Non-doctors whom I'm aware of who reportedly performed medical procedures for abortion providers include Paul David Bates (criminal case LAMC 31206712, 9-25-81, Los Angeles Municipal Court) and Shastia Khan (she allegedly prescribed drugs, installed IUDs and performed exams according to "The Abortion Profiteers" series which ran in the Chicago *Sun-Times* in 1978). According to an AP wire service story which ran on February 3, 1989, New York abortion provider Abram Zelikman allegedly let an unlicensed woman give anesthesia to Eurice Agbagaa, and told her to watch the African native after the abortion. Ms. Agbagaa bled severely after the abortion, then died a week later as a result, the article alleged. And according to an AP wire service story which ran on November 22, 1989, Connecticut abortion provider Hanan Rotem received a $2000 fine, in part for allowing his receptionist to administer painkillers and assist in abortions. Rotem, the article said, was investigated by state medical board officials over the abortion-connected death of Gloria Aponte. Bates, an ex-Navy corpsman, was also named in a lawsuit over the death of a woman who underwent unspecified uterine treatment. (The lawsuit— C102889—was filed in L.A. County Superior Court in the 1970s.)

4. Information on the judge's charge against Exxon's managers comes from an article in the May 6, 1991 issue of *U.S. News*.

5. Information on Morton Thiokol's reported illegal activities in connection with the *Challenger* tragedy comes from an article in the March 10, 1986 issue of *Newsweek*, an article in the May 19, 1986 issue of *Aviation Week*, and Richard

Lewis' book *Challenger—The Final Voyage.*

6. Information on General Electric's alleged $32 million rip-off of the taxpayers comes from an AP wire service article which ran August 15, 1991.

7. Information on Unisys' $190 million fine and the criminal activity which caused it comes from the settlement agreement Unisys officials signed with the Justice Department September 6, 1991, and from the related press release the Justice Department issued that day.

8. Information on the Wedtech scandal comes from Marilyn Thompson's book *Feeding the Beast.*

9. Information on Charles Keating and the Keating Five senators comes from an article in the December 11, 1989 issue of *Newsweek,* an article in the October 29, 1990 issue of *Time,* and an article in the November 26, 1990 issue of *Newsweek.*

10. Information on the offenses of American Airlines, Westinghouse, Lockheed, Gulf Oil, Phillips Petroleum, Diamond International, Ford, Firestone, Hooker Chemical, and A.H. Robins comes from Robert Bonn's book *Criminology.* I have personally seen several lawsuits which women have filed against A.H. Robins for gynecological damage.

11. Statistics on criminal and civil cases against big businesses come from Marshall Clinard's 1979 study, which Robert Bonn cited in his textbook *Criminology.*

12. Information on the Cleveland *Plain Dealer* affair comes from Ken Myers' article in the Akron *Beacon Journal* on April 19, 1987, and from articles in the March 30, 1985 and June 20, 1987 issues of *Editor and Publisher.*

Cleanup Work On The Private Sector

If you've ever done a massive cleanup in your house or work place after a move, an insect fumigation, a flood, a fire, a storm, an earthquake, or some other cataclysmic event, you're aware you never get it all clean on the first effort. You have to go back and do a little more cleaning, disinfecting, or debris removing. Usually, after a move, you'll have to clean and fuss for a couple of weeks before everything is all right. Sometimes, after a flood, you'll find leftover rats and snakes. Sometimes, after a fumigation, you'll find several dustpan loads of bugs.

"Good conversational topic, Kev," you're saying right now. "But what do dirt, debris, and dead varmints have to do with crooked business people?"

"Aside from the smell, not too much," I reply. But seriously, the connection between them is that I needed to write this chapter to finish the cleanup I couldn't get to in the first chapter on the private sector. The first private sector chapter covered so much ground so quickly that a lot of finer stuff sifted through my excavating equipment. So this chapter will cover some other important info on businesses that escaped the first chapter—info like a short list on which agencies monitor which kinds of businesses, a short list on which agents can make trouble for most businesses, a short report on insurance carriers, and a short report on public utilities.

The uses of this chapter are similar to the uses of the first chapter on the private sector. For "military" purposes, you can use the information in this chapter to find out about and expose the misconduct of unethical business people. For "civilian" purposes, you can check on business people and feel better about dealing with them if they come clean, or avoid them if they're dirty.

A SHORT LIST OF INFORMATION SOURCES ON TARGET BUSINESSES

You'll run out of time to check on many businesses before you'll run out of places to check. To help you concentrate your efforts on the most likely sources of info, I've put in this section a short series of paragraphs that will cross-index your target businessman's line of business with his natural predators—the government regulators.

These agencies' enforcement officers, auditors, contracts administrators, general counsels, and inspectors general will have some sort of negative information on your target company if it's as bad an outfit as you think it is (and if they've checked on its operators). Just like in the first chapter, I suggest you contact these people, or the freedom of information officer in each government agency that regulates your target's line of business. Ask these people for information on lawsuits, criminal actions, citations, enforcements, suspensions from programs, and any other kinds of dirt on your target they can send your way.

Defense Contractors. The U.S. Defense Department's Defense Criminal Investigative Service agents handle criminal cases against defense contractors. The DOD's Defense Contract Audit Agency agents audit defense contractors to make sure they aren't playing tricks with their billing. The DOD's Directorate for Information Operations and Reports publishes lists of nice-to-know info such as major contractors, colleges and nonprofit institutions that hold defense contracts, and money involved. Check in with these agencies to see if their agents have any negative info on your target.

Construction Trades Contractors. State licensing agencies for contractors and engineers and architects handle actions against these businessmen for professional misconduct and other types of wrongdoing. Government agencies which do business with construction businesses, especially the Federal Housing Authority (FHA), Farmers Home Administration (FmHA), and U.S. Department of Housing and Urban Development (HUD), maintain lists of contractors who are suspended or banned from contracts due to fraud or poor work. Local building code agencies have records on code violations. Local courthouses are full of lawsuits involving contractors. Check in with these sources.

Landlords. Local housing authorities enforce laws relating to rent, evictions, and habitability of premises. They will have info on whether a landlord has been cited for ripping off or merely gouging tenants, throwing them out in the street for no good reason, or maintaining flophouses. For more information on a landlord's possible slumlord tendencies, check with building code agencies and public health authorities.

Realtors. The state real estate commission might have some dirt on your target realtor. If he's an incompetent or a chiseler, he may have been sued for his poor or crooked job performances. Check your local courthouse for such cases.

Insurance Companies. See the section on insurance companies later in this chapter.

Stock Brokers. The U.S. Securities and Exchange Commission agents list brokers they've sued or prosecuted for fraud, mismanagement of investors' money, insider trading, and other kinds of wrongdoing. They also make brokers and investment firms file several different forms. Check with the SEC to get copies of forms they've made your target file.

Publicly-held Companies. The SEC makes companies which issue stock and are big enough file some sort of annual status report; this report is a public record. Even many smaller companies issue some sort of annual report to stockholders. The SEC has copies of these annual reports. (And often, the company's PR people may send you a copy of the annual report if you ask for one.) There are several kinds of other reports the SEC makes businesses file. Check with the SEC to get copies of these. The SEC's agents also investigate companies suspected of illegal stock manipulations, and they maintain lists of companies they prosecute or sue for such violations.

Bankers. The Federal Deposit Insurance Corporation, the Federal Savings and Loan Insurance Corporation, and/or the Federal Reserve System may have federal-level dirt on your local Shylock on any one of a number of unethical and illegal activities. Odds are good if someone's in the banking or the savings and loan business, he's been up to no good. Check to determine if your target is a banker or S&L exec who holds up the public.

(What happens when the regulators don't do their jobs? Bankers and S&L executives who go crooked have in recent years cost millions of people money, have bought senators and congressmen like whores to protect themselves from regulation and investigation, and have weakened the financial structure of this nation so seriously that the taxpayers will have to pay billions of dollars to clean up the mess. And that doesn't even count the billions of dollars in bad loans to bankrupt foreign governments that we the people will have to pay for because of the greed of the moneylenders.)

Credit Bureaus, Credit Companies And Bill Collectors. The Federal Trade Commission, through the Fair Credit Billing Act, regulates how credit companies bill customers and resolve disputes. The FTC, through the Fair Credit Reporting Act, makes credit bureaus tell people what's on their credit report. And the FTC, through the Fair Debt Collection Practices Act, tells bill collectors what is considered a fair collection technique and what is considered harassment. Check with the FTC for evidence your target company has been caught violating these laws. Likewise, check with your state's parallel agency to see what dirt its people have. Also, there are many books on the market about the credit business that can give you further pointers on how to uncover negative information on credit business people.

Importers. The U.S. Department of the Treasury, through the U.S. Customs Service, enforces laws on what and how much importers can bring into the country, and under what conditions they can bring it in. Also, the U.S. Department of Commerce's agents have records on whether your target has been helping unscrupulous foreign governments like Japan and Britain dump products in this country to keep their people working at the expense of our own workers.

Someone in one or both of these agencies also keeps records of violations of those who break other provisions of trade laws, like importing more than what's allowed, failing to pay enough customs fees on it, or fronting for smugglers and/or drugrunners, for example. Also, depending on your target's contracts, connections and lobbying skills, he may have to register with the U.S. Justice Department as an agent of a foreign country; failure to do so is a serious offense. Check with these agencies to find out how clean or unclean your target is.

Doctors, Nurses, Hospitals, Clinics. See the chapter on health care.

Lawyers. The state's lawyer board (or board of bar examiners) might have bad paper on your favorite shyster. But they probably won't. Likewise, the county or state bar association (a private association of lawyers) might—but probably doesn't—have complaints on file against your target shyster. Why? Because lawyers aren't usually going to investigate or punish one of their own. They'd be like the self-righteous whom Christ taunted, "Let one among you without sin cast the first stone."

However, there are some ways to check on lawyers. You could check the courthouse for legal malpractice suits filed against your target attorney. Or you could check criminal and civil case files at the courthouse to see how your target handles his clients' criminal cases and lawsuits. You may find he makes errors to prolong a case and get a bigger fee, or he may sell out his client and tell him to plead guilty to lesser offenses (or settle a case to a client's disadvantage if it's a civil case) because he quoted a flat fee and the case is going to run longer than he expected.

Food And Drug Sellers. The U.S. Department of Agriculture, the U.S. Food and Drug Administration, and the Federal Trade Commission all enforce laws related to food. Likewise, the FDA enforces laws related to drugs. Check with these agencies to see if there's dirt on those who sell the food you eat and the prescription drugs you take. Likewise, local public health officials and state agriculture officials keep records on code violators in these businesses. Check in with them to see if they have any dirt on your targets. Since food adulterers, overgraders, and unsanitary plant managers abound, you may find out your target is in their club.

These agencies are at this writing going after food companies for questionable ads and packaging practices. It's like the controversy surrounding oatmeal. I don't eat oatmeal because a company like Quaker Oats paid some scientists to do research to claim oat bran is good for me. I started eating oatmeal because my Grandpa Charlie—who came to America from Ireland—told me when I was a little boy that oatmeal made the Irish strong and tough. Likewise, I started eating spinach because my mom pointed out to me that Popeye could beat up the bad guys because of the nutrients he got from this vegetable. Who said cartoons have no educational value?

Weights And Measures. County weights and measures officials can check on anyone who sells goods by weight or by volume. You've seen their seals on grocery store scales and on gasoline pumps. If your target chisels customers by selling them less than their money's worth with crooked scales or flow devices, these agents may have cited him. Likewise, these agents can check on the octane level or the heating value of gasoline or heating oil. They can cite those who "water" these fuels. Check with these agents to see if they have cited your target. Or sic 'em on businesses you think are ripping you off. I've gotten several gas station owners cited this way!

Moving Companies, Trucking Firms, Other Transportation Companies. The Interstate Commerce Commission enforces laws on shipping rates, handling of goods being moved, unfair competition practices in transportation industries, and certain labor practices in transportation industries, among other things. Some states' public utility commissions also take part in regulating these industries. The U.S. Department of Transportation's National Transportation Safety Board can provide you with evidence from plane crashes, train wrecks, ship wrecks, and other

transportation industry disasters. These agents can also provide you with documents proving they cited, sued, or prosecuted a carrier for unsafe practices. Check these agencies' records for evidence of your target's wrongdoing.

Small (and Not-so-small) Businesses. The U.S. Small Business Administration runs a lot of programs to help small businessmen. Some con artists (like the officials of Wedtech) try to rip off these programs by lying about their qualifications for loans and contracts. Check with the SBA's agents; they can provide you with information on which businesses are benefiting from their programs, the paperwork the businessmen filed to gain SBA approval, and documents showing they took some sort of action against businessmen who violated the laws they enforce.

Utility Companies. See the section on public utilities later in this chapter.

Media. The Federal Communications Commission licenses broadcasters such as TV and radio companies. These companies are susceptible to complaints about bias, failure to give equal time, obscenity on the air, and other abuses. Newspapers and magazines are not really vulnerable to federal regulatory pressure. However, the marketplace is regulating them because fewer people read, so fewer advertisers advertise in print media. (You'd think editors would assign reporters to dig dirt on local educators to account for this literacy drop-off, but they don't!)

On the private side, watchdogs such as the Accuracy In Media group—AIM for short—document alleged media abuses. Also, certain other watchdog groups know which media types suck up to businesses to keep advertising money coming in. They may also know who the biased are. Check with these groups for further information.

A SHORT LIST OF AGENTS WHO CAN CAUSE TROUBLE FOR MANY BUSINESSES

Labor Law Enforcers. Many employers are potential labor law violators. They might be tempted to cheat workers out of money, force them to labor under unsafe conditions, discriminate based on any number of prejudices, or practice some other form of unethical treatment of their employees. See the chapter on labor for information on how to document labor abuses through U.S. Labor Department records and other sources.

Environmental Law Enforcers. Many manufacturers are potential polluters. Chemical plants, oil refineries, heavy industry plants, and (gasp) local government sewage plants are the most likely violators. Many mining companies, oil drillers, and logging outfits are potential land rapists. Any nuclear plant, if improperly run, might not glow in the dark, but it could cause people cancer. Check the chapter on the environment for information on how to document environmental abuses through records of the U.S. Environmental Protection Agency, the Nuclear Regulatory Commission, and other sources.

Prosecutors. The U.S. Justice Department actually sues or prosecutes many corporations and individuals suspected of federal-level unethical business practices. Likewise, each state attorney general office and each county prosecutor office handles similar cases at the state and local levels. Contact agents in these offices for information on cases against your target.

Licensing Bureau Agents. These people regulate those businessmen whose enterprises give them a special amount of control over people's finances or put them in a position to do a lot of harm if they become crooked. We the people really don't want real estate brokers to chisel buyers and sellers. And we really don't want gun dealers to sell firearms to the Mob. So our politicians license these and other businessmen.

Likewise, the agents regulate white collar professionals like doctors and lawyers and engineers and architects who need to demonstrate a certain amount of skill to prevent the public from suffering harm. Get a copy of your state's "red book" or "blue book" from your state's secretary of state office to figure out which licensing bureau agents monitor your target in his line of trade. Then contact the agents to see if they've ever taken action against him in any way. Documents on such actions, as well as info the agents have on the target's license and credentials and professional history, are good information to have.

Tax Collectors. An IRS agent sent Al Capone to Alcatraz when no other G-man could. That, to me, sums up the power of taxing agencies. Since government officials are addicted to our money the way junkies are addicted to dope, they'll do anything to punish those who don't give them their money fix by failing to pay taxes. I've covered tax information in the real estate chapter and in the first private sector chapter, but I'm just reminding you to check with the IRS, the state treasurer, and all the local taxing agents to find out if they've got some action going against your target.

We all hate the taxman, but nobody likes a tax dodger who makes the rest of us pay more to carry his load. And if the taxman has dirt on a target we can use, then maybe he isn't a complete ogre after all.

THE FEDERAL TRADE COMMISSION—A SOMETIME CROOK-BUSTER

The Federal Trade Commission's agents enforce a number of laws relating to unfair business practices and customer protection. (I hate the word "consumer" because to me it implies people lie around like loafers, eat like gluttons, and do nothing to earn what they buy.) You've seen energy efficiency tags on appliances, warranty information on products, and content and care labels on garments. You've also seen statements for loans or credit cards saying exactly how much these services will cost you in interest. You've also seen a number of other disclosures which tell you the terms and actual costs of goods and services. In most cases, the corporation bosses didn't give you this info out of the goodness of their hearts; they do it because the FTC makes them do it.

Likewise, the FTC can sue or prosecute businesses for a number of major business law violations. For example, the FTC's agents have gone after business people for the following violations:

- Unfair dealing with the public. The FTC's Bureau of Consumer Protection can attack company officials who engage in false advertising, credit violations (such as those listed above, and also discrimination in extending of credit), fraudulent telemarketing schemes, fraud and deception related to health care, or price-fixing among professionals such as lawyers or doctors or optometrists or morticians. The agents can also penalize those businessmen who fail to make known health or safety problems or mechanical defects in their products, and they can nail those who systematically fail to fulfill warranty or other contract obligations.

- Unfair competition. The FTC's Bureau of Competition can attack those who engage in restraint of trade, price-fixing, monopolistic practices, and in certain kinds of corporate mergers. Price discrimination is also illegal. It's OK for a manufacturer to give price breaks based on volume or the cost of making the sale, but it's not all right for the manufacturer to give one buyer a price break and gouge another buyer if both buyers are making similar buys. Some interlocking directorates are also illegal. (An interlocking directorate is a name for one or more people serving as director(s) of competing corporations.) Why? Because the alleged rivals, through these directors, could actually be working together to unfairly run other competitors out of business.

Two 1991 high-profile cases show the FTC's

muscle. In April 1991, FTC agents fined Nintendo, the Japanese-owned videogame company, for price-fixing. Nintendo officials, whom FTC agents said cornered 80 percent of the videogame market, agreed under the terms of a consent order (a cease and desist order) to refrain from price-fixing and from forbidding retailers from selling the videogames at reduced prices, agreed to refrain from cutting supplies of their videogames to retailers who discount them, agreed to refrain from making dealers who discount its videogames pay more credit costs, and agreed to refrain from making retailers report on other retailers who are discounting. Although a Nintendo official signed the agreement without admitting to violating the law, it's evident that company officials wouldn't have paid the fine and agreed to the cease and desist order if they hadn't been out of line somewhere. Some could argue Nintendo officials got off lightly; they only had to pay about $5 million in court costs and mail out $25 million in $5 rebate coupons good only for Nintendo videogames.

In the other case, FTC agents in December 1991 forced credit information giant TRW to clean up its act. The Feds had accused TRW officials of hurting people's credit ratings by maintaining inaccurate credit information on them, and by failing to correct these errors quickly when people pointed them out. A TRW official signed a consent order which is designed to make the company reform its practices.

Check in with the FTC's agents if you suspect your target businessman has engaged in any of the illegal practices listed above. They'll be more than happy to help you publicize the penalizing they've been doing.

INVESTIGATING INSURANCE COMPANIES

We all need insurance of some kind, but the cost of it bites everyone where it hurts! My own medical insurance has nearly tripled in the past three years, and the irresponsibility (or in some cases the misfortune) of a lot of people has helped cause the price jump. People who don't or can't pay their medical bills, homosexuals that engage in AIDS-causing sex, druggies with or without AIDS, smokers who undergo expensive cancer treatment, drunk drivers who kill and maim others and themselves, and hypochondriac wimps with low-deductible insurance policies who run to the doctor every time they have the slightest little problem are all to blame for honest people like you and me having to pay through the nose for medical insurance. Likewise, car insurance costs so much because a lot of jerks drive without insurance and hit other people's cars. This means the innocent people's

insurance companies pick up the tabs, and the companies' officials pass them back to their customers.

The irresponsibility of the individuals listed above gives professional lowlifes who are doctors, hospital operators, car repair shop owners, lawyers, and insurance company executives the opportunity to gouge you. Your insurance rates reflect the cost of other peoples' irresponsibility and/or crookedness.

But at least you've got a little piece of mind once you've got your insurance, right? Don't bet on it. Farmers in the Midwest who applied to buy drought insurance for their crops from the Chubb Group in 1988 suffered drought damage, then watched as Chubb welshed on paying their losses. Why? According to a published report, Chubb's agents sold farmers more than ten times as much drought insurance as the insurance underwriter had authorized. Chubb officials didn't get back to the farmers about the overselling of insurance, then simply told them they weren't covered when word came in from the Corn Belt that the drought was probably going to drop crop yields dramatically.

Also, insurance companies will sometimes not pay their clients' losses even when they are covered. At the heart of this problem is whether or not the client was so irresponsible that the company shouldn't have to cover the damage he caused. For example, if you decide to play "Bump Cars" during rush hour and deliberately damage other vehicles with your auto, your insurance company is probably within its rights to refuse to pay for all the damage you did. But sometimes insurance company people, in an effort to maximize profits, will stretch the definition of irresponsibility and decide not to cover the losses of people they should cover.

An even more common practice is for an insurance company's adjusters to give people less than replacement cost on items they've lost. This practice may or may not be legal, depending on the terms of the policy. And it may or may not be right. Insurance people can hold down other customers' costs if they don't overpay claimants. On the other hand, if they wield a sharp pencil needlessly against a legitimate claimant just to make some more bucks, then they aren't doing right by their customer.

If you want to check into a target insurance company, check for lawsuits involving the company at your local courthouse. People whom insurance companies have refused to cover or whom insurance companies have short-sheeted on claims payments do sometimes sue them, especially if there's a lot of money involved. Likewise, you may find dirt on your local shady insurance agent in the lawsuit files.

Another info source is your state's insurance commission. Call the insurance commission in your state capital, and ask the agents for documents and information on actions the state has taken against your target insurance company or insurance agent.

Then there are the federal folks. The Federal Trade Commission will go after company officials who don't back policies they sell. And the Justice Department might get involved if the insurance company's bosses are so crooked that the Feds could pin criminal convictions on them without too much effort.

Checking on insurance companies may help you save some money, help you decide which companies to do business with, and help you ensure your insurer lives up to his obligations to cover you. And if your insurer won't cover you, you could give the dirt you find to your local representative or TV reporter; they'll be sure to "cover" him!

PROBING PUBLIC UTILITIES

In exchange for allowing utilities monopolies in certain areas, state lawmakers set up public utility commissions to regulate the amount a utility can raise your utility bill. The purpose of this is to prevent the utilities' officials from engaging in wholesale price-gouging. But it doesn't mean they still don't try anyway.

Utility companies must file for rate increases, and the public utility commissions must set public hearings for these rate increases. The paperwork the utilities file arguing for the rate increases are public records. People in groups which fight rate hikes pore over the utility companies' reports to look for instances of the utility officials padding their figures, or asking for a rate increase to pay for items that a rate hike by law can't cover. Then, of course, they'll accuse utility people of lying on everything if they catch them cheating on anything. In my area, a watchdog group bit a local utility recently for hiding advertising costs and "charitable contributions" in its rate hike request. The rate hike opponents quite logically wondered why the utility should be allowed to gouge the public to buy good PR.

Other things the public utility commissions handle are regulation of utility company safety, service, and other items of concern to the public. In some states, the commissions also regulate public and private transportation companies. And any time the commission's agents or officers take action against utility companies or transportation companies for violations, it's a public record.

To get a copy of any utility's rate hike request, or to find out about any disciplinary action the public utility commission in your state has taken against utility companies, call the public utility commission in your state capital. Ask the agents what the procedure is for obtaining such information.

Don't overlook lawsuits against the utilities. Some may be filed at your county courthouse, at a courthouse in your state capital, or maybe at a courthouse in the county a utility's headquarters is in.

One other dirt source to check is your local utility watchdog group. Since they live for digging dirt on utilities, they may have already gotten their hands on some pretty interesting stuff. Be ready to separate the information they give you into two stacks—verifiable data and propaganda. But remember also this is their "cause", so they're bound to have something on your target you can use.

THE BOTTOM LINE ONE MORE TIME

Profit makes the world go around. If you're an employee, you earn your paycheck by doing work that enables your employer to make money off of your labor. By goofing off on the job, you cost others money and help make it easier for some corporate bigwigs to ship jobs overseas. If you're a businessman or a white-collar professional such as a doctor or a lawyer or an architect, you make your money by offering goods or services to people and businesses at a reasonable price. You're entitled to make a fair profit, but not an unfair killing. If only all of us would be honest, we'd be better off morally and economically. Until that day (which in my suspicious heart I think will never come), it's up to us to check on businesses so it will cost them less to do right than to do wrong.

END NOTES

1. Information on the Nintendo price-fixing case comes from the consent order (File No. 901-0028), the FTC complaint, and an FTC analysis of the consent order. Further information comes from an article in the April 22, 1991 issue of *Newsweek*.
2. Information on the TRW credit error case comes from the FTC complaint, the consent order, and a related FTC press release on the matter.
3. Information on the Chubb crop insurance fiasco comes from an article in the August 29, 1988 issue of *Time*.

This One's for the Working Man

The taxpayers of this nation have to give federal, state, and local governments at least a trillion dollars a year in taxes. "A billion here, a billion there," said Everett Dirksen, the late great Illinois senator, "and pretty soon we're talking real money!" At the rate our government taxers collect money, we could wallpaper the country in $1000 bills. Yet we're still in the red, and getting redder every day.

Well, I've griped enough about taxes for this chapter. Some of the guys I've voted for have raised taxes and chiseled the public, too. The guys who didn't do these things didn't get a chance to; they LOST their elections!

My taxes and your taxes, in paying for all this government, also help document unethical behavior on the part of many businesses and industries toward their workers. If your target businessman or industrialist is as evil as you think he is, there's bound to be some bad paper somewhere that the government agents have pinned on him. I'll admit the bureaucrats are good for something.

In fact, many of the agencies actually perform valuable services. The agents of the U.S. Labor Department and similar state labor agents have made many workplaces safer by enforcing workplace safety codes. The agents of the Nuclear Regulatory Commission protect workers in the nuclear industry and have kept nuclear power industry officials from causing repeats of Chernobyl in this country. State and federal labor agents have done much to improve the pay and the working conditions of American workers.

Without these agents, we'd all be like Koreans who routinely lose eyes, limbs, and lives in a land where the industry bosses are lords and the workers are impoverished serfs. I was with the 2nd Infantry Division north of Seoul in the early 1980s, and I saw the conditions the workers over there labor under. That's why the junk they produce for K-mart is so cheap. Korean businessmen pay their workers next to nothing and force them to work in conditions we haven't allowed in this country since before Teddy Roosevelt's time. And I'm not just picking on Korea. In other Third World countries, in Red China, and even in some of the agribusiness farms and sweat-

shops of this country where illegal immigrants toil, the lot of the worker is much the same.

Labor agencies make records available to the public. It's possible for you, as an average citizen, to find records which prove a corporation treats workers like peons, expendable bodies, or both. I can't tell you about the records of every agency involved in the fight to ensure justice for the American worker, but I can at least point you in the right direction.

In this chapter, I will cover checking on businesses for workplace safety violations, wage violations, discrimination problems, union-busting, and other illegal labor practices. I will also cover checking on union bosses for abuses, and I'll wrap up with a section on migrant labor conditions.

Finding out how a company or a union treats its people for "civilian" purposes can help you, your friends, and your loved ones decide whom to do business with or work for, and whom to avoid like the plague. Using these research techniques can also give you and your co-workers some leverage in dealing with your company bosses or your labor leaders to get better wages and conditions. You will be able to negotiate knowing a little more about what reasonable standards are for contracts in your industry.

The "military" uses of the techniques of this chapter include exposing a company's unethical treatment of workers to make it a boycott target or to make it the target of serious criminal probes. Other "military" uses include exposing the misconduct of crooked labor union bosses and getting company officials punished for other forms of unlawful behavior toward workers (like discrimination and contract violation).

MAKING IT UNSAFE FOR WORKPLACE SAFETY VIOLATORS

When "job safety" comes up in the workplace, most people laugh and make jokes about lame-brain OSHA inspectors who would put training wheels on cowboys' horses if they could. I laugh at the jokes, but I've seen people who lost eyes and hands at factories where I've worked. Government overkill is one thing, but in all too many work places, employers force workers to labor under unsafe conditions. It's up to the agents of OSHA (the U.S. Department of Labor's

Occupational Safety and Health Administration) and their state counterparts to punish these robber barons.

If OSHA or state occupational safety agents inspect a work place, the inspection paperwork is a public record. It will be on file at one of the agency's offices. If a government safety agent cites an employer for safety violations, the citation and related paperwork will be on file at some specified location. Call the agency in question and ask where records for inspections and citations for your area are kept. Make arrangements to review these files.

Certain industries, like mining, aviation, and nuclear power, live under a system where government agents are at the workplace often. The agencies which regulate these industries often keep inspection and citation files for each company. With these agencies, you can ask to see the inspection and citation files of the company you're checking and the agents can have them ready for you with little trouble at all. (Bear in mind that agencies like the Federal Aviation Administration and the Nuclear Regulatory Commission are independent agencies that are not affiliated with the U.S. Labor Department.)

If a company's officials have problems operating safe work places, federal or state labor agents can file civil cases against them to correct their attitude problems. If a company is a persistent or particularly vicious violator of worker safety laws, agents can file criminal charges against its key officials. Federal agents file cases in federal courts; state agents file cases in state courts. If your target company operates in your area, go to the county and federal courthouses in your area and see what kinds of cases government agents have filed against its officials.

If your target company operates in more than one area, you'll appreciate knowing the U.S. Labor Department's general counsel, the inspector general, other enforcement officials, or the freedom of information officer should be able to generate for you a list of all criminal cases and civil cases the agency has ever filed against your target company for job safety violations. You might also try checking with the U.S. Justice Department. Federal prosecutors may have filed some cases against your target also.

Remember, a case is public record once it is filed. So you can write to the Labor Department or the Justice Department with a Freedom of Information request, and ask for the freedom of information officer to list for you the safety cases the agency has filed against your target. This goes a lot quicker than trying to contact every federal courthouse in the country to find this kind of dirt on your target company. I'm sure your state labor department or attorney general probably has the same kind of file you can access for cases your state's agents have filed against your target.

A DIGGING PROJECT ON A HAZARDOUS WORKPLACE

I once used Labor Department documents to show a major coal mining company's officials were still running a Virginia mine with the same unsafe conditions that three years earlier had killed seven miners. The 1983 explosion in Clinchfield Coal's McClure No. 1 mine that killed the miners was a result of a dangerous buildup of methane gas in the mine. Methane gas buildup in coal mines is an extreme safety hazard. Methane, like natural gas, will burn or explode at between five percent and 15 percent levels in air. All it takes is a spark to ignite it. Miners use methane sensors to detect dangerous levels of methane and they use huge vent fans to blow it out of the mine before it can build up.

Mine managers are supposed to have the miners evacuate the mine when the concentration of methane gas is 1.5 percent or higher. This is so the miners can get to safety before the methane has a chance to build up to a level where it could burn or explode. In the McClure No.1 mine disaster, mine managers had failed to ensure adequate ventilation in the mine, so the methane gas built up to 6.0 percent (ignitable explosive level) in the mine, according to the U.S. Labor Department's Mine Safety and Health Administration investigation report. The resulting blast sent flames hundreds of feet through mine tunnels and killed the seven miners.

I found in MSHA's public file on the mine that mine managers had allowed the mine to become similarly explosive on at least four occasions after the tragedy. In such instances, a single spark could have touched off an explosion that could burn miners alive, cave in their bodies with blast shock, or cave in a tunnel over them so they would be crushed to death or would suffocate. On one citation, the agent wrote, "The underlying cause is that management is not enforcing the approved ventilation, methane, and dust control plans for the mine."

By checking MSHA's public records on accident statistics, I also found that Clinchfield's lost time accident rate, which at the time of the 1983 disaster was double the state average, had dropped substantially over the two years following the tragedy, but was still 50 percent worse than the state average for 1985. Neither officials of Clinchfield Coal nor officials of parent company Pittston had any comment on the above facts when I contacted them. They had plenty to say when the story ran, however.

SOME WRAP-UP NOTES ON WORKER SAFETY

I hope the story I told you about Clinchfield Coal won't make you hate all coal operators. Most of the coal operators I dealt with in Kentucky, Virginia, and West Virginia are people of integrity who DO care about their workers' safety. Almost all of them have worked in mines themselves. Plus, they're smart enough to know that accidents shut down the mine, idle workers, ruin equipment, and draw inspectors, which means they lose all kinds of money. The efforts of good coal operators, United Mine Workers leaders, and government mine safety agents are making coal mines safer places to work.

Just to give the nuclear industry equal time, I used publicly-available Nuclear Regulatory Commission reports and citations to write articles about managers of the Oyster Creek nuclear power plant in New Jersey. The NRC made worker safety records available to the public in the public library in nearby Toms River. Using these records of the NRC's actions, I noted NRC agents wrote up GPU Nuclear—the utility in question—for improper surveying of radiation hazards to workers. I also reported NRC agents cited company officials for failure to ensure some workers were wearing their radiation dosage detectors properly—a failure which caused some of these workers to suffer exposure to excess radiation.

However, like most coal operators, GPU Nuclear officials aren't ogres, and I reported this. NRC agents and International Brotherhood of Electrical Workers officials both said the plant had become a much safer place to work because of management's better attitude toward worker safety.

Believe it or not, hospitals, clinics and doctors rack up their share of NRC citations. This is because through neglect or worse, they cause their employees to suffer exposure to radiation. And radiation damage is radiation damage, whether it comes from Three-Mile Island or a piece of nuclear medicine equipment. NRC agents tend to give medical abusers of nuclear safety the same kind of scrutiny they give the power plants and the nuclear manufacturers. These citations are available from the NRC's freedom of information officer; the NRC is very good about giving info to people interested in who the NRC cites.

U.S. Labor Department people and state labor agency people are very proud of their work. Use this pride to your advantage. Call the public information officers and the freedom of information officers of these agencies to get their reports on all labor law violators they went after. One of the regular features I used to give my readers was a periodic wrap-up of which corporations and businessmen in our area drew fines or other punishment from state and federal labor agencies; the info I used came from very helpful labor agency officials.

UNFORTUNATELY, SIMON LEGREE LIVES

Harriet Beecher Stowe's *Uncle Tom's Cabin* was THE muckraking novel of the 1800s. In her story, the slave driving foreman Simon Legree beat an old slave to death and sent goons and dogs after poor runaway slaves. The hatred Miss Harriet generated against slave owners with her book was considered by many—including President Lincoln himself—to be a contributing cause of the Civil War. When Honest Abe met the lady author, he said to her, kiddingly, "So you're the little woman who wrote the book that made this great war!"

The Union Army and Honest Abe ended slavery in 1865. But some employers still haven't gotten the word. They exploit immigrants in their sweatshops, they hire on teenagers at minimum wages to run off adult workers, they reduce workers' hours enough so they won't have to pay benefits, they abuse the training wage provisions of the minimum wage law to short-change their new workers, and they pay less-than-equitable wages to workers after signing contracts that specify they must pay a prevailing wage.

Companies also illegally skin their skilled blue collar workers and lower-level white collar workers by making them "exempt" employees who have to do overtime work for little or no compensation. And companies bloodsuck their employees by not reimbursing them fairly for job-related expenses they have.

Some of the worst violators of labor laws, by the way, are newspaper publishers. They overwork their youngest reporters, pay them next to nothing, force them to work unpaid or underpaid overtime, and underpay them for using their cars on newspaper business. The line they use on young reporters is, "You're professionals." The underlying threat they use on young reporters is, "I can fire you, and screw up your chances of working on other newspapers if you cross me."

Young reporters who need to establish good work records for the future think they have to tolerate this abuse or else kiss their journalism careers good-bye. Maybe that's why so many of them think all employers are swine. The only time I tried to organize a union was when I worked at a newspaper, and the only employer I ever turned in for labor law violations was a newspaper publisher.

If federal or state wage and hour agents cite an

employer for wage and hour violations, the citation and related paperwork will be on file at some specified location. Call the agency in question and ask where records for inspections and citations for your area are kept. Make arrangements to review these files. If a company's officials have problems paying people fair wages, federal or state labor agents will file civil cases against them to correct their attitude problems. If a company is a persistent or particularly vicious violator of wage laws, agents will file criminal charges against its key officials. Federal agents file cases in federal courts; state agents file cases in state courts. If your target company operates in your area, go to the state and federal courthouses in your area and see what kinds of cases government agents have filed against them.

If your target company operates in more than one area, you'll appreciate knowing the U.S. Labor Department's general counsel, the inspector general, other enforcement officials, or the freedom of information officer should be able to generate for you a list of all criminal cases and civil cases the agency has ever filed against your target company for wage and hour violations. You might also try checking with the Justice Department.

Remember, a case is public record once it is filed. So you can write to the Labor Department or the Justice Department with a Freedom of Information request, and ask for the freedom of information officer to list for you the wage and hour cases the agency has filed against your target. This goes a lot quicker than trying to contact every federal courthouse in the country to find this kind of dirt on your target company. I'm sure your state labor department or attorney general probably has the same kind of file you can access for cases your state's agents have filed against your target.

DUMP ON THE DISCRIMINATORS

An unfair labor practice that can get your target corporation's officials in major trouble and give them black eyes besides is discrimination against workers on grounds of race, sex, ethnic origin, religion, age, or handicap. An employer's discrimination based on race, religion, ethnic group, age, sex, or disability that doesn't interfere with job performance (like discrimination against a computer programmer who is wheelchair-bound, for instance) is illegal.

Not only is it illegal for an employer to discriminate in hiring practices, it's also illegal for him to discriminate in pay rates, promotions, and in hiring for more desirable jobs and work conditions. Also, it's illegal for an employer to tolerate harassment based

on these grounds. No woman should have to put up with sexist BS, no racial or ethnic minority member should have to put up with bigot BS, no religious believer should have to put up with BS attacks on his spiritual life from godless lowlifes, and so on.

The U. S. Equal Employment Opportunity Commission investigates such charges and takes action against suspected violators. Specifically, they enforce the employment discrimination provisions of the Civil Rights Act of 1964, the Age Discrimination In Employment Act of 1967, the Equal Pay Act of 1963, and the Rehabilitation Act of 1973. These laws prohibit job discrimination based on race, ethnicity, religion, sex, age, and handicap (if these factors don't prevent a person from performing the job in question). And they look at patterns such as percentage of which groups hold jobs, pay differences for equal times in grade, schooling, seniority trends, numbers of complaints over discriminatory practices, and so on. Likewise, the equivalent agency in your state acts on such cases at the state level.

As you would expect, the EEOC's cases against employers are public records if they file actions. You can check with the EEOC to find out if their agents have brought civil or criminal charges against your target corporation for discrimination. The freedom of information officer, the general counsel, or the inspector general of this agency will be able to supply you with this information. Likewise, the equivalent officers of the parallel agency in your state can provide you with information on any state charges filed against your target.

A word to the wise—discrimination charges are sometimes made by liars or worthless employees whom the employers had every right to fire. For example, umpire Dave Pallone—the umpire who poked Pete Rose during a 1988 game before the Cincinnati manager shoved him back—claimed he lost his umpiring job because he was a homosexual. (Pete probably didn't like being touched by a guy who was looking for love in all the wrong places.) Pallone should have been fired earlier for interfering with the outcomes of games, if a certain sports columnist is correct. Why? Because the scribe wrote that Pallone announced publicly at a 1987 sports officials' convention that he deliberately interfered with Reds shortstop Dave Concepcion during games because of a long-running feud between himself and the player!

Use your common sense when you review files. If an employer can show the employee he fired was counseled for poor performance, didn't get trade-required licenses or certificates, or was caught breaking the law or a well-defined and fairly-enforced company policy (like pilfering or sleeping on the job), then he probably was within his rights to take action against the employee. The employee won't win in court unless the judge is bigoted, brain-dead or bribable.

Also, jerks sometimes file false discrimination complaints. Again, let your common sense be your guide when you review such cases. For example, let's consider the case of a woman who sues a fire department for discriminatory hiring because she couldn't get a firefighting job. If the fire department's chief can show he didn't hire the woman because she couldn't drag a set amount of weight in a fireman's crawl (an objective test which shows whether an applicant is strong enough to perform a task needed for the job), and can show he has refused or would also refuse a male's application if he couldn't do it, she wouldn't have a leg to stand on.

If you note a plaintiff fails to meet other obvious physical or mental or education or attitude requirements for a job he couldn't get, you can discount his lawsuit accordingly. For example, Paul Simon couldn't sue and win if a movie company didn't hire him for the role of one of the basketball players in a movie about the Harlem Globetrotters. A parochial school operator can refuse to hire a bisexual atheist druggie like Charles Manson because his orientation would in effect discriminate against the children's religion and the parents' religion and violate their rights as customers in a situation where they're paying for the service of a religious education. Shirley MacLaine couldn't sue because she was turned down for a rocket scientist's position. And a lesbian like National Organization for Women president Patricia Ireland couldn't sue a sperm bank because she couldn't physically be a donor...no matter *who* revs up her sex drive!

Also bear in mind that some EEOC actions are somewhat silly. Chicago columnist Mike Royko made public a misguided EEOC attack on a Chicago businessman named Mike Welbel for alleged discrimination in not hiring a black woman. When EEOC investigators showed up at Welbel's plant, they found he had 26 employees—21 Hispanics and five blacks. But despite knowing Welbel had a pure minority workforce, the EEOC agents determined he should have had 8.45 black employees because of the ethnic mix of the area. Royko said they wanted Welbel to pay blacks he didn't hire back pay for not hiring them. Welbel reportedly said, "They (the EEOC agents) want me to spend $10,000 on advertising to find people who didn't work for me so I can pay them $123,991 for not working for me."

Comparable worth? I'm not even going to get into that. All I'll say is that one feminist I once worked with bitched, "Garbagemen make more than I do." I suggested she ought to better herself and become a garbagewoman! The witch's attitude needed adjusting; who is SHE to look down on manual laborers?

HEARING THE WHISTLE-BLOWERS

Whistle-blowing employees serve the public by reporting illegal and unethical activities in their companies to law-enforcement agents. Well-known investigative reporters write many great muckraking articles off of the tips they get from these people who get fed up over seeing the taxpayers' money stolen by defense contractors or the public's safety endangered by faulty consumer goods. However, most whistle-blowers never get any reward except the ability to sleep at night with a clear conscience. Whistle-blowers often get hammered by their employers. Usually the preferred form of punishment a company imposes on a whistle-blower is demotion or reassignment or firing. Sometimes it gets a lot uglier. Whistle-blowers and their loved ones have been mugged, raped, or killed on the orders of unscrupulous employers.

To protect whistle-blowers, and to encourage people to become whistle-blowers as needed, state and federal public officials have enacted laws that make it illegal for employers to fire, damage the career of, or otherwise unjustly retaliate against a whistle-blower. (However, company officials are within their rights to fire, then sue for defamation, any jerk employee who files false complaints against them because he or she is unjustifiably angry about something on the job.)

Again, the U.S. Labor Department investigates such charges and takes court action against suspected violators. Likewise, the equivalent agency within each state's labor department acts on such cases at the state level. And you can get documentation of such actions from the freedom of information officer, the general counsel, or the inspector general of the agency.

DOCUMENTING OTHER UNFAIR LABOR PRACTICES

Union-busting. Failure to deal fairly with unions is a labor law violation. The range of lawbreaking by employers includes threatening employees who want to start a union, lying about unions to workers, obstructing union organizing efforts, refusing to deal with legitimate union bargainers who seek contract agreements, harassment on the job, retaliatory firings, and other illegal tactics.

Employers accused of these violations include many large and small companies, and even nonprofit groups. For example, officials of the League of Women Voters, the influential women's group which sponsors presidential debates, were not regarded as protectors of women in the workplace by a group of the League's own secretaries. These office workers picketed League headquarters in 1987 because the leaders of the women's group reportedly would not sign a contract with the local union representing the office workers.

The National Labor Relations Board supervises union representation elections and enforces laws relating to unfair labor practices. You can request information on NLRB files regarding your target business from this agency. Likewise, agents within certain states' labor departments deal with similar cases at the state level. Check with your state's labor department officials to see what laws they enforce in this area and what documents on employer wrongdoing are available to the public.

Worker's Compensation. Businessmen fight worker's compensation claims for a number of reasons. Sometimes the worker's claim is fraudulent, or sometimes he injured himself due to his own stupidity. Occasionally, you'll read of workers drawing benefits from fake back injuries getting caught later on moving heavy furniture with buddies. And every now and then, you'll hear of cases in which a cat burglar's widow sues for benefits because her old man died from a fall while plying his trade (stealing). Or you'll hear of cases in which a sailor's or traveling salesman's widow sues for benefits because her old man died of a disease he caught because his job-caused separation from her made him seek out sex with an infected prostitute.

However, many businessmen fight legitimate claimants, too. Why? Because the state will make them pay more taxes if the state's worker's compensation program has to cover a bunch of their employees. State agents figure, reasonably enough, that the employer whose workplace disables a lot of workers somehow ought to help the taxpayers bear the burden of paying for them. Businessmen figure, greedily enough, that they don't want to pay for the damage they cause their workers.

I know personally of one of these greedy corporations. I prepared the case of a former girlfriend of mine (who is still a good friend of mine) and argued it for her at a worker's compensation hearing. She is a nurse who hurt her back when an obese patient fell on her. Her hospital wanted to avoid paying for her back therapy treatments; she underwent these treatments on her off days so she could keep working! Justice was served in her case; the arbitrator ruled the hospital had to pay for the therapy.

If your target businessman is a worker's compensation deadbeat, a couple of sources will have dirt on him saying so. One such place is the county courthouse; workers whose claims your target fights will often sue him. If there's a union at your target's business, the union chiefs will be able to tell you plenty about him. And your state's industrial commission or labor department will have a listing of worker's compensation cases involving your target. Check into each of these sources.

Payroll Tricks. If an employer arbitrarily changes the terms of an employment contract with the workers while the contract is still in effect, and the change costs the workers wages or benefits, it could be a labor law violation. A trick I know of is for a company to rework the salary structure for a new fiscal year and drop workers' effective pay scales or force them to become "exempt" employees who have to perform voluntary overtime for inadequate payment.

The U.S. Labor Department investigates such charges and takes court action against suspected violators. Likewise, the equivalent agency within each state's labor department or industrial commission acts on such cases at the state level. And, as with other information requests, contact the freedom of information officer, the general counsel, the inspector general, or the designated enforcement official to see if your target company has been in hot water for these unfair labor practices.

A FINAL TIP ON CHECKING INTO LABOR LAW VIOLATIONS

A nice-to-remember item about unfair labor practices is that individuals whom the companies mistreated will often sue the companies. For example, many, many workers have received nice awards or settlements for injuries they suffered in unsafe workplaces. Whistle-blowers have won six-figure verdicts from crooked companies who have fired them unjustly. Women in public-view jobs have won judgments against companies who have fired them for not being pretty or for refusing to dress like sex toys. And in my own experience, I steered a Cuban friend of my dad to a high-powered labor law lawyer when his company laid him off due to his age. The lawyer got my dad's buddy almost $200,000 in an out-of-court settlement, so his revenge was sweet indeed. Cases like these are in courthouses across America. Check the appropriate county and federal courthouse for such lawsuits filed against your target company.

See if you can find a pattern of labor law abuses, as alleged in lawsuits.

DIGGING DIRT ON LABOR UNIONS

Labor unions have done a lot of good for this country. Union members made sacrifices, including imprisonment and death, so American workers could enjoy the eight-hour day, reasonable wages and benefits, and safe working conditions. Many of the most important labor wage and safety laws are on the books because labor unions helped muscle them into the books. Even non-union workers benefit from union members' activities, because employers had to raise their wages and improve their working conditions to keep them from unionizing or quitting to work for better employers.

However, unions have caused some problems. All too often, shop stewards and union local leaders consider a jerk who loafs on the job just as much of a union brother as the poor stiffs who bust their backsides to make up for the jerk's slacking. If they tolerate enough of this, productivity drops, and corporate weasels use this as an excuse to export everyone's union job to Taiwan.

Every now and then, union leaders are accused of Scrooging their own people. As this book goes to print, workers who staff the offices of the American Federation of Teachers are involved in a labor dispute with the militant teachers' union bosses. Why? Because the teacher bosses, claiming a tight budget, reportedly want givebacks from the staffers!

Then there are those thugs and thieves who give unions a bad name. Thanks to guys like Jimmy Hoffa, many Americans say "unions and the mob" just like they would say "ham and eggs."

A very useful report for the union dirt-digger is the *Labor Organization Annual Report*. The U.S. Labor Department requires unions to file these reports (known as Form LM-2) every year; the report lists union officials' salaries, the dues and other money the union took in, and the items the union spent money on. Investigative reporter M. Harry says in *The Muckraker's Manual*, "Basically, the report is designed to show how the union spent its money."

Harry tells dirt-diggers to alert if the Form LM-2 report lists a lot of people with the same last name on the payroll, because when people hire relatives, corruption often follows. Harry also said some unions do extensive business with one or two vendors, and suggested that investigators find out the owners of the vendor companies. His reasoning is that the union may be taking money from its members and enriching one of its leaders by doing business with a company he owns. Another item to check on the annual report is employee expenses. The leaders may be paying the employees excessive wages and then may be demanding kickbacks. Or they may have ghost employees on the payroll.

Criminal union leaders will have the same kinds of criminal records as other criminals. Check their criminal histories per instructions in the chapter on criminal records. Likewise, check their lawsuit track records and their personal records per the chapters on lawsuits and personal information just like you would on any other target.

Labor union leaders who violate labor laws may wind up in front of the National Labor Relations Board. Corporate heads sometimes bring these charges against unions, but sometimes a worker who believes a union action has hurt him will also make a formal accusation against the union. Check with the NLRB to see what cases have been filed against your target union leader.

Union leaders are no friends of workers if they don't negotiate a fair contract for the workers because management has bribed them. Eugene Methvin, a former member of the President's Commission on Organized Crime, said one mob thug told committee members some Teamster officials plotted with Fortune 500 executives to cut wages and benefits and ignore safety rules. The U.S. Justice Department prosecuted only seven defendants on this, he said, and not one of them was a Fortune 500 official.

If you think your leadership is corrupt in this regard, you can compare what your local union is getting to what other union locals are getting. You can check with other union locals or the companies which have contracts with them. Although union locals and companies are under no obligation to disclose the terms of their contracts to third parties, sometimes they will. If you fear reprisal from your own local's leaders, you might pretend to be a reporter when you contact another local and its company. Or you might be able to find similar contracts in the files of the U.S. Labor Department's Collective Bargaining Agreement Filing Room in Washington. Many union locals and companies file their contracts with these agents for information purposes, and their contracts are public records if they are in these files.

Union leaders are no friends of workers if they force their women workers to become call girls. Two waitresses sued Hotel Employees and Restaurant Employees union official Raymond Lane, a national magazine reported, for allegedly trying to make them become prostitutes.

Union leaders are no friends of workers if they

shake down their members for extra contributions or force them to pay daily kickbacks to get work assignments. G-men caught International Longshoremen's Association officials making dockworkers pay such kickbacks to stay on the job, Methvin noted. You could get an idea if these kinds of activities are going on in a target local union by talking to members as if you intend to join the union, and asking if there are any unwritten rules you should know about.

Union leaders are no friends of workers if they shake down businessmen for jobs or money, or if they rig bids, or if they file fake worker's compensation claims. The businessmen who are victims of these practices lose competitiveness, and have to lay off workers. If the thievery is bad enough, it gives the corporate bigwigs an excuse to ship jobs overseas. Methvin accused leaders of the Laborers' International Union of corruption so virulent that they helped add up to 20 percent to the cost of construction in New York City. You could get an idea if your target local union's leaders are shaking down small businessmen by talking to local businessmen as if you intend to start a business, and asking if there are any shakedown rackets you should know about.

Records of union racketeering will usually be in the hands of the U.S. Justice Department or in the hands of the U.S. Labor Department. Contact the general counsel, the inspector general, or the freedom of information officer of these agencies to get documentation of federal probes against your target labor leaders. Likewise, check the equivalent state agencies for evidence of state action against your target labor leaders.

Union leaders are no friends of workers if they discriminate against worthy members at the hiring hall. Likewise, they can't discriminate in charging union dues. If you meet standards as a worker, if you have the proper licenses or certifications, if your work record is good, and if your seniority is in order, you might be able to prove discrimination if your local labor bosses don't take care of you.

On the other hand, it's possible that big businessmen and anti-union politicians and social experimenting politicians help get minority group activists and radical feminists to attack unions on discrimination grounds when all the union leaders are trying to do is respect the seniority and the legitimate qualifications of their members. Or sometimes these groups attack unions on their own for stupid reasons. So if you're a local union official, document that you have a track record of respecting seniority and abiding by assignment and work rules, then countersue the idiots who are making trouble for you. Look into these groups' leaders' personal records, criminal records, lawsuit records, backers, and other items to dig as much dirt on them as possible. Then crush them in the media, in court, and on the street.

CHECK ABUSE OF FARMWORKERS

The most essential industry in the world is farming. Without it, we'd starve. And some of the most important workers in this country are the migrant workers and other farmworkers who do the labor needed to bring food to our tables. And yet these important workers live in conditions ranging from poverty to near-slavery in the good old U.S.A.

Under the law, farmworkers are entitled to the following:

- Minimum wage or higher, as spelled out in a fair contract.
- Knowledge that farm labor contractors are registered with the Labor Department.
- Payment of wages when due.
- Itemized statements of deductions for room and board. The employer can't gouge the farmworkers into peonage by charging hotel rates for the shacks he houses them in, either. The law clearly states he can only charge "reasonable cost" or "fair value" of food and lodging.
- Living quarters that meet minimum federal and state safety and health standards.
- Transportation (as applicable) in company vehicles that are insured and meet minimum safety standards.
- The right to purchase goods where they choose. This is designed to prevent employers with slave owner mentalities from paying workers in scrip redeemable only at a company store, where he sells goods at price-gouger rates.
- Information about their rights in a language they can read.
- Working in fields or other areas that comply with minimum safety standards.
- Working with equipment that complies with minimum safety standards.

The U.S. Labor Department's Employment Standards Administration enforces the laws relating to farmworkers. They will conduct most inspections and investigations relating to farmworker conditions. OSHA agents will conduct investigations and inspections relating to safety. Likewise, state labor or agricultural agents will make inspections and conduct investigations to enforce state laws relating to farmworkers.

Check with enforcement chiefs in the Employment Standards Administration or OSHA portions of the

U.S. Labor Department for any evidence your target agribusinessman exploits farmworkers. Also, the U.S. Labor Department's general counsel, inspector general, or freedom of information officer should be able to prepare for you a listing of farmworker-related cases and citations the agency has filed against your target. Likewise, the agriculture commission or labor department of your state may have info for you on your target's violations.

You can also find information on your target agribusinessman by talking to priests, nuns, preachers, volunteers, and social workers who minister to the migrant workers. Because they work to better the migrant workers' lives, these people are aware of a lot of abuses. Or you can check with local teachers or health agents who see the children of the farmworkers; they'll notice the children's poor conditions and maybe they'll have some info on whether their parents and older brothers and sisters are laboring for a tyrant.

THE DIGNITY OF WORK (AND DIRT-DIGGING)

We'll close this chapter with three thoughts. One, from St. Paul the Apostle, is, "The worker is worth his wage." The second, from Catholic teaching, is that St. Joseph is titled "St. Joseph the WORKER." And the third, from Catholic teaching, is, "There are four sins that cry to Heaven for vengeance." Right up there on this short list with murder, sodomy, and taking advantage of the poor is the sin of defrauding the worker of his wages.

What's my point? In exposing those who abuse workers, you are doing the will of God Himself!

END NOTES

1. My article on Clinchfield Coal's continuing safety problems appeared in the Kingsport (Tennessee) *Times-News* on June 30, 1986.
2. My articles on the Oyster Creek nuclear power plant appeared in the Ocean County (New Jersey) *Observer* in 1986 and 1987.
3. Allegations about umpire Dave Pallone come from Tim Sullivan's August 1991 column in the Cincinnati *Enquirer*.
4. Mike Royko's column on the EEOC's hassling of Mike Welbel appeared in the Chicago *Tribune* on September 21, 1990. It was reprinted in *Reader's Digest*.
5. Information on the League of Women Voters' labor troubles comes from a 1987 article in the Cincinnati *Enquirer*.
6. Information on the dispute between the American Federation of Teachers leaders and office workers of the union comes from an article in the December 30, 1991 issue of *U.S. News*.
7. Information on alleged corruption in the Teamsters' Union, the Fortune 500, the Laborers' International Union, and the International Longshoremen's Association comes from Eugene Methvin's article in the July 1986 *Reader's Digest*.
8. Information on alleged corruption in the Hotel Employees and Restaurant Employees union comes from Trevor Armbrister's article in the September 1983 *Reader's Digest*.

Pure As The Driven Sludge

At one time, people did pretty much as they pleased to the land. Indians set fire to the prairie to hunt buffalo, and white people cut down damn near every tree east of the Mississippi. And they cut down the Indians, too, while they were at it. Hunters left the carcasses of millions of buffalo to rot on the plains. Miners ripped huge scars into the earth, loggers left tree stumps as far as the eye could see, and farmers plowed their land in straight rows until the topsoil washed away or blew away. Industrialists' factories belched exhaust into the sky and poured waste into the rivers. They turned day into night with smog and night into day with stack fires. They made rivers light on fire and killed major lakes.

Teddy Roosevelt was the first prominent public official to preach conservation and proper land use. During the Great Depression, ugly pictures of starving farmers and clouds filled with topsoil led other public officials to push soil conservation programs. During the 1960s and 1970s, public outcry over strip mining abuses, smog, toxic waste dumping, the flaming Cuyahoga River, the "death" of Lake Erie, the Santa Barbara oil spill, and the panic of Three Mile Island led to tougher land use, pollution control, toxic waste disposal, and utility laws. And naturally, federal and state bureaucracies have mushroomed to enforce these laws. (However, some skeptics claim the only reason we appear to have made progress in fighting pollution is that our heavy industries have shut down in many places. We've traded millions of good blue-collar jobs for slightly cleaner air and a bottomless trade deficit.)

This chapter covers the kinds of information you can find on the public record on polluters and land rapists. This chapter also contains a section on checking on the nuclear industry. This chapter also covers checking on government abuses such as underenforcement, overenforcement, and pollution. (Sometimes the government isn't content to dump on us figuratively, as some Florida fishermen found out the hard way. They were fishing under a train bridge when human excrement from an Amtrak passenger train passing overhead rained down on them! In 1989 a Florida jury found the federal passenger carrier guilty of commercial littering.)

The "civilian" uses of this chapter include researching a company's environmental record so you can decide whether to do business with it, and researching a government agency's enforcement record to see how good a job its people are doing for your tax dollars. The "military" uses of this chapter include documenting a company's poor environmental record for boycott purposes, and forcing proper government action against violators. Or if you want to defend your job or a project, you can use the techniques of this chapter to dig dirt on your ecofreak opponents!

DUMP ON THE POLLUTERS

Corporations rob the public in a number of ways. One of the ugliest ways is by polluting the country. Corporations which pollute are ducking paying the legitimate cost of pollution control. What happens instead is that they belch poison gases into the air, flush harmful chemicals into the water, and dump a host of toxic wastes on land. This means the public has to pay for massive environmental cleanups and medical bills of poisoned people through higher taxes and higher insurance premiums. I'm no tree-hugger, but like most Americans, I believe everyone has to adhere to some minimum environmental standards.

In fairness to the companies, most of them are obeying the law as it is enforced. And they are laboring under one of the world's toughest environmental codes. Many American jobs have been lost because of the added cost pollution control laws put on American goods. Since too many of us have a K-mart mentality, we buy foreign-made junk produced by pollution-belching Oriental factories because these products are cheaper than American-made products. This is partially because of the pollution controls American factories must install, and partially because we have some reasonable labor laws to protect workers. Maybe a tariff based on a country's labor laws and environmental standards is in order.

Our taxes, in paying for Big Government, pay for environmental police such as the Environmental Protection Agency. These federal agents and state government environmental agents with similar functions are supposed to keep the corporations from making the entire country look like a cross between

Los Angeles and Chernobyl. These agents document environmental law violations. If your target businessman or industrialist is as evil as you think he is, there's bound to be some bad paper somewhere that government environmental agents have pinned on him. Environmental agencies make such records available to the public. It's possible for you, as an average citizen, to find records which prove a corporation treats the environment like a disposable diaper. I can't tell you the practices of every environmental agency, but I can point you in the right direction.

There are a number of laws covering punishment for corporate polluters. Some only allow agents to issue slap-on-the-wrist warnings or citations. But other laws, if used the right way (or the wrong way), can really hurt a company. For example, the EPA and state pollution control agencies have the power to revoke companies' exhaust stack discharge permits and wastewater discharge permits if they repeatedly and/or grossly violate air or water pollution laws. As you can imagine, losing the ability to discharge waste puts a serious crimp in most of these companies' styles.

When EPA or state environmental agents inspect a factory or other installation, the inspection paperwork is a public record. It will be on file at one of the agency's offices. If an EPA or state environmental agent cites a corporation for pollution violations, the citation and related paperwork will be on file at some specified location. Call the agency in question and ask where records for inspections and citations for your area are kept. Make arrangements to review these files.

If a company's officials have problems avoiding the temptation to foul the environment, federal or state environmental agents can file civil cases against them to correct their attitude problems. If a company is a persistent or particularly vicious violator of environmental laws, agents can file criminal charges against its key officials. Federal agents file cases in federal courts; state agents file cases in state courts. If your target company operates in your area, go to the county and federal courthouses in your area and see what kinds of cases government agents have filed against them.

If your target company operates in more than one area, you'll appreciate knowing the EPA's general counsel, inspector general, enforcement chief, or freedom of information officer should be able to provide you with a list of all criminal cases and civil cases the agency has ever filed against companies for environmental violations. In fact, each year the EPA publishes a book-sized report entitled *Enforcement Accomplishments Report*. This report lists criminal convictions, civil judgments, citations, and fines the EPA's agents hung on polluters the previous year. And the report lists corporate and government offenders *BY NAME*. Also, an information officer in the U.S. Justice Department could have info on federal pollution probes against your target.

Remember, a case is public record once it is filed. So you can write to the EPA with a Freedom of Information request, and ask the clerks to research what pollution cases the agency has filed against your target company. This goes a lot quicker than trying to contact every federal courthouse in the country to find this kind of dirt on your target company. You could also try writing to the freedom of information officer of the U.S. Justice Department for listings of civil and criminal cases against your target company. And I'm sure your state environmental department probably has the same kind of state file you can access.

One last source to try is your local environmental activist group. Since these people live for digging dirt on corporate polluters, they may have already gotten their hands on some pretty interesting stuff. Since these people are probably enemies of corporations like your target company, they might have some dirt on your target company and may be only too happy to share it!

Bear in mind you'll probably be dealing with very biased, almost cultlike people in some of these activist groups. (Activists range from people in the "wise use" portion of the environmental movement—many of whom are farmers, ranchers, and loggers—to people in the "green" portion— who more closely fit the public's image of an environmental activist.) Be prepared for aggressive soliciting for donations. Be ready to separate the information they give you into two stacks—verifiable data and propaganda. But remember also this is their "cause", so they might have something on your target you can use. If they don't, your inquiry might prompt them to witch-hunt your target company anyway! So you win regardless!

EPA-APPROVED DIGGING METHODS

Let's say you're so much of an outdoorsman that the four walls of a government agency records room give you claustrophobia. And let's say you've got the time and the patience to do observation work. The EPA's agents have written pamphlets for you showing you how you can make trouble for your target polluter simply by observing his actions. The pamphlets, entitled *Environmental Enforcement—A Citizen's Guide* and *Environmental Criminal Enforcement—A Law Enforcement Officer's Guide*, explain the EPA's codes and legal means of punishing polluters. They also explain how you can observe targets for evidence of pollution-related wrongdoing.

Without wholesale plagiarism, I'll cover the dirt-digging high points of the pamphlets. These include:

- Notice anything unusual about the type or source of pollution. Spotting a familiar smokestack which belches darker or smellier or more irritating smoke than normal, or finding your drinking water has a detectable change in taste or smell or color are examples. I once reported a chemical spill after noticing the usual slime-green flow of a stream near my factory had turned deep purple.
- Notice if pollution from a source in an area burns your eyes, mouth, nose, or skin. Notice if the smell of the air or the water which receives pollution discharges is hard to tolerate.
- Notice if pollution in an area looks foul enough or ugly enough to shock even the dirtiest slob you know. For example, a bizarrely-colored water discharge, terrible-smelling solid waste, an oil-like slick scum on water, smoke so thick you can't see through it, or smoke that is an abnormal color all fit the description of foul and/or ugly. (Then, too, foul and/or ugly is in the eye and the nose of the beholder. I think the multicolored flames at oil refineries and the spark showers at some heavy industry plants look pretty cool.)
- Notice if there are dead fish in water receiving wastewater or site runoff. Notice if there are dead animals and birds around facilities, or in water bodies receiving the wastewater or site runoff. Check for dead vegetation near pollution. Finding dead wildlife and plantlife are major tip-offs that some serious pollution is taking place.
- Notice unusual or suspicious human behavior. Night bulldozer operation in wetlands, trucks discharging wastewater on city streets or on roadsides, illegal solid waste dumping, and dumping waste into other companies' trash bins are valid examples of such behavior.

For the citizen investigator, the EPA books are good guides. My only complaint with them is that they don't tell you how to deal with noise polluters who play ridiculous music from any punk group, disco group, or heavy metal clown/freak group!

Noticing potential incidents of polluting, and then reporting these to environmental authorities will help cut down on the amount of damage your target can do to the environment. Getting the agents to cite your target will also give you ammo from the public record to shoot at your target. They can run, but they can't hide!

HOW ENVIRONMENTAL RECORDS HELPED PUT BUREAUCRATS ON THE SPOT

I once covered a story in which a gas station owner's knowledge of public record laws led to some trouble for his township. The gas station owner had been pinched by the state environmental agents because they found gasoline in an aquifer near his station. After he saw the report which listed the agents' findings, he compared the amount of fuel estimated to be in the aquifer with the amount of fuel he had bought and resold, and figured that there was no way his station could have accounted for the size of the spill.

The gas station owner figured most of the fuel fouling had come from a fueling point which the township maintained nearby. He knew township officials had replaced an old fuel tank with a newer tank two years earlier. So he had his lawyer file for records involving possible leakage testing on the old tank. When the township stonewalled his lawyer, his lawyer publicly accused township officials of covering up either a massive fuel spill or massive theft of fuel by township employees for their own cars. He and his lawyer were soon able to gain access to the township's records.

POLICING THE POLICEMEN

Now I'll say a few bad words about the environmental agents themselves. Sometimes they let off polluters with slaps on the wrist. Sometimes they are guilty of overkill. Following are two stories in which the muckrakers used the public record to show either inadequate or excessive government response to pollution problems.

Reporters from the Dayton *Daily News* in 1989 wrote an exposé about the amount of dumping going on in the Miami River. They paddled a canoe the entire length of the river from the source of the river in west-central Ohio through Dayton to the point just west of Cincinnati where it feeds into the Ohio River. They noticed people were using the river for a landfill and companies and local sewage authorities were using it for a cesspool. They reviewed the Ohio EPA's files and found hundreds of citations the agents had filed against polluters in 1987 and 1988. Yet they claimed environmental agents didn't revoke a single wastewater discharge permit!

The worst polluters, they wrote, were government sewer authorities. Fecal coliform, a bacteria which proves human excrement is in the water, showed up repeatedly in wastewater from these utilities. In all, they said, they found local government sewer authorities accounted for more than 2100 violations, roughly 60 percent of the two-year EPA total. The most-cited individual polluter they found was Dayton Walther Corp. The company's officials were cited 96 times in the two-year period, mostly because water from the firm's headquarters building was a source of thermal pollution, and also because of the water's acid or base pollution (unsafe pH swings). Also included in the 96 citations were write-ups for failure to report suspended solids.

By comparison, the reporters found, mighty Armco Steel in Middletown (between Dayton and Cincinnati), probably the Miami Valley's heaviest industry, was not even listed among the top five polluters in its county. However, the steel company's officials, they said, were negotiating to reduce fines they received for dumping excessive levels of zinc, lead, and cyanide into the river.

Remember what I said about environmental activists. They have very definite ideas not only about corporate polluters, but about government bureaucrats. They'll tell you which bureaucrats they think are slackers in the war against corporate polluters. Listen to what they tell you, but mentally separate their info into two stacks—verifiable data and propaganda.

Now I'll tell you a story from the other side of the file...public records showed government regulators were running amok.

The New Jersey Department of Environmental Protection hassled a small businessman in my county who reclaimed silver from X-ray film. For several years, he had discharged caustic soda waste from his reclaiming process into a septic tank with state permission. This made the groundwater very alkaline. He later switched to having the caustic soda hauled away for treatment.

The problem revolved around the businessman's efforts to clean up his site. He started pumping the alkaline groundwater out of the ground, neutralizing it with hydrochloric acid, and routing the treated water into the sewer system. At a public hearing on the issue, which I attended, a female DEP engineer with all the charm of an ice princess said the businessman refused to comply with her agency's orders to clean up the site, so her agency referred his case to the EPA Superfund program.

The businessman was in the audience, and he proceeded to make the DEP woman's life miserable. The businessman basically accused her of lying. He told the audience he had needed $100,000 to complete the cleanup and he had asked DEP officials for a loan to complete the job. They refused his request, he said, crippled his business, and told him they were going to order a cleanup study and cleanup project, all of which

he would have to pay for. He said he refused to comply with the DEP plan when the officials told him it would cost him $500,000 for the study and another $1 million for the outside contractor cleanup. He said if he went bankrupt, the people would have to pay for the cleanup. On the other hand, he said, he would have paid for the cleanup himself and would have had it done a year earlier if the DEP officials had loaned him the money.

The people in the audience grew sullen when the woman engineer admitted the businessman's charges were true. (The businessman had done his homework, and he had obtained the public records he needed to back his charges.) The people grew hostile when a male DEP agent admitted the state hadn't done any cleanup work of its own after ordering the businessman to stop his efforts. And the people grew irate when the DEP agents admitted under questioning they had stopped the county health department's agents from monitoring wells in the area for alkaline water (which could chew up a person's innards like Drano if he or she drank it), then had neglected to continue their own monitoring like they said they would. The DEP bureaucrats were lucky to get out of the public hearing hall without being mugged.

DIGGING DIRT ON LAND USE AND MISUSE

Just because someone owns land, it doesn't mean he has the absolute right to do anything he wants on it. Since his actions may affect other people, he has to get permits to do things. He will need a building permit to erect something as simple as a one-car garage. Or he will need more complex permits to perform activities such as office complex building, shopping mall development, steel making, electrical power generation, livestock slaughtering, chemical production, oil refining, or strip mining. To get government approval for such activities, the landowners (or the company officials using the land for the economic activity involved) will have to file a plan showing how they intend to comply with the laws regulating the way they want to use the land.

Not even the government is exempt from this process. Company officials who want permission for logging, livestock grazing, mining, or other commercial ventures on "government property" have to file the proper paperwork with the U.S. Department of Agriculture or the U.S. Department of the Interior or any other appropriate federal agency or state agency charged with managing the land in question. REMEMBER —WE THE PEOPLE REALLY OWN FEDERAL LANDS; THESE AGENCIES MERELY MANAGE THE LANDS FOR US.

All land use plans have one thing in common. The person submitting the plans has to show what he intends to do on the land in question, how his activity will affect the environment and other people, how he intends to keep others from being damaged by his activities, and how he intends to restore the land if resource extraction like mining or resource harvesting like logging is involved. These plans are public records. They contain a lot of information on the companies and the key people involved in the project, on the landowners involved in the project, and on the permits needed for the project. They also note what the land user considers the environmental impact is, and how he intends to control it.

Some environmental activists have used these publicly-available records to document that U.S. Forest Service officials are granting timber-cutting permits that bring in less money than what it costs to arrange the sale, plant new trees in the area, and repair the environmental damage the logging companies did to the area. This costs the taxpayers tens of millions of dollars. The Feds should be making money hand over fist on such deals.

Other activists have used these publicly-available records to prove British and Canadian corporations are trashing large portions of federal land in the American West in their search for gold. A reporter for a national publication noted the activists have found out these Anglo foreigners have been exploiting the General Mining Law of 1872. This law, enacted during the scandal-ridden Grant administration, allows anyone to mine for gold or any other metal on federal land under much less regulation than the Feds apply to coal companies.

Gold-mining in the 1990s involves large-scale strip mining, much like in the coal industry. But the reporter noted coal operators have to pay eight percent royalties on the coal they mine and they also have to pay to reclaim the land. Likewise, oil and natural gas companies have to pay a 12.5 percent charge on oil and gas they drill for on offshore sites. However, he wrote, corporate hard-rock metal ore miners who mine on federal land can do it for free. This means they can tear up thousands of square miles, use up scarce water, foul the water table, and create other problems without having to pay for them. The activists, citing publicly-available records and mining industry statistics, say these mostly foreign-owned mining companies make large profits, so they should be able to afford to pay royalties and clean up the land just like coal operators and oil companies have to do.

If you want to check on a target land use project, find out where the project will be. Then find out who owns the land. Then figure out what kinds of permits the land user will need, and which agencies he will need to get them from. This is a tall order, but someone in the county planner's office should be able to explain the appropriate laws to you. He should also be able to tell you which environmental, mining, utility, and/or building agencies the land user will have to seek approval from for his project. If your county planner's people are unhelpful, the zoning commission's people or your local elected official's staffers might be able to get you some answers. Also, local construction contractors might be able to get you this information.

Once you find out which agencies your target had to contact for approval of his project, contact these agencies' information people to make arrangements to view the plans your target has submitted for his project. (Report him in the name of good citizenship if he missed filing with any agency he should have filed with!) Then check your target's paperwork at each agency.

You may disagree with his analysis that operating an explosives testing facility in your city's downtown area will cause no one any possible harm, or that his intent to log Sequoia National Park will not degrade the environment of this magnificent area, or that his strip-mining plans won't trash the Gettysburg or Valley Forge historical sites and violate the peace of the brave men who consecrated these places with their blood, or his desire to set up a booth to sell Madonna CDs and video tapes on a California mission's grounds won't diminish the reverent calm of the holy landmark. And since he has to lay his cards on the table (filing an inaccurate plan could lead to rejection, or to civil or criminal penalties), you can peek at his cards while you build your own hand to trump him.

On the subject of land use permits, mining companies have to file detailed reclamation plans for restoring the land after they've mined the minerals out from underneath it in order to get permission to mine. (If you've ever seen old mine sites in Appalachia before the Surface Mining Control and Reclamation Act went into effect, you'll see devil's landscapes that angered people enough to get this law passed.) Such plans must include how, during the mining, the company's people will avoid fouling water supplies and water bodies, protect historical sites and archaeological sites, keep damage to plants and animals to a minimum, and compensate folks living nearby for any damages they suffer from the mining. Such plans must also include how, after the mining, the company's officials intend to replant trees, shrubs, other plants, and ground cover that were on the site before they started mining it. They must also try to reintroduce animals to the site if their mining killed them or ran them off.

Company officials also have to post a large bond as collateral to ensure they do the reclaiming. The company gets the money back if the reclaiming is proper. Otherwise, the government agents might fine them some of the bond money and use it to bring in a contractor to do some of the reclaiming. If the company's people are doing a poor enough job of reclaiming, the agency can make the company forfeit the bond, and the agency's people will use the bond money to bring in a contractor to reclaim the site. Depending on what state you're interested in, either the state mining agency, the federal Office of Surface Mining (a U.S. Interior Department agency), or both agencies get involved in permitting mines and enforcing reclamation (mining conservation) laws.

These agencies have the power to cite and fine mining companies for reclamation violations. They can also prosecute mining companies with lawsuits or with criminal charges if they are persistent and/or vicious offenders of reclamation laws. Of course, all of these actions are public records. Call the Office of Surface Mining agents in your state (or your state mining agency office, as applicable) to find out where mine site inspection files and citation records are kept for public view. Remember, the agency's general counsel or inspector general or freedom of information officer should have some sort of list of its cases and citations against your target company that you can access. Likewise, the state mining agency people keep similar state citation records for access.

A really nasty penalty these agencies can inflict on a mining company is to revoke the company's existing mining permits or refuse to issue the company permits to mine new sites if they don't follow reclamation laws on sites they are mining now. As you can imagine, losing the privilege to dig for minerals can put a major hurt on most mining companies.

However, some companies evade this punishment, too. For the following case, I used court records and public records in state and federal mining agencies to document that a mining company run by a politically active group of mining executives was still getting permission to mine for coal even though it had left messes elsewhere.

MUCK AND LUCK

In some states, the law forbids mining companies owing reclamation fines to get new mining permits unless the fines are under appeal. (It is possible for an overzealous agent to cite a company unfairly, so the ability to get new permits while appealing old fines protects companies from state enforcement agents' mistakes or wrongdoing.) Using state mine records, I was able to show a major coal company had received a permit to mine coal despite owing almost $100,000 in reclamation fines. This company's officials had contributed generously to the campaign coffers of the local congressman; they had also tried to buy several other Congressional friendships.

After checking records and dockets in state and federal agencies and courts, I verified none of the company's fines was under appeal. When I confronted state and federal officials on this situation, they had no explanation. The coal company's officials had no comment, either.

What's my point? Mining companies' reclamation plans and reclamation violations are public records. If your target is as dirty as you think he is, you should be able to find some high-grade dirt on him in these documents.

DIGGING RADIOACTIVE DIRT

I will preface this section by saying I favor nuclear power. However, the nuclear industry companies are run by humans just as imperfect as anyone else. So I checked on GPU Nuclear, my local nuclear power company, early and often when I was a reporter in New Jersey. I nicked its officials if they deserved it. For example, I reported instances in which company officials were at fault for excessive exposure of workers to radiation. And I reported that company officials may have known for years about a problem with the plant's drywell rusting (more on this below) before doing anything substantial to fix the problem.

However, I reported Nuclear Regulatory Commission agents and labor union officials gave GPU Nuclear good marks for honesty and safety. I reported on how one of the plant's managers caught workers trying to hide drug use and had them fired. In the wake of Jack Anderson's 1987 disclosure that some nuclear facility officials were using substandard Asian parts in their plants (cheap parts that were failing under normal use and were possibly posing safety problems), I was able to report GPU's Oyster Creek plant managers were having parts they bought tested to prevent such safety hazards from occurring.

People tend to panic when they hear anything negative about nuclear power plants. For example, in my first day on the job at the New Jersey paper, I learned GPU Nuclear wasn't going to restart the nearby Oyster Creek reactor on time. I've worked as a mechanic and as a technical writer, and my education is in engineering, so I asked the plant engineers the usual technician's question: "What caused the problem, and how are you going to go about fixing it?"

The plant engineers told me they had held up putting the plant back on line because of a rust problem on the drywell. The drywell is a huge steel and concrete vessel that encloses the reactor; its job is to prevent the escape of radioactive matter in case of a reactor failure. When I asked them how water could get into the drywell and corrode it, how they intended to stop the corrosion, and how they would fix the damage to the drywell so it could do its job if needed, they had plausible, mechanically sound answers for me. They even gave me blueprints showing me how they intended to get into the affected areas and repair them as needed. When my story came out the next day, it read like something out of *Popular Mechanics*.

However, journalists from Philadelphia to New York saw my story, and they rang the power plant PR guy's phone off the hook the next day. Part of their hyperness, I think, was because many of them were not overly bright mechanically. Another part of their hyperness, I think, was due to the antinuclear bias among many in the media. And part of the hyperness may have resulted from pressure they may have felt because I scooped them. Some of the stories I saw seemed to have a slant of mindless paranoia that mine lacked. Although in all fairness, my editor may have had a hand in that, too; he had the staff artist turn a drawing I had made from a blueprint into a three-color picture to accompany my story. The artist colored the affected areas of the drywell red!

The Nuclear Regulatory Commission is charged with keeping the nuclear industry in line. NRC agents inspect nuclear power plants and other nuclear installations (like atomic bomb plants) to verify the workers aren't being exposed to unsafe levels of radiation and that the company is operating the reactor and related machinery safely. They also check how the companies perform maintenance on their installations. The results of any inspection or any other action the NRC's agents take is public record.

The NRC maintains files of information on nuclear site inspections in locations near the facilities. To get information for some of my stories on the Oyster Creek plant, I used to review reports and citations on the Oyster Creek nuclear power plant in the public library in nearby Toms River. Call the NRC in Washington or in your state to find out where the agents make records on your local nuclear power plant available to the public.

The NRC's annual report is chock full of major criminal prosecutions and civil punishments its agents have hung on nuclear industry lawbreakers. This report also contains sections which sum up citations NRC agents have issued to the operators of nuclear power plants and other nuclear industry installations. Likewise, the NRC's Inspector General semiannual report contains information on NRC employees' wrongdoing that agency investigators have found. You can obtain these reports by contacting the NRC's information officer.

If you want to get specific dirt on your target nuclear industry people (nuclear power plant operators, nuclear bomb plant operators, radiation device operators, nuclear medicine managers, and so forth), the NRC's general counsel, inspector general, freedom of information officer, or enforcement agents can help you. One or more of them will be able to provide you with information on criminal cases, civil cases, and citations the NRC has filed against your target. U.S. Justice Department information officers may also be able to put this info together for you.

One other source to tap into is your local antinuke activist group. Since these people live for digging dirt on the nuclear industry, they may have already gotten their hands on some pretty interesting stuff. And many of them will be only too happy to share it with you. Since many antinukies are also environmental activists, they'll have much the same mindset. Many of them will be very biased, almost cultlike, in their outlook. And some of them will shake you down for donations. Be ready to separate the information they give you into verifiable data and propaganda. But don't hesitate to use any legitimate dirt they give you.

TURNABOUT IS FAIR PLAY

I believe in playing fair on environmental and land use issues. That means I will bash not only the corporate polluters and the land rapists, but also the trendy whiners who babble about Earth Day while they suck up all kinds of megawatts of power and tons of fossil fuel so their tennis courts can stay lit at night, the hot tubs in their mansions can stay at just the right temperature, their yachts can take them to the Caribbean, and their planes can take them on ski trips to Aspen.

Yeah, I'm talking about high-priced hypocrites like the Hollywood airhead set and the drug-fried rocker set. Any one of these "Beautiful People" all by himself or herself probably wastes more energy and consumer goods in a day than the people of an average Third World village use in many days to stay alive. Since many of these trendies are population control freaks, too, some wags suggest maybe they should commit suicide and save the planet of the resource drains that they are.

So the next time you are in a fight with these people over the location of a power plant, a landfill, a sewage treatment facility, a highway, a factory, or some other facility necessary for our excessively materialistic way of life, hit 'em below the belt. Show the public and the politicians just how extravagant these people are. Why not? Fair's fair, and these people want to deprive you of income by keeping a job-producing factory from being built, or they want to use your area as a pit for their filth.

Once you find out who their ringleaders are, find out where they live (covered in the chapter on personal information), figure out how much property and what enterprises they own (covered in the chapters on the private sector and real estate), and find out whatever else you can on their lifestyles of conspicuous consumption. Don't overlook divorce records, either. They contain lists of property to be divided, along with ugly accusations of bad behavior like infidelity, drug use, and child endangerment, among other things.

Take pictures of their mansions, tennis courts, cars, horses, private planes, country clubs, and so on. Pore over back issues of your newspapers and magazines for "society page" fluff stories about their entertaining and recreation activities. Then release details of their lifestyles to make them look like the spiritual descendants of Marie "Let them eat cake" Antoinette they often are.

CLEAN UP THE ENVIRONMENT WITH DIRT? WHY NOT?

I will close this chapter with a story I read about how some surfers out in California turned into diggers to expose and punish two paper pulp mill operators by using tactics like those which appear in this chapter. Several years ago, according to the article I read, surfers who took on the monster waves in Northern California's Humboldt Bay started noticing they were coming down with infections and other ailments. The surfers suspected their health problems were happening because the pulp mill operators were dumping toxic chemicals into the ocean nearby. So the surfer group's members did some digging and found the two companies had apparently violated the federal Clean Water Act 40,000 times since 1984. They also filmed "plumes of black discharge" (as the author of the article about the surfers put it).

Armed with this dirt, the surfer group's attorneys sued the companies in federal court and got the Feds to join the lawsuit. At this writing, the two companies—Louisiana Pacific and Simpson Paper—are looking at up to $3 million in fines. They will also have to spend millions more to make their pulp mills comply with the law. The surfers are proud they accomplished what they did, said a leader, who jokingly acknowledged, "Most people think of an organization of surfers as a self-canceling phrase."

What's the message of this chapter? Like the surfers, you don't have to be an organizational Napoleon to get a little justice. Just gather info and present it in a logical manner to people who can force change. The lives and health of people you save by exposing the wrongdoing of polluters (and conspicuous consumers) could well be your own and those of your loved ones. Plow through the public record for the dirt you need to soil the robber barons, government agents, and trendies. With a little hard work, you can sink your target in a morass of toxic mud he made himself.

END NOTES

1. Info about Amtrak's excrement dumping comes from an article in the December 11, 1989 issue of *Newsweek*.
2. The exposé on the Miami River appeared in the Dayton *Daily News* on July 16, 1989.
3. My article on the New Jersey DEP's questionable handling of a pollution site appeared in the Ocean County (New Jersey) *Observer* on February 26, 1987.
4. Information on the U.S. Forest Service's losses from timber sales (and the activists' exposure of the problem) comes from an article in the July 1, 1991 issue of *U.S. News*.
5. Information on the British and Canadian mining companies taking gold from federal lands comes from an article in the October 28, 1991 issue of *U.S. News*.
6. My article on the coal company's ability to get a new permit to mine coal when it still owed fines never ran in the Kingsport (Tennessee) *Times-News*. I turned in a draft of the article a couple of days before the paper's bosses fired me for publishing a child molester's name in another article. (Yeah, some editors are real bedwetters when it comes to informing the public about child molesters.) Since the article contained a lot of information that required a lot of legwork to verify, I can only assume they decided not to spend the time needed to retrace my steps. They never asked me for the boxful of documents I had on the case, either.
7. I wrote quite a few stories on GPU Nuclear and the Oyster Creek nuclear power plant in 1986 and in 1987. These appeared in the Ocean County *Observer*.
8. Jack Anderson's column about counterfeit Asian hardware in the nuclear industry appeared in early 1987.
9. My article on the delay of the startup of the Oyster Creek plant appeared in the Ocean County *Observer* on December 3, 1986.
10. Information on the surfers' actions against the California paper mill operators comes from an article in the September 16, 1991 issue of *Business Week*.

Government

Dig Dirt On Politicians

Just like Satan probably has a special low-rent section of Hell reserved for politicians who live a life of thievery and debauchery (in other words, too damn many of them), this book has a special low-rent chapter on how to figure out how politicians are able to continue in that kind of lifestyle. This chapter will concentrate on where your target pol gets his money and how he spends it.

Unfortunately, there is no limit to the number of terms most politicians can serve. Once someone gets into Congress, for example, he's like an intestinal parasite; he's in surroundings he enjoys and it's damn near impossible to get him out. Capitol Hill is the work address of influence peddlers, homosexual johns, statutory rapists, bad check passers, bribe takers, and weirdo quasi-racists who evidently enjoy hearing about how well-hung Clarence Thomas is...and that's just the leadership!

Some fools will vote for the incumbent, no matter how worthless he is, as long as they get their Social Security checks or their welfare checks or their business tax breaks. So until the people vote to limit all politicians to a set time in any given office, you'll have to impose your own term limitations on your targeted politicians by finding dirt on them and exposing them in time for the next election.

What if your target politician is a judge? Your row is a little tougher to hoe. Many judges are appointed for life or for long terms, so they act like they're royalty. However, if you can find enough dirt on your target judge, it will still be possible to give his career the death sentence.

This chapter will contain instructions on how to get politicians' and bureaucrats' financial disclosure records, and how to get politicians' campaign finances records. It also covers checking a public official's criminal, lawsuit, and personal records, and covers checking on his residence for election purposes. The "civilian" use for such info is for you to inform yourself on someone's past before voting for him or her.

A "military" use for this info is for you to help your favorite politicians and interest groups sling mud against politicians and other officials you don't like. If you do your homework on your targeted pol, you can give him an unwanted gift...free publicity on who buys and rents him.

CHECK FINANCIAL DISCLOSURE STATEMENTS

Politicians and bureaucrats have always been willing to use their offices to line their pockets or their friends' pockets with taxpayers' money. This tendency among our public servants caused reformers to enact laws to force them to at least make public their financial interests, so people could check if government policies or contract awards would make politicians or their buddies richer. As a result, candidates for elected office, incumbents, and high-ranking bureaucrats at the city, county, state, and federal level have to file financial disclosure statements to show what their property holdings, business holdings, and other financial interests are.

If your target is a federal officeholder, checking his financial disclosure records will be easy. Presidential and vice-presidential candidates have to file financial disclosure statements with the Federal Election Commission in Washington. As incumbents, George Bush and Dan Quayle filed their financial disclosure statements each year with the Office of Government Ethics (Ain't THAT name a contradiction in terms!) in Washington. These financial disclosure statements are public records. Contact the freedom of information officer of the agency to get copies of these records.

The president needs the "advice and consent of the Senate" for certain high-level appointees. These high-level folks—whose appointments can cause certain senators to work themselves into a televised lather if the special interest groups who own them start whining about the appointees—have to file financial disclosure statements with the agencies they will run. Agents of the Office of Government Ethics will actually review these documents which key presidential appointees like would-be Cabinet-level chiefs and independent federal agency chiefs submit before the president submits their nominations to the Senate for confirmation. You can get a copy of this statement from the agency the nominee hopes to run. You can also get a copy of the financial disclosure statement an incumbent official has to file each year from the agency he runs. Contact the freedom of information officer of the agency to get a copy of this record.

All lower-level presidential appointees must file their financial disclosure statements with their related agencies each year. Their financial disclosure statements are public records. All federal employees above pay grade GS-15 must also file their financial disclosure statements with their related agencies each year. These are also public records. Contact the freedom of information officer of the agency to get copies of these records.

Administrators in the various federal agencies are supposed to monitor lower-level employees for possible conflicts of interest. This means the lower-level employees have to file financial disclosure statements also. Each federal agency keeps the financial disclosure statements of all employees of the pay grade GS-15 and lower. The statements of these lower-level employees are not public records. However, someone suing the agency over something the lower-level employee or others in his portion of the agency did probably could get these statements if his lawyer demanded them.

Federal judges must file financial disclosure statements with the Judicial Ethics Committee in Washington. These statements are public records. Likewise, all employees in the judicial branch of the federal government above pay grade GS-15 must file financial disclosure records with this agency, also. These statements are public records, too. Contact the Judicial Ethics Committee in Washington to get copies of these records.

Candidates for the Senate (and sitting senators) have to file their financial disclosure records with the Senate Ethics Committee in Washington. So do Senate employees above the GS-15 pay grade. To get copies of financial disclosure records of senators and high-ranking Senate employees, contact the Secretary of the Senate in Washington.

Candidates for the House of Representatives (and sitting representatives) have to file their financial disclosure statements with the House Committee on Standards of Official Conduct in Washington. So do House employees above the GS-15 pay grade. To get copies of financial disclosure records of representatives and high-ranking House employees, contact the Clerk of the House in Washington.

You'd be amazed at the amount of good info you can find in these financial disclosure statements. Politicians have to list all the ways they make money on these statements. Some make money from businesses. Some make money from rental property.

(Check the violations files of the local agency that enforces the building code and related codes to see if your target is also a slumlord.) Many make money from stocks and bonds and bank accounts. (See if your target owns stock in companies which ship jobs overseas or in companies that he accepts contributions from or helps out while he's on the job.) Some make money from board memberships and director fees for companies. (See if any of you target's votes have benefited these entities.) Some make money from consultant fees, from land deals, and from other financial transactions.

Your target also has to report gifts and junkets. Honorariums—fees for appearances or other such services—are under attack right now. But our elected officials no doubt will find a loophole or come up with something sleazy to replace them.

Using one year's worth of financial disclosure records (and campaign finance records, which we'll cover later this chapter) of a congressman I covered, I noted the following:

The congressman was a lawyer by trade. He drew money from being a director of a bank. Further, he owned stock in CBS and in several other companies. One of them—a sports shoe company—shipped a lot of jobs to the Orient. Banking groups and entertainment industry groups poured thousands of dollars into his campaign coffers, according to his campaign finance statements. He received a free trip to New York to discuss legislation with a certified public accountant group and received a free 10-day trip to France from the French-American Foundation. He also received thousands of dollars in contributions from CPAs, according to his campaign finance records.

Getting financial records of federal officeholders is easy. Getting these records on state and local officials is harder, but by no means impossible.

Financial disclosure laws for public officials vary from state to state. The rule of thumb for checking on financial disclosure statements is to check at the level of government where your target is. Statewide office holders, state representatives, and key bureaucrats probably file their financial disclosure statements with the Secretary of State's office in your state's capital, or with their agency. Call the Secretary of State in your state capital to find out the info you need.

The county administrator's office is a likely storage place for the financial disclosure statements of all countywide elected officials and key nonelected officials such as department administrators, assistant prosecuting attorneys, and the like. Call the county administrator's office; ask where financial disclosure statements are kept for public viewing, and ask which elected officials and key county bureaucrats have to file them. Likewise, check in with a city administrator or a township administrator for financial disclosure information concerning a city or a township. If these people don't keep the records themselves, they can at least point you in the right direction.

CHECK CAMPAIGN FINANCES RECORDS

Money is the mother's milk of politics. So all successful politicians become good breast feeders. They also successfully blood-suck the taxpayers like leeches or vampires, but this section won't cover that biological function!

Some politicians have no shame when it comes to soliciting contributions. Lloyd Bentsen drew criticism during the 1988 presidential campaign for charging big bucks for breakfast meetings. Other politicians have soaked up honorariums like sponges. Many lap up PAC (political action committee) money like thirsty dogs. And many accept campaign contributions from special interest groups which oppose each other; maybe they figure the payoffs will cancel each other out so they can be impartial. Some stoop to take money from contributors who also cynically give to their opponents.

Some politicians will even take money from groups they supposedly oppose. I suppose the mindsets of some of these elected officials are like that of a prostitute who has so many johns she couldn't be partial to one even if she wanted to be! (Sorry, ladies of the evening. I realize you all, unlike the pols, actually give some satisfaction for the money you charge!)

A good example of politicians in action is their laughable collective behavior in the face of oil company price gouging. They make statements about the company executives' illegal conduct, then do nothing, because Big Oil owns or rents a lot of the pols. George Bush, an oilman from way back who is no favorite of mine, at least is man enough not to deny his fondness for some of the Seven Sisters (the major multinational oil companies).

Reformers forced the enacting of a number of federal and state campaign finance disclosure laws so people could figure out which special interests own or rent the politicians. The federal law applies to all federal campaigns, like Presidential, Senate, and House races. State campaign finance laws vary from state to state, but are usually like the federal law in that the laws generally require candidates for public office to disclose how much money they took in from individuals and organizations, who they got it from,

and how they spent it. Even politicians who run un-opposed or against token opposition are only too happy to take in money, so they can stockpile it for future campaigns, use it to help political allies' campaigns (and maybe buy or rent their votes), or stash it for their own use when they retire from a lifetime of feeding at the public trough.

Just like for financial interest disclosures, check for campaign finance records at the level of government where the politicians are. For county office candidates, ask clerks at the county board of elections or the county voter registration agency or the county administrator's office where campaign finance records are kept and how the public can view them. Also, the county people often keep such records on state representative candidates, and on candidates for city and township offices. Ask them if they keep these records. If they don't have these records handy, they can at least tell you where to go to find them.

Check the Secretary of State's office in your state capital for campaign finance records of candidates for statewide office, state representative, or other state-level posts. For congressional and presidential candidates, check with the Federal Elections Commission in Washington.

When you get your target politician's campaign finance records, check for contributions from political action committees (PACs) and from groups with a known political agenda. Also, pay special attention to contributions from various trade associations and to high-dollar contributions from individuals. These contributions often have strings attached. In fact, the campaign contribution records often list the affiliation of private donors, like their company, or their organization, or their government agency. You might think this is a bad idea on their part, but they understand it's a GOOD idea. They want recognition from the office-seeker that they took care of him when they call in at payback time. Check votes of public officials on contracts, grants, laws, or other items of interest to the pressure group.

Some campaign contributors are very straightforward about why they back certain politicians. Labor union men told me they endorsed certain politicians and gave them campaign money so they would take labor's side in legislation or specify in contract bidding they would only do business with companies that employed union workers. Also, a group's campaign contribution to a politician makes sense if the group has received the politician's support on issues of importance to its members. You as a dirtdigger can exploit this if you find contributions from controversial groups—like oil industry people, feminist groups, homosexual groups, or white supremacist groups, for example—listed on your targeted politician's financial disclosure records.

Whenever I researched my area's local elected officials and the Congressman, I always made sure to obtain their campaign finance records. The newspaper bosses might have whined about the cost (which was actually small, but most of my bosses were whiners by nature), but the records always paid dividends in good ugly stories about who owned or rented our area's public officials. Info from these files always came in handy when I suspected our area's politicians were paying back their campaign contributors.

A FEW MORE WORDS ABOUT POLITICAL ORGANIZATION GIFT-GIVING

The Federal Election Commission keeps tabs not only on politicians, but on political organizations as well. The FEC can supply you with a list of candidates which any particular political action committee or other similar pressure group financed, and how much money they gave to each of them. FEC agents make a number of other records available to the public besides the campaign finance records. You should be able to get reports on political organizations, and correspondence between the FEC and these organizations. (It's illegal, by the way, for a company or a labor union to donate directly to a campaign, but it is legal for company officials or union officials to form a PAC and solicit campaign donations.)

Some states have similar systems. In many counties, it is possible to go to the county election board and see a list of all political action committees doing business with politicians in the county. In such counties, each PAC has to file a donor list with the clerks at the election board. The list is a public record, and you can check out who's giving money to the PACs which are buying or renting your local politicians.

OTHER CHECKS TO RUN

Since every politician is a potential white-collar criminal, check him out like one. Check your politician's criminal record, his business interests and land holdings, his ties (via financial disclosure and campaign finance statements), his lawsuit record, and personal records per the chapters in this book which cover these topics. And definitely read the chapter covering crimes of dishonesty for further tips on how to check for evidence he's a white-collar criminal.

A MAN'S HOME HAD BETTER BE IN YOUR DISTRICT IF HE REPRESENTS YOU

Some politicians who publicly fuss over the plight of the poor don't necessarily want to live near them. After all, policemen keep the wealthier suburbs safer than the inner city. And besides, there aren't any great golf courses or chic cafes in the ghetto. So some politicians who want to get political office will rent apartments in low-income districts (which they will use as little as possible) for establishing residency, then will run for office from these districts. This may be legal, but it is clearly unethical. Not only is the perpetrator of such a trick trying to buy an office by hoping the locals won't know any better, but he defeats the whole purpose of representative democracy—people are supposed to send one of their own in spirit and community to represent them in government. The pol who plays games with his place of residence could be a racist or an elitist for not wanting to rub elbows with low-income blacks, Hispanics, and whites.

Of course, you as a citizen investigator can expose this carpetbagger for the migrating maggot that he is. Using appropriate chapters of this book, you can find out where the target has been registered to vote for the past few years, where he owns residential property, where he operates his businesses or where he operates as a professional, and at what address his cars are registered, among other things. You should be able to pin down the pol's real home location this way. You should be able to show his unfitness for public office just by exposing his attempt to fool the voters who he's counting on to put him in the government.

LEAVING ON A JET PLANE

Most people who go to the dentist or go skiing use their cars. John Sununu, the former White House chief of staff, had been using costly military planes.

Sununu drew all kinds of flak for his unethical waste of your tax dollars. I say we should have given the guy a break. As an engineer whose chief political experience was running the county-sized state of New Hampshire, he wasn't aware of all the neat tricks the lawyers who fill most top federal jobs and congress seats use to keep out of trouble while running up obscene expenses.

In fact, while I'm New Hampshire-bashing, why don't we force all those people, along with the young college punks and lace-curtain leftists in Boston and all the sapsucking marpies up in Vermont to merge with Maine, Rhode Island and Weicker Island (Connecticut) into one real state? New England could be like Illinois—a mid-sized state in area with about 12 million people, one large city, some good professional sports teams, and a historic baseball stadium. It would save government duplication of taxing, kill 10 Senate seats (meaning there would be 10 fewer crooks in Washington willing and able to sell our country down the river), and give sane voters across New England a shot at kicking Teddy Kennedy out of the Senate so he can sober up, learn how to drive, and learn how to handle women with a little more class.

Mapmakers would like it, because they wouldn't have to cram state names into county-sized areas. Schoolkids would rejoice knowing they won't have to spell words like "Massachusetts" or "Connecticut." Even lobbyists might like the idea; it would mean fewer officials to pay off.

Back to my topic. You've all read stories of Congresspeople (even Pat Schroeder might agree women can be just as sleazy in public office as men) junketeering to Hawaii in the dead of winter to personally inspect the quality of a federal public works project in that state while the folks back home in their districts are freezing their tails off. Reporters sometimes get tips on this traveling from enemies of the Congresspeople involved.

You can get documentation of junketeering on government money from the report of the committee whose business the representative or senator supposedly went on, or from other administrators in the House or Senate if his official trip was paid for with taxpayer money. You can get documentation of junketeering in the individual congressperson's financial disclosure statement if a private party (like a big corporation) paid for the trip. He'll have to list the lavish junket as a gift, but it's legal for him to accept a lavish junket as long as he reports it as a gift.

Junket records are fun to check. But the ways the branches of government handle reporting of junketeering on taxpayers' money, or junketeering on privately-donated money—like a mid-winter junket to the Virgin Islands as a freebie from some oil industry group for Congressmen to get away from it all and discuss oil industry tax structure issues—vary from branch to branch. They even vary within branches. For example, a House of Representatives member has to report privately-funded junketeering on his financial disclosure form. If he travels outside the U.S. on official business related to his committee, he or his House committee people will report the expense quarterly on committee paperwork.

The Clerk of the House will have info on official travel expenses a congressman racks up within the U.S. The House administration agents will have the dope on how much the congressman is spending to visit his district and maintain an office there. Check with the ethics agents assigned to monitor the branch of government you're interested in to get detailed information on travel and other reporting requirements.

I once wrote a story on a fact-finding trip about a dozen Congressmen took to the coalfields of Appalachia. Rick Boucher, a Congressman from southwest Virginia, helped recruit representatives for the field trip, which several coal companies paid for. Frankly, I thought the congressmen needed to learn a little something about coal, and I thought the junket was a good idea. But in trying to be a good journalist, I was the first reporter in my portion of Appalachia to question who paid for the trip. I found out who the corporate sponsors were by questioning congressional aides who came along for the ride, and I let my readers know about it. Later on, Washington reporters found from sources that most of the congressmen received $2000 honorariums as well. Boucher didn't take an honorarium, but I found out later by checking his campaign finances records that he accepted campaign contributions from one of the coal company's officials.

Boucher was upset as hell when I questioned him a couple of weeks later about the propriety of allowing corporations to pay for junkets and honorariums for public officials. He said, "I regret there was so much publicity over the procedures," of the by-now widely criticized junket, but added those who sponsored the junket "did what every major industry does to raise its profile." When I asked him, point-blank, if he thought it would be wrong for the Fortune 500 companies to take turns paying for Congressional junkets so the representatives would have almost no time at all to serve their people back home, he said he would leave the debate over junkets and honorariums to others.

Boucher ain't alone. Guys like him in both parties infest the government. And, like cockroaches, they scuttle only when folks like you put the light on them.

SLEAZIN' DOWN MEMORY LANE

Just in case you've forgotten how rotten our public officials can be, chew on these tidbits for a while.

Republican presidents Eisenhower, Nixon and Reagan lost control of their second terms because they didn't give their henchmen adult supervision, then tried to cover up for them or distance themselves from the problems caused when their henchmen got caught breaking the law. Eisenhower and Reagan were both given the benefit of the doubt because of their perceived grinning senility. Nixon, who was given credit for being sharp enough to know better and crooked enough to do the masterminding, was pressured out of office over the Watergate affair.

The Democratic "initial" presidents—FDR, JFK,

and LBJ—did things and allowed their henchmen to do things as illegal or even more illegal than the GOP presidents did or allowed. Read Victor Lasky's book *It Didn't Start With Watergate* to get the inside story on the forced internment of 100,000 Japanese-Americans during World War II, the possible theft of the 1960 election, the assassinations and attempted assassinations of world leaders, and the surveillance and harassment of Martin Luther King, among other classic Democratic executive branch crimes. Lasky, by the way, made the hilarious and true observation that the dirtiest trick of the 1972 campaign was the one the Democrats pulled on themselves by nominating a bozo like George McGovern as their standardbearer.

And how about our congressmen? The Keating Five—Senators Alan Cranston, Donald Riegle, John Glenn, Dennis DeConcini and John McCain—took campaign contributions from crooked financier Charles Keating, then criminally or foolishly caused federal investigators to back off from investigating him. Keating's Lincoln Savings collapse will cost the nation's taxpayers billions of dollars.

In other incidents, House Speaker Jim Wright of Texas and key House leader Tony Coelho of California had to resign in disgrace in 1989 when their corruption was made public. Wright evidently committed a number of offenses, most notably violating limits on outside speaking fees and conflict of interest. Coelho was accused of accepting favors from junk bond king Michael Milken and other businessmen.

Before that there was the Wedtech scandal. Bronx congressmen Mario Biaggi and Robert Garcia were convicted of bribe-taking type offenses in connection with the Bronx business whose operators won defense contracts improperly, bought off investigators, falsified documents to qualify for new loans, and looted the company. (Former Attorney General Ed Meese, who was involved in the scandal, somehow escaped prosecution, but he resigned under pressure in 1988 after one of his own prosecutors called him a "sleaze" during the Biaggi trial.)

Then there was the Bobbi Fiedler buyout offer. Ms. Fiedler, a congresswoman from a ritzy section of L.A.'s San Fernando Valley, and her boyfriend/campaign manager offered in 1986 to pay off the campaign debts of one of her rivals in the crowded race for a U.S. Senate seat nomination if he would drop out of the race. She was dumb as well as crooked. The rival was an ex-police chief of L.A., and she and her boyfriend were taped making the buyout bid. Bobbi escaped criminal prosecution.

And even earlier in the 1980s was the Abscam scandal. Pennsylvania congressmen Michael Myers and Raymond Lederer, New Jersey senator Harrison Williams and congressman Frank Thompson, New York congressman John Murphy, South Carolina congressman John Jenrette, and Florida congressman Richard Kelly were all convicted on bribery charges in connection with the FBI sting. John Murtha, another Pennsylvania congressman, escaped prosecution because he agreed to become a witness in two cases.

Then-House Speaker Tip O'Neill told a reporter, "It (Abscam) was a setup, a goddamn setup." ("It takes a thief to pity a thief," goes an old Jewish saying.) And the Washington *Post* editors whined, "No citizen, member of Congress or not, should be required to prove his integrity by resisting temptation…" The top dogs of the paper of Watergate (and later of the Janet Cooke faked story scandal) might have been upset that no one leaked the story to them.

Note that I didn't even have to bring up Teddy Kennedy!

How about the judges? Operation Greylord, an FBI sting run in Chicago in the mid-1980s, sent nine Chicago judges to prison for crimes related to fixing cases, taking bribes, and not reporting the dirty money at tax time. A tenth judge committed suicide before he could be convicted.

Chicago judges weren't alone in their venality. In Philadelphia, 17 of the city's 105 judges were suspended in 1987 by the state's Supreme Court for allegedly taking bribes from a local union. The Supreme Court removed 11 of the judges. Two others were convicted of crimes in federal courts. And another judge who was not one of the original 17 was convicted of bribe-taking in narcotics cases.

And three of the five justices of Vermont's Supreme Court were investigated in 1987 for trying to kill an investigation against a county judge. The county judge herself was accused of stealing $2800 of county money to throw a party for one of the three Supreme Court judges. One of the judges was cleared, one died while the case against him was still ongoing, and the third—William C. Hill—was found guilty of seven counts of judicial misconduct in 1989. A courthouse employee who allegedly walked in on Hill and Jane Wheel (the county judge in question) while they were embracing filed a complaint against Hill for becoming furious over the employee's "discovery motion"; this charge was dropped. Jane Wheel was found guilty of three counts of perjury and was sentenced to jail. Her case at this writing is under appeal.

And federal judge Harry Claiborne was removed from the bench in 1986 by the Congress. However, the senators and representatives waited until he was already in federal prison on tax evasion. (An earlier bribery case against him ended in a mistrial.) Ironically, Claiborne was the lawyer who helped the Senate Rules Committee probe Nelson Rockefeller. (A street American saying has it—"It takes one to know one.")

If your "favorite" public official didn't make my list, I'm sorry ...there are so many dirtbags and so few pages!

A nation's people never get politicians any better than they deserve. If we don't keep an eye on our politicians, we might as well lay back, submit, and try to tolerate the screwing they'll give us.

END NOTES

1. Information on Lloyd Bentsen's "Breakfast Club" comes from an article in the July 25, 1988 issue of *Time*.
2. Information on John Sununu's tax-supported travels comes from an article in the May 6, 1991 issue of *Newsweek*.
3. My articles on Boucher's coalfield junket and his defense of it appeared in the Kingsport (Tennessee) *Times-News* on June 10, 1986 and on July 6, 1986. An article I wrote on Boucher's campaign finances in the late summer of 1986 for the *Times-News* included info on donations he received from coal company officials.
4. Information on illegal activities committed by those in the FDR, JFK, and LBJ administrations comes from Victor Lasky's book *It Didn't Start With Watergate*.
5. Information on the Keating Five comes from an article in the December 11, 1989 issue of *Newsweek*, an article in the October 29, 1990 issue of *Time*, and an article in the November 26, 1990 issue of *Time*.
6. Information on Jim Wright and Tony Coelho comes from articles in the June 5, 1989 and June 12, 1989 issue of *Time* and from an article in the June 5, 1989 issue of *Newsweek*.
7. Information on the Wedtech scandal comes from Marilyn Thompson's book *Feeding The Beast*.
8. Information on Bobbi Fiedler's buyout offer comes from an article in the March 10, 1986 issue of *Newsweek*.
9. Information on the Abscam scandal comes from Robert Greene's book *The Sting Man* and from an article in the August 2, 1981 issue of *Time*.
10. Information on the Greylord scandal comes from James Tuohy's and Rob Warden's book *Greylord—Justice Chicago Style*.
11. Information on the Philadelphia judges scandal comes from a July 15, 1991 letter I received from Robert L. Keuch, the executive director and general counsel of Pennsylvania's Judicial Inquiry and Review Board.
12. Information on the Vermont judges scandal comes from a series of articles in the Burlington *Free Press* from September 20, 1989 through September 27, 1989.
13. Information on Harry Claiborne comes from an article in the April 4, 1983 issue of *Newsweek*, an article in the August 4, 1986 issue of *U.S. News*, an article in the September 29, 1986 issue of *Time*, and an entry in the 1987 *World Almanac*.

Check On How Government Officials Use Power

Are politicians and bureaucrats inherently more crooked or incompetent than anyone else? They certainly have more temptations than you or I do. They have more money to throw away and more power to abuse. Believe it or not, many of them are quite intelligent. However, when a lot of them devote their energies to wasting taxpayer money (and bouncing personal checks) when we're facing a multitrillion dollar deficit, we the people tend to wonder.

Why do government officials do so many dumb or crooked things? One obvious reason is that it's easier to win an election or an appointment than it is to develop the skills needed for the position. In this day and age, the right political packagers could get a brain-fried rock star or an airhead soap opera star elected over a proven stud like Abraham Lincoln or Teddy Roosevelt.

Then, for all officials, there's the problem of dealing with arrogantly jerkish pressure groups. At the local level, for example, it may be a government employees' union demanding unrealistic pay hikes. Or it could be the officials of a big company who falsely pump up employment hopes to get the public to pressure local officials into granting their company incredible tax breaks. At the state and national level, there are a zillion special interest groups willing, eager, and able to apply pressure to the politicians. All these kinds of pressure can spook and stampede normally intelligent officials into doing stupid things— like spending billions of dollars more every year than they take in.

The bottom line is this—public officials and government employees are people, too. Like the rest of us, some of them are lazy, some are incompetent, some are rude, some are tyrannical, some lie and cheat and steal, some give into pressure, and all of them make mistakes. The only problem here is when government people foul up, their foul-ups always have an impact on the public.

Government problems are understandable, but that doesn't mean you have to put up with them. If you want to dig dirt on your government, you'll run out of time to dig before you'll run out of places to dig!

Believe me, when you see the government records your tax dollars have paid for over the years, you'll feel like a mosquito that's just hit an artery!

In this chapter, I'll show you how to use public records to determine how government people exercise power. This chapter will cover how to check officials' voting records, executive orders and administrative decisions, judge rulings, and minutes of legislative and executive governing groups. It will also show you how to do some checking on government appointees. The "civilian" uses of this chapter include informing yourself on how government officials do business and monitoring how they have voted or acted on issues. The "military" use of this chapter is to dig up dirt on your target public official for use in an election campaign or some other event.

FOLLOWING HOW GOVERNMENT OFFICIALS EXERCISE POWER

All government in the United States has three branches—legislative, executive, and judicial. Legislative bodies enact laws, executive officials lead the government and their administrators enact and enforce administrative codes, and judges hear cases involving disputes over the law or cases involving people accused of breaking the law.

Dividing power among the three branches of government is called separation of powers. The framers of the Constitution must have done this because they guessed how lame a society we would become. If one branch had most of the power, or if the branches consistently worked together, the public would *really* be screwed!

How do you check on how government officials exercise power? There are several ways. One of the most usable records for checking on how government officials use or misuse power is the minute file. The minute file shows what actions the officials took.

The minute file is like a journal or diary that government agencies keep on their activities. The minute file has a bunch of different names, depending on the situation. It is known as "the minutes" at the local level, because city councils, town councils, county commissions, school boards, zoning commissions, and other such groups record their votes and actions this way. In courts, the minute file will be known as a docket (or some other name close to it). These books will show how judges handled the cases they heard.

Agencies at all levels of government keep similar records of what their top people have done; you'll have to ask the public information officer at the agency the name of the logbook the decision makers use to record their actions. In the state legislature, the minute file is often known as the record; it shows the debates, votes, actions, and reports of state representatives. And in the U.S. Senate and House of Representatives, the minute file is better known as the Congressional Record.

No matter what the minute file is called, you can read through it to see how government officials acted on various issues. You can also see what committees and other groups are mentioned in the minute file, and follow up on their involvement in issues.

Later on in this chapter, we'll talk a little more about how to use a minute file. We'll also talk about how to track down the actions of certain executive types—like mayors, governors and presidents—who aren't confined to using a minute file. We'll also talk about using courthouse records to track the activities of judges.

LOOKING INTO LEGISLATIVE LOWLIFING

Legislative bodies on the local level include city and town councils, county (or parish, for you folks way down yonder in New Orleans and the rest of Louisiana) commissions, and school boards. At the state level, state legislatures are legislative bodies. And at the federal level, the Senate and the House of Representatives are legislative bodies.

The records (minute files) of legislative bodies are relatively easy to review. Each legislative body has to keep a record on how its members voted, and this record is open to the public. To see it, all you have to do is contact the group's secretary or records keeper, find out where the record is kept, and make arrangements to see it. To review state legislative body actions, contact the secretary of state for your state or contact the secretary of the state senate or the secretary of the state house of representatives to get this information. (All states except Nebraska have state representatives and state senators. The Cornhusker State's citizens are smart enough to pay for only a one-house state legislature.)

To find out what your U.S. congressman or senator is up to, call your local public library, college library, or U.S. Government information officer. (The information officer's number will be in the phone book under U.S. Government listings.) Ask the librarian or the government information officer where a copy of the Congressional Record is kept in your area. Then go and review it to find out what you need.

The minute file (record) on legislative bodies will contain information on how members vote on issues, what they choose to spend money on, what appointments they make or confirm or reject, what they did in their committees, and what remarks (speeches or debates) they made about various issues during meetings of the legislative bodies. If you follow the minute file (record) for any length of time, you'll be able to gauge what your target legislative type has been up to, at least in public, anyway. (*Golf Digest* may have info on how Dan Quayle spends his idle hours and the tabloids might have info on your target's off-duty activities if his name is Hart or Kennedy!)

Here's a tip if you need to find out how a state or federal legislator has voted on certain types of issues, like gun control, abortion, environmental affairs, protection of American industry, welfare spending, and the like. Contact staffers of any special-interest group that takes a stand on the issue that interests you. Ask them what legislative actions have pertained to the issue over the past several years. Ask them how your target legislator has voted on these actions. They'll be only too happy to oblige you—and maybe solicit you for money. A word to the wise—these people have a bias (charitably called a point of view).

There are times when legislators from the U.S. Senate on down to your town council try to trick the public about what action they want to take. One such trick is a voice vote or a "show of hands" vote. This scheme keeps a member's vote on a controversial issue off the record if the majority of the legislative group wants to defy the public and do something selfish like vote themselves a whopping pay raise.

Another trick is for members to put a controversial issue last on the agenda at a night meeting, then go into "executive session" before the issue comes up, and "wait out" the public and the media. When most people have to go home and prepare for the next workday, and the journalists have to scramble to put on the 11 o'clock news or meet deadline for the morning paper, the officials emerge from their executive session hideout, come back into normal session, and vote on the controversial issue. This is often the trick of choice for local government officials.

An "executive session" is usually allowable only for narrow purposes, like when members discuss personnel matters to protect the privacy of those they discuss. This allows them to say honestly that a government employee or job applicant is a loafer or a thief or an incompetent dufus without publicly destroying that person's reputation. But officials sometimes misuse executive sessions to "wait out" the public or actually agree on taking legislative action. Doing the latter is illegal, because officials have to take such actions in public.

You can still find out what the officials are up to by checking the minute record (in the case of a government body taking action after a lengthy executive session). In the case of a non-recorded vote, or in the case of violations of the executive session law (doing business behind closed doors that should be done before the public), contact the officials who are in the minority on the issue in question. They are often happy to tell you why their colleagues acted like white-collar criminals.

EXCAVATING EXECUTIVE EXCESSES

Executive officials include people like mayors, local school and city and county administrators, governors, state administrators, federal administrators, the U.S. president, and members of his Cabinet. Executive bodies at the local level include city and town councils, county commissions, and school boards. They also include the various local administrative agencies, like zoning boards and utility commissions. At the state level, executive bodies include state administrative agencies. At the federal level, executive bodies include agencies headed by cabinet members, and "independent" agencies headed by people who are not cabinet members.

Presidents, governors, and mayors carry out their own programs. They also veto or ignore legislative votes or judicial rulings they don't like. They get friendly legislators or council members to fight for their programs in the Congress, the legislature, or the local council. And they appoint people to head agencies they have authority over. The appointed head usually tries to carry out the president's, governor's, or mayor's programs. Often, however, the bureaucrats in the agencies have their own agendas, and the appointed heads have to overcome these. Or the appointed head has his or her own personal agenda which may not always coincide with that of the elected official who gave him or her the job.

The mayor or the governor or the president doesn't have to hold a public hearing to act; he just acts. However, his veto or pocket veto of a bill, his signature of a bill, or his allowing of a bill to become law without his signature is public record. Check the record at the city, state, or federal level by checking the Congressional Record or by contacting the clerks who keep local or state legislative body records, as applicable.

Mayors, governors, and presidents tend to call press conferences to announce programs or get good day-to-day coverage in the media as to what they are up to publicly. Some of these officials will have their press agents release their scheduled activities on a day-to-day basis. Or they get their press agents to release or leak their propaganda to the media. Knowledgeable public officials realize reporters and editors aren't enemies to be fought—they're stooges to be manipulated!

If you want to know what an executive official has been up to on a day-by-day basis, you can check the newspapers (which will not print a lot of the info the executive types put out). You could also call the official's press people, identify yourself as a writer or a researcher, and get them to brief you *personally* and send *you* their press releases! You can then see what the newspapers haven't been printing. If some media people miss their opportunities to get info from the press agents because we the people are putting the press agents through their paces, them's the breaks. The best of the media types are no better than we are.

Politicians who support or oppose the president, governor, or mayor also usually know what he is up to. Contact the staffers for these politicians and find out from them any information they might have on the leader in question. Likewise, special-interest groups also watch the actions of mayors, governors, and presidents. You can contact staffers of these groups to find out what your target executive official has done with respect to the issues they fight for. Remember—these people have a bias.

Check on the actions of officials of executive bodies that are also legislative bodies (like town and city councils, county commissions, and school boards) per instructions in the section in this chapter on legislative bodies. Follow their actions through the minute files (records). Contact special-interest groups to see how members tend to vote on certain issues. And contact members who are in the minority when the majority tries to hide its actions in an executive session.

The hardest type of executive officials to keep tabs on are the administrators, agency officials, and other assorted bureaucrats. There are not enough reporters to cover their activities, and most of those who do cover them don't do that good a job. So the bureaucrats and officials are able to do a lot of things in the dark, away from the view of the public.

However, agency actions are public records. Such public records include agency regulations and minutes of administrative agency meetings at which governing body members take actions. Records open to the public also include agency citations of individuals, groups, and companies, inspection records, many types of reports, proposed regulations the agency officials intend to impose on the public, and the like. Actually, virtually all records of any agency, except certain personnel records, records pertaining to national security, records protecting valid company and industrial secrets, and some records involving personal privacy considerations are public records. Other chapters of this book discuss some of the most useful and commonly-checked government agency records.

The trick in digging dirt from administrative agencies' records is figuring out what kind of records the agencies keep. The best way to do this is to contact the targeted agency's public information officer or freedom of information officer and ask him or her for a listing of records the agency keeps.

Another way to find out is to contact a special-interest group or a politician who is a known critic of the agency in question. The special-interest group people will know quite a bit about the agency, and its staffers will be able to tell you a lot about what kinds of records the agency's people keep and what kinds of no-good the agency's people are up to. Likewise, the politician's staffers will know quite a bit about the agency in question and will be able to give you a lot of useful information. Again, separate usable info from propaganda in the info these people give you, but use what is legit.

Another source for agency activities is the proposed regulation log. Federal, state, and local agency officials have to publicize any regulations they intend to put on the books. This gives supporters, critics, and you the chance to see what the agency's higher-ups intend to do. Supporters and critics then attend the public hearings on the regulations or submit comments during the time the agency officials will consider them. Supposedly, this process gives the administrators a chance to receive input on how their proposed regulations will affect the public, then make any needed changes to their policies. Supposedly, this process also allows people to kill or change a bad proposed agency regulation. But cynics say in most cases, the agency bigwigs do what they want to do anyway.

To find out where the information for proposed regulations is kept, contact the public information officer of the agency in question and ask how you can obtain or view the agency's proposed regulation log.

At the federal level, the log for proposed regulations for all federal agencies is called the Federal Register; it's available from many sources.

Once you know what kind of information is available, cast out your dragnet and haul in whatever you want. You might even feel like the Apostles after Christ told them to throw out their nets; you'll likely catch enough fish to damn near bust your nets and swamp your boat!

HOW TO JUDGE THOSE WHO JUDGE

"Equal justice before the law," belongs right up there with belief in Santa Claus, the Easter Bunny, and the check being in the mail. In other words, it doesn't exist. If you check the arrest and sentencing data the local, state, and federal authorities keep, odds are you'll find richer criminals tend to get lighter sentences than poorer criminals, white criminals tend to get lighter sentences than black or Hispanic criminals, and female criminals tend to get lighter sentences than male criminals.

In the judiciary part of government, judges are obviously the officials to check on. And these little Hitlers need it. There are more courts and criminal cases and civil cases than there are competent reporters to cover them. So judges can run their courts like little kingdoms, letting off criminals or socking it to the innocent.

The problem with the legal system is that upper-income white male and white female lawyers run it. They might be oversensitive to criminals and give breaks to vicious thugs without thinking of the safety of the thugs' neighbors. Or they'll sympathize with white-collar criminals because of their social standings, their careers, and their college backgrounds and go easy on them, even though they have victimized people worse than most street hoods have done. Maybe it's the "there but for the grace of God go I" syndrome. Far too many judges have done unethical things for money or career advancement.

The flip side of the coin is that most judges don't have a feel for what real people have to deal with. This is why so many of them, for example, will sentence the winner of a streetfight to jail. They don't realize that many streetfights are rough justice in their own sense or are safety valves for young men to avoid committing serious acts of violence. Then there are the many judges who will take children away from parents whose only "crime" is being poor or being good enough parents to apply a little corporal punishment to their kids every now and then. This judicial attitude especially discriminates against strong parents who are blacks or Hispanics.

One Tuesday morning several years ago, I witnessed an unforgivable example of sentencing discrimination in an L.A. courtroom. The cops brought in a Mexican man whom they arrested the previous Thursday night for the heinous crime of throwing a beer bottle at an unoccupied parked car. The judge was out of town Friday, so the Mexican didn't get a chance to undergo arraignment. Since he didn't have bail money, he had to sit in the county jail over the weekend. Monday was a state holiday, so he remained in jail while the judge took the day off. So when he finally went before the well-rested judge, he had already spent 4-1/2 days in jail and had lost at least two days of work, not to mention the half-day he was losing now. The judge read the charges against the Mexican, and he pleaded guilty. The judge then fined the man $400 and sent him on his way.

The next several defendants were all white males charged with prostitution on the streets of Hollywood. They had been picked up (for arrest purposes, not for commercial sexual encounters) by the cops Monday night. Each of the male prostitutes pleaded no contest, and the judge slapped each of their limp wrists with a $500 fine. A black man in the court room and I both blurted out our unprintable expressions of disgust at the same time. The judge and the bailiff both stared at us, then went back to the business at hand. The black man and I met out in the hall a little later, and our discussion of the judge's sense of fairness was in language that would have shocked Larry Flynt. Suffice it to say that we both cursed the judge for giving the call-boys basically the same fine as a harmless bottle thrower.

What's my point? If you review the cases any judge hears, you're likely to find at least some evidence of inequity of sentencing or other instances of unequal treatment before the law. And if your target judge is as biased and/or corrupt as you think he is, odds are you'll find a pattern of injustice as ugly as a swastika and as brazen as a red flag. However, Chicago columnist Mike Royko, perhaps anticipating the Operation Greylord case that sent a number of Chicago judges to prison for bribe-taking, once wrote, "Surprisingly, the fixer said, not all judges suspected of being fixed really are. Often people become suspicious of a judge because he makes a lot of weird rulings. But he might be completely honest and make strange rulings only because he is dumb."

If you want to check on the kind of job your local judge does, just check the local criminal or civil docket for his court. Different court clerks keep different court records, but almost all of them should be able to tell you which cases your target judge heard.

If your area has a law newspaper or journal which lists all cases heard in your area's courts, you might be able to check the cases your target judge has handled if the paper or journal is set up properly. Or the publisher may be able to run a computer search by judge for you. You can see if your area has such a paper by calling the court clerks or local lawyers and asking.

You might have to check judges the hard way—pull each case file in the county, then see which judge handled it. As this book goes to print, I wrapped up an investigation of an Ohio judge suspected of giving lenient sentences to child molesters. To check his record, I had to check the Common Pleas Court (upper court) criminal docket, write down the case number of each accused sex offender for several years, then check the case files for the charges, the plea bargains, the convictions, the sentences, and the judges. I was able to prove the judge in question was letting child molesters get probation. (I also showed, depressingly enough, that county prosecutors and county child welfare agents kept their mouths shut about the judge's injustice toward child victims. They, in my opinion, compounded the injustice by their silence.)

As you go through the cases, note the kinds of criminals and the kinds of cases the judge has heard. Check for race, sex, and evidence of income (bail vs. jail, private attorney vs. public defender, etc.). Check for differences in the amount of bail the judge set, check for evidence of cozy or cold relations between the judge and the defense attorneys in the briefs and the orders, and check for differences in sentencing for the same crime if no other factors are involved (like an extensive criminal record). See if the judge excuses himself from the cases of his supporters or his business partners or his opponents. See the kinds of remarks he makes toward the defendants or the prosecutors. Make copies of anything that seems particularly damaging.

This tactic also works well for civil cases. See how the judge treats certain types of plaintiffs and defendants in lawsuits. And believe me, some of these little Hitlers in black robes will inflict incredible amounts of abuse on people or will allow their lawyer buddies to do the same.

One of the cruelest outbursts I ever heard of came from the mouth of Judge Harvey Sorkow, the judge in the infamous Baby M surrogate mother case. Mary Beth Whitehead, the woman who was paid to bear and give birth to Baby M, was from the New Jersey county where I was working at the time, so our paper had a reporter at the trial every day. Mary Beth had gone through the trouble of carrying Baby M, bonded to the little infant, and offered to give back the $10,000 her family could desperately use if only she could keep the child.

The Stern couple demanded the baby and they had lawmen seize her from Mary Beth, so the custody trial was on. When Sorkow ruled that Mary Beth had to give up her child and could not have visiting rights, he said, "Mrs. Whitehead is manipulative, impulsive, and exploitative... she is a woman without empathy... " Sorkow also called Mary Beth's parents "unworthy." Sorkow had earlier let a shrink named Lee Salk call Mary Beth "a surrogate uterus and not a surrogate mother." Basically, Sorkow allowed this poor woman to be treated no better than a breeding animal; he, the lawyers and the "expert witnesses" trashed her.

If you want to dig dirt on a judge whom you suspect is soft on crime, just check for evidence he sets bail unreasonably low for murder suspects, child molesters, and other criminal scum. Check what evidence he won't allow; check what ridiculous technicalities and defense tactics he allows. Check how often he lets people go free; check how often he gives criminal scum slaps on the wrists if juries do find them guilty despite his best efforts to sabotage the cases on technicalities. If your county or state keeps statistics of this sort, check the conviction rate in his court against the rates of other judges, and check average sentences from his court against those of other judges to see if he is much more of a criminal-coddler than the norm.

This tactic worked well for crime-beleaguered Californians in 1986. They wanted to get rid of Rose Bird, the lawyer who Jerry (Governor Moonbeam) Brown hand-picked to run the California high court. They researched her track record, and they made sure her bizarre rulings became public knowledge. They publicized the fact that Rose Bird voted to overturn 61 death penalty sentences (and voted to uphold none of them). Soon some wags started joking, "Free the Night Stalker. Confirm Rose Bird." (The Night Stalker was a Satan-worshipping murderer who gouged the eyes out of his victims; Rose Bird had to be confirmed (rehired) by the voters in 1986.) These Californians were so successful in getting media publicity for their targeting effort that the voters beheaded Rose Bird when she came up for confirmation in the fall of 1986.

Conversely, if you want to show that your target judge would feel right at home in Red China, research the record for instances in which he needlessly bullies defendants or their lawyers. Check for evidence he sentences people unreasonably harshly for crimes that don't really require imprisonment. Check for evidence he sets ridiculously high bail. Check for evidence he tolerates prosecution witness perjury and police perjury (if you read the trial documents, these things can leap out at you).

If your county or state keeps statistics of this sort, check the conviction rate in his court against those of other judges. Check average sentences from his court against those of other judges to see how harsh he is. Check to see how many of his convictions are overturned on appeal, especially if the overturn was due to some stupid or fascist thing he did.

A dirt-digging shortcut is to contact labor unions, citizens' groups, special-interest groups, police groups, the ACLU, local Republican or Democrat bigshots, or anyone else who is in a position to know how a judge performs (or fails to) in any area you can think of. If the group has a gripe against the judge, the members will let you know specifics in a heartbeat. Then use these specifics as dirt if your aims are similar to those of the complainers. Once again, separate usable info from propaganda in the info these people give you, but use what is legit. A note to the cynical—if people from a group many people despise (like the Bar Association or the ACLU) have good things to say about your target, use *THESE* specifics as dirt also!

This section wouldn't be complete without mention of one of the most worthless judges ever to waste oxygen—Hugo Black. Black, a notorious anti-Catholic bigot, first gained notoriety as a lawyer in getting an Alabama Klansman/priest-killer off the hook by appealing to the jury's ignorant bigotry. Black, a Klansman himself, rode his bedsheet to a seat in the U.S. Senate, and in the 1930s received an appointment to the U.S. Supreme Court from FDR. Black continued to make anti-Catholic rulings as a justice.

Black was worthless on some other issues, too. For example, he was in on a number of pro-criminal rulings on the high court. Some of Black's leftist supporters explained away his Klan membership as nothing more than allowable cynical political opportunism in his state in his time. (The underlying message of this excuse is that it's OK to pose as a vicious racist or some other type of scumbag as long as you're doing it only to advance your ambitions.) Black, along with Rose Bird, is a perfect example of why judges should not be appointed to any bench for life.

CHECKING GOVERNMENT APPOINTMENTS

It's the practice of almost all government officials to appoint their friends and allies to government jobs.

Sometimes this is legal; sometimes it isn't. Often government officials reward people with positions they're not qualified for. Or they might install someone who is qualified, but bypass people who are much more qualified. I've covered both kinds of political appointment stories.

My opinion is that any government group's officers should hire the most competent people their taxpayers want to pay for. So if you think your local school board members have hand-picked a pliable stooge for their school superintendent, or if you think your city council members gave a plum city job to a political crony, check the position's job description (which the hiring group has to make available to you by law), and see whether or not the new jobholder meets the minimum requirements. If he or she doesn't meet the minimum standards, you can challenge the hiring or appointment on fitness for office grounds.

Check to see if the government group's officers even solicited applications other than the application of their favorite. If they didn't, you may be able to force them to do so, depending on the law that applies to the group's hiring practices. Check to see who the job applicants were, and try to find their resumes or qualifications. If the resumes are filed publicly, you've got what you need. If they're not filed, demand to see them, if it's legal to do so. (And don't take the officials' word on legality; verify it independently.) If you can't see the resumes, contact the unsuccessful applicants. Often, they'll be happy to tell you their qualifications and explain why they think the government body's members passed them up. Also, contact officials who voted in the minority against hiring the person who was hired. They'll have their own reasons for why they thought the subject in question wasn't the right person for the job, and they might share them with you.

And don't forget the old standby of checking on the appointee's criminal, personal, lawsuit, and financial disclosure records. Other chapters in the book provide the details.

A WAR STORY ON WASTE

Now I'll tell you a story about how I tied together local government minutes, federal agency grant program records, and lawsuit records to document how leaders in an Appalachian town let a $1.5 million grant for a public housing project slip away and ended up being snarled in red tape and lawsuits.

I was covering a county supervisors' meeting one day. The mayor of the sleepy little burg that served as the county seat asked the supervisors to help him turn a vacant building site into a parking lot for the county courthouse. The supervisors, saying they heard there was legal action on the land, wanted no part of any such project.

As a newcomer to the area, I didn't know the story behind the vacant land. But being nosy, I checked into it and found an ugly story of waste, racism, classism, and mismanagement.

The site in question, a block or so away from the county courthouse, was to have been the location of a housing project for the working poor. But the Farmers Home Administration revoked a $1.5 million grant for the project a month before I came to the area, and the site was lying vacant. I interviewed the chairman of the county's housing authority board, the agency which owned the site. He said he hoped the county would buy the property, because the housing authority had no definite plans for the site once the Feds revoked the grant.

Why would a federal agency revoke a grant? And what lawsuits could possibly revolve around a vacant tract? I spent several hours reviewing grant records of the Farmers Home Administration. The bulky file contained grant proposals, housing project designs, financial justification paperwork, letters between agencies, memorandums, bid solicitations, construction bids, and other documents pertinent to the case. I then spent another couple of hours reviewing the minutes of the county housing authority board, and a couple of more hours at the county courthouse reviewing site ownership documents, liens and lawsuits tied to the site, and lawsuits involving the housing authority. These documents, all public records, enabled me to put together the following story on the history of the homeless housing project.

The housing authority bought the five-acre site in 1980 for $100,000. The man who ran the authority then applied for a grant for the housing project and tentatively received a $1.5 million grant in 1982 from the Farmers Home Administration. Then the trouble began.

Three couples filed suit against the housing authority in 1983. They claimed the housing project for the working poor would lower the value of their properties, which were nearby. Then the town council also came out against the housing project. The council members argued the project would overload the town's public services. The housing authority director retaliated with an equal-opportunity complaint against the couples and a similar complaint against the town council members.

The Farmers Home Administration put the project on hold because of the clashing. The agency's officials told the housing authority director not to do any work on the project until they took the grant approval off hold. Otherwise, they told him, he would lose the grant and the Feds wouldn't pay for the work, either.

The lawsuits were dismissed in 1984. The housing authority director had to re-submit the project for construction bids because of the long delay. The construction firms now wanted more than $1.5 million. The director changed the concept of the housing project to a fewer-unit, higher-rent project, and a construction company came in with a bid under $1.5 million in 1985. This would lead to trouble, because the housing authority was going to have to pay back some of the grant with money raised from rents.

But before the Feds approved the redesigned project, the housing authority director allowed the contractor to start excavating the site in the fall of 1985 "to get a jump on the winter." Then the Feds suspended the contractor from the project and all other agency projects for alleged nonpayment of bills. They lifted this suspension a couple of months later, but by now the weather was too lousy to complete the excavating.

In January of 1986, Farmers Home Administration agents told the housing authority director they wanted a survey from him proving he could fill the redesigned housing project with enough working poor people who could afford the proposed higher rents. The director couldn't do it, and the housing authority board members fired him late that month.

The board members had no greater success. They couldn't generate the survey, either, and Farmers Home Administration officials revoked the grant a couple of months later.

The board members, at the time I did my digging, were trying to get a new grant for the redesigned project which Farmers Home Administration officials had never formally approved. Meanwhile, the contractor's subcontractor put a mechanic's lien on the site, claiming he never got paid for work he did on it the previous fall. The fired housing authority administrator told me he was going to sue the board members for breach of contract over his firing. And neighbors of the vacant five-acre site were talking of suing the housing authority over muddy runoff from the partially-excavated site.

The county's taxpayers were going to have to shell out big money for this mess. The lawsuits involving payment for work done on the site and the lawsuits over the mud runoff would cost a bundle of money to fight in court, even if the county ended up winning. Likewise, the wrongful firing suit was going to cost money to fight. And then there was the waste of all the money paid to the fired director and other county employees and outside consultants to put the two failed plans together in the first place. And even if the second project had been approved, it would have cost more to build, would probably cost too much rent for working poor people of the area to afford, and very likely would have had a high vacancy rate.

No one held a gun to people's heads in that county to prevent them from finding out about that project. And no one's preventing you from reviewing the public records to see if your public officials are misusing their power to do things that will hurt you and other people. Tax reformer Howard Jarvis of Proposition 13 fame used to say, "Only the knowledge that the people care will keep the politicians honest." The bottom line is this: By reviewing the public record and applying pressure, you can hold government officials accountable and maybe accomplish the impossible— make them do the right things every now and then. After all, they're not operating in a vacuum—their abuses hurt your loved ones and you!

END NOTES

1. Mike Royko's quote comes from his column "An Attorney for the Fix," which is dated October 23, 1975. It appeared in his book, *Sez Who? Sez Me*.
2. Quotes concerning the Baby M trial come from articles in the January 19, 1987 and April 13, 1987 issues of Time and from Mary Beth Whitehead's book *A Mother's Story*. My own opinions and observations come from talking with my former co-worker Cathy Carroll and from reading her stories and wire copy stories on the Baby M case in the Ocean County (New Jersey) *Observer* in 1987.
3. Information on Rose Bird comes from an article in the September 15, 1986 issue of *Time* and from an article in the November 17, 1986 issue of *U.S. News*. Information on the Night Stalker comes from articles in the September 9, 1985 issue of *Time* and a September 16, 1985 issue of *People*.
4. Information on Hugo Black came from Michael Schwartz's book *The Persistent Prejudice*.
5. My article on the public housing project which went awry appeared in the Kingsport (Tennessee) *Times-News* in the fall of 1986.

Check On How Government Officials Spend Your Money

What's the definition of a fiscal conservative nowadays? One who favors "SMALL" tax increases!

Some government spending is necessary. Almost everyone except crooks, thugs, rapists, arsonists, and faith healers believe police, firefighters, and paramedics are good to have. Trash pickup, utilities, and sewers are also items I'm sure most of us can appreciate. And I'm sure the vast majority of Americans are glad we spend enough money to keep our roads paved and our defenses strong.

Almost all other government spending, good or bad, is the result of some politician buying votes with your money. Social welfare programs and other government entitlements, for example, keep a lot of folks fat, happy, and Democrat. Republican lawmakers reward their fat-cat constituents with breaks for businesses. Regulatory agencies, as vital as many of them are to the public good, are largely the result of special-interest group pressure on the politicians.

The pork barrel is a great way for a bunch of legislators to simultaneously boost their re-election chances. The idea here is, "As long as we politicians are going to keep wasting tax dollars, some of the waste ought to look like I did something for my district." So a major appropriation bill will contain a little something for almost everyone who's voting on it. Even a "dove" might vote for a wasteful military bill if he can say he got defense contract work for his district. Even a "fiscal conservative" might vote for a mindless social program if his district gets a piece of its action and he gets the proper credit.

Even our nation's public schools came into being in many states as the result of politicians prostituting themselves for votes. An idea as natural as school attendance for children wasn't the law of the land until about a hundred or so years ago. Starting with Horace Mann in Massachusetts, many politicians who wanted public schools sleazily courted the anti-Catholic bigot vote blocs on the left and on the right by promising the public school system would combat alleged Catholic subversion through the Catholic schools.

In this chapter, I'll show you how to use public records to determine how government people spend your money. This chapter will cover how to track items in government budgets, how to check on government officials' behavior in relation to government contracts, and how to uncover various tricks the bureaucrats play with the budget. The "civilian" uses of this chapter include informing yourself on how government officials do business and monitoring how they spend your money. The "military" use of this chapter is to dig up dirt on your target public official for use in an election campaign or some other event.

A FEW EXAMPLES OF WASTE AND FRAUD

There's a multitrillion dollar national debt already on our backs, so I shouldn't have to say too much about government waste and fraud to fire you up. But just in case, here are three quick cases that should motivate you to do some checking.

In the first case, Ohio community college officials are at this writing under investigation for reportedly using school money to make campaign contributions to state legislators. It is legal to use school budget money to pay for facility expenses, lab supplies, salaries, and other such items; it's a no-no to use school budget money to buy politicians!

In the second case, a scientist/manager at the U.S. Department of Agriculture's animal parasite research laboratory in Auburn, Alabama got caught in 1991 illegally diverting agricultural research money into AIDS research. No, you sickos, he wasn't caught teaching "safe sex" to farm animals! But the research leader *WAS* caught injecting calves with the AIDS virus, then sending body fluids of these animals all over the country and to Mexico. USDA agents, acting on a tip from a whistleblower, also found evidence the research leader lied about his actions and wasted roughly $90,000 on his unauthorized research.

And in the third case, the editors of *Aviation Week*, in their July 4, 1988 issue, ran a six-page special section on waste and bribery involving military procurement. The key charge the journalists of this pro-military magazine reported was that Pentagon officials were wasting up to $40 billion a year on military procurement alone. Another major charge they reported was that more than 90 percent of all weapons procurement programs are more costly than first estimated—not even counting the effects of inflation or lower numbers of items purchased. (Both of these factors jump per-unit costs of weapons.)

As long as the politicians are spending your money to buy votes, take care of their buddies, or advance their own agendas, you might as well know how to find out which ratholes they throw your money into. Here's how.

CHECKING THE LEDGER

The most usable record for checking how government officials use or waste your money is the ledger. The ledger has a bunch of different names, but the concept of a ledger is similar to the concept of your checkbook.

The administrators of every government body with spending and collecting authority have to keep a ledger. At the local level, the ledger is often a very real and very heavy set of books which you can review. At higher levels of government, the agency or legislative body in question will use more sophisticated budget documents to track finances, but they will contain the same kinds of information as the ledgers at City Hall.

Every government body has income from various sources. These monies are entered into the ledger as payments received. Every government body has expenses for various programs. These are entered into the ledger as payouts. Each payout has a number assigned to it so government bureaucrats and auditors (and you, the citizen investigator) can track down where the money went.

The ledger must show to the penny how and when money came into the government agency's budget (like from tax collection, matching funds from another government agency, user fees, interest, and so on). Likewise, the ledger had better show every expenditure. And each expenditure entry had better show who received the money, when he received it, and the amount he received, down to the penny. There had also better be a control number which ties each expenditure to paperwork authorizing the agency to pay it. This applies to everything from payrolls to contracts with vendors. The agency has to keep paperwork on file by control number. This information is usually on a requisition form or a similar government form, a vendor's bill, and/or a receipt. This paperwork will also show who authorized the purchase.

Reporters from a Pennsylvania newspaper tracked down government spending actions this way when they did some digging on state legislators' use of state money for office furnishings and office supplies. Using state budget records, the reporters noted one state lawmaker spent $222,000 on office expenses in a two-year period. (It seems he bought everything except a Poconos-style heart-shaped honeymooners' tub for his office!)

They noted the state's lieutenant governor William Scranton III (who also served as the president of the state senate) ordered himself a $74,000 copier the same year he ran for the governor's office, then had his staffers run off tens of thousands of extra press releases per month during his losing campaign. They also noted the representatives enjoyed perks ranging from free briefcases to lilac-scented after-shave and hair mousse at the state capital barber shop to the privilege of sending $255,000 worth of honorary citations to voters in their districts.

U.S. senator Bob Smith did the same digging on the federal budget in 1991. According to a published report, the New Hampshire Republican found a number of pork barrel projects—many of which were slipped into the budget without a vote or a debate— like some of these gems:

- Some senators anonymously added $6 million to an appropriation bill so they could upgrade their perfectly good private subway system. No recorded vote was taken for this action.
- Arkansas senator Dale Bumpers got $2.7 million earmarked for a catfish farm in his state. (Does Bumpers think pork should smell fishy?)
- Minnesota congressman Martin Sabo got $1 million for a study on why more people don't commute to work by bicycle. (Pedaling 20 miles to work in Duluth during a blizzard might save energy, but will also boost worker compensation payments for frostbite damage!)
- Iowa congressman Neal Smith got his colleagues to spend $15 million to plant trees on land owned by local governments. "Are you for tree planting or not?" the Congressional tree-hugger reportedly snapped when put on the spot about his project.
- New York congressman Stephen Solarz sneaked into a Navy procurement bill an extra $5 million for erecting a government building for the Solomon Islands parliament. When questioned, he reportedly said he viewed the spending as a monument to American fighting men who fought at Guadalcanal in World War II.
- Florida congresswoman Ileana Ros-Lehtinen brought home $1.4 million worth of pork to brighten up Miami's Biscayne Boulevard with tropical plants and brick walkways. (In most

urban areas, graffiti-painters will "decorate" for free!)

Since the ledger and the related paperwork are public records, let's run through how you would check an expenditure item on a ledger. Let's say you as a resident of Steelburgh, Pennsylvania, want to check on whether your city officials are wasting money on out-of-town travel. You call the city administrator's office, find out the location of the city's ledger, and go down to City Hall to check it out. Since the city has several departments, and you read in the paper that the city's budget is $50 million for this fiscal year, your city's records should reflect that all $50 million was distributed into the city's various accounts (the police department account, the fire department account, the city administrator's account, the sanitation department account, the public works account, and so forth).

Next, you go through each of the city's accounts in the ledger. You notice the city administrator account lists three travel expenditures totalling $40,000. The dates are 1/11, 2/15, and 7/5; the control numbers are A1015, A1098, and A1179. You notice the public works department account lists two travel expenditures totalling $25,000. The dates are 1/22 and 2/24; the control numbers are P1022 and P1102. Finally, you notice the city sanitation department account lists three travel expenditures totalling $35,000. The dates are 1/15, 2/20, and 8/13; the control numbers are S1018, S1099, and S1197.

Your next step is to ask to see the paperwork for each of the control numbers. When the city clerks retrieve these items for you, you pore over the paperwork. You notice the city administrator and an employee named Quarrel went to three "better local government" conferences. Receipts for plane tickets and hotel rooms indicated the two winter conferences took place in Florida and in the Virgin Islands, while the July conference took place in the Catskills.

You notice the city public works director and a city engineer named Sonono went to a concrete industry convention and a "city construction contracts workshop." Receipts for plane tickets and hotel rooms indicated the January convention took place in the Bahamas, while the February workshop took place in New Orleans. You notice the city sanitation chief and an air pollution technician named Ferrari attended a "substance abuse in the workplace" conference in January, a landfill technology seminar in February, and a dumptruck industry trade show in August. Receipts for plane tickets and hotel rooms indicated the drug/alcohol convention took place in a ski resort near Middlebury, Vermont, the landfill seminar took

place in Palm Springs, and the dumptruck trade show took place in Atlantic City and included a side trip to one manufacturer's plant in Queens, New York.

Your next step is to get the clerks to make photocopies of the requisitions and the receipts. After all, you'll need hard-copy proof that your city spent $100,000 on travel at a time when city officials are calling for a property tax hike, a city sales tax, or both.

Your discovery on the city's travel expenditures leads you to conclude the city is wasting money elsewhere, too. So you zero in on the three departments spending big bucks on conferences, seminars, work shops, and trade shows.

You check the city administrator's account and notice there are several expenditures for copying machines. You write down the control numbers, review the requisitions and purchases, and notice the city administrator didn't ask for competitive bids even though he bought $100,000 worth of copying machines from Bidet Copying Company. It is illegal almost everywhere for a government official to buy goods or services over a certain dollar amount without soliciting bids from several vendors. Of course you'll want to photocopy these documents, and note there was nothing in the records to indicate city officials sought competitive bids.

You next check the city public works account. By scanning the ledger, you notice the department's officials have bought all building supplies from a couple of businesses whose owners are big contributors to the mayor and a majority of city council members. This may not be illegal, if the businessmen in question sell the supplies to the city at fair prices, or if the city bosses have to buy from locally-owned businesses or certain other businesses because of some sort of ordinance or court order. But you may want to copy the invoices anyway and see if you couldn't get a better price on comparable quality items from another supplier in the area.

You then check the city sanitation department account and notice two payments of $100,000 each to Kessinger Transportation. You write down the control numbers, review the related paperwork, and see the city bought two Mercedes Benz trash trucks from this dealer. "Gee-zus!" you say to yourself; "I could buy a HOUSE for less than what the city pays for trash trucks!" Reviewing the paperwork further and checking the truck specifications from competitor Mac-Namoron Motors, you see MacNamoron's American-made vehicles could haul just as much garbage at half the cost!

One or more of several things is wrong here. It could be the contract specification is so complex and unrealistic that a well-made product that could do the job is bypassed because it didn't meet some non-essential specification or its manufacturer didn't submit it to some screwball product test. It could be that the city bureaucrats mistakenly concluded the cheaper truck didn't meet the contract specification. It could be that a minor error in the lower bid caused the city bureaucrats to reject it. It could be that the city bureaucrats don't know they should accept the lower bid if both vendors' bids meet the specifications.

We don't even want to speculate about any bad blood between MacNamoron and city officials or speculate about kickbacks, bribes, or political connections involving Kessinger and city officials, do we? Needless to say, you'll want to copy the requisitions, the receipts, all bidding paperwork, and anything else out of the records that would cast any doubt on the vehicle buying abilities of the sanitation department officials. MacNamoron's reaction might be interesting, too, if you ask him for one.

CHECKING GOVERNMENT CONTRACTS

Reviewing contract paperwork can uncover other ways in which city purchasers (or any other government body's purchasers) can waste taxpayer money or get rooked in their purchases. One of these involves the "change order." A "change order" is what a government agency or a private client issues to a contractor to change some aspect of a project the contractor has already agreed to do. Of course, the contractor will get more money to do the extra work.

Often, "change orders" are necessary, because a problem or a need for more items or features in a project arises. I ran across these situations down in Appalachia from time to time. In one instance, a school board's officials had to file a "change order" and pay thousands of extra dollars to contractors who were performing school building renovations because lawmakers ordered them to add asbestos removal to the project after it started. In another instance, state highway officials had to issue a "change order" to cover added costs of routing a highway around an unstable rock formation on a hillside; geologists had earlier underestimated the problems it would cause.

But many "change orders" translate into unneeded expense for you the taxpayer. A classic example is when government officials solicit bids for a project without having a firm idea of what they really want or need. Contractors who know the incompetence of these officials often take advantage of it by submitting a very low bid for the contract; when they win the contract, they overcharge the hell out the government agency when its bumbling officials submit change orders every time they change their minds about what they want the contractor to do. Since government contracts (except a few involving national security) are public record, you can check a contract to see whether the change orders are for good or for questionable reasons.

Another scam that costs the taxpayers money or services is contract noncompliance. This means the contractor doesn't perform the job to the specifications of the contract. He might have laid nine-inch sewer pipe when the contract called for 18-inch sewer pipe. He might have used cheap junk hardware from the Orient when the contract specified all materials were to be American-made and meet legitimate industry standards. He might have built a building slightly smaller, or used cheaper materials than what the contract specified. Some violations are hard for you to prove, but others are simple to verify.

You could physically check for contract noncompliance at the project site (when the public is allowed access or even when no one's around to run you off), or you could check the paperwork of the contract and try to figure it out. For example, doing a little math would tell you it takes a certain number of cubic yards of asphalt to black-top a five-mile stretch of a four-lane highway to a depth of eight inches, if that's what the contract called for. (Remember also pavers have to steamroller the asphalt to pack it firmly.) But if the bill shows a purchase of about half that amount, there could be a problem; the contractor may not have paved the whole five-mile stretch, or maybe he spread less than eight inches of blacktop over the road.

Or you may check a water works contract and notice the utility bought a large number of pumps from the contractor as part of the contract, and the pumps are supposed to deliver a specified minimum amount of flow. You could call the pump manufacturer's sales engineers and check whether the pumps are powerful enough to pump the needed volume of water into the system's pipes.

If you're not that sharp in the hard sciences or in the industrial arts, you can still accomplish something with these records. Make photocopies of the records of a suspect project and have an engineer or building trades friend of yours review the paperwork. He might be able to spot problems.

The government's wrongdoing in these two situations (questionable change orders and contract noncompliance) involves not monitoring the contractor adequately. The reasons could range from simple incompetence to bribery to political ties between the contractor and the government.

A third scam that costs the taxpayers money is

charging the government more than private customers for services. It is illegal for a contractor to charge the government more money for goods and services than what he charges the nongovernment customer. Why? Because you the taxpayer would end up giving him extra profit or subsidizing the price breaks he gives to private customers. But many contractors overcharge the government anyway because they believe government purchasing agents don't really know the fair market value of most goods and services. Again, the government's wrongdoing here involves not checking the contractor's business practices adequately.

Cheaters who overbill the government this way try to justify their thievery by complaining about the amount of paperwork involved or the lags in government payments for their services. But, hey, no one held a gun to these people's heads to force them to do business with government agencies! The extra cost of doing business with the government usually isn't large. Besides, since the government often buys in large amounts, the businessmen could easily cover the added costs with the volume of business they will be doing. At any rate, why should they bloodsuck off of us taxpayers?

The way to prove this kind of scam is to first get from the contract file the figures for what the government agency paid the contractor. Next, contact competitors of the contractor in question to determine what are the fair market values for the goods or services in question. (Suspect problems if the government agency's people paid much more than the fair market value for the goods or service in question.) Then approach the target contractor and ask for a quote for the same kind of goods and services. If his quote is lower than what his government contract shows the government paid, you've caught him.

What I've showed you is how to check on simple contracts of local government agencies. Actually, most government agencies, from the smallest township to the Pentagon and the Department of Health and Human Services, do business this way. Only the figures and the complexity and size of the contract files are different. If you want to check on block grants, industrial park grants, HUD projects, defense contracts, or any other large or small expenditure or contract your heart desires, just figure out which agencies are involved in the project. Then call public information officers or freedom of information officers or contracts administrators of the involved government agencies and arrange to see the project files. For more specific information, check out the chapter on government contracts and grants.

MISCELLANEOUS BUDGET TRICKS TO WATCH OUT FOR

Pressure groups in and out of government put a lot of energy into ensuring their pet agencies will have enough money to waste on programs they support. The press releases, the public posturing, and the other stunts they pull to get their pets their share of the pork are called "budget negotiations" by the media. You or I would call such behavior "whining" or "tantrum-throwing" or "lying."

I ran into an example of this when the governor of a state I was working in was putting together his budget. Some teachers' groups started bitching that the governor wanted to cut funding for education. I looked into their charge, and I found out the state's education department people wanted about $300 million more for the coming year than they got the previous year. The governor was proposing spending about $200 million more on education for the coming year, so some of the teacher groups were calling this a "cut." When I confronted some teacher association people on their "New Math", they said they had been doing their figuring anticipating the public schools were going to get the amount the education department higher-ups had asked for.

Another budget dirty trick that is akin to fraud on the taxpayer is needless spending by the agency in the final months of the fiscal year to justify getting more money in the coming fiscal year. Instead of trying to save the taxpayers money by running fiscally responsible bureaus, the bureaucrats worry about getting even more money to waste. They think if they save money, the budget people who allot them money will give them less in the coming fiscal year, because they've proven they don't need the excess if they have any money saved. (If the budgeters are on the ball, that's what they SHOULD do!)

A U.S. Environmental Protection Agency official drew fire in 1991 for being dumb enough to put the "spend every tax dollar" mentality in writing. He sent a memo to his people urging them to go on all scheduled trips and "use the remaining travel dollars, if possible." Media people got their hands on the memo somehow, and published it. The EPA's critics roared in anger when the memo became public. The critics said EPA officials were encouraging waste or were failing to use money to conduct more inspections of polluted sites.

I ran into a similar mentality when I was serving as a young Army officer in Korea. My colonel assigned me the job of preparing the battalion's budget for the next fiscal year. I noted what we had spent during the present year, and what we were going to spend to become combat-ready. I then planned out what I thought we'd need for the coming year to maintain our level of strength, and I added a request for more fuel and ammo and rations than normal so we could conduct the extra training we would need to bring ourselves up to snuff. I also made some allowances for purchases of sporting goods and TVs for the soldiers' recreation. And since I had to do this budgeting during the Carter Administration, I anticipated double-digit inflation would continue. So I added a 15 percent inflation factor to my figures.

When I presented the figures to the colonel, he ranted about how I was low-balling the battalion. He ordered me to redo the budget so he could get his hands on more money. I refused. I told him, "Sir, if you don't like my figures, redo them yourself. Then sign your own name at the bottom of the report." I don't know if he took my advice or simply farmed the job out to a subservient staff puke in our outfit. At any rate, my days as a government budgeter were over.

You can check for evidence of this abuse also. All you have to do is check the final months of the ledger of any agency. If you notice a spending frenzy, and if you notice the agency is buying seemingly trivial items or is going crazy on travel spending, you may have valid evidence the top dogs of the agency are padding their budget figures to justify their request for even more money for the coming year.

GET INSIDE HELP

Believe it or not, each government agency has auditors and investigators who search for waste and fraud on the part of government employees. Waste and fraud are enormous problems, but they would be much worse if it wasn't for the work of these government agents.

When a government inspector or investigator gets disciplinary action started against a government employee, it's usually a public record. The general counsel, the information officer, the contracts administrator, the inspector general, the freedom of in-formation officer, or someone else in the agency should be able to get for you documents showing lawsuits, citations, and criminal cases the agency's lawmen have filed against employees. A federal agency's Inspector General semiannual report and the General Accounting Office's monthly report lists contain many examples of fraudulent and wasteful behavior by our bureaucrats.

THE BOTTOM LINE

No one's preventing you from reviewing the public records to see if your public officials are throwing your money down some gold-plated rathole. To quote my Uncle Chuck, "As long as they're taking money from me, they might as well take care of my money." The bottom line is this: By reviewing the public record and applying pressure, you can hold government officials accountable and maybe accomplish the impossible— keep them honest. After all, they're spending YOUR money!

END NOTES

1. Information on Horace Mann came from Michael Schwartz's book *The Persistent Prejudice*.
2. Information on Ohio community college officials' alleged use of school money to make contributions to state politicians comes from articles in the Cincinnati *Enquirer* on May 28, 1991 and August 21, 1991. Some information also comes from an Associated Press article which ran on August 15, 1991.
3. Information on the scientist/manager's reported misuse of agriculture money for AIDS research comes from the USDA Office of Inspector General Audit Report No. 02091-1-At and from the USDA Inspector General's FY 1991 (first half) Semiannual Report To Congress.
4. Information on allegations concerning military procurement waste and fraud comes from articles in the July 4, 1988 issue of *Aviation Week*.
5. The article on Pennsylvania lawmakers' spending was in the Philadelphia *Inquirer* on February 22, 1987.
6. The article on Sen. Bob Smith's checking for pork barrel projects in the federal budget was in the April 22, 1991 issue of *Time*.
7. The information on the EPA official's spending plea came from an article which appeared in the Cincinnati *Post* on September 20, 1991.

Contracts And Grants–Your Taxes At Waste

Government officials handle more money than anyone else in the country. Most of them don't have much experience in business management. Also, all of them are susceptible to pressure. Politicians are susceptible when running for re-election. The top bureaucrats whom the politicians appoint are susceptible to pressure from the politicians. The people who serve underneath the top bureaucrats are susceptible to pressure from the top bureaucrats when performance reviews, promotions, and layoffs are involved. Put these ingredients together with the insatiable greed of many contract-seeking businessmen and consultants and the insatiable greed of many grant-seeking scientists, medical types, social workers, social experimenters, academics, and artsy types, and you have a recipe for massive waste and fraud at the expense of the taxpayers.

This chapter will cover (in more detail than the chapters on government spending, the private sector, public health, schools, and crimes of dishonesty) how to find evidence of government, contract-seeker, and grant-seeker wrongdoing. The other chapters hint at these digging methods. But since documenting fraud and waste in connection with government spending on contracts and grants is so important and has a lot of detail, such digging deserves a chapter all its own.

The "civilian" uses for this chapter include informing yourself on how government officials handle grants and contracts and monitoring how well they take care of your money. The "military" uses for this chapter include exposing and punishing contractors or grantees for fraud or waste or other wrongdoing, and exposing and punishing government officials for crookedness, negligence, or other wrongdoing.

CONTRACT DIRT-DIGGING

Uncle Sam and his state government and local government nephews are by far the largest group of customers for goods and services in the country. If your target is a businessman, odds are good he is selling something to one or more government agencies. Now, government needs for goods and services are legitimate, and good businessmen should provide good products and services to government. Unfortunately, the amount of money available is so huge,

and the competence of government purchasers is often so poor that a lot of fly-by-night types leech off the taxpayers by winning government contracts, then delivering substandard goods and services, or over-charging for the goods and services. Your target businessman may be one of these leeches.

Staffers of each government agency keep a ledger or a list of every contract program they operate. These lists are public records. These lists will indicate the contracts the agency awarded under each contract program by the name and ID number of each awarded contract. The agency staffers also keep records on who won each contract. It is possible for you to find out from an agency which contracts it awarded to your target businessman.

Once you have the identity and ID number of each of the contracts the agency awarded your target, you can file for the paperwork on each contract. The paperwork will include the specifications of the contract, your target's bid (proposal), the amount your target will get for fulfilling the contract, and a number of other items of interest. Again, virtually every document in a contract file except those pertaining to national security secrets or trade secrets will be open to you. (The target's bid for any contract that is still open—unawarded—will not be public record to prevent business rivals from getting unfair advantages on him. But once the contract is awarded, the documents are public.)

The hardest part of this drill will be figuring out all the contract programs an agency runs. Generally, you can get information on contracts an agency awarded in any given year. Although the agents of an agency like the U.S. Department of Defense will probably ask you to narrow your request to the businesses you really want to check on. Why? Because their contract list is probably thick enough to stop tank gun fire!

Check with the agency's contracts administrator, controller, related finance people, or freedom of information officer for this information. Once you get the list of contracts your target company has received, the rest should be cake. All you'll have to do is request to see the file on each contract, using the contract ID number as an identifier. Then you can have photocopies made of the documents in each file.

While it's perfectly legal to run a business on government contract money, many people attach a stigma to it. To many, running a business on government contract money is evidence the businessman is at the very least a less-than-adequate businessman who isn't man enough to compete head-to-head in the marketplace against other real businessmen. (There are exceptions; the country needs some companies to manufacture items like ballistic missiles, aircraft carriers, and artillery pieces. These things have a limited civilian market.) To many, running a business on government contract money is a sign a businessman could be crooked. If you find out your target businessman does a high percentage of his business with the government, you might want to look into this possibility.

Knowing what government contracts your target businessman has also provides you with a scalpel to cut through the red tape and view a lot of his business dealings. You can analyze your target's contract paperwork and check for any possible wrongdoing on his part. The contract documents of an unscrupulous businessman may reveal that he's cheating the public while he's doing taxpayer-funded government contract work. For examples, check the chapter on government spending for information on how businessmen use change orders (low-balling competitor bids, then plugging in costly extras to the contract after winning it), how they overbill the government compared to what they bill private customers, and how they engage in contract noncompliance (cutting corners on a government job to pocket extra bucks) to cheat taxpayers.

You could see evidence in the contract paperwork that your target is engaging in wasteful behavior that, while legal, is costly. For example, your target might be selling $600 hammers to the Pentagon because he's taking advantage of a bureaucrat's crazy requirement the hammers withstand ultracold temperatures at a height of 50,000 feet. He may have been the low bidder because other thieves in the tool industry submitted higher bids, but he "justified" his unjustifiable figure by saying he had to do design work on the hammers, run a special production line for them, and have them tested at an exotic environmental testing facility.

If he actually does all this work at the demand of the bureaucrats, the paperwork proving it will have to turn up in the file sooner or later. Obtain the documentation, then call your congressman to complain about the wasteful bureaucrats. But if he merely delivers off-the-shelf hammers to the government or only does minimal research and testing on them (like looking up in a book to verify the steel in his hammers won't get too brittle at extremes in temperature and altitude), then you might have evidence he's cheating—or at least gouging—the taxpayers.

You might find in contract documents evidence of fraud or perjury on your target's part. For example, if you can prove he has misrepresented something about himself or his business for profit motives (like saying his business is minority-owned or female-owned to get a "set-aside" or a "quota" contract when he's a white male), you've caught him in an illegal act.

There's also another use for this kind of information. You can use it to prove the bureaucrats supervising the contract are incompetent, wasteful, or both. An easy way to hurt a bureaucrat's reputation is simply to link him with a well-known wasteful project. I'll bet it wouldn't help the careers of the bureaucrats involved in buying $600 hammers for the Pentagon to be linked to such a fiasco.

Likewise, a more thorough review of the contract records could show systematic evidence of government wrongdoing. If you can find in contract paperwork evidence of errors, cost overruns, a large number of change orders that shows the government's people don't know what the hell they want, failure to check on the contractor to make sure he complies with the contract and delivers what he's obliged to deliver, a price for goods or services that you can show is higher than what the target charges private customers, money improperly accounted for, or money improperly paid or withheld, you've got evidence of government wrongdoing.

Here's a note on improper withholding of money due. This is a killer for small honest contractors! My dad was a construction boss working on refurbishing a public housing project; he told me the bureaucrats' delays in getting the subcontractors their money caused many of them to lay off workers and to lose money when they had to reschedule business loans. Some firms went out of business; the cost in unemployment benefits, in bankruptcy court costs, and in finding and breaking in new workers and contract firms made the job cost the taxpayers more.

Another note on contracts—there seem to be a select few who get a lot of them, and many red-headed stepchildren who get none, even though their bids are competitive. It could be that government agencies are playing by the book in awarding contracts. But do you expect a negative guy like me to buy that for all cases? I didn't think so.

Bureaucrats know the score. They know a certain amount of contracts are used to reward friends of government. They know which businessmen are friends of the political bosses and contributors to the party till. They also know which businessmen aren't contributors. And they certainly know who the enemies are! So they could be illegally helping their favorites get government contracts or keeping others from getting the contracts.

One obvious tactic to use in establishing a possible motive for favoritism is to check on the targeted businessman's political contributions. (See the chapter on politicians.) If he has a track record of supporting those in power, it will often translate into business for him. Major corporations, through political action committees, routinely buy or rent politicians with campaign contributions. Corporate bosses often contribute to the two major contestants of races to ensure themselves an in no matter who wins!

Another tactic is to research ties between the contractor and the local politicians. Enemies of these people in the other party can tip you off. So can other businessmen in the community. So can lawsuits, land records, corporation records, and the like. Check the chapter on politicians for other tips on checking for their possible ties to the contractor.

Then there's the work of documenting possible instances of favoritism. When you scan contract paperwork, look at winners' bids. Often, their language dovetails with what the government agency wants. This is evidence they know the process well (perfectly legal) or got insider information on the contract to be let (illegal) or they got help from the bureaucrats in putting together a bid (also illegal).

Check the winner's bid for pricing. If the winner's bid is higher than the losers' bids, and the lower bids also comply with the specifications of the contract, you've found evidence of illegal favoritism and/or government stupidity. If the winner's bid is the lowest, check for obvious lowballing in preparation to receive massive change orders. For example, a winner might not honestly account for problems that could lead to more expenses, or his bid will look unrealistically low in comparison with other bids. Also, check for the possibility of noncompliance down the road in the way the winner words his offer.

Scan losers' bids, too. If their bids were lower than the winner's bid, the government could be ignoring them to reward friends. Or the government agents could be subtly disqualifying losers by flagging shortcomings in their bids while overlooking similar flaws in the winner's bid. Or the government agents could be asking for overly strict or needless conditions that the legitimate businessman will not accept. Or the government agents could use discretion in determin-

ing the winner's bid fits the requirements better than other bids.

In any case, you can use contract documents (including the proposals of those who lost out) to show a pattern of favoritism toward a businessman or a pattern of discrimination against certain classes of businessmen.

SIFTING THROUGH THE GOVERNMENT'S OWN DIRT

Believe it or not, each government agency has auditors and investigators who search for fraud, price-gouging, noncompliance, and other wrongdoing of those who get government contracts and/or grants. Without them, we the people would be in the hole even worse than we already are! Most of these agents are excellent civil servants, but they're simply overworked. There are so many crooks out there grabbing money from the government that these agents are like refs in a hockey game—they can't catch every penalty-deserving act!

When agents do catch contract crooks and grant larcenists, their agencies can blacklist them (put them on a list for nonparticipation in government contract or grant programs). They can also file criminal charges against suspected abusers of grants and contracts, or they could sue to make them repay money.

At any rate, such government actions are public record. The general counsel, the information officer, the contracts administrator, the inspector general, the freedom of information officer, or someone else in the agency should be able to get for you documents showing lawsuits, citations, and criminal cases the agency has filed against your target. Likewise, someone at the U.S. Justice Department or in your state's Attorney General office should be able to retrieve these documents for you, or at least tell you which agency actually has them. It's nice to know there are some government employees who are actually on the taxpayers' side!

A CLASSIC EXPOSÉ OF CONTRACT FRAUD

The operators of the Bronx-based Wedtech manufacturing firm got so crooked that they screwed themselves into prison. But they had company. Their money-waving helped Bronx congressmen Mario Biaggi and Robert Garcia get greedy, take bribes, and end up convicted also. Wedtech's officials got into trouble by lying about ownership to Small Business Administration agents to get minority set-aside contracts. A newswoman with a nose for public records digging helped uncover their wrongdoing.

The wrongdoing came to light when a Bronx

businessman refused to give 10 percent of the stock of his company to Bernard Ehrlich (the law firm partner of Mario Biaggi's son) when Ehrlich reportedly tried to shake him down for it. He tipped off reporter Marilyn Thompson that Wedtech's officers may have given Ehrlich and Biaggi stock shares as bribes. Working on this tip, and using publicly available documents, Ms. Thompson was able to show Wedtech officials evidently used stock to bribe officials, and evidently cheated the taxpayers out of millions of dollars by posing as a minority-owned business.

Marilyn Thompson started out by obtaining copies of the annual reports Wedtech filed with the Securities and Exchange Commission. (Companies with receipts greater than a certain level whose stock is traded publicly have to issue these reports, and they are public record.) She noted in the reports that Wedtech got many Defense Department contracts, and also got many minority set-aside contracts from the Small Business Administration. She also found out who owned stock in Wedtech, and she found out Biaggi's son and Ehrlich together received 225,000 shares.

Further, Ms. Thompson found by checking the documents that John Mariotta (the Puerto Rican whose ethnicity got Wedtech its minority business status) owned far less than the 51 percent of the company he needed to qualify it as minority-owned. It would come out later that Mariotta and Jewish (but nonminority status) partner Fred Neuberger had been bribing others with stock so heavily, that when the company offered stock for sale to the public, Mariotta no longer owned 51 percent of Wedtech. Further, she discovered from checking the records that Wedtech officers put together a stock transfer scam to make it look like Mariotta still held majority interest. But the fix was so transparent Marilyn saw it as she reviewed the company's records. She also found evidence in the documents that company officials eventually cancelled this sham stock arrangement.

By checking the publicly available documents from the Small Business Administration on Wedtech against the SEC documents she already had, Marilyn Thompson also noted Wedtech officials may have violated two other provisions of the minority set-aside contract program. One was that Wedtech eventually grew into a major company, exceeding the size limit for program participants. The other was that Mariotta himself was no longer disadvantaged, as the program specified. Ms. Thompson checked his home and other assets to determine he was now a wealthy man.

The result? A string of stories from Marilyn's word processor starting in 1986 helped expose Wedtech and the politicians who helped company officials steal money from the taxpayers. Roughly 20 people associated with the scandal were sent to prison, and former Attorney General Ed Meese had to resign under pressure when it became evident he had ties to the corrupt company.

FINDING FLAGRANT GRANT ABUSES

Grants, like government contracts, involve mind-boggling sums of money. Some grants are for scientific research, in which the research institution will perform a certain research project, and the government will pay for it. Other grants are for community programs, like block grants for public housing, utilities, and industrial parks. In these, the federal and state governments will give money to local entities, who will in turn negotiate for specified goods and services, and monitor the contracts involved. Other grants involve giving money to people who run job-training programs or some other sort of people programs.

Other grants serve as the government's way of providing freebies to certain groups in society. For example, government grant money sends kids to college, and trains artsy types in those art forms that aren't popular enough to make it on their own. (I believe about the only opera that is self-supporting is the one down in Nashville that features Loretta Lynn, Connie Smith, Wanda Jackson, Bobby Bare, Charley Pride, and other great country singers!) Often, the receivers of this money don't have to pay it back. Do you want an all-inclusive definition for grants? Grants provide opportunities for bureaucrats to spend your money.

Government officials do need a certain amount of work done (like research or community programs) that they can't get done by any other means than by using grant money. Many people get grant money from state and federal agencies to perform projects that someone in the agency with the authority to cut payment checks approves of. Unfortunately, the amount of money available is so huge, and the guidelines for giving it away are so loose that a lot of fly-by-night types sponge off the taxpayers by using grant money for their less-than-useful projects. Your target businessman may be one of these sponges.

As you would expect, checking grant records is similar to checking contract records. Each government agency's staffers keep a ledger or a list of every grant program they operate. These lists are public records. These lists will indicate the grants the agency awarded under each grant program by the name and ID number of each awarded grant. The agency staffers also keep records on who received each grant. It is possible for you to find out from an agency which grants it awarded to your target businessman or other grant-getter.

Once you have the identity and the ID number of each of the grants the agency awarded your target, you can file for the paperwork on each contract. The paperwork will include the specifications of the grant, your target's proposal (protocol), the amount of grant money your target will get, and a number of other items of interest. Virtually every document in a grant file except those pertaining to trade secrets or patient privacy will be open to you.

The hardest part of this drill will be figuring out all the grant programs an agency runs. Generally, you can get information on grants an agency awarded in any given year, although agents of an agency like the U.S. Department of Health and Human Services will probably ask you to narrow your request to the grant-getters you really want to check on. Why? Because their grant list might well have more entries than New York City has panhandlers! Check with the agency's contract administrator, controller, related finance people, or freedom of information officer for this information. Once you get the list of grants your target has gotten, the rest should be easy. All you'll have to do is request to see the file on each grant, using the grant ID number as an identifier. Then you can have photocopies made of the documents in each file.

While it's perfectly legal to run a business on government grant money, many people attach a stigma to it, even more so than to those who get contract money. People have heard stories about the government awarding scientists lots of grant money to study silly subjects like the sanitation habits of the fudge tunnel gerbil.

Knowing what government grants your target businessman has also provides you with a scalpel to cut through the red tape and view a lot of his business dealings. You can analyze your target's grant paperwork and check for any possible wrongdoing on his part. The contract documents of an unscrupulous businessman may reveal that he's cheating the public while he's performing taxpayer-funded government grant work.

If the user of a government grant doesn't perform the community project work or people project work or research work he's supposed to perform with the grant money, he's cheating the public. If a developer uses block grant money earmarked for public housing to build a mall, he's cheating the public. If a research scientist gets money to find a cure for sickle-cell anemia but instead goes into researching breast enlar-

gement schemes, he's cheating the public. If an agribusinessman gets a crop subsidy not to grow a particular crop for price support reasons, but enrolls land in the program he was going to have to let lie fallow anyway, he's cheating the public.

In fact, I saw a case in which dissident members of an Ohio nonprofit group with a semi-feminist bent sued their own trustees in 1985 for allegedly misusing private grant money. They said the trustees collected thousands of dollars of grant money for specific projects, then stashed the loot in their general expense account. The dissident members argued that such actions were unethical, and could cost the group grant money in the future. The lessons? Some nonprofit groups' leaders may be crooks or power abusers. Also, any lawsuit involving your target is worth checking for possible fraudulent behavior.

You could see evidence in the grant paperwork that your target is engaging in wasteful behavior that, while legal, is costly. For example, I'm sure you've all read accounts of how people get grant money to do the most ridiculous things on the face of the earth at your expense! If your target actually performs the ridiculous research project or the asinine art project the government paid him to do, the paperwork proving he did so will have to turn up in the grant file sooner or later. Obtain these documents, then call your congressman to complain about the wasteful bureaucrats. But if your target doesn't use the money to perform the stupid stunts the government bureaucrats were perfectly willing to pay for, then you'll have evidence he's cheating the taxpayers.

You might find in grant documents evidence of fraud or perjury on your target's part. For example, if you can prove he has misrepresented something about himself or his business in an apparent attempt to get money (like saying his business is minority-owned or female-owned to get certain "quota" grants when he's a white male), you've caught him in an illegal act.

There's another use for grant documents. You can use them to prove the bureaucrats supervising the grant program are incompetent, wasteful, or both. An easy way to hurt a bureaucrat's reputation is simply to link him with a well-known worthless project. Believe it or not, some fools with the National Endowment for the Arts thought it was a good investment of your tax money to pay $30,000 to put together a traveling exhibit of the pictures of homomoronic photographer Robert Mapplethorpe. Mapplethorpe, who died from AIDS, had taken pictures of a guy drinking another guy's urine while he was urinating, a guy with another guy's fist and forearm stuck up his rectum, a nude little boy on a chair, and a little girl being caused to show her vagina; these pictures were in the exhibit.

I guess you have to be a "real intellectual" to call piss-drinking, sphincter stretching and child pornography "art." The stooges on a Cincinnati jury were unable to find museum director Dennis Barrie guilty of obscenity for showing these snapshots for profit at the Contemporary Arts Center in 1990. (The prosecutors evidently lacked the savvy to bring child pornography charges against him.) Maybe their heads were where the sun doesn't shine.

Other mental midgets in the NEA granted Andres Serrano $15,000 for a "work" entitled "Piss Christ." Yep, the maggot put a crucifix in a bottle and filled it with his own urine.

In some instances, giving public officials evidence of such stupid wastefulness will get them to come down like a ton of bricks on the bureaucrat and his bosses. Letting people in the bureaucrat's neighborhood or social circles know he's the idiot who okayed such a ridiculous and wasteful grant will reap him the abuse he so richly deserves (unless he hangs out with people as goofy as he is).

Likewise, a more thorough review of grant records could show systematic evidence of government wrongdoing. If you can find in grant paperwork evidence of failure to verify the grant getter uses the money for the purpose the government gave it to him, or if you can find evidence government agents didn't check questionable items which the grant getter listed as expenses, or if you can find evidence government agents are shielding a grant getter from legitimate inquiry, you've got evidence of government wrongdoing.

Here's another note on grants. There seem to be a select few who get many of them, and some who get none, even though their proposals are at least as worthy as those of the winners. It could be that government agencies are playing by the book in awarding grants. But, like with contracts, do you expect a negative guy like me to buy that for all cases? I didn't think you would.

Agency bureaucrats know a certain amount of contracts are used to reward friends of government and the agency. They know which grant seekers are friends of the political bosses and contributors to the party till. They know which grant seekers share their agendas (very important in human services and education agencies). They also know which grant seekers aren't their buddies. And they certainly know who the enemies are! So they could be illegally helping their favorites get government grants or keeping others from getting the grants.

One obvious tactic to use in establishing a possible motive for favoritism is to check on the targeted businessman's political contributions. (See the chapter on politicians.) If he has a track record of supporting those in power, it could translate into grant awards for him.

Likewise, check the politics or the personal agenda of the agency chief and his top people. Agency people tend to award grants to people who share their agendas. They tend to keep grant seekers who aren't "with the program" out in the cold. Find this info out from a "cause group" staffer or a special interest group staffer; they monitor how agency people conform or fail to conform to their own agendas.

Once you figure out the bureaucrats' agenda, check to see how often the grant getter shares their viewpoint on life. If the agency staffers and the grant getters seem to be ideological buddies, then you might be able to prove favoritism. Likewise, losers who can show that a given agency that shuts them out at grant awarding time has key people who don't like their politics might be able to make a case for discrimination or violation of civil rights.

Another tactic is to research ties between the grant getter and the politicians. Enemies of these people in the other party can tip you off. So can other grant applicants. So can lawsuits, land records, corporation records, and the like. Refer to the chapter on politicians for other tips on researching ties between politicians and your target grant getter.

Then there's the work of documenting possible instances of favoritism. Check the winner's proposal for the amount of closeness to the agenda of an agency. Check the winner's proposal for closeness to the published purpose of a grant. These could be indicators of good grantsmanship (which is legal), or of illegal favoritism and help on the part of the government grant giver.

Scan losers' proposals, too. If their proposals are better than the winner's proposal, the bureaucrats could be ignoring them to reward friends. Or the government agents could be asking for overly strict or needless conditions that the legitimate grant seeker will not accept. Or the government agents could be subtly disqualifying losers by flagging their proposals' shortcomings while overlooking similar flaws in the winner's proposal. Or the government agents could be using discretion in determining the winner's proposal fits the requirements better than other proposals.

In any case, you can use grant documents (including the proposals of those who lost out) to show a pattern of favoritism toward a grant seeker or a pattern of discrimination against certain classes of grant seekers. Once you find such evidence, you can release it so the authorities will show favoritism toward the idea of punishing the biased government agents and the mooching grant getters.

SOWING THE SEEDS OF DISCONTENT

I wrote some stories several years ago about a plum agricultural subsidy program that many farmers in my area of Kentucky didn't apply for. The program in question was the Payment-In-Kind (PIK) program of the U.S. Agriculture Department. PIK was designed to reduce surpluses (and raise prices farmers could get for crops) by paying farmers with money and with stores of the crops from federal surplus stocks for promising not to grow certain crops they normally raised. Of course, getting paid not to produce is a benefit most of us would kill for, and only some producers in each county would get a crack at this prize.

In the county I was working in, there were allegations that friends of the local USDA county agent were getting enrolled in the PIK program, while most farmers hadn't even tried to enroll. After finding out the nuts and bolts of the program from the USDA, I called a number of farmers who had tried to enroll, but later backed out. They told me the amount of products they would get from federal surplus stocks was small. I got them to tell me the acreage of crops and yield of corn and wheat they could show they raised over the previous few years, and I calculated for them how much free grain they could get, and how much cash they could get from the program if they had taken part in the program.

The farmers said, "It wasn't explained to ME that way!" Some of them told me they were unaware of the cash payments. Apparently, the local USDA agent was misinforming the farmers. And with the reduced competition for enrollment, some of her supposed friends apparently got enrolled.

Although the USDA did send an agent out to our county to investigate the local agent, he evidently did a poor job. He found no apparent evidence of wrongdoing, but he didn't seem to investigate the local USDA people properly. One irate farmer told me the investigator called him from the local USDA office within earshot of all the bureaucrats in the office to ask him if he had any complaints. (This would be like the cops calling from Mob headquarters to ask shakedown victims if they had any beefs with the boys.) The farmer naturally worried about giving the man an honest answer because he thought local USDA officials would get even with him. He said the agent "would have heard different" if he had driven out to farms and interviewed the farmers so they wouldn't have to fear reprisals.

The stories I wrote about the situation didn't lead to any sensational criminal trials or resignations under fire. However, complaints about the program from several areas kept the staffers of Kentucky senator Walter Huddleston busy because Huddleston had helped get the PIK program enacted. Huddleston lost his bid for re-election the next year; how much the discontent of PIK'ed-on farmers in heavily rural Kentucky had to do with this I couldn't say.

A CONTRACT FOR DEATH

Servicemen have long joked about having to use military equipment made by the low bidder. The 1986 *Challenger* space shuttle tragedy drove this cruel joke home to the public.

NASA officials figured they could keep the shuttle program's costs down by re-using many components. They also envisioned they could make the shuttle program make some money by stepping up the flight schedule to deliver more satellites and conduct more space experiments. These were good ideas, but the space agency bosses were apparently tempted to cut corners on safety in designing their low-budget space program.

Even while a presidential commission was gearing up to investigate the tragedy, NASA's inspector general investigated charges that top dogs at rocket engine manufacturer Morton Thiokol were demoting engineers such as Allan McDonald who opposed launching *Challenger* in near-freezing temperatures. Morton Thiokol employees and executives also accused NASA officials of pressuring them into okaying the launch of *Challenger* despite the problems the cold weather was causing. At least one NASA official, Stanley Reinartz, was evidently caught falsely or incorrectly claiming that McDonald didn't try to talk NASA and Morton Thiokol officials out of launching *Challenger*.

It eventually became suspected that a pressure seal failure on one of the rocket motors led to the destruction of *Challenger* and the deaths of six astronauts and teacher Christa McAuliffe.

While the other presidential commissioners, NASA officials, and Morton Thiokol officials sparred over theory, scientist Richard Feynman dropped a suspect seal into a glass of ice water, let it sit several minutes, then removed it. He noted the seal wouldn't return to its normal shape like it was supposed to do when he pulled it out of shape. Feynman's low-tech experiment and his humorous explanation for it amused the onlookers at the hearing and led to the eventual finding that the seal did fail due to the cold weather launch.

But it would be about the only moment of levity for the whole affair. It was revealed that NASA officials and Morton Thiokol officials knew about the problems a seal failure would cause, but made no effort to design a backup to prevent a seal failure from endangering the crew members. It also came out that there was no way for the astronauts to make their capsule escape from a rocket engine explosion or similar catastrophe.

It also became known that NASA's overambitious shuttle launch schedule had led to large amounts of worker overtime, worker fatigue on the job, and major mishaps which caused shuttles damage in 1985. Three weeks before the *Challenger* tragedy, fatigue probably caused one overworked operator to accidentally dump so much liquid oxygen from the shuttle *Columbia* during countdown that the launch had to be scrubbed 31 seconds before liftoff. His mistake cooled the engine so greatly that it probably wouldn't have had the thrust to put the shuttle into its proper orbit.

NASA's low-ball approach, NASA officials' apparent sensitivity to criticism from journalists over launch delays, NASA officials' apparent pressure on Morton Thiokol, and Morton Thiokol officials' apparent desire to keep profits from the space shuttle program as high as possible all played their parts in causing the *Challenger* tragedy. Feynman and the other presidential commissioners found NASA and Morton Thiokol were both at fault for the *Challenger* disaster. As Feynman later put it, NASA and Morton

Thiokol officials' decision-making was "a kind of Russian roulette" in which they lowered safety standards because previous launches succeeded despite safety problems.

THE FINAL ACCOUNTING

The *Challenger* disaster was funded with government money. Your tax money, spent improperly, led to the deaths of seven brave people and the loss of a multimillion dollar spacecraft. It's YOUR money the politicians, the bureaucrats, and the special-interest group people are talking about when they refer to "government funds" or "government resources" or "government revenues." As long as they're taking it from you, you might as well make sure they're spending it wisely.

END NOTES

1. Information on the Wedtech scandal comes from Marilyn Thompson's book *Feeding The Beast*.
2. Information on the group whose dissidents sued their own trustees for reportedly misusing grant money comes from Case A8500586 in Hamilton County (Cincinnati), Ohio Common Pleas court.
3. Information on the NEA's grants for the Mapplethorpe and Serrano outrages comes from an article in the July 3, 1989 issue of *Time*. Information on Dennis Barrie's obscenity pandering trial comes from an article in the October 8, 1990 issue of *Time*.
4. My articles on the PIK farm program appeared in issues of the Whitley County (Kentucky) *Republican* on March 24, 1983, and on June 16, 1983.
5. Information on the *Challenger* tragedy came from a March 10, 1986 article in *Newsweek*, a May 19, 1986 article in *Aviation Week* and Richard Lewis' book *Challenger—The Final Voyage*.

Public Health And Safety

Flunk Failing Educators

Years and years ago, teachers were respected in society, but were grossly underpaid for their efforts. Many of America's brightest women were teachers because businessmen wouldn't hire them for the professional positions. And school board members tended not to allow women to run school systems, either. In fact, until a generation or so ago, about the only women who were even running major enterprises like school systems or hospitals or colleges or charitable organizations on a regular basis were Catholic nuns!

Times changed. As more opportunities opened up for women, the best and the brightest of them stopped going into the teaching profession. Nowadays, most teachers make decent to good money, but they don't seem to get the job done in the classroom. It doesn't take an Einstein to see that too many public school systems today (with the help of parental neglect) are dumping functional illiterates on society. There are still many dedicated professionals in our nation's schools today. But they seem to be outnumbered by the misfits, losers, and pension-seekers.

One time a woman who was a public school teacher complained to me that the garbagemen in our area made two-thirds as much money as an entry-level teacher. I replied that our area's garbagemen were picking up the trash like they were supposed to do, so they were earning their pay. But since our area's kids were among the dumbest in the state, as far as state testing scores showed, I said it proved the teachers in our area weren't worth the money our taxpayers were paying them. Needless to say, the schoolmarm wasn't thrilled with my analysis.

In this chapter, I'll show you how to use public records to grade your local school's teacher performance, check on your school district's finances, and derail its social engineers. I'll also show you a thing or two on how to check how college staffers use grant money and how some profs cheat the students out of some of their education with substandard teaching skills and "politically correct" fascist thought control methods. And I'll show you how to check on student loan deadbeats.

GRADING SCHOOL PERFORMANCE

The mission of grade school and high school teachers and administrators is to turn out reasonably educated young people who can function in college, the Armed Services, or in trades. In other words, the interests of children and teens must come before the interests of the public education bureaucracy. However, too many educators seem to have forgotten this.

In fact, public school teachers have been doing so poor a job in recent years, they have had to lie massively nationwide to try to cover up their failures. In 1987, members of the citizens' watchdog group Friends for Education surveyed 3500 school districts around the country and filed for test averages in the 32 states which at the time conducted statewide student basic skills testing. They found that 82 percent of all school districts released figures claiming their pupils scored above-average in basic skills testing. They also found that education officials in all 32 states which used student basic skills testing reported their students scored above-average scores. They further noted some of the states which rank at the bottom nationwide in high school graduation rates and college entrance exam results were among the 32 states with allegedly above-average public schools.

When the Friends for Education folks saw these figures, they knew something was rotten in Denmark. All 32 states surveyed reported above-average scores? Four-fifths of all school districts surveyed reported above-average scores? How could this be, when someone HAS to finish below average? Common sense and basic math told them that either the remaining school districts and 18 states had schools full of kids so stupid that their idiocy could balance these other students, or that the school officials were lying.

After doing a little more digging, the Friends for Education people found out the public school officials were comparing their kids to a group of hand-picked dummies who took the basic skills test almost a decade earlier. They were not comparing their kids to other kids at the same grade levels in other states. Dr. John Jacob Cannell, the West Virginia physician who founded Friends for Education, then issued a report in late 1987 which blasted public school officials for misleading the public and for "teaching to the test" (prepping kids to get politically acceptable scores on the basic skills exams without really boosting their learning). Dr. Cannell got effective publicity for his efforts; Associated Press ran a lengthy story on his report in November 1987.

In a similar scam, California public schools superintendent Bill Honig admitted in 1988 that educators at 38 public elementary schools in his state monkeyed with test papers for the state's basic skills test. What a rotten message his employees sent: Those who can, do; those who can't, teach; those who can't teach, cheat!

The Friends for Education people performed a major public service. Not only did they expose public school officials as liars, but they reminded people across the country that school basic skills tests are public records. As their research indicated, most states' officials now make students take basic skills tests in elementary school, junior high school, and high school so they can see just how ignorant the kids in their schools really are.

While an individual child's test score on such a test is private information, the school averages on these tests are public records. If you want an indicator of how good or bad your kids' school really is, file for the school's achievement test averages at your local school system central office, or with your state education department in your state capital. Also, try to get your state's basic skills test averages so you can see how your kids' school stacks up against other schools in the state.

Another gauge of teacher performance at your local high school is student performance on the SAT or ACT college entrance tests. Once again, while an individual child's test score is private information, the school averages on these tests are public record. If you want an indicator of how good or bad your kids' high school is, file for the high school's SAT or ACT test averages at your local school system central office, or with your state education department in your state capital. Also try to get the state and national achievement test averages so you can see how your school stacks up against other schools in your state and across the nation. The College Board, a New York City-based association of colleges that sponsors admissions exams and other college placement affairs, has these scores if you get stonewalled by your local or state education officials.

Yet another gauge of teacher performance is union apprenticeship program entrance testing. The union chiefs may or may not release these scores to you. After all, they are not the government, so they don't have to. But many apprenticeship program administrators will level with you about just how ignorant the incoming high school graduates really are. After all, the union men have nothing to gain by lying about the problem. You can contact these men by calling local unions, and asking for the phone numbers of the apprenticeship program administrators.

There is another test in wide use at high schools around the country that federal officials say is a very good indicator of youths' intelligence and schooling. The test is called the Armed Services Vocational Aptitude Battery (ASVAB); it checks students' verbal, math, and thinking skills, and their aptitudes for a number of electrical and mechanical trades. The U.S. Department of Defense pays for it, and its people give it to high school students who volunteer to take it at their high schools.

The armed services administer the ASVAB to high-schoolers to gain access to potential recruits. The payoff for school officials is that the armed services provide them with test information, and they are able to use the data to assess their students' general abilities and occupational training. You may be able to get statistics on this test from your local school district office. It will probably be harder to get it from the Pentagon unless you file a Freedom of Information request for information or ask your congressman to get it for you. Pentagon paranoids do not routinely release information on the ASVAB, even though it is not classified, and is paid for by the taxpayers.

Then there are school accreditation inspections. Accreditation inspectors come around every so often to check on each school. Ugly rumor has it that officials in the wealthier school districts put on well-orchestrated dog-and-pony shows for the inspectors, so they'll go easy on them and instead beat up on inner-city schools or beat up on the rural school districts which have small tax bases and few voters. The inspectors pass most schools, but they do write reports on the schools, and they do tell school officials where they need improvement. These reports should be available from your school district or the state education department.

There's another indicator of teacher expertise—the written communication skill of teachers. Check notes they send home; you'd be surprised how often these educators of your children can't put a coherent sentence together. I embarrassed the hell out of a high school teacher by running a photocopy of a writing sample of his along with an article I wrote on him. This man was also a freeholder (county commissioner) in the New Jersey county where I worked.

The freeloader (sorry, Freudian slip) was angry

when a clerk in his town dunned him for owing 62 cents on his sewer bill. The clerk later alleged he got town officials to lay her off. I reviewed the bill stub the freeholder sent back, and on it was written this nasty little note, "Keep the change—obviously the sewer utility need (sic) it more than I do. $1. (sic) cash enclosed (sic)" I ran a copy of the stub with my article on the incident, and I was told the teacher/freeholder bitched up a storm at my publisher over the article. He may have been sore his writing weakness became public knowledge.

PRACTICAL EXERCISE TIME

Now I'll tell you about how I flogged the public school system in this same New Jersey county over its performance. Bear in mind the records I used are open to you, the average citizen.

I started out by writing an article on the amount of money the state was spending on remedial education for college kids. By interviewing state school budget officials, I found out the taxpayers of New Jersey were shelling out millions of dollars each year so students could learn in the state college system the things they should have learned in high school. I checked the records for these programs at my county's community college to give it a local angle. The college's remedial program administrator implied her college was spending this money because the local high school educators hadn't been doing their jobs.

Meanwhile, I was doing some school budget stories which seemed to some like an attack on local school board members. All I was doing was telling people how much budget hikes and school bonds were going to cost residents, because the school board members weren't releasing these figures in a timely manner. But teachers and other irate supporters of the school board members called my editor and told him things like, "Your hillbilly reporter probably counted on his fingers and toes to come up with the figures, didn't he?" They said this about me because I'd just moved up from Appalachia, I hadn't changed the plates on my beat-up old Plymouth yet, and my accent is non-New Jersey.

I was angry these idiots had insulted me and my former readers in the hills. My response was swift. It was an article showing how poorly the county's public high school kids did on the SAT tests. I filed for the test results at the county school system central office, then got state and national averages from a woman with the College Board. The figures showed that the county's high school kids did worse on the SAT than the kids across America, and also did below-average work by New Jersey standards! I noted a lower per-

centage of kids in the county took the test than the national average; this made the results look even worse. Also, I wrote, virtually all our high school kids were whites, so the school administrators couldn't blame the poor showing of the kids on low-income blacks and Hispanics.

By now, I was told I was Public Enemy Number One to teachers, school officials, and high school boosters in the county. People were calling in and cursing me, and in reply I made fun of their intellect and parentage. I got into a number of confrontations at school board meetings, and more than once I had to physically back off my antagonists. A couple of honest school officials admitted they weren't doing a good enough job. But most officials who would make on-the-record statements said the kids choked or said the SAT test wasn't a valid measure of the school system's effectiveness. They said most kids didn't take the test because they were interested in going into trades. They didn't want to admit they were doing a poor job or imply the local voters' kids were all dummies.

You can guess what my next step was. I interviewed a number of union apprenticeship program administrators about the ability of kids coming out of our county. One told me, "They're so (expletive) dumb, they're lucky they can sign their own names!" Another one told me they had to lower the difficulty of the entrance tests to an eighth-grade or ninth-grade level. The comments of the other union men were similar. After this article ran, the negative phone calls slacked off some.

TEXTBOOK TROUBLES

Sometimes the teachers aren't totally to blame when your kids come home with bad info in their heads. Sometimes their textbooks are screwed up.

As this book goes to print, a national publication reported the Texas Board of Education approved the use of four new history books in state high schools—on the conditions the publishers fix close to 4000 errors reviewers found in the books and pay about $240,000 in fines for submitting the grossly flawed books.

People with a textbook watchdog group known as Educational Research Analysts reportedly caught most of the errors, the article's author noted. Some of the prize bits of misinformation they found in the books contained include the statements that Napoleon won the Battle of Waterloo, that we ended the Korean War by using nukes (I wish!), and that Abe Lincoln issued the Emancipation Proclamation in 1963 (the year JFK was murdered). After the books were re-examined in 1991 and certified as error-free, the reporter noted, reviewers found 162 new mistakes, including the statement that the Battle of Vicksburg was fought around "Vicksburg, Tennessee" (sic). (Vicksburg is in Mississippi.)

You can review books before your school board buys them. In fact, groups of parents have reviewed certain books and have pressured their school board members not to buy them. Don't hesitate to use your right to check these books for orientation and accuracy before your school officials use your money to put them in your kids' hands.

EXTRA CREDIT

I've run my mouth enough on the teacher competence topic for now. I'm going to share with you some tips an insider gives parents.

This "insider" is Krista Ramsey, a teacher who became a reporter and a syndicated columnist to boot. She made these recommendations in two 1989 columns:

- Compare your school's basic skills test results and college board test results with results from school districts of similar demographics in your county and state. For example, Beverly Hills schools might look good going head-to-head with schools in Watts, but they might not do as well going against schools in similar or even somewhat less affluent areas in California.

- Check test scores for patterns. Consistently poor math scores, she chose as an example, could indicate teaching weaknesses in math.

- Ask what percentage of students go on to college, need remedial classes in college, and earn a degree. "Be suspicious if the school doesn't know," she wrote. "All good businesses check to see how their product performs in the marketplace."

- Check failure rates. Check what measures the school officials use to try to educate failing kids.

- Find out if the school offers solid core courses and at least a few specialized courses.

- Walk through the school's facilities. Vandalism, cleanliness, type and condition of equipment, and discipline (or lack of it) you observe will tell you quite a bit about how the school is run.

- Find out how many teachers apply for jobs at the school and how long they stay there. "Teachers usually know the good schools," she wrote. "They apply there in large numbers. They stay there many years."

Krista Ramsey said you should get the information from the school district's staffers, the schools' principal, and the schools' teachers. She also noted, "Your

conversations with administrators and teachers will also show you how the school treats parents."

Nicely said. And for some of you out there, her gentle but firm voice was a little bit of a breather after listening to my foghorning.

BUDGET MATTERS SHOW TEACHERS CAN'T FIGURE

School officials waste money just like any other bureaucrats. And school officials are also just as quick to con the public about their finances as any other government officials.

When I was reporting in New Jersey, I wrote two articles in which I estimated what school board actions in two townships were going to cost taxpayers. Why? Because school board members in the two townships would not give me or anyone else in the public timely financial statements on what their actions would cost. In one township, I estimated a school bond would cost property owners an extra 11 to 16 cents per $100 of assessed property value for 20 years. In the other article, I estimated a school budget in another township was going to jump local taxpayers' property taxes by 50 cents per every $100 in assessed value if it passed.

Naturally, my figures generated controversy, even when I showed my calculations in the text of each article. After each article, teachers and other irate supporters of the school board members called my editor to complain about my math skills. They may have been right. Because when school board members in each township finally got around to releasing their figures, the taxpayers got even worse news than what I had first given them. In the first township, the school board members released a financial statement showing the bond would cost property tax owners 13 cents per $100 of assessed value for 25 years. In the second township, school board members released figures showing they wanted 57 cents per $100 in assessed value more that year from each property owner!

In another incident, school officials and state tax officials screwed up in figuring property tax rates when they put a levy on the ballot for the Cincinnati public school system in 1987. The officials figured they'd need to get the voters to approve a nine-mill property tax increase to bring in the extra money they wanted. The voters approved the measure in 1987, and the school officials in the next six months raked in $2.5 million more than they figured they'd get. It turned out a seven-mill increase would have been high enough to raise the money the Cincinnati school board members said they wanted, so the board members had to return the money to the taxpayers.

No wonder your kids are having problems with math. The *educators* can't figure, either!

You can be your own financial analyst on local school spending measures. All you need to know is the amount of a bond or a budget, then figure in any interest, then divide by the number of years the bond or budget will be in effect. Once you calculate this figure, divide it by the total amount of ratables (assessed property values) in your school district. (Local school officials and/or county tax officials should have this information; it's a public record.) The figure you come up with will be the amount of property tax per dollar of assessed property value the spending measure will add to your property tax each year. If the good the school spending issue will accomplish is worth the increase in property taxes you as a homeowner will be stuck with (and you as a renter will pick up when your landlord jumps your rent), then vote for it. If not, shoot it down come election time.

If you want to figure how much money the taxpayers are spending on your state's public school system, talk with your state education department's financial officers. They are located in your state capital, and they can give you figures on federal, state, and local money going into education. They can also give you specific dollar figures for a lot of state education items.

A FEW WORDS ON CLASS SIZES AND TEACHING METHODS

Teachers and administrators moan about class sizes as if handling 25 to 30 kids is a job tougher than brain surgery. I went through eight grades of a working-class Catholic elementary school, my smallest class had 47 kids in it, and we came out of the school with more learning than our public school friends. So I don't necessarily buy that line.

And today's figures indicate my own experiences weren't lost in The Good Old Days. A special feature in a national publication noted Catholic schools spend only about half as much per student as do public schools, yet their students complete high school and go on to college at much higher rates. Why? Because, the publication noted, the Catholic school's educators still stress moral values, discipline, tough no-frills courses, and parental involvement. And roughly one in four Catholic school students is either black or Hispanic (and almost all the other kids have ethnic European or Filipino backgrounds), so the lower expectations many have for non-WASPs doesn't hold water, either.

A friend of mine who's a school board member in a California town doesn't buy the class size argument, either. He routinely taught large classes in a rural school district and claims he didn't pass on any functional illiterates, so I'll take him at his word. As a school board member, he headed off a teachers' strike *AND* made them do more work at the same time with this little gem of an offer—let us increase average class size from 24 to 30 kids, and you'll get a good pay raise. All of a sudden, the teachers in his district stopped whining about their work loads and took the deal. He either proved the class size issue is a red herring or that teachers will put their pocketbooks ahead of their kids. I hope for the kids' sake the first of the two is correct!

Speaking of kids' welfare, an ugly story out of Texas aired on national TV in 1991 to show just how little some school system administrators and teachers really care about kids. Thaddeus Lott, the black principal of an elementary school in a poor black section of Houston, runs an old-fashioned kind of school. Lott actually believes in disciplining kids. Lott also has thrown out the Houston school district's curriculum; he makes his school's kids drill in phonics, take part in group recitation, repeat math "times tables", get grades daily, and do other kinds of things that went out of style a generation or so ago (before so many schools went into the crapper). His kindergartners know the names of all 50 states from memory, his first-graders are doing third-grade arithmetic, and his fifth-graders are reading novels most kids don't see until high school.

The poor kids at Lott's Wesley School test in the top quarter of Texas elementary schools. They also do work up to two years ahead of their grade level. But Houston school officials attacked Lott and accused his teachers of cheating for the school's scores to be so good. The reporters interviewed a first-grade teacher at Wesley School, and told viewers two officials from the Houston school district walked into her classroom, accused her of feeding test answers to pupils, and rifled through her classroom for hours.

"I was in tears because I was upset," said India Williams, the pleasant, attractive black woman whose classroom was evidently invaded by Houston school system goons. The woman who runs the Houston teachers' union charged the district's officials were after Lott and his teachers. She termed the school district officials' behavior as "racism of the worst kind. It's a racism of lowering your expectations for minority students."

The reporters contacted Houston school superintendent Joan Raymond for a response. Ms. Raymond—looking like a cornered she-weasel— claimed the school system's officials weren't trying to undermine Lott and his teachers and kids. The reporters countered with evidence Lott's school got cut out of a lot of funding. They also said out-of-town educators visit Lott's school often for ideas, but Houston school system officials never asked Lott to train teachers. She had no convincing response to these charges. Ms. Raymond was forced to resign, they said, but over matters other than her henchmen's treatment of Lott's school.

This story may have been news to the public, but Lott, the kids' parents, and his supporters in the community knew about it for a while. They all used publicly available records to make their case.

DERAILING THE SOCIAL ENGINEERS

A lot of educators are heavily involved in running worthless social programs in schools across the country. Sometimes they forget to stick to the basics, like providing a safe environment for kids to learn in, and actually *TEACHING* the kids the basics which will help them in adult life.

Two fairly controversial social programs made it into the school systems in Los Angeles and New York City in recent years without the school board members ever voting publicly on them. L.A. school board members used a committee approval to spring the notorious "Project 10" homosexual advocacy program on students. They deputized a lesbian counselor to talk to high school kids around the city during school hours about homosexuals in a positive manner. They did not make their decision public for four years. Their scheme was uncovered only because parents and students at heavily black and Hispanic San Fernando High School made enough of a stink about the lesbian counselor's visit to the high school that they forced public disclosure of the program in the process.

And in the Big Apple, a newspaper reporter in 1986 revealed that state-funded teen sex clinics had been operating in nine high schools for up to two years without the approval or knowledge of the city's school board members. Nonwhite school officials, noting that all of the clinics were in schools with large numbers of minority students, wondered aloud why minority girls were being targeted for population control.

If your local school system is in the clutches of some screwball social experimenters, detoxify them by denying them their money fix and voting against school system measures. But to get people to join you, you'll have to dig up and present enough dirt on these social programs to get their attention. Here's how to do it:

Go into the school system's central office and ask to see the school system's minutes, budget, and financial records. These are all public record. Pore over these records to see exactly how your school board members and administrators are using your money. If you find they're funding a program you think the kids can do just fine without, make copies of documents showing who voted for the program, and how much the school system is spending on the program. Also, ask for all documents which outline what the goals and methods of the program are. And then go public with your findings.

If school-based sex clinics concern you, for example, demand a copy of the clinic's program and budget from the school. See how much money it will soak up and what the staffers intend to do with the money. See what worthy education programs will be scrapped or short-changed because of its presence in the budget. See if the regular school nurses will be fired to make room for the clinic staffers. See how the school board members intend to handle malpractice lawsuits in case teen girls get AIDS, VD, or female organ damage from botched abortions resulting from staffers' referrals. After all, the money a school system loses over such lawsuits is money taken away from legitimate school purposes.

But don't stop there. Research the backgrounds of the people who are supposed to run and staff the sex clinics. You may find everything from lesbian activists to workers without valid nurse licenses to child-exploiting felons are involved. You can also find out if any local abortion provider is supporting the high school sex clinics, if he's donating money to the schools, and if any of the staffers have ties to him. If you find evidence of any of these, the abortion provider could be paying kickbacks for steering pregnant girls to him.

And then go public with your findings. Let parents know they are paying taxes to support some nutcase program at a time when the school board members and the teachers' union are moaning about tight budgets. Suggest publicly that if the school officials have enough money to distribute condoms to high-schoolers, for example, then they surely don't need to inflate their budget with another school levy.

What if a single teacher with a bad attitude and a personal agenda is the problem? Sometimes a friendly talk with the teacher can square her away. However, some teachers aren't willing to respond to reason. To crack these nuts, you'll have to do your homework on them. Get your kid to bring home the teacher's reading list, then check the readings to see what percentage of the books or articles push a certain viewpoint. If the teacher doesn't show any diversity in this area, she has done you a favor by documenting her own biases. If the teacher is the sort who tries to put down kids whose families' values irk her in any way, you can probably convince these kids' parents to get their kids to testify about her thought fascism.

Check the public files for the teacher's criminal and civil record, and for other negative information on her. Check the curriculum vitae she filed with the school board members when they hired her; it will say where she went to school and where she taught before she came to your area. As needed, check with officials who knew her from these periods in her life. Organize other parents when you've got her unmentionables in your hands. Then expose her before your school board members, let them know about parental concerns about her, remind them of your kids' First Amendment rights, and suggest they take personnel actions against her for her wrongdoing.

I've got one bit of advice for you when you deal with the keepers of school records. Many of these people are not used to seeing parents in their office demanding to look through school records. They will try to treat you like unruly students who need discipline. Your response will be to treat them like you'd treat a pimple-faced geek who's messed up your order at the local fast food place. Explain the facts of life to them. If you need to, talk to their supervisors about their performance, and let the superintendent know he and his clerks are YOUR servants, not the other way around.

COLLEGE DIRT-DIGGING 101

Most people, when college scandals are mentioned, think of athletic department scandals. They think of how Barry Switzer forgot to tell his Oklahoma Sooner football players not to rape women, shoot people, or peddle cocaine. They think of *Ripley's Believe It Or Not* producers considering sending a camera crew to Southern Cal to show Trojan athletes actually attending class and not sniffing up the chalk lines on the practice fields. They think of UCLA boosters buying Bruin basketball players everything from cars to abortions for girlfriends. They think of Southern Methodist and the "death penalty", Florida and the crooked coaches, Kentucky and cash payments to recruits, and a president at Ohio State who got caught trying to book a quiet getaway to England with a woman who raised money for the school after it was whispered he fired a coach for the "sin" of playing the ponies.

Since I root for Notre Dame, I don't have to worry about how the Irish conduct themselves on the field of combat, in the classroom, or around town. I also

don't mind having my ethnic group—the Irish—associated with a bunch of toughs who can pound any opponent in the country into dogmeat on any given Saturday. I view Notre Dame's team name as a tribute to the toughness of my ancestors. I don't associate college scandals with athletics scandals or with the frat punks abusing one of their pledges, either. I associate college scandals with the kinds of misbehavior other public figures engage in, like theft, for starters.

The 1991 price-fixing scandal in the Ivy League, for example, shows what I mean. The U.S. Justice Department filed antitrust charges against all of the colleges in this pompous bunch and put enough leverage on the elitist colleges' officials to get them to agree to a judgment forbidding further price-fixing. The Ivies' professors may quote Marx, but their administrators act like robber barons. And the punks on campus were evidently too busy protesting against American foreign policy to see their own school officials were playing their mommies and daddies for suckers.

STUDYING RESEARCH FRAUD

You can investigate colleges in several areas. One that comes to mind immediately is research fraud. Research fraud can entail cheating the public by over-billing the government on tax-supported research. It can also involve allowing bogus research to gain legitimate status.

In 1991, federal agents of the U.S. General Accounting Office evidently caught Stanford University's officials trying to cheat the taxpayers out of millions of dollars through a government research program billing scam. The federal agents said they caught Stanford officials billing everything from depreciation on a yacht to worker salaries at a college-owned shopping center to silverware at the college president's residence as expenses for government research programs. And for sheer gall, Stanford officials take a back seat to no one. They have reportedly been pressuring the Feds to fire the auditor who caught them reportedly cheating the taxpayers!

A few years ago, some of Stanford's students and profs thought it was politically incorrect to have an Indian mascot, so they got the teams renamed the *Cardinal*—after a school color, not after any clergyman. In light of this recent scandal, and in light of the fact that the school was founded by robber baron Leland Stanford, it ought to have a white-collar criminal as a mascot!

If you want to see how your target college uses research money, ask the college's public information people to give you a list of all government-sponsored research programs and other projects the college is involved in. The college staffers should give you the list, or at least inform you of which government agencies the school is taking money from.

If the college officials get uppity with you, use the info in the chapter on contracts and grants to check on contracts the college might hold with the U.S. Departments of Defense, Health and Human Services, Education, and Agriculture, for starters. Other federal and state agencies pay for college research, too, but these agencies are the biggies. These agencies' agents can make available to you information on research program contracts their people have let to colleges. Later on, you can accuse the college officials of Nixonian stonewalling.

Since government research programs involve government contracts, each program's financial paperwork is public record, too. You are entitled to see the proposal or protocol (a document spelling out the goals of a project and the kinds of tests or experiments involved). You are entitled to see the paperwork which shows what the college billed the government for. Depending on the type of project, a lot of the research results are public record, too, except for personal privacy matters, proprietary information, and national security information. You can gain access to these through the college's own publicist, or through the freedom of information officer or the contracts administrator of the government agency paying for the research.

For evidence of money waste and fraud, check the paperwork and see how the college officials spent the money the government agents gave their school. See if they wrongfully billed the taxpayer for non-project goods and services. Check to see how closely the college people stuck to the research protocol and the terms of the contract. See if you can spot any evidence of laziness, like five people doing the work of one.

Digging into government grant irregularities at colleges is similar to checking contract irregularities. Since government grants are public record, the financial paperwork, proposal or protocol, and other paperwork related to the grant are available to you. Check with college officials to see what kinds of grants they're getting. Again, if they stonewall you, contact the grants administrators of major federal and state agencies to see the grant paperwork so you can see how much grant money they're throwing at the college, and why.

College officials have certain rules to follow in using government grant money. Namely, they have to do the research or put on the fine-arts programs the money is meant to support. Once you have the grant paperwork, check it to determine whether the college people are using the grant money according to the rules of the grant. For further pointers, check the chapter on contracts and grants.

As bad as regular money fraud can be, bogus research fraud is a more sinister kind of fraud. Sometimes researchers commit research fraud to enhance their reputations and careers. Sometimes researchers commit research fraud to attract more money to their labs and keep their jobs. Either way, this kind of fraud is harmful. It can lead scientists and medical people to harm people unknowingly because they relied on faked lab work or bad research of others. And even at less critical levels, it can cause legitimate researchers to waste time and money by building their work on bad research, or it can cause them *NOT* to check an area because its false conclusions steer them away from the area.

No school is really safe. Even Massachusetts Institute of Technology had such a scandal recently. Margot O'Toole, a young Irish-born medical researcher, blew the whistle on her supervisor at this school for faking medical research. The supervisor and another doctor, a Nobel prize winner named David Baltimore, co-published a research paper on the body's immune system based on the phony work. Ms. O'Toole told Baltimore about the bad work her supervisor did, and she said the conclusions weren't supported by lab notes, but he ignored her. She then lost her job for being honest. Eventually, congressmen and federal agents investigated Ms. O'Toole's allegations, and they found she was telling the truth. The supervisor, Dr. Thereza Imanishi-Kari, was exposed as a fraud. Dr. Baltimore had to admit he was wrong.

For evidence of bogus research fraud, see if you find reported results that are radically different than the established body of knowledge on the subject. Then check the results against the reported testing that the results are supposedly based on for problems. Another indicator of possible research fraud is bizarre productivity reported. For example, if you see a document where a scientist reports he performed 600 large animal dissections over two days, question his figures.

If you aren't knowledgeable in the field the research involves, get a friend or prof who *DOES* know about the field to check the data, any calculations and conclusions, and the report for problems. Check to see how closely the college researchers stuck to the research protocol. Check the paperwork for evidence of submission of an article on the project to a science journal or in some other publication. Then check the publication in question for evidence other scientists question the validity of the project.

AND NOW, A LAB EXERCISE

It's said honey attracts more flies than vinegar. Keep this in mind if you want to con college officials into telling you what they are up to.

Colleges, like bimbos, brag about how well-endowed they are. If college officials think you're a gifted student who might enroll, or a businessman who might donate, they'll tell you all about what a great research institution they're running. Flirt with them or tomcat with them a little. Con them into telling you how well-endowed they are, and how much more gold they'll be digging from contributors, private foundations, and government sugar daddies. Press them for documents proving their involvement in government and private industry research projects. You may want to trap them into overstating their abilities; it's false advertising for them to claim their college is involved in certain types of research to lure students and/or money if it is *NOT* involved in the research. Or you may want the college officials to confirm their participation in a research program you oppose, like animal testing or fetal experimentation, for example.

My cousin Elaine, a charming and lovely young lady who is an animal-rights activist, wanted to check if her local college was involved in animal testing. When she asked me for help, I faced a moral dilemma; I favor animal testing because it's saved many, many human lives. Also, as a hardened carnivore, I have eaten the usual beef, pork, poultry, and fish. And I've also eaten the flesh of dogs, cats, raccoons, rats, gators, snakes, eels, octopuses, squids, lizards, and bugs. And one time I made a hand puppet of the piglet I dissected in biology lab to gross out some of the coeds in the class. So I have no problem with knocking off a few animals in the name of science or nutrition!

But my cousin wanted to do some dirt digging on the college, and I felt a little hypocrisy on my part just this once wouldn't hurt anything. So I told her to contact the school's chemistry and biology departments, the school's financial officers, and the school's PR people to find out a little about the noble work for mankind they were doing. I told her to get project names and project paperwork from the college and the government agencies and private groups funding the research. I suggested she look at the school's records to see if certain medical, pharmaceutical, or cosmetic companies were donating money to the school, and for what purpose. At this writing, Elaine is doing her digging. The next ugly exposé of animal abuse might be the result of her work!

LAB DANCE

Sometimes bimbos do more than just talk about their assets. They let others rent them for a while. They thus cross the line from bimbohood to whoredom.

Colleges sometimes cross this line, too. Certain groups will fund research that tends to prove their point or bolster their business. For example, a tobacco company might need research "proving" smoking isn't necessarily harmful to people's health. Or a homosexual group might need research "proving" their sexual habits aren't responsible for their high risk of contracting AIDS.

The groups which fund such dubious projects are of course buying the college people like prostitutes, and the college people know it. But they think, "Oh, what a feeling," and work hard for the money. After all, a fat cat's contributions can keep people on staff until money for legitimate projects comes along.

You can contact the college's publicist to find out which companies and groups are sponsoring research at the school. Then find out what the research is about by talking with the publicist, the college researchers doing the work, or the sponsors' PR people. If you approach them as a writer, or maybe as another researcher who's legitimately interested in the work, you may get them to send you proof of funding and proof of what's being researched.

If the school is a state school, the contracts or donations should be public record. (A private college's listing of private contracts and donations probably won't be public record in your state.) Also, some colleges, or the research portions of them, might be set up as nonprofit corporations. Follow the instructions in the portion of this book on nonprofit corporations to file for tax records; these records often contain names of donors and research contracts as income sources.

Since college people like to pretend they're above rooting for money, your releasing proof that some of them are *NOT* above it will motivate others on the campus to make trouble for the rooters. Further, some of the college's donors might not like the lab people's corporate and pressure group johns. And some government agents will attack collegians whose research deliberately leads to tainted results, especially if these results eventually harm the innocent.

GRADING COLLEGES ON QUALITY OF EDUCATION

When you attack college officials on the quality of

education their institution provides, they can go hyper in a hurry. These eggheads may be spineless on a number of issues, but when you attack their competence, you'll hit a nerve. They'll squirm like worms on a hot pavement.

Actually, it's not too hard to see what kind of an education they are providing. You can check with industry people to get a feel for the quality of people a college graduates. You can check some colleges' figures on how many of their graduates got hired into certain fields. Industry personnel officers and employment search firms should also have such data.

You can also check directly on the credentials of instructors. Colleges publish catalogs, and the catalogs list the credentials of the profs. It will take a few phone calls to find out what other colleges' officials know about profs in the years before they came to teach at your target college. You can also check any of a number of *Who's Who* reference books on certain types of profs, and see what the book's authors say about your target prof.

I once got stuck with a lousy prof for a nighttime organic chemistry class. She was hopeless as a teacher. She contradicted the book, made errors in presenting material, and was very disorganized in her lectures. I obtained class notes from an excellent chemistry prof who taught me at a nearby technical college, and at my own expense I copied her excellent class notes for my classmates. The lousy prof was highly upset by this move, because she felt I was openly criticizing her ability by doing it. So when she attacked me in class, I shot her out of the water. The upshot of it all was she tried to have me suspended, and I demanded my money back from the school for her failure to educate.

I filed charges against the teacher, and she filed charges against me. At a hearing, which I taped, the department head and some other egghead professor told me I misunderstood the role of chemistry at a liberal arts college. They were more into chemistry as an ethereal theoretical learning experience (like, heavy, man) than they were into trying to teach it to me and the other students so we could perform in industry and medicine. I told the two what I thought of their out-of-touch view of the needs of students and the workplace, assassinated what was left of my prof's character by getting her to agree with me on the mistakes she made in class, and left.

I told officials at the college (a public university in southwest Ohio) their chemistry program wasn't designed to help students for the real world, and I had them refund me my money. Later on, I let the trustees

of the college know about their prof and their chemistry program. I met with one of the trustees, and at this writing she told me she took my charges seriously and she was forcing an investigation on the matter.

My episode brings up a common problem for night school students. They work during the day, and the taxes on their labors helps pay for the college. But the college offers very few night courses, and the ones they do offer are staffed by too many rookies because too many tenured profs don't want to teach at night. So the working night school student pays tuition and taxes to subsidize a substandard form of education for himself or herself. To find proof of this rip-off, simply check the credentials of the day profs and the credentials of the night profs in the college's own catalog. Contact the night profs' former schools to see if they had any problems there. And check professional societies and state professional certification agencies to see if there's any bad word or bad paper on them.

COLLEGE THOUGHT FASCISM IS POLITICALLY CORRECT

Another college quality of education issue, "politically correct thinking," has become a public controversy recently. "Politically correct thinking" on campuses, of course, involves embracing things like feminism, loony leftism, and homosexuality, and discriminating against religion, America, and normality. Students and professors who object to the ravings of these thought control freaks can suffer damage to grades and careers.

Since "politically correct thinking" is as close to institutional fascism as America has, maybe I should have stuck it in with the section on crime, because its practitioners willfully violate the civil rights of others. However, it's a quality of education issue, too. Why? Because if a college allows a bunch of these losers (who probably couldn't cut it in the real world) to dictate curriculum, they cut off a large amount of learning students should have, and fatally slant other parts of the learning. This leaves students with a poor-quality education.

To document evidence of "politically correct thinking," check the backgrounds of the professors and department heads at a college. Do this just like you would for profs who teach night school. Check their schooling, their previous jobs, their published works, and their related activities. Check their reading lists for evidence of one-sided coverage of issues. Tape their lectures. If the school is a state institution, you might be able to bring this evidence to a friendly legislator (or major donors) for action.

You might also be able to find out the infected department benefits from government grants. You may be able to get government agents to cancel these grants if you can document evidence of discrimination and obvious slanting of curriculum in violation of civil rights laws, First Amendment laws and other such laws. If the school is a private institution, you might be able to use many of the same tactics, especially with the school's big-bucks donors and alumni. Either way, you might get someone with enough pull to pull the plug on the thought police.

MARKING THE MOOCHERS

Not all campus wrongdoing is the fault of faculty and staff. Students who commit crimes like rape or theft or pledge abuse at school, and those who act like "politically correct" goons in disrupting the rights of others are certainly swine. But this section concentrates on student leeches who obtain a college education, then don't pay their loans back. Sometimes they even fraudulently use money made available for education to buy sports cars and other luxuries.

Eventually the public pays for this dishonesty, so the perpetrators are basically thieves. A particularly galling point about college loan abusers is that they are able to make more money than the average worker because of their educations, but these selfish jerks don't repay the money that made their financial betterment possible. This leaves less money for others to better their lots.

The college's financial people can release the names of students who default on student loans, but they usually don't. If they file civil lawsuits to collect the money, however, then the lawsuits are public records. Defaults on student loans which the U.S. Department of Education has guaranteed can become public record. This is because the government has to collect loan money which it has backed with the money of the taxpaying public. However, the thought within this agency is that they can't give out the names of students who default on student loans.

But any Freedom of Information Act challenge you filed would probably crumble their position. Why? Because the Feds report loan defaults to collection agencies, which make money in collecting loans. They also report loan defaults to commercial credit bureaus, which provide the information to others for money. So the Feds *ARE* releasing the dirt to those who, unlike you, want the info so they can make money! Why should the education bureaucrats discriminate against clean people like you?

Also, lawsuits to collect money from student deadbeats are public records in the courts in which they are filed. And people who are delinquent about paying off property taxes or business-related taxes get negative publicity in local tax records. Student moochers should get the same treatment.

For those of you who say, "So what if a target welshes on a student loan? Lots of people do it. Making it public won't cause the target much trouble," I'll reply with this thought: People need to have good reputations to find and hold jobs, borrow money, and do a lot of things that require a clean record. Showing your target is a deadbeat will hurt him or her somewhere down the line!

To show you what I mean, I'll tell you about a case I knew of when I worked in Kentucky. It was revealed that Grady Stumbo, a public official and a doctor who was running for governor in Kentucky in 1983 as the "white horse" candidate, owed money for an unpaid student loan. The money he borrowed—and didn't repay—made it possible for him to become a doctor and an important political figure. Although Stumbo repaid the loan soon after he was publicly exposed as a deadbeat, the damage was done. He lost the primary election, and Martha Layne Collins went on to govern the Bluegrass State instead.

VALEDICTORIAN TALK

America needs healthy schools for its continued survival and success. Those of us who care about our children and our country need to hold educators accountable for the performance of the school systems. Abraham Lincoln—a man with almost no formal education—still realized the importance of schools and the importance of making them responsive to the needs of society. Honest Abe went along with getting state colleges jump-started with federal money, but he made sure they would research agriculture; the farmers of this nation have been the most productive on earth ever since. Mr. Lincoln was a believer and practicer of the idea that if government officials are going to take people's money, they ought to see the people get a return on it.

There are still some good folks in the education field, and they need your support. And all educators, like parents, need to be reminded of their purpose in life—to train the young so they can perform adequately in life.

END NOTES

1. Information on the Friends for Education exposé of basic skills test result inflation comes from an AP article which appeared in the Columbus *Dispatch* November 27, 1987.
2. Information on California teachers who tampered with basic skills test scores comes from a San Francisco *Chronicle* article that was quoted in an article that appeared in the

Cincinnati *Enquirer* September 1, 1988.

3. Information on the incident involving a freeholder/teacher who made a number of mistakes in writing an insulting note to a local utility comes from my article in the Ocean County (New Jersey) *Observer* on December 31, 1986.

4. The articles I wrote on the New Jersey schools' performances appeared in the Ocean County *Observer* from December 1986 through March 1987.

5. Information on the flawed Texas textbooks comes from an article in the January 27, 1992 issue of *U.S. News*.

6. Krista Ramsey's columns appeared in the Cincinnati *Enquirer* on February 20, 1989, and February 27, 1989.

7. The articles I wrote on New Jersey school bonds appeared in the Ocean County *Observer* from January 1987 through March 1987.

8. Information on the Cincinnati public school tax levy rate screwup comes from an article in the Cincinnati *Enquirer* on May 10, 1988.

9. Statistics on Catholic schools' performances relative to the public schools comes from an article in the December 9, 1991 issue of *U.S. News*.

10. Information on the Thaddeus Lott case comes from a transcript of the show *Prime Time Live*. The TV show segment, *"Readin', Writin', and Right,"* aired June 6, 1991.

11. Information on the Los Angeles school system's *Project 10* homosexual advocacy program comes from an article which appeared in the L.A. *Daily News* in June 1988.

12. Information on the New York City school system's teen sex clinics comes from a series of articles Jane Perlez wrote for the *New York Times* in October 1986.

13. My satirical remarks on college athletics at several schools are based on the following sources:

—Oklahoma Sooners: an article in the February 27, 1989 issue of *Newsweek*.

—Southern Cal Trojans: articles in the October 27, 1980 and May 16, 1982 issues of *Sports Illustrated*, and an article in the February 11, 1991 issue of *People*.

—UCLA Bruins: mention in Murray Sperber's book *College Sports, Inc.*

—Southern Methodist Mustangs: an article in the November 14, 1988 issue of *Time*.

—Florida Gators: an article in the October 30, 1990 issue of *Sports Illustrated*.

—Kentucky Wildcats: an article in the May 29, 1989 issue of *Sports Illustrated*.

—Ohio State Buckeyes: an article in the November 25, 1987 issue of the Columbus *Dispatch*.

14. Information on the Ivy League's price-fixing scandal comes from the case U.S.A. vs. Brown, Columbia, Cornell, Dartmouth, Harvard, Massachusetts Institute of Technology, Princeton, Pennsylvania, and Yale. The case, No. 91-CV-3274, was filed in U.S. District Court in Philadelphia May 22, 1991. That same day, according to a U.S. Department of Justice press release and the court record, the Ivies settled with Uncle Sam. (MIT, by the way, is not a member of the Ivy League, but the other eight schools are.)

15. Information on Stanford's research contract and grant money misappropriation scandal comes from the U.S. General Accounting Office report T-RECD-91-18. Info on Stanford officials' gall in trying to get fired the government auditor who evidently caught them comes from an article in *USA Today* September 20, 1991.

16. Information on the fraudulent medical research scandal at MIT comes from an article in the May 22-28 issue of *Irish Echo*. As a follow-up, an article in the 1991 year end edition of *U.S. News* noted MIT officials paid $27,000 to Washington lobbyists to try to keep Congressmen from investigating the fraud.

17. Information on Grady Stumbo's college loan deadbeatism comes from articles in the Lexington (Kentucky) *Herald Leader* on April 8, 1983 and September 4, 1983.

Bust Bad Cops and Shyster Prosecutors

Why make trouble for the guardians of public safety?

Some of my friends criticized me when I told them I would include in this book a chapter on how to check on policemen and prosecutors. After all, they argued, policemen and prosecutors are about the only government employees whose job it is to protect the public from criminals. "Remind THEM what their job is," I replied. "Too damn many of them have forgotten."

Policemen and prosecutors are government employees who can cause people the most trouble. And because of their abilities to cause trouble, they, more than any other groups of government employees, have to be accountable to the public.

Cops have powers of arrest that most people don't have, and they have the weaponry to back it up. Most people are conditioned to obey the police; even hardened thugs like Bugs Moran's gangsters put up their hands when Al Capone's mobsters, impersonating coppers, told them to do so on that infamous Valentine's Day many years ago. Capone's goons then machine-gunned Moran's men. (Jack McGurn, whom my Grandpa Charlie once arrested, was the man who masterminded the hits. McGurn, by the way, was shot to death in a bowling alley the day before Valentine's Day of 1936. One of the killers left a valentine card in his hand. I just thought you'd like to know.)

Prosecutors decide how criminal cases will be handled. Defendants' lives are in their hands, and since prosecutors are always lawyers and often politicians, justice can take a back seat to the prosecutor's personal interests when he decides how to handle a criminal case. Many guilty escape punishment and many innocent are coerced into plea-bargaining because of shyster prosecutors.

I really didn't want to write the police portion of this chapter when I sat down to write this book. Why? Because policemen have a dangerous and thankless enough job as it is trying to protect the rest of us from criminal vermin. Both of my grandpas were Chicago coppers who were wounded in the line of duty. (My Grandpa Leo once jumped a squad car over a rising drawbridge to collar a carload of criminals.) I myself served military police duty in Korea. Some of my friends are policemen. So why, I thought, should I help criminals and ACLU wanna-bes cause them more trouble?

I finally decided to show you how to go after bad cops after recalling how many of you suffer at their hands. Since the pay and the standards for policemen aren't what they need to be, the profession attracts a certain amount of bullies, Nazi-type authority freaks, and others who use a badge to hassle or exploit people. (Even good-paying forces attract some guys like these, but they're easier to exclude.) This means there's a hard core of scum in blue whose brutality, jerkism, and crookedness deserve uncovering and exposing. And those few of you who ARE scum in blue have forced me to make it harder for your brother policemen as well as for you.

On the other hand, I never had any trouble at all with writing about prosecutor abuses. Why? Because prosecutors are lawyers and politicians and bureaucrats first, and all too often are public servants in name only.

Prosecutors of America, too many of you view your jobs as a game or as a stepping stone to higher public office or a lucrative private practice. You've got too much power and you abuse it too freely. A lot of you are at heart lazy paper-shufflers who couldn't get a second look from a real law firm. You'll cover for crooked politicians, plea-bargain with murderers and sex offenders, and bully the innocent. Too many of you jerks are playing "beat the other lawyer" instead of serving justice. So even the "good" ones among you can suffer for the sins of the bad, because you don't have the guts to police your lawless brothers and sisters.

In this chapter, we'll cover checking on police brutality, police shootings, police corruption, police lying, police incompetence, and police nuisance ticket-writing. We'll then hit prosecutors for plea-bargaining, taking dives on cases, reneging on promises, wasting time on nonsense cases, and committing legal malpractice that hurts the public. In short, we'll hit prosecutors for acting like lawyers!

You can use this info for the "civilian" purposes of monitoring the performance of policemen and prosecutors to ensure they enforce the law instead of break it. After all, people lose respect for the law when those who are supposed to uphold it subvert it by breaking it. You can use this info for the "military" purposes of getting a bad cop or a shyster prosecutor punished or removed from office. Don't feel bad about doing this, either; a bad cop or shyster prosecutor is worse than a common criminal.

ARE YOUR COPS MALE METER MAIDS?

The cop who is quick with the ticket book is law enforcement's version of Barney Fife, the dodo deputy who Don Knotts portrayed on the *Andy Griffith Show*. The ticket-fixated cop is a male meter maid who thinks law enforcement is nothing more than hiding along streets and highways and ticketing motorists. Meanwhile, real criminals get opportunities to commit crimes because this kind of cop and his buddies are wasting valuable patrol time and stakeout time writing tickets.

It isn't an exercise in higher math to show what a waste these guys really are. Since it takes about 10-15 minutes to issue a citation, a cop wastes an hour for every 4-6 tickets he writes. Granted, most people pulled over are violating the law, but how many of them are *REALLY* posing a threat to highway safety? What ever happened to warnings?

Speaking of safety, how many accidents are caused because of excessive ticket-writing? Many cops stall traffic and create collision opportunities by blocking traffic lanes when they fail to get their patrol cars out of the roadway. Also, a cop who's pulled over a motorist is an "attractive nuisance" in that there are enough fatheads who will slow down to check out the curbside action. (These peabrains are probably the same idiots who follow ambulances and fire trucks to accident sites and victims' homes.) And every year people get hurt by policemen darting through traffic to make traffic stops.

To add insult to injury, there are police forces who actually profit from the number of tickets they write. In certain areas, the taxpayers are too cheap to pay for real law enforcement, so they pay their police and sheriff's deputies and constables (elected policemen) by the fee system. In other words, the lawman gets a certain percentage of the fine from each ticket he writes that is paid. It doesn't take a Sherlock Holmes to figure out the motive behind these officers' zeal with the ticket book. (I once worked in a Kentucky county that had this lousy system in place. I-75, the main highway from Cincinnati to Atlanta, cut through this county. It was a real testimony to the county lawmen's integrity that they didn't spend all their time on this road waylaying out-of-state motorists. Unfor-

tunately, these men's wives had to get jobs also so they could keep their families fed.)

Law enforcement officials try to justify their meter maid tactics by claiming their officers have a better chance of apprehending fugitives by making frequent stops. What a laugh that claim is. How many fugitives do officers *REALLY* catch on chance traffic stops? The good cops cue in on unusual behavior, observe and follow suspicious motorists, and maintain better overall vigilance to capture criminals. A more professional officer can still stop traffic violators and run their records without having to write them tickets— and can get back to patrolling and other police work more quickly. A cop writing tickets is a cop *NOT* watching other people!

One reason the less professional forces stoop to writing tickets is to make it look like they're doing something. Catching real criminals is a risky and uncertain business which is beyond the scope of a lot of policemen. So to make it look like they haven't spent all their patrol time taking donut breaks, the cops write tons of tickets to pad their statistics.

To check if your local police force has a "meter maid" mentality, do the following:

Find out the number of tickets your local police issue by contacting the state motor vehicles bureau in your state capital. In this agency are agents who maintain traffic ticket data on a county-by-county basis. They can provide you with traffic ticket statistics for all counties in your state. Once you get the printouts, figure out the ticket per resident ratios of your city and county and other cities and counties in your part of the state. For each city and county, simply divide the number of tickets written by the number of people in the city or county. (Unless you live in a lightly-populated county with an interstate highway running through, the number of tickets your people get out of the area should even out with the number of tickets nonresidents get in your area.) If your city or county has a high ticket per resident ratio compared with other jurisdictions in the area, odds are your local police or sheriff's deputies are meter maids instead of real lawmen.

Take it one more step—see if your local cops are fiddling with tickets while your city or county burns. To do this, find out how many reported major crimes take place in your city and county and find out how many arrests for such crimes your local police make.

To do this, contact the FBI's Uniform Crime Reporting Special Programs Unit in Washington and ask for your state's "crime by county" report and your state's "arrest by offense" report for recent years. The first report breaks down by county and city the reported major crimes (murder, rape, robbery, aggravated assault, burglary, larceny (high-dollar theft), vehicle theft, and arson). The second report breaks down by city and county all police and sheriff's deputy arrests for these major crimes; it also contains arrest data on roughly 20 other less serious offenses.

Using the FBI data, figure out your locality's crimes per resident ratio by dividing the number of major crimes by the number of residents. Then figure your local police force's arrest ratio by dividing the number of arrests by the number of reported major crimes. (Note there will always be fewer arrests than reported crimes. This is because many crimes are never solved, but also because some people commit many crimes. Arresting one thief or one rapist may clear quite a few crimes.) Like with the tickets, compare your local police force's arrest ratio with the ratios of other police forces in your part of the state. If your local force's arrest ratio is low compared to other forces but its ticket ratio is high, Barney Fife and his buddies have come to roost in your area.

I did this kind of digging as a favor for the residents of Clinton County, Ohio. This county, halfway between Cincinnati and Columbus, is notorious locally for its ticket-happy cops and deputies. Using the methods described above, I showed its local yokels wrote several times as many tickets per resident than the police forces of every other county in the area. I then compared Clinton County's crime and arrest statistics with neighboring counties. It turned out the police and sheriff's deputies of neighboring Fayette County (a county with about as many people as Clinton County) in 1990 made 200 arrests for major crimes on 921 reported major crimes. Meanwhile, Clinton County's "finest" made 128 arrests for major crimes on 966 reported major crimes. The stats screamed the obvious—Clinton County's cops wrote four times as many tickets and made roughly half as many felony arrests as the cops in Fayette County.

I released the data to a newspaper in Clinton County, and the resulting article about the local lawmen's priorities did not "make their days." In fact, the reporter took my project one step further; he decided to find out how the ticket fine money was being spent. He found out the county officials let the sheriff buy new patrol cars with extra money his men brought in by their ticket-writing. Since using fine money for such a purpose is illegal in Ohio, the state auditor is at this writing investigating Clinton County's public officials for possible misuse of money in allowing the patrol car purchases.

The only way you can stop meter-maid behavior is to pressure your local elected officials. They control hiring and firing of officers, and they also have a fair amount of input over what kind of law enforcement program the sheriff or the police chief runs. (Believe me, this happens a lot more often than the media will tell you. In an Appalachian county I once covered, the county supervisors had a petty vendetta against the sheriff—so much so that they wouldn't vote him money for decent patrol cars. As a result, he had to buy high-mileage castoff vehicles from other police forces to keep his men on the road. If the supervisors—and not the state—had power over how many deputies the sheriff could have and how much he could pay them, they may well have laid off and/or short-changed his deputies, too.)

If the local cops are writing nuisance tickets on their own, give a friendly word of protest to your local elected officials. Show them a spreadsheet of the force's ticket and arrest figures compared to the rest of the state; it might be all you need to convince them to shorten the cops' chain. However, if the cops are writing tickets as a sort of unenacted wheel tax to help the local government budget, you may have to purge the sheriff, the police chief, and the pols in charge (or trace the money to verify local officials are using it illegally, then tell the state auditor about it) to get this practice to stop. If you don't, then you deserve what you get.

STRIKE BACK AT POLICE BRUTALITY

The most common complaint against policemen that's a serious one is police brutality. Like rape, it's an easy charge to make and a hard one to prove. Like paranoid feminists who accuse virtually all men of trying to rape all women, the ACLU and others in the upper-income liberal white whiney set accuse virtually all cops of brutality against all prisoners. Officers respond with much justification that many suspects are dangerous people who often attack them. And cops also can claim honestly in many cases that many prisoners with bad attitudes make trouble for them and could ignite a jail riot or a prison riot.

Also, in a copper's defense, most of the people he deals with in an adversary situation ARE criminals! Many of them are blatant scum, and after seeing his fill of these human louses, an officer starts to think all suspects are subhuman, and the temptation is great for him to treat them accordingly. It's a tribute to our officers' professionalism that there aren't *MORE* instances of police brutality!

It's easy to defend a cop for beating up a suspect in a fit of anger because the suspect has tried to kill him or has committed a sickening crime like molesting little children. But too many police brutality incidents involve a bully with a badge simply beating up a prisoner or a suspect because he doesn't like him and he thinks he can get away with it.

Bully cops believe they can get away with their behavior, and they're almost always right. After all, who's going to believe some criminal scumbag, even one who's suffered a fearful beating, if he accuses a policeman of brutality? Not most folks. The cop can claim the suspect tried to escape, or attacked him, or did something else that led the cop to give him a well-deserved beating. His buddies will cover for him, and the local cops' union will attack anyone trying to determine the truth.

But brutality, like other crimes, has physical and circumstantial evidence. And some of this evidence will show up on documents. A prisoner who's been beaten by police hard enough to require medical attention will have a medical record. Police departments or other government agencies maintain accounts to pay for medical care for prisoners.

These should be public records. If you push hard enough, you should be able to make the accountable agency come up with records showing how much money was spent on treating prisoners who suffered beatings and who reportedly gave them the beatings. Also, police runs of prisoners to hospitals for care should be public records in some states. Even if a person isn't charged with a crime and is later released, a photocopy of his treatment record (with identifying data blacked out) might be available to you. However, it may take the help of a friendly politician for you to get this data.

Likewise, government emergency services records and county hospital records might contain evidence of police brutality. Ask for records for paramedic runs and hospital admissions of people in police custody. You might get a fight from the keepers of these records, and they'll claim privacy is involved. Just fire back that the names of the prisoners are already known because all arrests are public records. Add that tax dollars are going for treatment of these prisoners, because government employees (policemen) are responsible for the injuries requiring this outlay of treatment money. It may take the help of a friendly politician for you to get this data.

Since policemen are often experts at covering up physical evidence that might implicate them in crimes, you'll also have to look at circumstantial evidence. For example, why would black businessman Arthur McDuffie be irresponsible enough to attack several Miami-area cops who pulled him over in 1979? And how could McDuffie pose so much of a threat to them all by himself that they had to beat him to death? Or why would Long Beach State football player Ron Settles become so despondent over an arrest for a traffic violation in 1980 that he would hang himself in his cell, like Southern California police claimed?

Yeah, these cases smelled bad to me, too, when I first heard about them. Later on, police witnesses admitted McDuffie had not resisted arrest. Also, a coroner's inquest jury members determined Settles "died at the hands of another, other than by accident."

Other sources of evidence on police brutality include civil rights complaints lodged with local prosecutors, state attorney general offices, and the U.S. Justice Department. A civil-rights violation lawsuit or criminal prosecution seems to have more success at punishing police criminals than a criminal prosecution for brutality. Why? Prosecutors tend not to lean too hard on cops, and jury members tend to give cop defendants every break in a criminal trial involving homicide or felony assault charges.

Another old standby to check is your police department's lawsuit record for other cases. When the "justice" system lets bad cops off the hook, victims (or their survivors) of police brutality find the lawsuit is about the only weapon they have. Plus, it's easier to get a verdict in a civil case, because in a civil case, it doesn't take a unanimous vote of the jurors to reach a verdict, and the plaintiff's burden of proof is easier. As an example, we'll use the case of Rafael Acosta, a restaurant worker in Chicago.

In 1981, two Chicago cops followed Rafael into his apartment, handcuffed him, beat him, and threw him down a flight of stairs over a lousy traffic violation. His wife and children were among the witnesses who saw the police mug him. Rafael suffered brain damage so severe as a result of the police mugging that he became truly dangerous to himself and others—he attempted suicide, sexually assaulted women, and attacked strangers—and he had to be confined to a mental hospital for several years.

Chicago police authorities ruled the two cops didn't use excessive force in the attack on Rafael, and no prosecutor filed criminal charges against the thugs in blue. However, Rafael's wife and children filed suit against Chicago, and won $3.5 million in an out-of-court settlement with the city's leaders in 1987. (It's a sad commentary on the justice system that it took a lawsuit for the Acosta family to get any justice at all.)

Local civil rights groups and the lowly ACLU probably have some dirt on the police for brutality cases. And the even lowlier media can provide leads on cases of police brutality. Since most journalists are liberals, they're more prone than most to look into charges of police brutality. And since they've got a paper or a station behind them, they'll make more headway than most people. And sometimes, stories in the papers and in the electronic media will give you clues on police brutality even when the reporters aren't looking to expose it.

For example, former L.A. police chief Daryl Gates was more or less forced to retire as a result of the national uproar that followed his cops beating a speeding motorist named Rodney King into a bleeding pulp in 1991. Gates had previously been inadvertently exposed for tolerating police brutality. Gates' gestapo brutalized a number of pro-life demonstrators in 1989. Some of these peaceful demonstrators suffered major injuries at the hands of his thugs in blue. The media reported the brutality in a few stories dealing with the trial of these people. But since most reporters are pro-abortion, they didn't consider the 1989 brutality a big enough problem to give it continued unfriendly coverage.

TAKING AIM ON POLICE SHOOTINGS

Most police shootings are justified, or at least unavoidable. However, there's a percentage of trigger-happy cops out there who will shoot even unarmed suspects they could have beaten up. These jerks give other cops a black eye they don't deserve. In fact, one researcher who studied 900 fatal police shootings noted roughly 30 percent of the victims were not involved in any criminal activity, and one-quarter had no weapon of any kind when police shot them to death. One in four of these people was shot in the back.

If you want to check into a police shooting, you can check the suspect's criminal file (if he survived and was arrested). Even in a police cover-up, you'll find some leads to indicate a problem exists, and you might find some statements that contradict the evidence. Since police investigations of shootings are often confidential, you'll have to enlist the aid of a friendly local official to get the dirt for you. (You can file for the report, but odds are you'd have to go to court against the police to get them to turn over any information; you can bet they'll "forget" to include a lot of items.) Also, don't expect to see the record while the investigation is still ongoing, because charges could result, and the officers deserve the same kinds of legal protection as anyone else who's being investigated for a crime.

Like brutality, a police shooting will have physical evidence. Check the police report and the criminal file of the shot suspect (and the coroner's report, as applicable, per the chapter on death records) for the following items:

- Was the person shot in the back, or in the back of the head? (Some who get shot this way deserve it because they've killed someone on the scene and are trying to escape. Or the police outmaneuvered them during hostage situations and took them out in the most effective way possible. But many of those shot from behind are the victims of wrongful use of deadly force.)
- Did the person have a firearm or any other kind of weapon in his possession at the time of the shooting?
- Was a weapon recovered from the scene that may have been a policeman's "alibi" weapon (a weapon a policeman "planted" at the scene to make it look like the shooting victim had it)?
- Was there any evidence the suspect was even committing a crime (or was wanted for a crime and was trying to avoid capture) at the time of the shooting?
- Are there any witnesses?
- How many police witnesses are there? A lot? Did an "officer in trouble" call go out before half the force showed up at the scene of the shooting?
- Was the person drunk enough or high enough or out of control enough to have done something stupid like attack a policeman?
- Was the victim caught between police and a suspect, was it apparently a tragic accident in which the victim surprised a police officer, or was the victim a victim of a poor police marksman?

Police shootings will often have circumstantial as well as physical evidence. For instance, why would a 230-pound cop have to shoot a 140-pound man who was alone, unarmed, sober, and not a suspect in any crime? Evidently, the cop panicked and thought he saw a gun, or the cop is truly incompetent in nonlethal subduing techniques (in other words, he's a lousy fighter), or he's lying.

Other circumstances will come into play—like the experience or fighting ability of the police officer and the shooting victim, or the likelihood of the shooting victim to even be mixed up in a crime or a confrontation with lawmen in the first place. For example, was the police officer a rookie, a woman, or a small man? (These cops seem more prone to use deadly force wrongfully.) Or what is (was) the victim's situation in life? (A stable employed family man, for example, is generally not prone to attack a policeman or commit other crimes. A police account would be more suspect here than a police account of shooting an escaped murderer.) Was the victim black or Hispanic? (Members of these groups get shot by police at a much higher rate than whites, and members of these groups maintain police have an itchier trigger finger for them than they do for whites.)

The police report will contain the officer's account of the shooting, as well as other information. Go through the report with a fine-tooth comb to find inconsistencies and possible pieces of circumstantial evidence of police abuse or poor judgment.

Like with brutality incidents, check for lawsuits filed against the police department. If someone (or his survivors) has sued the force because one of its men or women in blue shot him, the case paperwork will contain a lot of helpful information. Other sources of evidence on police shootings include civil rights complaints lodged with local prosecutors, state attorney general offices, and the U.S. Justice Department.

Also, checking with local civil rights groups can get you some leads on checking into police shootings. The local groups have a pretty good feel for police brutality aimed at the people they defend. Also, the ACLU and the media people may have some data on police shootings they've compiled for lawsuits or for news stories.

A word of advice—don't be disappointed if you don't find evidence of total police racism or viciousness. Most wrongful police shootings happen because the cop in the wrong needs more training on the rules for using deadly force, or because he was under stress and didn't consider his other options, or because he needs more training on using his stick or his mace or his fists and feet to subdue a suspect. Also, you may well find a large number of these shootings involve young cops, or involve female cops or small male cops who need training on how to handle suspects or therapy on how to cure their "Jane Wayne" or "Little Caesar" authority hang-ups.

CHECKING FOR CROOKED COPS

Do cops in your area take bribes or steal from businessmen …like from mooching merchandise on up to taking heavy shakedown money for protection? Do cops steal guns, narcotics, or money from evidence rooms?

It's not that hard to gather evidence of bribe-soliciting or shakedown activity. Just check in with businessmen in the area. Represent yourself as a businessman who's new to the area. After chewing the fat a little with other businessmen in their stores, ask them what the ground rules are in the area—like which officials and cops need to be taken care of. Some businessmen will show you the door. Others might tell you the truth.

If you find evidence of police bribe-soliciting or shakedowns, you'll probably have to take your evidence to the FBI or to a government officials who is a police critic. Police who blatantly break the law this way are often working for a force whose top dogs aren't out checking their men, and probably won't punish them, either.

On contraband theft, the police have to inventory all contraband at regular periods or account for it if they sell it, return it, or destroy it. File for these records; disposition of contraband property may be a public record. (Again, you may need a friendly public official to get it for you, and even he might not be able to get all of the info for you due to an ongoing investigation.) Check for unexplained differences in the amounts of drugs, guns, money, or other items seized and amounts disposed of. Check the auditing procedures of the department. Who has access to the contraband? Who is the custodian, the supervisor, and the auditor in the custody and disposal of contraband? How is it verified that property is being disposed of properly? Are reports filed when items are missing?

Other likely sources of information on police criminal activity include civil and criminal cases filed at the courthouse, complaints filed with the state attorney general's office or the U.S. Justice Department, and police critics in the community.

JUST BECAUSE A COP SAYS SO DON'T MAKE IT SO

Cops lie just like everyone else. In fact, the police code, like the Mafia's code of silence, may well encourage them to lie to protect brother officers. Unfortunately, cops' lying is much more harmful than other people's lying, because when they lie, innocent people can go to jail or guilty people can stay out of jail. Filing false reports and suppressing evidence are serious police abuses.

Some cops lie in court. Some cops also lie when they file incident reports. You can check a cop's report for falseness, for contradictions with known fact, and for contradiction with other documents. Use this info to attack his credibility if you need to do so.

Once I was arrested for disorderly conduct because I argued with two police punks about a traffic ticket. They lied several times on their report. But the two lies that really fried their credibility were them claiming I refused to sign the traffic ticket and them claiming they gave me a copy of the ticket. In fact, the ticket had my signature on it, and all copies, including the copy they refused to give me, were in the court file the day the case went to trial.

I defended myself in court against these two, and I

questioned the first cop on these lies after I got him to talk about every action that led up to my arrest and jailing. (I had the judge make the other cop wait outside the courtroom.)

The first cop claimed I refused to sign the ticket. Then I asked for the case file, and from the file I presented a signed ticket. I asked the first cop if he and his partner were admitting to forging my signature, because the ticket was signed. He said no, then claimed I signed the ticket just after he and his buddy arrested me. I then asked him how a man in handcuffs could sign a ticket. He drew a blank. I also asked him why he claimed he gave me the ticket when all copies were in the file, and had never been separated from each other. The judge shut up the prosecutor when he tried to object.

The other cop behaved just as poorly when he was on the stand. I cleared myself of the charge, and later got disciplinary action taken against the bad cops for making an improper arrest and for committing perjury.

In another ticket case of mine, a cop claimed on the ticket that I didn't come to a stop until my car was 30 feet into an intersection. The truth was that the engine compartment of my car was over the white stop line at the intersection. I went to the intersection with a 50-foot tape measure, took measurements, and discovered if the cop's statement was correct, my car would have been in the middle of the intersection and I would have struck him as he was trying to make a left turn from the crossing street of the intersection. Needless to say, I showed up in court with the tape measure and pictures of the intersection. The judge reduced the ticket to its true nature (engine compartment over the line), and didn't fine me.

You can do the same kind of work on police reports. Look for blatant lies (like above), and look for suspicious circumstances. For instance, why would cops take another cop involved in a fatal car wreck away from the crash site and not give him a test for intoxication (or give it to him several hours later)? Either the cops have no idea of how to investigate a vehicle accident or they are trying to cover up for a buddy. Or why would several cops claim an unarmed guy whom they beat to death tried to attack all of them when they made a traffic stop on him and he wasn't a suspect for any crime? Yeah, this excuse would smell, too.

Again, other likely sources of information on police wrongdoing include civil and criminal cases filed at the courthouse, complaints filed with the state attorney general's office or the U.S. Justice Department, and police critics in the community.

DOCUMENTING COP INCOMPETENCE

Lawmen make mistakes on the job just like anyone else. Some of them also do lousy jobs on certain days out of laziness, temporary dumbness, or because they've brought home-life problems to the job. However, their work problems cause people more harm than do yours or mine. Their foul-ups can send innocent people to jail or keep criminals on the loose.

In his book *Helter Skelter*, Vincent Bugliosi, the prosecutor who convicted Charles Manson and four of his followers for the Tate and La Bianca murders, said policemen made a number of boneheaded moves in working the case. For example, he said, a policeman was dumb enough to grab the pistol used in the slayings by the grips from the boy who found it. By doing so, the cop messed up the fingerprints on the gun. The boy had been alert enough to handle the gun by the barrel to preserve the fingerprints.

Bugliosi said police interrogators routinely overlooked important statements that Manson Family members and other witnesses made to them. He said policemen wiped out other fingerprint evidence and clumsily destroyed pieces of physical evidence while transporting them. Further, he said, professional jealousies between the teams of detectives working the cases prevented them from working together and solving the case more quickly. This meant Family members committed other crimes while they were still free.

Bugliosi had some harsh words for other officers. He said a parole officer let one of the Family's suspected killers roam free because he was afraid of him. And he said a female guard at the women's jail repeatedly refused to allow Susan Atkins' cellmate to come forward and tell police investigators all the information about the case that Susan—one of the killers—told her. What makes this woman guard's headless stupidity even more incredible was that she was the girlfriend of one of the detectives working the case! Her lights were on, but no one was home.

One of the sorriest incidents of police work I ever heard of took place in Santa Barbara, California in 1983. Police there arrested three members of the Harlem Globetrotters after they received a call about a robbery committed by three black males. Since blacks are rare in this somewhat snooty community, the cops evidently grabbed the first three black guys they could find—and that's how they nabbed the Globetrotters.

Evidently the cops were too stupid to figure out they had the wrong guys because two of the three Globetrotters they arrested were 6'5" or taller, while the tallest suspect was 5'10"! Further, the police saw the Globetrotters get into a taxi, while the suspects reportedly escaped in a gray Caddy. And the Globetrotters were dressed quite a bit differently than the suspects. Besides, why would a Globetrotter feel the financial need to stick up a store? The cops' stupidity cost the taxpayers of Santa Barbara $75,000 in an out-of-court settlement with the three basketball stars.

Cops routinely make needless arrests due to laziness and due to the need to show superiors they're "doing something." Cops will arrest the winner of a streetfight even if the loser started the fight or was a voluntary participant if the loser is enough of a wimp to press charges instead of taking his whipping like a man. Cops will often make improper arrests in domestic disturbances or in child abuse claims without checking for the truth. The attitude of too many cops is "make an arrest and let the courts sort it out." This is a worthless attitude to take, because many innocent people end up having to fight groundless charges in court. This costs them money, damages their reputations, and causes them problems on the job due to absences or innuendoes about why they're in court.

A related police abuse is to overcharge a defendant. They may charge a streetfight winner with felony assault, even if the loser suffered little or no damage. They may charge a petty shoplifter with felony grand larceny. Or they might charge a suspect with resisting arrest just to do it. Police commit these abuses to hurt the defendants, to give prosecutors leverage in plea-bargaining, and to pad their personal felony arrest statistics. After all, policemen like to get promotions, too.

Likewise, police officials lobby for money, and the best way is to point to numbers of arrests made (especially felony arrests). They can argue that their cops are effective and need more money to keep their edge. Or they can argue the arrest numbers prove the community is crawling with criminals and they need more money to control them. Unless the police chief or sheriff becomes enlightened (and the public officials who vote on police budgets become enlightened), don't expect these police abuses to disappear any time soon.

The flip side of the police negligence coin is their failure to act when a situation screams for it. For example, three stooges on the Milwaukee police force reportedly returned a 14-year-old Laotian boy to killer Jeffrey Dahmer when he claimed he and the boy were homosexual lovers. They ignored the obvious evidence that the boy had escaped from Dahmer's apartment naked and was bleeding rectally. They also ignored the fact he was underage, which means they should have arrested Dahmer on a statutory rape charge. They also reportedly told the women who witnessed the boy's escape and reported it to "get lost." The result of these cops' evident stupidity? Dahmer strangled and dismembered the boy. Thanks, cops.

You can check your police force's actual effectiveness in a number of ways. Check the number of felony arrests they make against the number of convictions that result. Check for how often felony charges are downgraded to misdemeanors. If your police force has a low conviction ratio relative to other police forces in your county and in the state, odds are they are below-average performers.

If your force's average is low compared with the state average, but is roughly comparable with other police forces in your county, either all your county's forces are below-average, or maybe your county prosecutors aren't getting the job done. (You can check misdemeanor rates also, but they will be harder to check due to the large number of courts involved. Besides, common sense says these statistics will be similar to felony statistics.)

CASE CONCLUSION

Police have a hard job, so it's not fair to hassle them for no good reason. However, they volunteered to become cops, so they have to meet minimum standards just like everyone else. Don't feel bad about digging dirt on bad cops. An incompetent cop poses a threat to the community just like any other incompetent professional. And a crooked cop is worse. If you can expose him, you're doing the public a favor. After all, a bad cop not only criminally victimizes others, but he also rapes, assaults, and steals the public trust!

JUSTICE DENIED

Usually a person found guilty of a crime IS guilty of something, and is often guilty of more! However, some innocent people are convicted of crimes. Much of the blame for this belongs to poor prosecutor and police work. Some of the blame belongs to the way the judges and the lawyers handle cases. All too often, the prosecutor and defense attorney play "beat the other lawyer" instead of getting together, looking at the facts of the case, and trying to determine the truth. Judges don't help, either. It is rare for judges to ask questions of witnesses, accusers, or defendants to get at the truth; they let the attorneys play their games. And some jurors are knotheads who don't think clearly, who let their emotions sway them, and who push to enter guilty verdicts because jury duty is inconvenient for them.

A case which had elements of all of the above was the Randy Ayers case in Cincinnati. Some of you might have seen the show about it on TV. Randy Ayers, a teenager, was tried in 1982 for raping and shooting a girl in Cincinnati in 1981. The crime *DID* take place; the tall, attractive 15-year-old girl—an honors student at a Catholic high school—suffered a brutal and painful rape, losing her hymen and suffering vaginal damage in the process. She was also robbed, and she was shot in the throat and the back of the head. And the conscienceless animal who raped, robbed, and shot her looked a lot like Randy Ayers.

Ayers became a suspect after one of his pals found the girl's purse and he and they had handled it. He went to the police station with his buddies and one of his buddies' mother to turn in the purse. He looked a lot like the described suspect, and police showed him a drawing of the suspect. Ayers reportedly told his friend's mother he was going to leave town because he thought the authorities were going to pin the rape on him.

The girl later identified Ayers as her rapist after Cincinnati police had her pick Ayers out of a "lineup" of one. (They only showed her Ayers.) She also identified Ayers when police took her to a high school near the crime scene and had her watch kids in the hallways.

Ayers said he didn't assault the girl. He said he was drinking beer and smoking marijuana with some of his buddies at the time she was being raped. He was also shorter than the girl; she had told investigators her attacker was a couple of inches taller than her.

The rape exam performed on the girl didn't eliminate Ayers as a suspect. The rapist's semen contained Type O blood cells, and Ayers—like millions of other American males— has Type O blood. (DNA identification technology which could have eliminated Ayers as a suspect hadn't been made reliable yet.) The examiner could not find any pubic hairs in the vaginal combing performed on the girl that were not her pubic hairs.

At Ayers' trial, his lawyer made a big deal of his height, but it didn't help him. When the girl was made to stand next to Ayers to prove she was taller than he was, she broke down and wept. The jurors didn't buy Ayers' buddies' story that Ayers was getting stoned with them while the girl was being raped several blocks away. Nor did they give a girl who was Ayers' friend any credence when she said she was also with Ayers and several other teens the night the girl was raped, robbed, and shot. They also dismissed her testimony that Ayers had not taken advantage of her when she had passed out while she was alone with

him. They convicted Ayers, and he received a 14-to-50-year sentence.

For eight years, Randy Ayers served time. But one day in the summer of 1990, he was freed. Why? Because Robert Minton, who was a suspect in the rapes and murders of two young women in 1990, confessed to the rape which sent Ayers to prison. Minton looks a lot like Ayers, but is several inches taller. In 1991, Minton was convicted of raping and gruesomely murdering the two young women. He tried strangling one woman, then ran over her with a car, then beat her to death with a hammer. He slashed the throat of the other woman.

Staffers of the TV show *A Current Affair* reported the authorities and the defense attorneys may have found out some time before the end of Randy Ayers' trial that Minton was possibly a better suspect in the case than Ayers. And yet, they said, they still kept Ayers on trial. I interviewed John Johnston, the producer of the show on the Ayers case, about this claim. He stood behind the allegation. He said he understood prosecutors didn't want to bring Minton into the case because they had a strong case against Ayers and they didn't want to confuse the jurors.

Prosecutor Michael Barrett and defense attorney Elizabeth Agar pointedly refused to talk to me about the case. Defense attorney Scott Croswell told me he believed Ayers was innocent all along, but said he didn't recall considering Minton a more likely suspect. Prosecutor Carl Vollman angrily denied ignoring Minton to go after Ayers. After all, forensic evidence didn't exclude Ayers and the victim identified Ayers as her assailant.

Judge Thomas Crush, who heard the case, told me he personally didn't look into the possibility that someone other than Ayers was the culprit. He said it's the job of the prosecutor and defense attorney to establish what happened. He said defendants often claim someone else committed the crimes they are accused of.

Judge Crush also told me the defense attorneys told him about Minton during the trial, and he said he suggested they show the girl a picture of him to see if she would identify him as her real attacker. Crush said the defense attorneys never did this. When I asked him why, he said the defense lawyers might have thought the girl would stick to her story that Ayers was the one who raped her, robbed her, and shot her. This would have hurt Ayers' chances for acquittal.

I checked the hundreds of pages of reports and transcripts on the case, and I found no evidence that the prosecutors held back a better suspect or that defense lawyers pulled any punches in defending

Ayers. However, many prosecutor records never make the public file. And off-the-record discussions between judges and lawyers don't make the public file, either. Like Randy Ayers, Judge Crush and both sets of lawyers denied any wrongdoing. They could probably get each other to testify for them, like Randy Ayers' delinquent buddies did for him. However, like the forensic exam, there is nothing to prove beyond the shadow of a doubt that the lawyers and the judge are innocent of misconduct.

To add a "perfect" ending to this tale, let's look at the remarks two of the jurors made after Ayers was cleared. In a newspaper interview, one juror who said he believed Ayers was innocent due to the height question said he caved in when other jurors—especially the women jurors—badgered him. A woman juror said she and other jurors looked down on Ayers and his scruffy pals. She implied the jurors judged Ayers and his friends by their appearances rather than listening to their testimony to judge if they were telling the truth.

Prosecutors and defense attorneys, working together instead of as adversaries, could have established Ayers' innocence in this case. Several witnesses said Ayers was with them when the girl was raped, robbed, and shot. No forensic evidence tied him to the crime. He looked like the rapist, but was shorter; girls and women tend to remember if boys and men are shorter than they are. They would have saved Ayers from prison, and would have saved Sandra Barrett and Georgeanne Gatto from being raped and murdered. However, the legal system isn't set up for co-operation. Searching for truth and working for justice might get the lawyers and judges in trouble with the bar association!

At the very least, the Randy Ayers case was a miscarriage of justice. Randy Ayers languished in prison for eight years while Robert Minton roamed free, raping and killing. Ohio taxpayers had to pay Randy Ayers $400,000 for his wrongful imprisonment, but it didn't compensate Randy for his loss of eight years of his life. (Judge Crush told Ayers not to spend it all in one place.) Nor will any gesture bring back to life the women whom Robert Minton murdered.

And if anyone—policemen, lab people, lawyers, jurors, or Judge Crush—failed to work honestly or competently on this case? Then the Ayers case was more than a miscarriage of justice; it was an *abortion* of justice!

PROSECUTING THE PROSECUTORS

Prosecutors wrap themselves in the American flag and claim they protect the public. If it were up to me, I'd wrap a lot of them in concrete and sink them in the Pacific Ocean to protect the public. After all, these guys are LAWYERS first, bureaucrats second, and public servants in name only.

A recent case in Cincinnati can serve as an example. Edward Cook, a 46-year-old black mechanic, lost his four children in a garage fire in 1991. He and his children had to live in the garage because city officials evicted them from an apartment complex after a fire had damaged it, and they could afford nothing better. Since the garage was in a dangerous part of town, Cook locked his children in the garage for their protection one night while he ran to the store for some groceries.

When Cook returned, the garage was ablaze. Cook suffered head burns trying to rescue his little angels. Firemen tackled him to keep him from losing his own life. Fire investigators determined later the children had started the fire by playing with matches.

Now the tragic story turns hateful. Some yuppie geeks in the Hamilton County Prosecutor's Office tried to get Cook indicted for child endangerment and involuntary manslaughter. Obviously, none of them ever had to really scuffle for a living. None of them evidently had any appreciation of how hard it is to try to raise children on little money in a dangerous area.

Cook's relatives and friends made an angry outcry over the prosecutors' misconduct. People came forward to say what a good father Cook was, how well his children did in school, and how well-taken care of they were. They raised money for him so he could bury his children. (Cook's plight touched even my steel heart, and I sent a $50 check to the fund.) People kept vigil at the courthouse to monitor the injustice against Cook.

Eventually the prosecutors put Cook's case before the grand jury. Cook testified before the grand jury, and the grand jurors told the prosecutor pukes to stick their case where the sun doesn't shine. Justice was served, but not by the prosecutors who are supposed to uphold it.

PROSECUTOR PROBLEMS

How can prosecutors rape Ms. Justice? Let me count the ways.

Plea-bargaining. Prosecutors plea-bargain anywhere from 65 to 95 percent of all criminal cases. Of course, most people who are charged usually are guilty of something, but that's not always why prosecutors plea-bargain so freely. Prosecutors claim they care about people, but many of them really look at criminal cases like statistics. The more convictions they can show, the better it will look for them when they run for office or go into private law practices.

So many prosecutors will plea-bargain with criminals to pad their statistics. After all, a murderer who pleads guilty to the reduced charge of manslaughter or felony assault counts as a conviction just as much as if the prosecutor had to work a little and try him and convict him on the more serious charge and keep him locked up awhile. Prosecutors who plea-bargain too freely endanger the public because the truly dangerous and crooked criminals will avoid just punishment and will be able to prey on the people much quicker.

For example, prosecutors cut a deal with Ricky Slaughterhouse (the killer whose criminal career I covered in the criminal records chapter) which allowed him to plead guilty to "hindering prosecution" for shooting a Kentucky man to death. He had previously been convicted of murder in the case, but a federal appellate judge had thrown the case out on a technicality. So instead of retrying Ricky, the prosecutors cut the deal with him. In other words, Ricky agreed he "hindered prosecution" of a felony assault-with-a-gun charge by mortally wounding the man he assaulted with a gun. Ricky, who was also serving a concurrent (at the same time) sentence for stabbing a man to death in Ohio, was then free to walk out of prison and start a whole new life of assault-related crime.

Another key reason why prosecutors use the plea bargain so readily is that they're bureaucrats. Many of them have lots of cases to review, and they get lazy on some of them. This means they don't review many of their cases thoroughly to see whether the alleged victims are vindictive liars, or to see whether they have the right person charged for crimes which some criminals *DID* commit against the victims. Too many prosecutors take the easy way out instead. They threaten the defendants with massive prosecutions and long prison terms unless they accept plea-bargains.

Some defendants are innocent, but scared. They know there are enough worthless judges and dopey jurors out there who could rule the wrong way on them, so they cave in to the pressure and accept the plea bargain. And in such cases, since the plea-bargaining defendants had nothing to do with the crimes, the real perpetrators are still on the loose to prey upon the public.

Failure To Prosecute. Prosecutors also commit crimes against public safety when they fail to prosecute dangerous or clever criminals even if they *KNOW* they're guilty. Prosecutors pull this stunt in cases where they'll have to work a little to get a conviction. For example, reputed homosexual J. Edgar Hoover had his FBI agents concentrating on bank robbers and spying on Martin Luther King instead of going after more of the sophisticated Mob and white-collar criminals. (Hoover was aided and abetted in this wrongdoing against Dr. King by JFK, LBJ, and top aides in their administrations.)

A sleazy example of failure to prosecute was the Hillside Strangler case. Cousins Kenneth Bianchi and Angelo Buono raped and murdered ten women and girls in the L.A. area in 1977 and 1978. Bianchi later moved to Washington with his girlfriend, and he murdered two more women in the Evergreen State in 1979. He confessed to these two murders later that year. While in custody, Bianchi more or less confessed to the L.A. killings and implicated his cousin.

According to Darcy O'Brien, who wrote the book *Two of a Kind* about Buono and Bianchi, the Hillside Strangler case unfolded as follows:

Bianchi—pretending to be suffering from a multiple personality disorder—changed details of his story constantly. Police detectives found some forensic evidence and plenty of circumstantial evidence linking Buono with the slayings. They believed the prosecutors could get Buono convicted if they worked a little. However, Roger Kelly, the prosecutor assigned to the case, belittled witnesses who said they saw Buono help Bianchi abduct women. Kelly also ignored forensic evidence a woman police technician had found to link Buono to a murdered teenage girl. One of the detectives thought Kelly was trying to sabotage the case against Buono by this behavior.

But why would a prosecutor act this way? One of the detectives thought Kelly might drop the murder charges against Buono because he would have to work hard and chance losing the case—and hurt his conviction rate as a prosecutor. His fears seemed to be realized when in 1981, Kelly and his boss, Los Angeles County District Attorney John Van de Kamp, decided to ask the judge in the case to let them drop all murder charges against Buono.

But Judge Ronald George refused to be "a rubber stamp," as he told me in an interview for this book. Judge George refused to let the prosecutor take a dive on the case. He refused to let the murder charges drop, and he ordered Van de Kamp to prosecute the case or get the hell out of the way so the state attorney general could send a prosecutor to try the case.

Van de Kamp still had cold feet; he decided to pull his prosecutor out of the case. California Attorney General George Deukmejian jumped on the case with both feet. He sent two prosecutors and an investigator to take care of business. Immediately the Buono trial took on political overtones because Deukmejian, a Republican, was going to run for governor in 1982 on a tough-on-crime platform. And Van de Kamp, a Democrat, was going to run for Deukmejian's attorney general job. If Buono was convicted by election day, Deukmejian would look good, and Van de Kamp would look bad. On the other hand, Deukmejian would look foolish and Van de Kamp would look like less of a sissy if Buono walked.

However, the case lasted well into 1983. Meanwhile, Deukmejian became governor and Van de Kamp became attorney general. Finally, the jurors found Buono guilty of nine of the ten murders he was charged with. They gave him life in prison for his crimes. Judge George—again showing some concern for justice—said he was sorry the law wouldn't allow him to overrule the jurors so he could sentence Buono to death.

Weak Prosecution. Another prosecutor offense is putting on a weak case against defendants, especially against those with the right political ties. For example, federal lawmen accused federal prosecutors in New Jersey of failure to prosecute a number of public officials connected with the Abscam scandal. Higher-ups in the U.S. Justice Department took the cases away from the New Jersey federal prosecutors, and sent others into New Jersey to handle the prosecutions. Robert Del Tufo, the highest-ranking federal prosecutor in the Garden State accused of foot-dragging, soon resigned. Two other prosecutors kicked off the case later appeared as witnesses for the defendants when they appealed their convictions.

In Cincinnati, local TV investigative reporters evidently caught county-employed building inspectors playing golf when they were supposed to be on the job. The reporters also evidently caught the inspectors falsifying mileage claims to get more money. But when a Hamilton County prosecutor brought the case to a grand jury for indictment in 1991, the grand jurors didn't indict the inspectors. Hamilton County Prosecutor Art Ney wouldn't comment on whether his assistant had introduced the TV film of the goofing off as evidence. If Ney's people deliberately withheld the film or other relevant evidence (Ney is a friend of the family of one of the accused inspectors) for no good reason, they committed an act similar to obstruction of justice.

Bad-Faith Bargaining. Prosecutors sometimes renege on deals they cut with witnesses. Prosecutors pull this crap because they know it's their word against the testimony of convicts, and people won't usually believe the lousy criminals. I covered such a case in a federal court—it involved a prisoner who witnessed two of his fellow biker gang "brothers" kill another prisoner by locking him in his cell, splashing a flammable liquid on him, and throwing lit matches at him until the liquid ignited and he burned to death. According to the suit the prisoner filed, he claimed state officials promised him if he testified against the killers, they would keep his identity secret until the trial, they would keep him locked up in another prison in the state, and they would reduce his armed-robbery sentence.

The officials went back on their word big-time, the prisoner charged. He said other gang members showed him a copy of his signed statement a month before the trial, and they proceeded to make his life a living hell. He testified against the gang members anyway, and his testimony convicted them. As his reward, he said, the officials decided to move him out of state and decided not to reduce his sentence. The prison warden and the local prosecutors I spoke with about the case told me circumstantial evidence was totally on the prisoner's side. They said they believed he wouldn't have jeopardized himself unless the state officials made those promises to him.

Wasting Time And Money On Nonsense Cases. One of my earliest articles concerned an L.A. city prosecutor who saw fit to waste an unspecified amount of money to prosecute a priest who had drowned some nuisance stray cats that had been hanging around his high school. (The priest, who had once been a farmer, evidently still had a farmer's seemingly harsh but realistic attitude toward pests.) Steve McKee, the prosecutor in question, got involved after a few bozos picketed the priest's high school. With all the *REAL* crime that goes on in L.A., I said to McKee, why was he prosecuting someone for doing what local animal control people do all the time—kill strays?

McKee said he thought the drownings were serious offenses. McKee denied he was going after the priest to showboat for the lunatic mainstream in L.A., but he also refused to say whether or not he was a churchgoer, an atheist or an anti-Catholic bigot. He did say his boss Ira Reiner (a one-time Manson Family defense attorney who was city attorney for L.A. before becoming the district attorney for L.A. County) had given the go-ahead to prosecute the case.

Simple Malpractice. Prosecutors rape Ms. Justice often by intentional misconduct. Sometimes they merely shaft her due to garden-variety negligence. I've covered the Raymond Tanner case before, but as an example of prosecutor error, his case bears repeating.

Prosecutor Robert N. Piper III told me he decided not to prosecute Tanner for cutting off his wife's head on Valentine's Day of 1990. Why? He said two state-retained psychologists who interviewed Tanner many weeks after he beheaded his wife believed Tanner thought his wife and the Masons were involved in a plot to kill him.

I asked prosecutor Piper why he hadn't checked with the two psychologists who examined Tanner in the Butler County (Ohio) jail the day after he killed his wife and concluded he was faking insanity. The prosecutor replied, with some astonishment, that he wasn't aware of any other evaluation. When I told Piper the sheriff had reported to the media he had ordered the two shrinks to examine Tanner a couple of days after the examinations took place, the prosecutor confessed he was unaware of their findings. In short, the prosecutor overlooked a huge piece of evidence in the murder case of a man who cut off his wife's head.

Was Raymond Tanner insane? Maybe so. Most rational men don't decapitate their wives on Valentine's Day (or any other day, for that matter). But jury members who received all the evidence should have made that decision, not a prosecutor who might have mishandled the case. Tanner was found not guilty of killing his wife by reason of insanity in June 1990.

Oh, by the way … Tanner can walk free as soon as some shrink convinces a judge he's sane.

COMPILING THE EVIDENCE

Dirt-digging on prosecutors is not an exact science. However, there are ways to get the job done.

You can check the percentage of felony cases in which prosecutors get convictions. Likewise, you can check the percentage of felony charges that are downgraded to misdemeanors. If your county has a low conviction ratio or high downgrading ratio relative to other counties in your state, your county prosecutors may not be getting the job done. (Or maybe your local police have trouble making arrests that stick.)

You can check for evidence of inequities in plea-bargaining, failure to prosecute, weak prosecution, wasting time with stupid cases, and incompetence in the criminal case files. Using the instructions in the chapter on checking crimes, go through the criminal case files as follows:

- Note the kinds of cases the prosecutor has tried.
- Check for race, sex, and evidence of income of defendant.
- Check for how rigidly authoritarian or how

ridiculously lax the prosecutor is in arranging to lower charges and sentences in exchange for guilty pleas.

- Check the pattern of plea bargaining—how far the prosecutor will go depending on what evidence he has, whether or not he drops numbers of charges or drops the most serious charges, or whether or not he insists on imprisonment. Check for evidence of discrimination based on race, sex, or income. How does he handle crimes of violence? How does he handle non-violent crimes?
- Check for evidence of a strong defense case and evidence of a prosecutor bullheadedly trying to prosecute the case or trying to secure a plea-bargain by ridiculously overcharging a defendant.
- Check for evidence the prosecutor isn't presenting a strong case when damaging evidence might be available to him.
- Check for evidence the prosecutor has mishandled the case in some other way.
- See what kinds of sentences the defendants receive if convicted. See if they are convicted on a lesser charge because the prosecutor couldn't make a more serious charge stick.
- Note how often defense attorneys get judges to issue directed verdicts. A judge, in issuing a directed verdict, is in effect throwing out the case because the prosecutor hasn't proven the defendant committed the crime. Note how often juries or judges find defendants innocent. Note how often defendants successfully appeal the convictions.

Also check to see if the prosecutor gives a damn about victims. Too many prosecutors treat victims as mere pieces of evidence instead of as people who have been hurt deeply by the criminals. Does the prosecutor seek restitution for victims? Does he consider victims' wishes and concerns? Does he shield victims from abusive and unwarranted cross-examination in court while still allowing the defense attorneys to defend their clients?

You can also check for civil suits filed against prosecutors. Victims' survivors might sue over botched prosecutions. Acquitted defendants might sue over the hassles the prosecutor caused them by prejudice or by failing to screen cases. Plea-bargaining witnesses might sue because prosecutors broke their word on deals.

A shortcut way of determining a prosecutor's effectiveness is to contact defense attorneys, citizens' groups, special-interest groups, police groups, the ACLU, local Republican or Democrat bigshots, or anyone else in a position to know how a prosecutor performs (or fails to). If any of these folks has a gripe against your prosecutor, they'll let you know in a heartbeat.

THE VERDICT

It's important to know how good or how bad your prosecutors are, especially if they run for higher office. After all, justice and public safety rest uneasily in their slimy hands.

And on that note, I'm going to let you consider a textbook example of a mismanaged criminal case—the truly terrifying McMartin Preschool case. According to published accounts of the case, this is what went down:

In 1984, Los Angeles County prosecutors charged Peggy McMartin Buckey, her son Raymond Buckey, and five other staffers at the big-name preschool in Manhattan Beach, California with several hundred counts of child molestation. They made the charges after police investigators determined staffers had sexually abused 369 children.

In the pretrial hearings, the Buckeys' lawyers subjected the first 13 child witnesses to savage and repetitive cross-examination. The little children—who had been raped, sodomized, and reportedly forced to watch little animals being killed—broke down, fidgeted intensely, started lisping, and displayed other signs of systemic emotional abuse as the lawyers' cross-examinations continued. Judge Aviva Bobb allowed this abuse to continue, and she also refused to allow the children to testify via closed-circuit TV, even though the children's parents got the law changed during the 13-month pretrial hearing period to allow this setting for testimony to protect little children.

Prosecutors made no major effort to get Judge Bobb overruled or removed from the case. Instead, they decided not to call other children as witnesses. Bobb then dismissed roughly 200 charges against the defendants. Ira Reiner inherited the case from Deukmejian buddy Phil Philibosian (who replaced John Van de Kamp as the L.A. County District Attorney when he became attorney general) when he beat Philibosian in an election to became the district attorney; Reiner dropped charges against the five other staffers in early 1986.

Eventually, Peggy McMartin Buckey was acquitted in early 1990. Her son Raymond survived two trials; each ended in a hung jury. As the jurors put it, the evidence proved the children had been molested, but the prosecutors couldn't prove who had done the molesting. Prosecutors decided to drop the case after the second trial ended in mid-1990. The case cost the taxpayers $13.5 million.

If the Buckeys were innocent, they paid a terrible price. Peggy Buckey spent two years in jail and Raymond Buckey spent five years in jail. They'll never run another preschool or enjoy any kind of a normal life, either. But, if they were guilty, they got off pretty damn lightly. And in either case, THE REAL MOLESTERS ARE FREE TO MOLEST MORE LITTLE CHILDREN.

Some wags, noting that Ira Reiner briefly served as a lawyer for Manson Family murderess Leslie Van Houten, commented sarcastically, "In that trial, it's a good thing Reiner worked for the DEFENSE!"

If your prosecutors are like the shysters who handled the McMartin Preschool case, it's up to you to purge them. If you don't, they'll waste your tax money, and let criminals roam free.

VIGILANCE AND THE LAW

Cops and prosecutors almost always protect the rich. Sometimes they take care of the working blue-collar and white-collar people. Only seldom do they protect the poor. People know this, and some have gotten desperate enough to become vigilantes. Even anti-gun people like Carl Rowan are now capable of shooting criminals on their property. Vigilantes are proof that cops and prosecutors aren't doing their jobs properly. If everything was hunky-dory, people wouldn't feel the need to protect themselves, their loved ones, or others in the community.

Cops and prosecutors tell women to submit to rapists. They don't say how many women avoid the degradation of a rape by fighting back. (Although in fairness, one of the Chicago policemen interviewed for the book What Cops Know said, "You should fight like hell if you get attacked on the street or in your home.")

Cops and prosecutors more or less tell people to limit their involvement in crime-fighting to paying their taxes, locking their doors, and calling in tips. They're mighty quiet when it comes to talking about how many men stopped crimes by attacking criminals and beating them into submission. Remember, several Mexicans accomplished what a statewide police dragnet in California couldn't do...they caught the Night Stalker.

Cops and prosecutors preach sermons against gun ownership. Well, they're right up to a point. Many people are killed by firearm accidents and irate relatives. However, some wags might say this is Darwin's law of natural selection in action; the smart survive, and the stupid kill off themselves or their kin, leaving fewer "stupid" genes in the nation's gene pool. What cops and prosecutors don't tell you is that the Liberty City rioters (the Miami rioters who tore up the city following the acquittal of the police thugs who killed Arthur McDuffie) stayed away from a trailer park whose blue-collar residents were well-armed and vigilant. The residents put up barricades and took turns guarding their homes with rifles and shotguns. These people weren't anti-black racists; they even told reporters they sympathized with blacks who were angry over white cops escaping justice for beating Arthur McDuffie to death. They just didn't want their cars burned, their trailers trashed, and their lives jeopardized by the rioters.

Cops and prosecutors don't like to be reminded of their impotence in many situations. That's why selfless protectors of the people like the Guardian Angels catch so much flak from the cops and the prosecutors. The Guardian Angels are serving the people by reminding folks to stand up for themselves and others because it's the right thing to do and Big Brother can't do it for them.

One of my favorite moments in TV news involved the Guardian Angels. I was warming up my TV set for the *Morton Downey Show* (quality programming in my book), and I caught the last few minutes of a newscast that preceded the show. An official in a big city was telling reporters about how the local authorities in his town had tried to "sting" the Guardian Angels. All of a sudden, a woman reporter with all the brass of a Laverne DeFazio stuck a mike at him and asked him why he was wasting time messing with the Guardian Angels when there was *REAL* crime to be dealt with on the mean streets of that city. She made that official look and sound like Elmer Fudd.

VIGILANCE AND YOU

It would be great if we who call ourselves men adopt the Guardian Angels' "street-knightly code" of protecting women, children, old people, and handicapped people from the criminal scum. And it would be great if we the people adopt the attitude of community spirit and concern for others. However, until more people come around to this way of thinking, we will still have to suffer the "protection" of a justice system loaded with bad cops and shyster prosecutors. And it will be up to you—even if vigilante methods aren't for you—to keep an eye on your police and prosecutors to ensure they're serving Ms. Justice instead of raping her.

END NOTES

1. Statistics for traffic tickets in Clinton County and other counties in Southwest Ohio come from the Ohio Bureau of Motor Vehicles. Statistics for reported crimes and arrests in these counties come from the FBI's Uniform Crime Reporting Special Programs Unit.
2. Information on police and sheriff ticket-writing practices (and financing for new patrol cars) comes from an article in the Wilmington (Ohio) *News-Journal* on January 30, 1992.
3. Information on Arthur McDuffie's death at the hands of Miami-area police comes from the June 2, 1980 issue of *Newsweek*. McDuffie was beaten to death by the police in December 1979. An all-white jury acquitted the police in May 1980, touching off rage in South Florida's black community which culminated in the Liberty City riots of 1980.
4. Information on the 1980 hanging death of football player Ron Settles, who was in the custody of Signal Hill, California police for resisting arrest over a traffic ticket, comes from the October 26, 1981 issue of *Time*. A coroner's inquest jury decided Settles died "at the hands of another, other than by accident" in September 1981.
5. Information on Rafael Acosta's brain-damaging beating at the hands of Chicago policemen comes from an Associated Press wire service story which ran in 1987.
6. Information on the beating that L.A. policemen gave speeding motorist Rodney King comes from an article in the March 25, 1991 issue of *Time*. Information on L.A. police chief Daryl Gates' retirement comes from an article in the August 5, 1991 issue of *U.S. News*.
7. Information on L.A. police brutality against pro-lifers comes from a photo in an article in the May 1, 1989 issue of *Time* and from a federal lawsuit they filed against Los Angeles over another incident. (The case — No. CV8-4766AWT — was filed in U.S. District Court in Los Angeles; in deposition, L.A. police chief Daryl Gates admitted his men broke a protester's arm.) Further information on L.A. police brutality against the pro-lifers comes from September 14, 1989 articles in the L.A. *Times*, the L.A. *Herald-Examiner*, and the L.A. *Daily News* about the trial of the leading demonstrators. Jurors said they acquitted the protesters of resisting arrest charges because they saw films of the brutality the police inflicted on them.
8. Statistics on police shootings of innocent and unarmed people come from a study by Arthur Kobler which was cited by Robert Bonn in his textbook *Criminology*.
9. Information on blunders committed by law enforcement officials who were connected to the Manson Family case comes from Vincent Bugliosi's and Curtis Gentry's book *Helter Skelter*. Bugliosi, a former L.A. County prosecutor, was the attorney who prosecuted Manson and co-defendants Susan Atkins, Patricia Krenwinkel, and Leslie Van Houten. He also prosecuted Manson Family member Charles "Tex" Watson in a separate trial. Bugliosi noted many more police screwups than those I covered in this chapter. Further, he charged law enforcement and prosecutor higher-ups were too willing to plea-bargain in the case; he said only Manson's hold over Susan Atkins kept this killer from profiting from an incredible plea-bargain the L.A. County District Attorney officials gave her. Bugliosi also accused his own boss, former District Attorney Evelle Younger, of hypocrisy in throwing a prosecutor off the case for talking to the press when Younger himself spoke about the case while running for the attorney general's office in California.
10. Information on the Globetrotters' wrongful arrests in Santa Barbara, California in 1983 (and their subsequent lawsuit against the city for the arrests) comes from articles in the Santa Barbara *News-Press* on December 14, 1983 and October 13, 1984. Further, in the controversy surrounding the policemen's pinheaded arrests, the *News-Press* on January 16, 1984 carried an article that noted the city's liberal white Democrat mayor Sheila Dodge was accused of defending the police by more or less implying blacks look alike. And the article also noted councilman Gerry DeWitt, a liberal Democrat, claimed the media people were slanting coverage of the Globetrotters' arrests; he admitted he slanted news himself when he was a reporter!
11. Information on homosexual killer/cannibal Jeffrey Dahmer comes from the August 5, 1991 issue of *Newsweek* and from the August 18, 1991 issue of *Our Sunday Visitor*.

12. Statistics on plea-bargaining come from separate studies by Herbert S. Miller and David A. Jones that Robert Bonn referred to in his textbook *Criminology*.

13. Information on the Randy Ayers case comes from his case file (Case No. B820102, Hamilton County (Ohio) Common Pleas Court). Further info on his case and the case of Robert Minton comes from articles in the Cincinnati *Post* on July 20 and 24, 1990 and on August 3, 1990, and from articles in the Cincinnati *Enquirer* on July 21, 1990 and December 10, 1991.

14. Information on the Edward Cook case comes from articles in the Cincinnati *Enquirer* on November 17, 18, and 19, 1991, from articles in the Cincinnati *Post* on December 23, 1991 and January 22, 1992, and from an *Enquirer* article on January 23, 1992.

15. Information on the FBI's surveillance of Martin Luther King comes from Victor Lasky's book *It Didn't Start With Watergate*.

16. Information about the attempt to drop the case against Hillside Strangler suspect Angelo Buono comes from Darcy O'Brien's book *Two of a Kind*, and from my interview of Judge Ronald George in 1991. Judge George, according to O'Brien, accurately slammed L.A. County prosecutors John Van de Kamp and Roger Kelly by saying, "In making the decision to prosecute, the prosecutor should give no weight to the personal or political advantages or disadvantages which might be involved or to a desire to enhance his or her record of convictions."

17. Information about the foot-dragging of federal prosecutors in New Jersey in prosecuting public officials tied to the Abscam scandal comes from Robert Greene's book *The Sting Man*.

18. Information on prosecutor handling of the cases of Cincinnati area building inspectors who were accused of theft in office and tampering with records comes from articles in the July 2, 1991 issue of the Cincinnati *Post*.

19. Information on L.A. city prosecutor Steve McKee, who prosecuted a priest for putting nuisance strays to sleep while cases against real criminals backlogged, comes from my 1982 article in the San Fernando *Sun*.

20. Raymond Tanner's murder case is CR 90-02-169, Butler County (Ohio) Common Pleas Court. Besides interviewing prosecutor Robert Piper, I interviewed police officials, Butler County Sheriff Richard Holzberger, two of the shrinks who checked Tanner (neither would comment), the coroner who conducted the autopsy on Maria Tanner, and family members of both Raymond Tanner and Maria Barker Tanner. I also reviewed the autopsy, some psychiatric evaluations on Tanner, and several newspaper articles on the case, as well as the criminal case file.

21. Information on the McMartin Preschool case comes from an article in the April 9, 1984 issue of *Newsweek*, an article in the June 24, 1985 issue of *Newsweek*, an article in the July 8, 1985 issue of *People*, an article in the December 15, 1986 issue of *Newsweek*, an article in the January 29, 1990 issue of *Time*, and an article in the August 6, 1990 issue of *Time*.

22. Information on Ira Reiner's involvement in the Manson Family case comes from Vincent Bugliosi's and Curtis Gentry's book *Helter Skelter*.

23. Information on Carl Rowan, the black writer who shot a white intruder, comes from articles in the June 27, 1988 issue of *Time* and the July 4, 1988 issue of *Jet*.

24. Information on the trailer park residents who protected their homes and loved ones during the Liberty City riot comes from an article in the June 2, 1980 issue of *Newsweek*.

25. Information on the Mexicans who captured the Night Stalker—the demon who raped, killed, and mutilated his way through Southern California in 1985—comes from articles in the September 9, 1985 issue of *Time* and the September 16, 1985 issue of *People*.

Who's Hazardous to Your Health?

It used to be that doctors and hospitals were considered above reproach. But in this day and age of AIDS-infected doctors, revelations of massive malpractice, skyrocketing medical bills and insurance premiums, and reports of old people suffering abuse at nursing care facilities, maybe a little dirt-digging on the health care professionals is in order. After all, they're people like everyone else; for every Albert Schweitzer there can be a Josef Mengele.

In fact, the sad case of Diane Boyd sums up what level some of our health care professionals seem to have sunken to. Diane, a mentally retarded teenager, was raped in a state-run mental hospital in Missouri. She became pregnant, and her mother gave the go-ahead for Dr. Robert Crist to abort the child at the Reproductive Health Services facility in St. Louis.

Diane's mother got more than she bargained for. The abortion not only killed the baby, but Diane too, she would later charge. According to the wrongful death lawsuit Diane's mother filed, Crist or someone else at the abortion facility gave Diane drugs without checking what prescription drugs Diane was being given at the state mental hospital. She charged Diane suffered depressed respiration (not breathing enough) and died as a result.

Ironically, the state of Missouri, a co-defendant in this case with Reproductive Health Services, would later go before the Supreme Court against the abortion facility on another matter. This latter case is better known to the public as the landmark 1989 *Webster* case. And now you know the rest of the story.

In a situation just as ugly, Kim Bergalis has just died as this book goes to print. A sentence of death hung over this beautiful young woman for two years because her dentist David Acer gave her AIDS. Kim, an attractive, personable college coed, could never know the love of a husband because of her affliction. She was also a virgin; yet government health officials seemed so intent on discrediting her that they subjected her to humiliating exams and they interrogated and tested her former boyfriends. Like a modern-day Joan of Arc, Kim Bergalis fought for realistic AIDS testing for health care professionals while she waited for the Reaper to come for her.

Believe it or not, there are doctors and dentists out there who make light of Kim's tragic fate, even though 6800 doctors and other health care workers are known to have AIDS. Some medical bozos go even farther off the edge. Manhattan dentist Jack Rosenberg, who founded a dental guild for homosexuals, has been quoted as saying he knows several dentists who are HIV-positive and he told them not to let their patients know!

In all fairness to health care people, they are at risk from AIDS-infected patients thanks to the stupid behavior of most of these patients and thanks to the insane confidentiality laws in this country. In particular, nurses, dental hygienists, and paramedics will be the innocent victims of this madness.

In this chapter, I will show you how to check doctors for malpractice and how to check hospitals and clinics for substandard health care. I'll also show you how to check on other kinds of public health menaces using Food and Drug Administration records and local public health department records. Then I'll show you how to trace how your medical target gets public assistance from federal and state social welfare agencies, and how he might be defrauding the public.

You can use the techniques in this chapter for "civilian" purposes like deciding whether to entrust yourself or a loved one to the care of a particular doctor or hospital or nursing home. You could use the techniques to help make up your mind on whether to do business with a certain market, eatery, or food processor. As for "military" purposes, you can use these techniques to find out just how much of a butcher, quack, or thief your target doctor is, or find out just how much of a slaughterhouse your target hospital or clinic is. Then you could expose them for the health menaces they are.

EXAMINING DOCTORS

The strongest union in the country isn't the United Auto Workers, or the United Mine Workers, or even the Teamsters, whose toughs make the meanest biker gang look like fairies. The strongest "union" in America, in my opinion, is the American Medical Association, the professional group doctors belong to. (Some call it a *CARTEL* instead of a union.)

There are ways you can find out whether your

doctor is a threat to your health. But the AMA's initials aren't on any of them.

In fact, calling the local medical association is usually a waste of time. Most doctors ARE competent, and they'll tell you about other doctors who are good, but they don't often blow the whistle on the bad ones. Their group isn't in the habit of collecting dirt on dues-paying members. So you can bet they won't snitch on each other to strangers, like malpractice lawyers looking to sue, or malpractice insurance agents looking to cancel policies, or members of the public looking for info on physician competence.

You could try calling the state medical board in your state capital to see what info they have on your subject doctor. If that agency has taken any action against the doctor's license, the agents will send you a copy of the record. However, if the agency's people investigated the doctor but took no action against him, the record is not open to the public. In some states, the agency will investigate doctors who seem to run up a lot of malpractice cases. In others, the agency won't really get involved unless a doctor is accused of criminal misconduct.

It's possible your target doctor has violated the law. I've found criminal cases against doctors for things like public health fund fraud (which we'll cover later), drug trafficking (selling prescription drugs with junkie appeal to street pushers, who in turn peddle the drugs to their favorite dopers), sexually molesting female patients, criminal negligence in connection with running grossly unsanitary facilities, and negligent homicide in connection with the wrongful deaths of their patients. Check on your target per instructions in the chapter on checking criminal records.

One way to gauge a doctor's safety compared to others in his field is to go to the county courthouse and see if anyone has sued him for malpractice. Malpractice cases against your target doctor will be in the civil section of the upper court of the county he practices in. Look up your target doctor's cases per instructions in the chapter on checking lawsuit records to find out just what kinds of mistreatment former patients of his (or their survivors) accused him of.

In either court situation, MAKE COPIES, MAKE COPIES, MAKE COPIES of documents that show evidence of a doctor's unsavory behavior.

So let's say you're a woman who's looking into an OB-GYN (instead of vice-versa). Malpractice insurance carriers and government agents tell me the average OB-GYN gets sued once every five years. Documents a spokeswoman for the American College of Obstetricians and Gynecologists sent me shows member doctors average a malpractice suit every eight years. Doctor's associations, malpractice insurance carriers, and state health departments or medical boards or insurance bureaus also have such malpractice statistics.

If your suspect has had one case against him in the past 10 years, odds are he's a pretty good doctor, or he's good at scaring women into not suing him. Two or three cases over 10 years? Not so hot, but maybe he was just unlucky. Four, five or more cases in the past 10 years? Even the butchers' union might not want him! At the very least, he's probably a below-average practitioner in his field.

Some groups have used this tactic in several states to expose local abortion providers as harmful to women's health. Pro-lifers in Chicago found roughly 200 malpractice cases which women or their survivors filed against the busiest abortion providers in the Windy City. In these cases, the women sued the doctors for items of malpractice such as leaving parts of the baby inside them, perforating their uteruses, lacerating their cervixes and vaginas, causing them massive infections, damaging their bladders and bowels, and severing their uterine arteries.

In a number of cases, the women's survivors sued the abortion providers for causing the women's deaths. Likewise, abortion opponents in Southern California found hundreds of malpractice cases which women or their survivors filed against the busiest abortion providers in that area.

Despite what the doctors' lobby claims, not everyone who sues for malpractice is a greedy jerk retaining an ambulance-chasing lawyer. (Many of them are, however, and sometimes juries get out of hand in awarding damages to patients whose suffering wasn't all that great.) Doctors who average a lot of malpractice suits will argue they've been sued by relatively few people out of the thousands they've treated. That's a sorry argument. For one, a doctor with a lot of malpractice suits relative to the average for doctors of his specialty in his area compares unfavorably with his peers and is therefore probably substandard. Also, a large number of lawsuits ought to tell a doctor maybe he'd better slow down, take a little more time, and give a little more care to his patients. A doctor who sees a bizarrely large number of patients compared to his peers might be cutting corners on health care.

Most people are afraid, or lack the time and money to go after doctors who have hurt them. For example, how do you think the average woman feels about having to face intimate questioning from the lawyer of the gynecologist who caused her damage, especially if the lawyer is big on implying she's a sweathog who doesn't practice basic sanitation on her plumbing or is a shameless slut who hops from bed to bed?

And for every person who sues a doctor, there are scores who have received substandard medical care from a doctor at one time or another. For example, University of California researchers who conducted a survey of roughly 250 doctors released results in 1991 revealing 45 percent of the doctors anonymously reported making mistakes—most of them serious— when treating patients. Of the errors which these doctor anonymously reported to the researchers, 31 percent allegedly caused or sped up patient deaths, 24 percent kept patients in the hospital longer, and 38 percent forced patients to undergo extra treatment. The doctors admitted anonymously they often did not tell their superiors what they did wrong, and only 24 percent of them told the patient's family when they made mistakes in treating their loved ones.

Some state medical boards are starting to require doctors or their malpractice insurance carriers to report any malpractice settlement or loss of $25,000 or more. This is so state medical agents can investigate them for misconduct. They wouldn't be wasting their time if there wasn't some merit to this approach.

Checking a doctor's malpractice record in the courthouse will take you a little time. But it's as good an indicator of the doctor's safety as is available to the average person. Unless, that is, you're able to spot vultures circling his medical building!

EXPLORATORY DIGGING ON HOSPITALS, CLINICS, AND NURSING HOMES

Most people who enter hospitals either get well or are too far gone to save. However, many people die or deteriorate after undergoing negligent treatment in a hospital.

Consider these sick statistics which a national publication carried: Roughly one of every 18 hospital patients gets sick from germs in the hospital; 80,000 people die this way every year. Many more die each year due to medical malpractice.

Hospital and clinic operators are supposed to check on the credentials of the doctors and other health care professionals they sign up. However, they don't always do the job well enough. For example, officials of the giant Kaiser Permanente hospital chain may wish they had done a better job of checking on former staffer Vilis Kruze before the staffers of *60 Minutes* did it for them on national TV in 1990. According to the staffers, this is the sleazy curriculum vitae on Dr. Kruze:

Dr. Kruze was a member of the Nazi SS during World War II, and emigrated to Ohio after the war. He was convicted in connection with botching an abortion he performed on a 19-year-old Cleveland go-go dancer. The teen hemorrhaged and passed the baby away from his office, then she committed suicide a few days later. Ohio authorities made Kruze receive psychiatric treatment at a hospital for the criminally insane, and later made him receive treatment for reportedly locking his secretaries in closets and for forcing them to urinate in bottles at their desks.

Later, Kruze moved to Hawaii, got a contract as a fill-in doctor for Kaiser, and reportedly treated a child so negligently that the child suffered permanent brain damage. The child's parents brought suit, and eventually, Kruze's evil past was revealed. But by now Kruze himself was dead. He was stabbed to death by the revenge-seeking brother of a teenage girl who overdosed on drugs Kruze gave her in exchange for her giving him sex.

Most states' public health department agents do some sort of monitoring on hospitals, nursing homes, and free-standing clinics. In some areas, the state public health department's people will inspect hospitals and nursing homes regularly and will conduct surprise inspections or conduct inspections in response to complaints. In other areas, the county health department's people will handle inspections of hospitals and nursing homes.

In some states, agents inspect free-standing clinics. But too many states' agents treat clinics like doctor's offices and don't check them unless they receive a lot of state public health money or receive a lot of complaints.

Public health codes vary from state to state. In some states, public health officials have the tools to go after slipshod health care providers. In other states, the doctors' lobby and the facility operators' lobby keep the public health people handcuffed. But even states with 19th Century health codes do occasionally send out inspectors to facilities that receive state public health care money; they go to check on the quality of health care the public is paying for.

In one well-known example, inspectors visited Cincinnati's Drake Hospital in the wake of the Donald Harvey killings. According to published reports, this is the chart on the Donald Harvey case:

Harvey, an orderly, killed two dozen people at the hospital in roughly two years. He usually killed old people on his ward with arsenic, cyanide, rat poison, or cleaning fluid. Harvey's co-workers became suspicious of him because of the high numbers of deaths on wards where he worked. They voiced their suspicions to their supervisors, but were reportedly threatened to keep quiet about him. Harvey, under investigation for a patient death, admitted he killed the man, and claimed he did it to put him out of his misery. Cincinnati authorities closed the case a day later without investigating the other deaths.

Concerned staffers at the hospital finally called local TV newsman Pat Minarcin and told him about the situation. Minarcin did some digging into the case, and soon he was able to show the extent of Donald Harvey's killings. When hospital officials reportedly threatened Minarcin, he responded with a special half-hour newscast in June 1987 on how Harvey had been killing people at the hospital. After the newscast, local officials belatedly began re-examining the hospital. Harvey pleaded guilty to the killings and received three consecutive life prison sentences. The hospital was reorganized, and top administrators had to leave.

During this time, state health inspectors turned the hospital upside-down looking for violations. Why were the state folks there? The main reason the state got involved, a health agent who took part in the investigation told me, was that state public health money was being spent at the hospital.

Inspectors write reports and citations when they inspect. These reports often contain shocking, gruesome, and sickening information on hospitals, nursing homes, and clinics.

For example, Los Angeles reporter Betsy Bates in 1988 wrote a stomach-turning series of articles, based largely on public health records, about California public health officials' efforts to shut down Inglewood Women's Hospital.

She wrote that doctors and staffers of this facility, at the time one of the busiest abortion facilities in America, had been investigated and cited for offenses ranging from grossly unsanitary conditions to substandard patient care to falsifying medical records to complicity in the deaths of at least five women who had undergone abortions. These accusations by and large had been in health inspection reports Los Angeles County health inspectors had been writing on the place for years. State public health officials finally revoked the facility's hospital license. But owner Morton Barke found a loophole in the state's public health code and re-opened the facility for abortions a day or so later as an unlicensed clinic and doctor's office.

You may have read reports of abused or neglected old folks at nursing homes around the country. The reporters who wrote these stories no doubt checked into the nursing homes after receiving tips from angry relatives or guilt-tormented staffers. To flesh out their articles, they simply checked public health records on the nursing homes to find out what citations these places had been hit with.

A truly frightening story that broke when I was working in New Jersey involved how a politician "stung" a state-run mental hospital. According to newspaper accounts, this is what happened:

State senator Richard Codey, operating as an undercover agent in early 1987, applied for work at the hospital using the name of a convicted sex offender and the Social Security number of an armed robber. Hospital officials hired him without a hitch. He then went to work in the facility, and he said he saw employees sleeping or watching TV on the job, watched one aide prod patients with a blackboard pointer, and witnessed one staffer give a patient a cigarette butt to eat. He said staffers at the mental hospital told him they would "play with" (have sex with) the pretty women and teenage girls who were patients at the facility. Codey then went public with his investigation, and got the director of the facility fired.

Later in 1987, Codey held a public hearing on mental hospitals, and witnesses told of abuses such as staffer drug trafficking, a patient losing his foot to gangrene because staffers delayed getting him medical treatment, staffers beating patients, staffers drugging and raping female patients, and staffers getting female patients pregnant. The questions I'm sure most people asked themselves when they heard about these terrifying abuses were, "How could the bosses tolerate this?" and "How deep a problem is staffer misconduct nationwide?"

Clinics aren't immune from criticism, either. For example, L.A. County public health inspectors cited a Planned Parenthood abortion facility in 1986 about the same time one of Planned Parenthood's own lab technicians—a native of Egypt—reported his bosses for a string of health code violations. The lab technician claimed Planned Parenthood officials then fired him for reporting the substandard conditions of the facility to public health officials. Planned Parenthood officials later settled out of court with the Egyptian after he sued them for wrongful firing. This story was made public by a citizen investigator, who found an account of the incident in the public files of the L.A. County Department of Health Services. He also found the unlawful firing lawsuit (and a number of medical malpractice lawsuits against Planned Parenthood) at the L.A. County Superior Court Clerk's Office.

And you, too, can find evidence of bizarre, shocking, or plain old unsanitary conditions at your local hospital, nursing home, or clinic. Or you could set your mind at ease if the facility you or a loved one wants to check into has a clean bill of health. You can check public health records on health care facilities just like the reporters and citizens I told you about did, and then strike your own blow for health care reform.

The first thing you'll need to know is who's responsible for monitoring your targeted facility. To figure out who your state and local public health agents are, check the government listings in your phone book. There you will find the name, address, and phone number of your local public health agency or county health department. You might also find the name, address, and phone number of your state public health agency in your phone book. If the listing isn't there, call the information operator in your state capital for the info. Or call your county health department for the info.

If county agents check hospitals and nursing homes in your county, the records of their inspections will be at the county health department. If state public health agents do the checking, the records of their inspections will be at the state public health agency in the state capital, or will be in regional state public health agency offices around the state.

Health inspection reports are public records, so you can see them and photocopy them. To view these inspection records, call your county health department or call the state public health agency's information officer for instructions on how to view the records. Agents usually file records by name of hospital, clinic, or nursing home, so you can ask for the public file by the facility's name.

Once you get the facility's public file, check it for routine information such as:

- License.
- Owners and/or officers of the owning corporation.
- List of doctors with staff privileges.
- Key administrators.
- Any info showing a staffer or corporation officer is a convicted criminal or proven addict. (This will appear in health records in some states.)

Next, check the facility's public file for evidence of serious health code violations such as:

- Patient deaths due to substandard medical treatment, staff care, or basic sanitation.
- Unsafe, hazardous, or questionable surgical, treatment, or other medical practices observed.
- Unsanitary conditions, breaking scrub, unsterile implements, blood on floors, etc.
- Lack of control over drugs.

- Lack of proper emergency equipment.
- Doctors' orders not being carried out.
- Patients being given drugs without doctors' orders.
- Medical record falsification, absence, or incompleteness.
- Anesthesia deficiencies.
- Shortage of nurses and other staffers.
- Uncertified, unlicensed, or unqualified people performing duties.

Mark all pages that contain information that will come in handy.

Next, ask for the facility's medical aid program file. (This should be a public record also, but some clerks will routinely (and probably incorrectly) tell you it's not. Do what you have to do to see this file.) Once you get the facility's medical aid program file, you'll notice it contains some rehashing of information in the public file. It might also contain records of any investigation for state health program fraud or insurance fraud.

Check the medical aid program file for allegations of abuses, such as:

- Overbilling the state. By law, no facility can charge the state more for giving a public-assistance patient treatment than it charges cash or private insurance patients. (The only exceptions usually allowed are reasonable billing to cover interest in case the government is lax in paying the facility's bill, and reasonable billing to cover extra state-ordered paperwork.) The reason for this is obvious. Overbilling the state for treating public assistance patients means the taxpayers are supporting price breaks which the facility gives to other clients or are paying for the operator's excess profits. Many facility operators succumb to the temptation to cheat the taxpayers this way.
- Fee splitting and kickbacks. It's illegal for facility officials to pay for referrals they get. Why? Because the person receiving the kickback may be steering patients to the payer of the kickback for money instead of for the patient's best interests.
- Outright fraud, such as billing for services not performed, or multiple billings for these services.
- Substandard medical practices.

Make photocopies of documents that show evidence of wrongdoing. You'll now have evidence that your target facility is one sick puppy indeed. And you may make a vow never to get sick again!

FINDING DIRT IN FOOD AND DRUGS

Muckraker Upton Sinclair in 1906 published *The*

Jungle, a book about shockingly unsanitary conditions in Chicago's meat-packing plants. That same year, Teddy Roosevelt signed into law the Food and Drugs Act and the Meat Inspection Act to put health controls on what Americans eat, drink, and ingest. The Food and Drug Administration was created in 1927 to administer these laws. The U.S. Department of Agriculture had done so until then, and there is still some overlap between the two agencies.

FDA regulators set standards of sanitation and content for food, drugs, and cosmetics. They also set testing standards for drugs, and they set safety standards for medical devices. They have some law-enforcement authority over food processors and importers, and over drug manufacturers and importers. They have more inspection and seizure authority over cosmetics firms, blood banks, other biological products facilities, and medical device factories.

FDA inspections and citations are public record. For example, I have seen FDA citations on blood banks whose officials didn't ensure blood donors were giving AIDS-free blood. If your target is in a business that the FDA inspects, you can get copies of such citations by contacting the FDA's freedom of information officer, the FDA's general counsel, or the FDA's inspector general.

Likewise, USDA inspections and citations are public records. For example, I've seen cases in which USDA inspectors have caught meat packers selling adulterated meat. I've also seen a USDA report which noted 30 percent of dairies its agents inspected were so unsanitary that USDA agents wouldn't grade their products. If your target is in a business the USDA inspects, you can get copies of such citations by contacting the USDA's freedom of information officer, the USDA's general counsel, or the USDA's inspector general.

As an aside, the FDA can provide you with information on product safety, as well as information on food, drug, and cosmetic content. Some of this information can be helpful, and some (like allowable insect content in foods) is downright amusing.

For example, medical reports generally draw the same broad conclusions about food products. But occasionally crazy medical reports have surfaced damning perfectly good organic substances like caffeine. (When they first claimed caffeine was bad for us, my immediate response was, "Then why do real men like truck drivers, sergeants and petty officers drink their coffee black?") Then other reports came out showing many coffee companies were using dry-cleaning chemicals to decapitate (I mean decaffeinate) coffee. (Since I have decaffeinated real

coffee in a lab using methylene chloride, I knew that bad rumor was true. Sniff a can of decaf next time you open it; you can smell chemicals in some brands.) Thus enlightened, other researchers came out and said maybe caffeine isn't so bad for you after all.

(Some wags note Ronnie Reagan's doctors may have put him on decaf, and Our President acted like Rip Van Winkle and slept through his second term. Maybe some "medical saboteurs" got George Bush to kick the caffeine habit, too, and eat raw fish, barbecued dog, and stir-fried broccoli at state dinners in Japan. Who can you trust?)

FINDING DIRT IN YOUR LOCAL HEALTH DEPARTMENT

Public health agents enforce the health code as it applies to markets, eateries, and other places where food is handled. This means your city's or county's public health department agents inspect such businesses. If you're curious, you can check the agency's records to see which markets and restaurants have the highest cockroach, mold, bacteria, and virus counts and the lousiest sanitation records.

You can also check with your local public health agents to see if your target business has food handler certificates or similar documents on file. In certain areas, food handlers have to undergo checks to verify they aren't carriers of contagious diseases, so they won't pass the sicknesses on to those who eat the food they prepare. If you suspect your target food joint employs another Typhoid Mary, check to see if she's been getting her inspections. If not, you can always make noise about it in the interests of public health.

The only problem with using local public health files are the inspectors themselves. Most of them are conscientious, but they're overworked. However, others are lazy, are on the take, and some might be close buddies of your target (especially if he does business in a rural county). Just because dirt isn't in a target's health department file, it doesn't always mean there isn't any filth on his premises!

Food isn't the only area of concern to your local public health officials. Public health department agents also inspect sewer hookups and plumbing, water works, sewage systems, housing, trailer parks, camps, sources of air and water pollution, swimming pools, gyms, landfills, and incinerators. Further, they inspect public health nuisances like sewage backups, infectious wastes, insect and animal infestations, derelict buildings, rotting large farm animals, and other such hazards. You can check these inspection and citation files for any dirt on your target.

Local public health files also contain other interesting data. If you want, you can check the files for evidence of weird behavior which caused your target businessman to get cited. For example, workers at a pizza parlor frequented by business associates of mine caused their boss a heap of trouble when they served a woman customer a pizza with a topping she didn't order ...a sanitary napkin! *Bon apetit!*

WHEN GOVERNMENT IS UNHEALTHY

People can whine all they want about the inadequacy of government health care programs. The simple fact is that we taxpayers end up paying for government programs, and we're running out of money to give to *ANY* program! It's not fair to blame federal, state, and local officials for the state of health care when they are honest enough to tell us everything on our wish list can't be funded.

However, government officials are to blame when they fail to take valid action against medical people, food products businessmen, and drug company magnates who endanger the public. They are also to blame when they mismanage health care budgets or steal from the public.

The inspector general of the U.S. Department of Health and Human Services looks into waste, mismanagement, patient mistreatment, fraud, and theft by government public health employees. You can obtain information on this kind of government misbehavior by making a freedom of information request to the agency's freedom of information officer, inspector general, or general counsel. The inspector general's semiannual reports outline various investigations he and his people carry out against government employees. I'm sure your parallel state public health and welfare agencies could provide you with similar information about abusive, crooked, or incompetent state and local public health employees.

Then there are times when a government agency is directly accused of public health and welfare meddling. Reporter Elizabeth Sobo, using public documents, reported in 1991 that the U.S. Agency for International Development and the CIA were targeting Latin American, Asian, and African people for population control. She noted a U.S. government-funded birth control program set up in the Dominican Republic after the 1965 U.S. invasion of that nation has led to the sterilization of one-third of Dominican women. She also reported AID officials, through a $15 million contract with Johns Hopkins University, have bombarded the people of Nigeria in recent years with thousands of population control ads, stories, songs, and other propaganda messages.

For further evidence of government wrongdoing in the health care field, check out the following section on health care spending. The waste and mismanagement problems in these government programs cost taxpayers big money.

FOLLOWING THE HEALTH CARE MONEY TRAIL

The U.S. Department of Health and Human Services and state and local public health departments dole out billions of health care tax dollars to provide basic health care to those on public assistance. They also dole out big money to support other health care programs. Some of these programs are good; others are not so good. It's your right as a taxpayer to see how these agencies are spending your money.

How do you get your hands on these records? Call the public information officer or the contracts administrator for the public health agency whose records you want to see. Ask for information on what projects the agency funds. Often, you can get a summary of all programs the agency funds if you ask for it.

Once you have this information, check the summary for the name, purpose, and amount of money in each program. Once you find the program you are interested in checking on, call the information officer or the contracts administrator back and ask for the procedure for viewing financial records (or ask for the procedure for getting these records photocopied and mailed to you if you live too far away from where they're kept). Follow the official's instructions, and you should be able to haul in the information you're seeking.

A citizens' group in California used these kinds of public records to show Planned Parenthood and other groups were targeting the state's black, Hispanic, and Asian communities for population control. They released a booklet which said the state's Office of Family Planning had given Planned Parenthood and other groups $9.4 million in 1984-1985 for 28 separate programs aimed at cutting the numbers of racial minorities in California. They named the facility, purpose, and funding of each of these projects. Eventually, the governor terminated this agency's programs.

You can also ask a state public health agency's public information officer for records of the state's public health payments to your target doctor or facility (hospital, clinic, nursing home) operator. Likewise, you can find out how much money your target doctor or facility operator pocketed from the Feds by asking the public information officer of the U.S. Department of Health and Human Services in Washington for records of federal payments to him.

Other sources of dirt on your target doctor or facility operator are the inspector general and the general counsel of the Department of Health and Human Services. These law-enforcement administrators investigate, cite, prosecute, and sue doctors and facility operators for medical fund fraud, for substandard health care, and for other abuses. Contact them and ask them to provide you with copies of punitive actions they took against your target. Likewise, contact the officials with similar jobs at your state or local public health department for information on actions they have taken against your target.

To give you an idea about how widespread the theft/fraud problem is, chew on these stats which the HHS Inspector General released in 1990 (and which I obtained through a freedom of information request). HHS agents secured at least 1300 criminal convictions in Fiscal Year 1990, took administrative actions against at least another 900 people in FY 1990, and recovered about $50 million in fines and restitution from those who stole or misappropriated federal public health care money. The Inspector General's people investigated doctors, hospitals, nursing homes, medical equipment companies, and medical services providers for virtually every kind of medical fraud imaginable. The most common type of fraud seemed to be overbilling the Feds for goods or services.

If you suspect your target is breaking the law, overbilling is where to look first, and it's not all that hard to do so. Since virtually any bill a government pays is a public record, you can obtain copies of your target's bills to each public health agency. Then look for one of the following items:

- Billing the agency more than private customers for the same goods and services. We've already talked about why this is illegal. To figure out what a health care provider charges a private party, just call his office and ask for a quote. Then compare this figure to what he charged the government (taxpayers) for similar goods or services. If you find he's billing the government more, you've caught him. You can report him to the agency and maybe save the taxpayers some money.
- Seeing an extremely high number of patients or performing an extremely high number of tasks. For example, California public health officials investigated the doctors of San Vicente Hospital because if the reports of the doctors at this abortion facility were accurate, they were spending less than eight minutes per woman to perform most second-trimester abortions. The state officials knew this speed was unsafe for the women

the doctors were operating on, so they checked the doctors' claims. If you see similar instances of undue speed, question the doctor's commitment to his patients and to quality health care, and question his honesty as well.

A PRESCRIPTION FOR REFORM

Reporters who wrote a series of investigative articles in the Chicago *Sun-Times* in the late 1970s and similar articles in the Chicago *Tribune* in the late 1980s and early 1990s have used public health care payment records to spotlight the methods—many of them illegal—Chicago's leading abortion providers were using to get government money for their businesses. The reporters wrote that some of these doctors billed government public health agencies hundreds of thousands of dollars each year.

According to published reports, one of these men—Arnold Bickham—served time in a federal prison for fraud in connection with the way he overbilled the government on employee salaries. He was implicated in the abortion-related death of one of his women patients before he went to prison. After he got out of prison, he was implicated in the New Year's Eve 1986 death of a teenage girl whom he threw out of his facility and left to bleed after he performed an abortion on her.

According to published reports, another man—Henry Pimentel —is at this writing fighting state public health agents who are trying to revoke his doctor's license over his medical fund fraud conviction. State agents took his abortion facility's license in early 1991 after they evidently found unsanitary conditions, outdated drugs, and unqualified staffers. They had earlier suspended him from receiving public health funds because he and his people performed what they termed "grossly inferior work."

Much of the documentation the reporters based their stories on came from readily-available public records from the files of the U.S. Health and Human Services Department and Illinois state public health financial records. There's nothing stopping you as a citizen investigator from finding evidence of this kind of misconduct, either. Use the dirt you dig to lance your target like a boil. It will make your area a healthier place.

END NOTES

1. Information on the abortion-related death of Diane Boyd comes from St. Louis City Circuit Court case 812-11077. As a follow-up note, Crist is being investigated as this book goes to print for the death of Latachie Veal. This 17-year-old Texas girl died in November 1991 after Crist performed an abortion on her. The source for this case is an article in the

November 6, 1991 issue of the Kansas City *Star*.

2. Information on AIDS victim Kim Bergalis comes from an article which appeared in the July 29, 1991 issue of *Time*. Likewise, this article was the source of the reported quote and other information on Jack Rosenberg, the dentist who urges AIDS-infected dentists to stay in the closet when it comes to disclosing their affliction with patients. Further information on Kim Bergalis comes from an article in *USA Today* on September 12, 1991, and from an article in the Dayton *Daily News* on December 9, 1991.

3. Information from the American College of Obstetricians and Gynecologists comes from the group's report *Professional Liability and Its Effects: Report of a 1987 Survey of ACOG's Membership*.

4. Information on the UC survey of 250 doctors who admitted to harming patients comes from an article in the May 6, 1991 issue of *U.S. News*.

5. Statistics on illnesses and deaths of people from diseases they contracted in hospitals and deaths from doctor malpractice comes from an article in the August 5, 1991 issue of *U.S. News*.

6. Information on Vilis Kruze comes from the transcript of 60 Minutes broadcast of November 4, 1990.

7. Information on the Donald Harvey killings (and the story of how Pat Minarcin uncovered them) comes from an article in the August 24, 1987 issue of *Time* and from an article in the October 1987 issue of *Cincinnati* magazine.

8. Betsy Bates' articles on the Inglewood Women's Hospital abortion facility appeared in the L.A. *Herald-Examiner* on February 11, 12, and 17, 1988.

9. Information on New Jersey official Richard Codey's crusade against patient abuse at mental hospitals (and his related "sting" against state mental health officials) comes from articles which appeared in the Newark *Star-Ledger* on March 1, 1987, on March 10, 1987, on April 10, 1987, and on October 18, 1987.

10. Information on Planned Parenthood's 1986 health code violations in L.A. County, California, comes from a cease and desist order dated April 8, 1986, and a 36-count deficiency report from an April 3, 1986 inspection. Both documents were issued by the L.A. County Department of Health Services. The wrongful firing lawsuit against Planned Parenthood is C618798; it was filed in the L.A. County Superior Court.

11. Information on the unsanitary dairies comes from the U.S. Department of Agriculture Office of Inspector General Semi-annual Report for the first half of FY 1991.

12. Elizabeth Sobo's two-part exposé on AID and the CIA population control effort in Latin America and Africa appeared in the May 26, 1991 and the June 2, 1991 issues of *Our Sunday Visitor*.

13. Information on the California Office of Family Planning's funding of population control programs aimed at ethnic groups comes from the booklet *The Office of Family Planning: Analysis of a Tragic Failure*. Information on the end of this agency's population control funding comes from an article in the L.A. *Times* on January 11, 1989.

14. Information on the people whom federal health agents got convicted or punished in some other way comes from the U.S. Department of Health and Human Services Office of Inspector General Semiannual Report for the second half of FY 1990.

15. Information on San Vicente Hospital staffers' questionable abortion practices comes from the California Department of Health Services case DHS SUR 78-0067. The report noted there were a number of billing irregularities worth thousands of dollars, but stopped short of accusing the facility's operators of fraud.

16. Information on abortion provider Arnold Bickham comes from *The Abortion Profiteers* series which ran in the Chicago *Sun-Times* in 1978, from an article in the Chicago *Sun-Times* on March 13, 1986, and from an article in the Chicago *Tribune* on September 14, 1989. Information on abortion provider Henry Pimentel comes from articles in the Chicago *Tribune* on July 28, 1990 and on February 8, 1991.

Grave Digging—Coroner Files and Death Certificates

This chapter is not for the squeamish. But this chapter might help you prove your target is responsible for the death of another. Short of proving your target is a homosexual child molesting killer like John Wayne Gacy or Jeffrey Dahmer, there's nothing worse you can pin on someone.

Evidence showing people have died at the hands of another turns up all the time—especially in lawsuits at courthouses. People sue motorists who kill someone with their cars. People sue bosses when their loved ones are killed in unsafe workplaces. People sue doctors whose malpractice kills their loved ones. And sometimes people will sue criminal killers for damages because it's often easier to make someone pay money under civil law than it is to convict him of a serious crime under criminal law.

Records of people's deaths will also show up in criminal cases at courthouses, in vital statistics files at the county health department, and in autopsies and inquests at the county coroner's office. Since we've already talked about researching civil and criminal cases, this chapter will cover researching coroners' records and death certificates.

The "military" use for death records research is obvious. Proving your target was responsible for the death of another will usually trash his reputation pretty thoroughly. But there is a pretty important "civilian" use for these kinds of records—you might be able to convince people to stop self-destructive behavior by examining the horrible deaths of others who engaged in such behavior.

Before we really dig into this gruesome chapter, I'm going to tell you about how a Connecticut man used public records to solve a decades-old mystery about a little girl's death in a fire.

THE CASE OF LITTLE MISS 1565

Let's go back to the first week of July in 1944. When the circus came to town this week in Hartford, Connecticut, World War II was in full swing. Our men were pushing east across France, north through Italy, and westward through the Pacific Islands. This very week, Americans would liberate Saipan (reportedly only a couple of weeks too late to save courageous aviatrix Amelia Earhart from probable decapitation at the hands of a Japanese swordsman). Many women and children, whose husbands and daddies were away fighting the war, would go to see the show under the big top in Hartford on July 6...maybe to get away from worrying about their loved ones for just a little while.

But they would soon be caught in a spectacle almost as dramatic and terrible as the war itself. The circus tent burst into flames, and the 7000 or so spectators and circus people had to flee for their lives. Sadly, 168 people didn't make it. One of these was an eight-year-old girl whom authorities could never identify. Perhaps she was a neighborhood girl who tagged along with friends to the circus; perhaps she was a runaway; perhaps she had just wandered in to see the show. But no parents came forward to say their little girl was gone. The young girl lay unclaimed, and on her toe the coroners put the tag 1565. She was eventually laid to rest under a stone that read, "Little Miss 1565."

Many years later, a picture of the young girl touched the heart of Rick Davey, a Hartford Fire Department investigator. In 1982, he began reviewing files of the fire, which were public records. He developed leads from these records, and he interviewed people connected with the case in any way. By March 1991, he had solved the mystery of who the little girl was. He publicly identified Little Miss 1565 as Eleanor Cook.

Davey went one step further. Using clues from the files, he identified a possible arsonist. The suspect, who was a 14-year-old circus worker at the time, later served time for arson elsewhere. The suspect, now living in Ohio, was tracked down and questioned. He denied setting the Hartford circus fire. But at this writing, Connecticut authorities are deciding on whether to re-open the case. You see, there is no statute of limitations for murder.

Davey, commenting upon the case, said, "These (fire victims), even in death, have a right to expect that the truth be known." There is nothing stopping you from being as relentless a digger as Rick Davey—and making the truth known yourself.

FINDING CORONER CASES

Coroners perform the ugliest, saddest work in America. They cut up dead people to figure out what killed them. I watched an autopsy only one time. It took place on a cold gray wintry day in Cleveland, and I watched the coroners dissect a poor young woman. It was awful. But there is a purpose to the corpse cutting; coroners have helped convict many a killer, identify many a missing person, and determine many a health threat so other people could survive.

A coroner, in performing an autopsy, will try to determine if foul play, an accident or negligence, suicide, unusual circumstances, natural causes, or some kind of public health threat caused a person's death. Some states still call any public official who fulfills this role the coroner. Others call him the medical examiner. His functions are basically the same state to state. For the purposes of this chapter, I will call the county-level public official a coroner.

Most counties in each state have a coroner's office. In larger counties, the coroner is a doctor and he has a large staff of medical examiner doctors, lab technicians, and clerks. In the smaller counties, an individual undertaker or doctor serves as the county coroner, and one of his competitors serves as the deputy coroner; state-retained doctors who serve as medical examiners perform the autopsies for these counties. For the rest of this chapter, I will call state-connected autopsy-performing doctors "medical examiners" to avoid confusion.

In most states, the county coroner's files (and state medical examiner's files) on deaths are public records. There are only two tricks to getting into the coroner's files. One is that the coroner has to have performed an autopsy for there to be a file in the first place. Coroners don't get involved in most deaths. They usually handle only the suspicious deaths, like homicides, suicides, certain accidents, certain special public health cases, or certain instances of therapeutic misadventure (what they call a case in which a doctor kills a patient by his negligence). Since you're looking for dirt on your target, remember this: If he might have caused someone's death, assume the coroner will be involved.

The other trick to getting into the files is having the name of the deceased, or at least an identifying number. That's how the coroner's employees file the autopsy files. In some instances, you'll know a dead person's name already, so you can easily gain access to the coroner's files.

But what if you don't know the names of any possible victims of your target? You can still find out the names of these victims and gain access to most coroner's office files if you do a little legwork. Here are some angles to try:

- Start by checking the courthouse for wrongful death lawsuits against your target. Check also for criminal charges against your target. You might find charges ranging from negligent operation of a motor vehicle to maintaining an unsafe establishment to negligent homicide on up to premeditated murder. Don't forget the federal courthouse; the dead person could be from out of state, your target could have business in several states, the Feds could have lodged a civil or criminal complaint against your target, or a lawyer representing survivors could have found a federal law like deprivation of civil rights or RICO (racketeering-influenced corrupt organization) to file a lawsuit under so he could go for really big money from your target. All such cases will contain the name of the victim somewhere.

- Even if government regulators don't file formal criminal charges against your target, you can check government agency records (such as those at a labor agency or a health agency) for proof that he killed someone. The agency's file on your target or his business might contain names of victims. If it doesn't, the agents in many cases will still give you the name of the deceased (or at least the deceased's death certificate number or the autopsy number). In several cases, I found government agents cited businessmen for worker deaths on their job sites; in most cases, the record contained the name of the victim(s). In another probe I conducted, I discovered that public health inspectors had written up an abortion facility operator for health code violations that helped cause a woman to die. The file on this facility didn't contain the dead woman's name, but it did contain enough information on her that I was able to get her name and autopsy number from an agent who was familiar with the case.

- If your target is in the medical field, you could check your local health department for the death lists the agents keep for each hospital, clinic, nursing home or other such establishment. Each licensed facility's operator probably has to report deaths on a monthly or quarterly basis. If your target is a doctor or another kind of medical professional, you might find something on these lists that might tie him or her to a death. These lists should contain dead people's names and/or death certificate numbers.

■ If you suspect your target killed someone in a traffic accident or through some other form of negligent behavior (and he wasn't cited, charged, or sued), your local police force's officials may give you some helpful general information, like a list of all accident victims or homicide victims in a given year. Likewise, fire department officials and rescue squad and paramedic officials might keep and release copies of similar lists. Check in with any of these public safety agencies via the agency's information officer; he or she may be able to get you this info without too much difficulty. If some sort of ordinance (or basic cussedness) prohibits them from releasing such information, you might consider having your policeman friend or local private investigator approach the authorities on the sly for the info.

■ Sometimes, a local newspaper's files will contain an article that will tie a person's death to your target. If the paper's librarians are good, you might be able to get them to find the article in their morgues (yeah, this is what newspaper clipping files are called). Scanning newspaper obituaries also can help. When I was a reporter, I helped people who were looking for this kind of information by pulling copies of old articles for them and providing them with obituaries to scan.

■ Some undertakers will help you if you approach them the right way. Ask the undertaker if he can remember anyone he had to bury as the result of a certain kind of accident, medical malpractice, or the like. Likewise, see if you can find an honest doctor or nurse who might have the guts to expose a bad doctor or discuss the case of a victim he or she treated who was admitted as the result of foul play. Try to get a victim's name, or at least get the time frame for the event. Then check obituary files and newspaper articles in this time frame for the names of victims whose demises fit the account given by the undertaker, nurse, or doctor. Investigators tell me newspaper files, obituaries, friendly undertakers, and honest doctors and nurses have enabled them to pin wrongful deaths on targets.

■ Check coroner office records by cause of death. The records of larger coroner's offices and state medical examiner agencies are set up so agents can search death cases by the manner in which a person died. Many coroner's offices' clerks can search by a broad category, such as by homicide, suicide, accident, therapeutic misadventure, natural causes, or undetermined.

Once you have a dead person's name, you can gain access to the coroner's files. But even if your searching only turns up death certificate numbers instead of names, you're still in luck. If you at least have a death certificate number, you can ask a clerk at the vital statistics bureau in the county where the person died to get you a photocopy of the death certificate. Or you could contact the state's vital statistics bureau (usually a part of the state's public health department) to get a photocopy of the death certificate.

Once you get the death certificate, check it for the deceased person's name, check it for a note that an autopsy was performed, and check it for listed causes of death. In some states, the death certificate will note if the coroner investigated the person's death. And even if the death certificate doesn't contain this note, chances are good that the coroner investigated this person's death if the cause of death was homicide, suicide, accident, or therapeutic misadventure.

DISSECTING CORONER CASES

Once you have a victim's name or coroner case number, you can gain access to the coroner's files. Call the coroner's office and find out what the procedure is for viewing coroner case files. Then go to the office, give the name or number to the coroner's clerk so she can get the file for you, and review the file once she gives it to you. Here's what to look for:

■ Check the investigator's report (or similar document prepared by the first agent to investigate the death) for the victim's name, address, age, race, probable cause of death, and time and location of death. The report will also give a brief initial summary of the case.

■ Check the autopsy report (or similar document prepared by the coroner or medical examiner) for the cause of death. Also check this gruesome document for the condition of the person's body and for the organ-by-organ check for clues of foul play, other wrongful activity, disease, or substance abuse. The document will describe in detail any wounds the corpse might have, and any other relevant observation on its external and internal condition.

■ Check the toxicology report (or similar document prepared by a lab specialist who tested the victim's body fluids) for evidence he confirmed or ruled out drugs, booze, or poisons as factors in the victim's death.

■ Check the facility report (or similar document prepared by a doctor suspected of killing a patient with his malpractice). It's interesting to see whether or not he admits to wrongdoing, shows he's truly innocent, or tries to weasel out of the blame for the patient's death. Just think of what effect this document, written in the doctor's own hand, would have on potential patients!

■ Skim through the rest of the file for information. Check for interesting, useful, or gruesome information. A real heart-tugger is the body release request a victim's loved ones have to sign. Imagine yourself in the shoes of a loved one of a victim, having to see the corpse in a drawer, then having to sign for the body and the clothes and the personal effects. I like to think I'm a hard guy, but I've never been able to read the body release request for a child's body or a teenager's body without feeling a twinge of sadness and at least a few tears in my eyes.

Make copies of these documents. By all means, you want hard-copy proof of what your target did to cause the person's death.

We'll follow now with a story on how a medical examiner's autopsy cleared a man wrongly accused of killing his wife. Then we'll discuss how a woman was able to use autopsy information to finger a coal company over the death of a miner.

HOW A MEDICAL EXAMINER CLEARED A WRONGLY-ACCUSED WIFE-KILLER

When I was a reporter in Appalachia, I stumbled onto a story that taught me the value of withholding judgment until all the facts are in. It involved the case of a man who was charged with beating his wife and leaving her for dead on a barroom floor. And I would later use autopsy information available to the public to tell my readers he was not the killer.

I heard from the police that a man got into a fight with a bouncer at a tavern the night before, then struck his wife in the head during the fracas and knocked her unconscious. They said he left the scene when police were called, and was later arrested for drunk driving. "What kind of scum leaves his wife like that?" I thought.

However, I soon overcame my initial disgust at the man and decided to look into the case. The fight had taken place in a town in Tennessee which had a bad reputation for mistreating outsiders. The man was from just across the state line in Kentucky. Maybe, I thought, there's more to it then what the police are saying.

There was. I tried to interview witnesses, but no one wanted to talk. However, I learned that the man had broken up a fight between his wife and another woman. Then the bouncer told the couple to leave the premises. The man for some reason decided he wasn't going to leave, and a fight ensued between the two men. The wife may have tried to jump in to help her husband against the much-bigger bouncer, and somehow she received a severe blow to the head. I also found out the man had stayed at the club to make sure paramedics would come for his wife, ran away when lawmen came for him, drove to the hospital where the paramedics took his wife, kept vigil in the hospital's emergency room, then fled when lawmen showed up at the hospital. He drove back into Kentucky, where sheriff's deputies arrested him on the drunk driving charge.

Meanwhile, the woman and the four-month-old baby she was carrying died in the hospital. The man, who was being held in Kentucky, was now looking at one and maybe two murder charges.

I found out state lawmen who were assigned to handle the case were having no more luck than I was in finding witnesses willing to talk. One of the investigators complained to me, "There was a bar fight and 75 people said they were in the john. And it was only a two-hole can!"

I printed the investigator's comments. In the same story, I also printed a police source's report that both sides of the wife's skull were fractured, and one fracture may have been caused by a sap or a blackjack. To me, this indicated she may have been struck very hard on one side of her head by the bouncer (who could easily have had such a weapon), then fell very hard on the other side of her head. At any rate, the article generated considerable comment in the area our little paper covered. All of a sudden, people started to talk to the authorities about what may have happened. Some of these people finally agreed to talk to me, too.

I then interviewed the man while he was being walked from the courthouse to the county jail, and he claimed he was innocent. He did not fight extradition to Tennessee, and he vowed he would clear his name. What led me to believe him was not his protesting, but his size. I've been in many fights inside and outside the ring, and I could see he was too small to have the strength to have crushed his wife's skull with a chance shot to the head with his fist.

(I also was able to reconcile the facts regarding the man's running from the bar, and later, from the hospital. We all have "fight or flight" reflexes; we can never predict how we'll act in stressful situations. The man, under a great deal of pressure he had never even considered when he and his wife had gone out for a little fun that night, had simply panicked—like all too many of us would have done. But he at least had shown concern for getting his wife medical attention, even though his judgment in running away was questionable.)

Needless to say, I was soon wearing out the telephone of the Tennessee medical examiner who was set to do the autopsy on the man's wife. Even on days when I had no new information on the case, I'd still print a little blurb on the case to keep it in the public eye so maybe someone would come forward with the truth. Eventually, the medical examiner determined a blunt object or maybe the woman's fall to the floor had caused her head enough damage to kill her. He determined there was no way a fist could have caused that kind of damage to the woman's head.

The medical examiner's work was proof positive of the man's innocence, and I reported it. The grand jury members in Tennessee refused to indict him, and he was cleared of any wrongdoing. Unfortunately, the person who was responsible for the woman's death was never punished for his actions. But at least the medical examiner, by his work, saved an innocent man from wrongful imprisonment and maybe execution.

HOW AN AUTOPSY HELPED A MINE WORKERS MUCKRAKER

Now I'll tell you about how a reporter put together a truly ugly story based on coroner records, medical examiner records, and labor agency records that are open to the public. Marat Moore, the reporter in question, worked for the *United Mine Workers Journal*, a magazine put out by the United Mine Workers union. She wrote a story on how mining company executives may have used undue pressure to cover up the cause of death of one of their miners in a mine in Buchanan County, Virginia. (This county is deep in Appalachia, where Kentucky, West Virginia, and Virginia come together.) According to Ms. Moore, this is what happened:

Bruce Ballard, the miner in question, was found face down near a roof bolter in a nonunion mine owned by Consolidation Coal on the morning of September 20, 1985. (Miners use electrically-powered roof bolters—machines the size of small lawn tractors—to drive steel rods into the rock above coal seams to prevent cave-ins. These rods, known as bolts, have replaced timbers in underground mines.) Later that morning, the county coroner pronounced Ballard dead by electrocution. He noted Ballard's corpse was clothed but barefooted.

Meanwhile, an agent from the U.S. Mine Safety and Health Administration investigated Ballard's death. He determined the roof bolter and its power supply were not faulty and that no one had moved the machine or worked on it before he (the inspector) reached the mine. State mine safety officials showed up later in the day to check the machine, but miners were already using it again. So they noted they couldn't finish the investigation because the accident site had been disturbed.

A medical examiner for the state medical examiner's office later performed an autopsy on Ballard. (As I said earlier, state medical examiners perform autopsies for counties too small to keep a full-time medical examiner's lab busy.) He also ruled electrocution was the cause of Bruce Ballard's death. A forensic scientist, however, decided there wasn't evidence of metal in tissue taken from Ballard's body to prove he made direct contact with an electrical conductor. U.S. Department of Defense pathologists called into the case said Ballard's wet clothing could have made it possible for enough electrical current to enter his body and kill him without burning his clothing or his body. However, they couldn't agree on how Ballard died, so they ruled he died of undetermined causes.

(Ballard's widow had to produce a receipt before Consolidation Coal officials would give her what they claimed were Bruce's steel-toed boots. Ballard's father, a retired federal prosecutor, told me his daughter-in-law said the boots were in good shape, then threw them out without checking if they were Bruce's size. He told me they were not examined for burning, melting, or otherwise having passed electrical current.)

Consolidation Coal officials monitored the investigation, contacted some of the examiners, and also discussed the case with a U.S. Mine Safety and Health Administration official. The official sent the case for a cause-of-death review, because his agent said the mining machine checked out and because there was not a unanimous conclusion among the medical experts that Ballard was electrocuted. The MSHA review board members—none of whom was a doctor—ruled Ballard's death could not be blamed on electrocution and therefore didn't count as a mine-related death.

Bruce Ballard's widow and family members were angry over this ruling. And they were furious when Consolidation Coal officials reportedly sent Bruce's widow a letter congratulating Bruce for helping the company achieve its goal of "zero accidents" for 1985.

Marat Moore reviewed local rescue squad records and discovered miners at the Consolidation Coal mine had suffered injuries severe enough in 1985 that the rescue squad had to make five ambulance runs to the mine that year. She interviewed rescue squad members to confirm this. Needless to say, United Mine Workers officials used her account of the Bruce Ballard case to push for changes in the way MSHA conducted business.

Admittedly, Marat Moore was not an "objective journalist." She was working for a labor union magazine, and the death occurred at a non-union mine owned by a company with which her union had clashed. However, her use of the autopsy paperwork and the additional forensic reports and her inspection of rescue squad records (and of course, her research on the mining agency's records) enabled her to write a first-rate muckraking story.

Even though I wasn't covering the county where Bruce Ballard died, Marat's effort interested me enough that I interviewed most of the principals myself to see that she had accurately reported what they told her. I then filed for the records on the case myself, and found Marat Moore's account meshed with what the records noted. The records on the case were all open to the public, and Marat Moore knew how to get her hands on them. In fact, she did such a good job of getting the public records tied to the case that she probably could have written a story almost as ugly without conducting a single interview.

INSPECTING INQUEST RECORDS

Another place where wrongful death dirt on your target might be is the coroner's inquest file. A coroner's inquest is like a grand jury session in that the coroner's inquest jury members have to determine if there is probable cause the suspect wrongfully caused the death of another through criminal negligence or through criminal actions. Unlike a grand jury session, the coroner's inquest is a public event, and it can sometimes even be a notorious event. It's no fun for the defendant, even if he's not investigated further.

Ask Teddy Kennedy—he talked his way through an inquest in Massachusetts after Mary Jo Kopechne died in his car. In their book *Death at Chappaquiddick*, Richard and Thomas Tedrow used records of the inquest on Mary Jo's death, along with other records on the case, to conclude she survived for several hours on air trapped in the car and died when the oxygen ran out.

If this was so, Mary Jo could have been saved if Teddy had gone for the cops right away. (By the way, an autopsy was never performed on Mary Jo's body; Teddy's people had her body shipped to her parents in Pennsylvania.) Judge James Boyle, who conducted the inquest, determined there was probable cause to believe Kennedy was driving negligently, and that his negligence apparently helped cause the death of Mary Jo Kopechne. Boyle could have recommended criminal prosecution of Teddy, but did not.

The coroner's inquest file is like a criminal file; it's a public record and you can review it. Treat it like a criminal file; see what your target was suspected of doing or failing to do which led to the death of another, then follow the documents down to the final decision to recommend prosecution or recommend dismissal of the case. Figure out why an inquest ended the way it did; figure out why the jurors or judge did or didn't recommended criminal prosecution. And by all means, make copies of documents you can use.

The worst thing the jurors or judge of a coroner's inquest can do to someone is recommend he be charged with criminal misconduct. The recommendation can make him look bad even if he gets off the hook later. After all, how many people even *undergo* something that serious? You can still say your target was investigated, explain how he was able to avoid criminal prosecution, and let people make up their own minds about whether your target is an unethical lowlife who's unsafe to be around.

AND NOW A FEW WORDS ABOUT DEATH CERTIFICATES

Most deaths don't come to the attention of the coroner's office; only the suspicious ones like homicides, suicides, certain accidents, and certain therapeutic misadventures do. However, a person's just as dead by wrongful conduct even if his death isn't investigated by the coroner.

Almost all deaths cause some authority to fill out a death certificate on the deceased, and list his opinion on how the person died. In most cases of death, a doctor or a paramedic will pronounce the person dead and sign the paperwork so an undertaker can dispose of the body.

Using the methods I laid out above, you can find whether or not your target has been suspected of causing someone else's death, obtain the name or the death certificate number of the victim, and then obtain a copy of the death certificate.

As I noted earlier in this chapter, death certificates in most cases are public records. (In a few backward locales they aren't; they're restricted to the viewing of police types or family members. In a pinch, you might try getting a policeman friend or a private eye to get a death certificate for you if you need it. Or you might represent yourself as a relative or a researcher with a need to know.) County health departments' vital statistics bureaus keep death certificates on file. Also, state health departments' vital statistics bureaus keep backup copies. Contact these people for info on the procedure for obtaining copies of death certificates.

Many vital statistics agents key death certificates with ICD-9 codes so public health people can search for people's deaths by ICD-9 code causes of death. (ICD-9 codes—short for International Classification of Diseases—are recognized by medical professionals around the world. And don't let the word "diseases" fool you. ICD-9 codes cover other causes of death, ranging from train collision to drug overdose to execution by penal authorities!)

If you want to check out which people have died in your county or state from a particular cause, go to a college library (preferably one with a medical school, dental school, nursing program, or mortician program), find the ICD-9 code books, and figure out which codes match the kind of deaths you are interested in. Then, armed with these codes, get your vital statistics clerks to generate a list of names (or a list of death certificate numbers, depending on the agency's bookkeeping) for you. Using this list, you can gain access to the death certificates you want to review.

Death certificates typically contain the dead person's name, age, sex, race, date and place of birth, date and place of death, Social Security number, residence, occupation, education level, and next of kin. They also typically contain information on who reported the death, who certified the death, who embalmed the body, and who buried or cremated the body. They also typically contain the primary cause and the contributing causes of the death, the circumstances of the death, and information on whether the body was autopsied. Check each death certificate once you receive it for all this information.

Most of the information on a death certificate is good. However, the causes of death may sometimes be inaccurate.

There are two major reasons why the real cause of death might not appear on the death certificate as the primary cause of death. One is that the person recording the death is the kind of stickler who will list the last item that pushed the person through Death's door. He might list the underlying causes later on in the death certificate, or he might not list them. Such a person is the kind of nit-picker who might note Jayne Mansfield—the blonde bombshell actress who was decapitated when she ran her car under a truck on a New Orleans road in 1967—died from "heart stoppage."

The other reason is that the person who signs the death certificate may be covering up something connected with the death. For example, a doctor may cover for his patient if the patient died of an embarrassing disease brought on by his own sexual activity (like the way a doctor may have decided to report Liberace did not die from AIDS). Or the doctor may cover up for himself or a colleague if either one of them was responsible for the patient's death.

Remember what I wrote about the study of doctors covering up mistakes. Almost one-third of them reported making mistakes that killed their patients. And only one-quarter of the doctors admitted to telling the patients' families they made mistakes in treating their loved ones. In cases of abortion-related deaths I have investigated, I've seen the doctors try to cover their tracks (or their colleagues' tracks) by noting the women died of embolisms, "cardiopulmonary insufficiency", old female organ wounds, and "ovarian gangrene"—anything but the abortion itself.

In any case, the falsifier of a death certificate is endangering lives. Why? Because a person who covers up the death of a patient with a communicable disease keeps people he came in contact with from seeking medical attention. And a doctor who covers up patient deaths he or a colleague caused defrauds survivors of their just awards and keeps a health menace in practice where he can do still more damage to people.

There are several other reasons a death certificate may contain bad information. Someone friendly with the deceased or the deceased's family might enter bad info on a death certificate so the family can claim benefits they might otherwise lose. For example, a kindly doctor might write down a man died of a heart attack while working when he really died of a heart attack while having sex with his secretary or Gal Friday (like Nelson Rockefeller may have been doing when his ticker crashed for good). This way, the man's widow can get certain work-related death benefits for herself and the children, even though her old man died like a heel.

Or company officials might want to avoid legal problems associated with a person dying on the premises. (See the miner's story, above.) They simply lean on or bribe the person who fills out the death certificate, and he puts down what they want him to put down. Likewise, a crooked doctor or someone else who caused a death through his own negligence might bribe or pressure or con the person who fills out the death certificate into listing a false cause of death so he can escape criminal prosecution or a wrongful death lawsuit.

Then there's the guy who enters a fake death certificate on himself so he can create a new identity. Why? He may want to escape creditors, lawmen, ex-wives, Mob hitmen, IRS agents, or other persistent and vicious people who don't wish him well. Or he may be helping his "widow" collect on his life insurance policy so they can live it up on the money they take by fraud from the insurance company.

Then there are those who fill out a death certificate in as noncommittal a way as possible to avoid being named in a lawsuit. My brother, an undertaker, says he has had to sew up many a body that forensic people have torn apart in search of clues of what killed the victim. And he says the victim's families are heartbroken and disappointed when the death certificate cause reads "Undetermined."

At any rate, look at the whole picture when you check a death certificate. Try to find out as much as you can about the circumstances of the person's death or disappearance. Try to figure out who would benefit by the cause of death being listed the way it is. A little extra digging will exhume the truth, or at least provide you with some leads.

CIVILIAN USES FOR CORONER FILES

Every so often, teenagers commit suicide in a bizarre fashion, often to draw attention to themselves. They're depressed, and they really don't weigh out all the consequences of their actions before they attempt suicide.

In a few cases, a teen commits suicide because he or she is clinically depressed or is the repeated victim of an ongoing abusive situation. You adults and teens should learn the outward behaviors which may clue you to a kid you know who is suffering from one of these conditions. Such signs of suicidal tendencies might, for example, include changes in eating and sleeping and hygiene habits, withdrawal from friends and family, violent or rebellious or withdrawal behavior, substance abuse, boredom, lack of concentration, drop-off in school performance (and similar declines elsewhere), loss of interest in favorite activities, refusal to accept praise, giving away cherished belongings, and certain phrases. "I wish I was dead," "I feel rotten," "I won't be seeing you again," and "I can't take it anymore" are such verbal clues.

But in many cases, the kid offs himself or herself for some stupid reason. This stupidity makes the suicides bad people because they throw their lives away and they set bad examples for other teens who may be moping around in a self-pitying funk because of parental discipline or a puppy love affair gone sour.

It's up to you to dig out the dirt from between their ears. Maybe you can use suicide records found in the coroner's office to make would-be copycats wake up and smell the coffee, or at least give them something to think about if they're considering suicide.

The surest way to make an impression on teens is to give them the ugly truth about self-inflicted death in the coldest way possible. My dad recommends making a suicide prevention film like the old "splatter films" you saw in high school driver's education class.

But if you don't have the money or the stomach to produce such a film, you can still get your point across with the right approach. Research some teen suicide coroner cases, make copies of some of the most sickening paperwork, and make copies of pictures in the file. For example, if you find a case in which two teenage girls lay down in front of a commuter train, find the document that shows how many pieces the train tore their bodies into. See if you can find in the death scene investigator's report any measurement or estimate of how far the girls' heads rolled down the tracks after the locomotive wheels severed their heads from their bodies.

If you find a case in which a youth hanged himself, see if the forensic examiner determined he died of strangulation. In other words, his neck didn't jerk hard enough in his drop for the neck bone to break and the spinal cord to sever, so he took several minutes to twist slowly, convulse, and choke to death.

If you find a case in which a teen slashed his wrist, see if the examiner noted he found several cuts on the wrist before the kid "got it right" and severed an artery. This could mean the teen made his first cut or two, hesitated or panicked, and probably grossed out at seeing his own blood gush and feeling the pain before he made the slash that killed himself—quickly, or slowly and agonizingly.

If you find a case in which a girl overdosed on pills, see if the coroner ruled she choked to death on her own vomit. Or maybe he determined she drowned with her head in a toilet bowl when the pills triggered her vomit reflexes and she ran into the bathroom to throw up.

By all means show copies of pictures of suicides. In a coroner file, I saw a picture of a woman whose throat was slashed from ear to ear, and the sight of her severed windpipe sticking through the gash in her neck is something I'll never forget. (I'm not easy to gross out—I have physically put the remains of fire victims and car wreck victims into body bags, and I have seen a girl's headless torso and severed head at a crash site—and I've been able to go on with my work.) If the teens don't react with revulsion, either openly or privately later on, then they're probably beyond your help anyway.

Also, tell kids point-blank that five, ten, or more years from now, people aside from their loved ones will talk about them like they were low-grade morons for killing themselves—not tragic young teens who sent anyone a message. Only their loved ones will hurt. If a kid's parents are as mean or as worthless as he or she thinks they are when he or she melodramatically commits an "I'll make them sorry" suicide, they probably will shrug it off, say good riddance, and get on with their lives while the kid's body rots in the ground.

Opponents of Sherlock's shock treatment might call it "sick." Others might view it as violation of the privacy of the dead. My response? All this goofy "counseling" that school officials use in the wake of a teen suicide disrupts the surviving kids' learning, doesn't force the kids to get back to work, and doesn't force them to grow up by confronting ugly reality.

As for the privacy of the dead, those who kill themselves stupidly didn't want privacy. They CHOSE to drag other people, like witnesses and paramedics and nurses and policemen and coroners, into their own trivial lives by mindlessly killing themselves. My method may sound sick, but it's the only way others could find use for these kids' lives—lives these kids thought little enough of to throw away.

There are milder uses than suicide prevention for coroner's files. They are also aimed at modifying potentially destructive behavior.

Despite all the efforts of police authorities and parents and even bartenders nowadays, there are still those pinheads who will drive while drunk or strung out on drugs. Short of taking people by the hand, marching them down to crash sites and making them witness freshly-killed people, you can show them documents and pictures of folks killed by drunk or stoned drivers (including the drunk or stoned drivers themselves). Most such accident victims who die don't die instantly, or cleanly. Maybe, just maybe, some of these substance abusers will think twice before getting behind the wheel after downing several beers or doing several lines.

Another form of behavior that kills people is smoking in bed. The urge for a late-night nicotine fix or a post-coital smoke is so great in some people, they'll die for a smoke. And they do die, literally, from smoke inhalation or from burning to death after smoking in bed. I'd show people pictures of a house fire I covered. A woman was smoking in bed, and she fell asleep, never to awaken. Her mattress caught on fire, and soon the whole house burned to the ground. Even the

metal roof on her house melted. And her corpse? All that was left was the back of her skull, her spinal column, a little of her collarbones, a little of her pelvis, and a few strands of barbecued flesh. Her flesh, her organs, her arms, her legs, and most of her head were literally burned off of her spinal column.

The smell and the sight were so sickening, the men who gathered to help fight the blaze and the women who got the men refreshments either vomited or cried, or did both. I personally put what was left of the woman in a body bag. I'd like to think a review of that woman's death might cause a few people to give up lighting up before nodding out.

The death of someone from a drug or alcohol overdose can be pretty sickening to watch or read about. In some cases, blood vessels in the brain explode, killing the druggie. Or the heart speeds into takeoff mode, then shuts down forever. Or large sections of the liver die, then fail to filter wastes from the blood. The intoxicated fool then dies of infection or another less-than-delightful ailment. Or the person falls and bonks his head on a table (like William Holden reportedly did), or drowns while swimming loaded (like Natalie Wood reportedly did), or chokes on his own barf while lying in a drug or booze-induced stupor (like John Belushi). In any case, sharing paperwork on sordid deaths like thess with people might keep them from partying too crazily.

Believe it or not, the bedwetters, mental midgets, and space cadets who seemingly form a majority in L.A.'s entertainment community pressured local officials to remove L.A. County Coroner Thomas Noguchi when he reported, without cover-up, the circumstances surrounding the deaths of the celebrities I mentioned above. Noguchi may have had his faults, like reportedly not managing his people well enough. But the "Coroner of the Stars" performed a public service whenever he released the sleazy details of how some celebrity died because of his or her own stupid behavior.

THE FINAL WORDS

No one should die in vain. Using public records on people's deaths to punish bad people who caused them and using records of people's deaths to dissuade others from doing stupid things that can produce similar results will ensure fewer people die in vain.

END NOTES
1. The story of Little Miss 1565 comes from an article in the April 21, 1991 issue of *Newsweek*.
2. The articles I wrote on the man wrongly accused of killing his wife ran in the Whitley County (Kentucky) *Republican* in the

first half of 1983.

3. The story of the Bruce Ballard case comes from an article in the September 1986 issue of the *United Mine Workers Journal.*

4. Information on the inquest into Mary Jo Kopechne's death comes from Richard and Thomas Tedrow's book *Death at Chappaquiddick.*

5. Information on questions surrounding Liberace's death come from articles in the February 16, 1987 issues of *Time* and *Newsweek.* Liberace, who was effeminate in public, had long been suspected of being a homosexual. Liberace denied he was a homosexual, said he disapproved of homosexuality, and fought a lawsuit a former employee filed against him for "palimony". Was he or wasn't he? For the purposes of this book, we'll assume he was telling the truth.

6. Information on the innuendo surrounding Nelson Rockefeller's death comes from articles in the February 12, 1979 issues of *Time* and *Newsweek,* and the February 19, 1979 issue of *Newsweek.*

7. Information on the deaths of William Holden, Natalie Wood, and John Belushi (and on the trouble Thomas Noguchi got into for leveling with the public about their deaths) comes from articles in the March 22, 1982 issues of *Time* and *Newsweek,* an article in the March 28, 1983 issue of *Newsweek,* and from Stanton Peele's book *Diseasing of America.*

Special Projects

Real Estate Mudslinging

In the earlier chapter on real estate records, we covered the basic ways to uncover information on your target in the course of checking real estate records. This chapter will be more fun; it will show you how to find serious dirt pertaining to land ownership and how to use the dirt to make trouble for your target. And if you're a property owner, I'll show you a thing or two about reducing your property taxes fairly.

This chapter will cover special projects you can perform relating to real estate. Assuming you've developed some basic land research skills by following the instructions in the earlier real estate records chapter, I'll show you in this chapter how to track down government-connected land scams, how to do your own assessing and appraisal checking to double-check the politicians at tax time, how to find out who's ducking paying property taxes, how to fight zoning and planning schemes, how to check on building code violators, and how to expose hidden owners of property.

TRACKING DOWN GOVERNMENT-CONNECTED LAND SCAMS

Since money and land go hand in hand, there are all kinds of opportunities for bad people to make money illegally off of land. Real estate fraud comes to mind immediately for many people. (Check the chapters on researching criminal records, lawsuits, and private sector misconduct to track this kind of behavior from your target.) Other good methods of making money illegally involve using government purchasing and taxing authority to unfair advantage.

One classic method of making money dishonestly off of land is selling land to government agencies at inflated prices because the government purchasers don't know any better, or because they are crooked and can be bribed to okay a ridiculously high asking price. A related method is getting inside information about a government agency's intent to buy land or construct an eminent domain project (one in which the agency will seize land from owners, then compensate them), buying up land in the area of the project as cheaply as possible, and letting the government buy it back at higher costs.

If you suspect people have pulled such scams, check the property records. If someone has sold land to a government agency at an inflated price, the assessment records and sales records of comparable properties in the area will hint at it. In other words, similar properties in the same area with the same zoning should have roughly equal assessed value and should sell for about the same prices. When you check on land in the area, watch for the inflated assessment (especially one that happens just before the land sale, and a review of the deed and building permit records shows no improvements that can justify the jump), and watch for the inflated selling price relative to other assessments and sales in the area. These items point to possible wrongdoing on your target's part and point to possible wrongdoing or negligence on the bureaucrats' part.

Likewise, checking sales in an area will indicate if someone has bought up a lot of property in the area of a government project. If your target bought up land in the affected area a short period of time before the project became known to the public (especially if your target has ties to people in the government agency performing the project), suspect your target and/or government agents of wrongdoing.

Another scam involves getting an auditor or an assessor to give property a ridiculously low assessed value. Since property taxes are based on assessed value, a lower-than-normal valuation means the property owner beats paying his fair share of property taxes. And guess who shoulders the added burden caused by this freeloading? You and me, buddy.

If your target has political connections, check the assessed value of property he owns with a number of other similar properties in the area. If his properties seem undervalued relative to other properties, this may be evidence of bribery or favor-getting on his part, and evidence of bribe-taking, favor-giving, or honest incompetence on the assessor's part. At this writing, Joseph DeCourcy, the former auditor of Hamilton County (Cincinnati), Ohio, is under indictment on charges he really *DID* lower taxes— allegedly by illegally lowering the property assessments of Republican fat cats to give them $1.4 million in improper tax breaks. As you might have guessed, this county is basically run by a GOP machine.

Yet another scam involves simple refusal to pay property taxes for a while. People who do this on a large scale treat the county treasury as a low-interest bank, because even if they eventually do have to pay the taxes and the interest and penalties, it's often cheaper and easier for them to pay back money this way than for them to finagle a banker into loaning them big money. You can check your county's property tax rolls for evidence your target owes back taxes. If he's not in a bankruptcy situation, or even if he is, such apparent deadbeatism on his part is evidence he might be loaning money to himself at taxpayer expense. (This assumes, of course, the county doesn't sock it to tax deadbeats with high interest charges and penalties.)

Then there's the scam of misusing zoned land. For example, a property owner might overbuild a residential area by putting up more houses than the zoning allows to make extra profit. Or he might shoehorn in more rental units in apartment complexes than the zoning code allows. These are relatively simple for you to catch if you check your target's project against the zoning and double-check to make sure he didn't get a variance (exception) from the zoning officials to do what he wants. If they give him a variance, but you find in the public records of the zoning commission minutes that they routinely don't grant variances, you may have possible evidence of an unethical relationship between your target and the officials.

However, the misusing zoned land scam may not always seem apparent on paper, because the property owner might be using high-dollar land for a purpose better suited for lower-dollar land. An extreme example of this would be using prime Beverly Hills real estate for a junkyard. Crooked people aren't stupid. If (and only if) there's money to be made from a low-rent business operating illegally in a high-priced area, they'll try it. For example, a target might be operating a manufacturing facility in a commercial area near a manufacturing area because he couldn't get the land elsewhere or because he'll get less scrutiny. Or he may be operating an illegal landfill or a waste treatment facility on prime farmland because there's a demand for the service, or because the local authorities won't come out to check on him.

Do your homework on the zoning for the land, then check out your target's usage against the allowable zoning. Again, check for variances, and check on how tough it is for most people to get them if your target seems to be able to get them. If he's misusing the land, you've caught him...and maybe you've also caught the zoning officials not doing their jobs.

OTHER WAYS TO MAKE LAND-BASED TROUBLE

Do Your Own Bond Evaluating. Knowing property assessment records and property tax records allows you to prepare your own financial impact statement of any bond issue. You can do this by first finding out from your county assessor the total assessed property value in the school district, city, township, county, or other special tax district subject to the bond issue. You then can calculate a ballpark figure of how much the bond will cost the taxpayers by multiplying the amount of the bond times the interest rate times the number of years it will take to pay off the bond, and adding this figure to the amount of the bond to obtain the rough cost of the bond. (The actual cost of the bond may be less due to amortization and other bond payoff factors.)

Then divide the rough cost of the bond by the number of years it will take to pay off the bond to get the rough cost of the bond per year. Divide the rough cost of the bond per year by the total assessed value of property in the taxing district to come up with the fraction extra the taxpayers will have to pay each year. Multiply this fraction by 1000 to estimate how many dollars per $1000 in assessed value this bond will add to each taxpayer's property taxes.

For example, your government taxing district has a total assessed property base (total ratables) of $1 billion. The district's officials want approval of a $10 million bond. At an interest rate of 5 percent over 20 years payback time, the rough cost of the bond will be about $20 million ($10 million times 5 percent per year times 20 years for interest plus $10 million for principal). Divide $20 million by 20 years payoff time to get a rough bond cost of $1 million per year to the taxpayers. Divide $1 million by $1 billion in total assessed property base to get a fraction of 0.001. Multiply this figure by 1000 to get one dollar per $1000 assessed property value per year. By this figuring, a homeowner whose house and property have an assessed value for tax purposes of $50,000 will have to pay roughly an extra $50 a year in property taxes (one dollar (per $1000) times $50,000 divided by $1000) for 20 years if this bond measure passes.

In several elections, I made reasonably accurate estimates of what local bonds would cost in property taxes before the local officials released the official impact statements. My readers knew ahead of time what kind of a tax hike they were in for, and if they thought it was worth it, they could vote for the bonds. Needless to say, many bond supporters did not like it when I gave the taxpayers this free financial service!

Double-check The Officials. Sometimes the

taxers screw up bills. If you suspect your bill is one of these, check with the county assessor to see what the total weight of levies is on your property, then multiply the total weight of levies on your property by the amount of assessed value of your property that the assessor uses in calculating your taxes. If you find a difference between your figures and the assessor's figures, point it out to the assessor, especially if he made a math error in the government's favor!

In 1987, Cincinnati public school officials got a school levy passed, and they overbilled the public. It turned out the educators didn't know their New Math well enough (although some cynical souls no doubt accused them of being crooked), so the taxpayers got dunned for $2.5 million more than the school officials said they needed. After the error was made public, the red-faced educators offered tax rebates. The media folks covering the levy issue earlier should have done their own math instead of trusting the school officials.

Do Your Own Real Estate Appraising. An article in a national publication in 1991 noted many homeowners were getting unfairly high property tax bills because bureaucrats in assessors' offices across the country were making mistakes in assessing the values of homeowners' properties. Homeowners who checked their property records at the assessors' offices reportedly said the government employees had overstated the size of their houses, had entered improvements and features the houses didn't have, or had mistakenly overvalued their lots.

Since the article's author reported homeowners who contest their tax assessments get the assessments reduced from 40 to 80 percent of the time (depending on locale), it shouldn't hurt you to check on your own property records at the assessor's office for errors that are costing you money. If you find any errors, or if you find evidence your neighbors are paying substantially less in taxes than you are for the same kind of property, you can challenge your assessment and maybe save yourself some money.

Correct Other Government Problems. When I was working on a paper in New Jersey, I got a call one afternoon from a lady in distress. The cause of her plight was a snarl of red tape that was keeping her and her husband from putting up a prefab house on a small homesite they had bought. Buck-passing between bumbling bureaucrats in the township's sewer authority, the state Department of Environmental Protection, and the U.S. Army Corps of Engineers kept the couple from getting a sewer line installed on their property for over a year; no sewer line meant no home. So they lost the prefab home they wanted, they had to shuffle between friends' and relatives' houses

and live out of boxes for more than a year, they ran up engineering and lawyer bills, and they got socked by the township for more money in the process.

Since the woman kept records of her land title, her application for the sewer line, and the bureaucrats' responses to her (all of which were public records), the woman's story wasn't too hard for me to verify. I contacted the officials in question, listened as they made lame excuses for their screwups, and quoted them in a story I wrote the next day that read like a script for a Three Stooges feature. A week later, the bureaucrats developed the brainpower and energy to solve the lady's problem, and she sent me a nice thank-you note. But even though I gave the woman's problem the media attention it needed to maybe help get it solved, I couldn't have done it so easily if she hadn't done her homework.

Publicize Deadbeats. You can check tax rolls to see who owes back taxes on land. It's possible your target is one of these. Imagine his embarrassment if he's exposed as a tax deadbeat. Or let's say you don't have it in for anyone in particular, but you want people to pay their taxes so the politicians don't squeeze honest folks like you for even more money to make up the difference. You can check the tax rolls at your county treasurer's office to see who the leading deadbeats are, then release this info to media people, politicians, or other people in a position to make trouble for the tax deadbeats.

One of my most popular articles resulted from just such a search. In a county in Appalachia which I covered, county school officials wanted county supervisors to tax people more to pay for the bills they were running up. (The school board members didn't have their own tax levying authority.) One of the supervisors, in commenting about the school board's money situation, complained about tax deadbeats. That led me to check the tax rolls. As luck would have it, one of the leading deadbeats in the county was one of the school board members!

I laughed like hell when I saw this, but my resulting article was no laughing matter for the school board members. The public hearing on the tax levy took place after my article ran in the paper. As you could imagine, the meeting hall was packed to the rafters with angry mountaineers, and they made life miserable for the local officials. The school board member in question prudently ducked the meeting—and probably avoided a good old-fashioned beating. Angry taxpayers settled a lot of scores in the next election.

Fight Turf Wars Over Zoning And Planning. You can fight developers who want to trash your area or someone else's area. And you can fight those who want to put a nuisance or a crime-magnet business in your area or someone else's area. To win such a fight, you need to know how to research planning and zoning records. Let's illustrate what can happen with an example or two.

Let's say Mister Haney Developers want to build a planned community for oil company executives in your county (which we'll call Crude Acres) on land that is being eyed for use as a state park. The county planner didn't recommend it as a subdivision he wanted to include in his land use plan. After all, he figured the oil execs could live in Kuwait and sniff burning oil wells daily for the next year or so. But the developers and the executives find out about the planner's thumbs-down by checking his report on the developers' plan and by checking the agenda of the planning commissioners' public hearing. So they put on a low-key dog-and-pony show at the planning commissioners' public hearing and suavely lie about the economic and environmental good the ritzy gated subdivision will do. They then make phone calls, twist arms, and offer bribes so the planning commissioners vote their way when the project comes up for recommendation.

In order to allow the Crude Acres subdivision, the zoning commissioners will have to approve the recommendation of the planning commissioners, then re-zone land to accommodate it. By now, opponents of the oilmen may materialize after seeing or hearing the news about the project. They'll show up at the zoning commission's public hearing and fight the robber barons. If they've done their homework, they'll have checked for evidence of campaign contributions, business ties, or other connections between the oil company people and the public officials. (Finding this kind of dirt is covered elsewhere in the book.) And they keep checking the agendas and showing up to meetings until the zoning commissioners vote on the issue. If need be, they'll apply leverage on the county supervisors to reject the scheme if the zoning commissioners okay it.

Or let's say the operators of Aqua-Goose Partners, Ltd. want permission for a homosexual bathhouse on property they own that is zoned for commercial use. However, the property is near schools and churches, and the city's zoning code contains a rule that states anyone putting up a new building or business establishment near a church or a school must get zoning commission approval due to public safety and morals concerns. So Aqua-Goose Partners asks the zoning commissioners to approve their business plans.

In most normal communities, the zoning commis-

sioners would show the Aqua-Goose people the door and tell them not to let it hit their backsides on the way out. But let's say your zoning commissioners aren't up to speed. They allow the Aqua-Goose project to make the agenda of their next public hearing on zoning variances. If you don't check agendas of your zoning commissions, you'd better hope a reporter did (and wrote a story on it), or a vigilant friend at the courthouse did, or one of the token commissioners with common sense raised a stink about the application. Or maybe you or someone you know read the local newspaper's classified ads for public hearing notices and saw the notice for the Aqua-Goose project there.

At any rate, you find out about it through one of these sources. You leg it to the zoning commission office and the planning commission office to review the plan. You compare it to the code to find obvious instances where the bathhouse will be in violation. You then see how the operators claim they are going to be able to operate such a place without offending the morals of churchgoers, putting young schoolboys at risk of molestation, or posing a threat to public health by leaving AIDS-contaminated condoms around in the parking lot and the garbage bins. You then look for evidence of Aqua-Goose bigwigs' campaign contributions, business ties, social relationships, or other connections to local officials per other chapters in this book.

You then show up at the zoning commissioners' public hearing with about a zillion of your closest friends to make the bathhouse set wish they'd never left the closet. And you send a message to the zoning commissioners who they'll really have to suck up to when they get ready to vote whether to allow the bathhouse. Make sure you and a zillion of your closest friends attend the meeting at which the zoning commissioners vote on the bathhouse, too, and make yourselves heard. Follow the situation to the county commission or the city council as needed. Apply pressure to get the bathhouse project dumped, or else your side will get it in the end.

EXPOSING BUILDING CODE VIOLATORS

Most investigators overlook the humble building code, the fire code, the electrical code, the plumbing code, and the waste code in their scramble to dig dirt on targets. But knowing what these laws cover in your area could lead to some interesting dirt digs.

Cincinnati's ranking public health official was pinched by public health agents for allegedly owning several tenements. City health inspectors cited him for owning a roach-infested apartment building, and for owning four vacant derelict buildings that were not barricaded. He certainly hasn't benefited from this public disclosure.

Down in the hills, a black man I know (whom I'll call Fred Douglass after the heroic runaway slave, abolitionist, and diplomat) was a constant candidate for local office in one of the small Kentucky counties I covered. The racism of too many of the local people kept Fred out of the winner's circle, but he still found a way to serve the public. Fred was an electrician, so he became a building inspector for the government. He waged war against the coal camp/sharecropper-mentality of landlords in the area by staging constant building inspections and citing the owners of these substandard shacks on a laundry list of building code violations. Building by building, Fred improved low-income housing in the area.

The citations Fred wrote are public records, just like such citations are in your area. Check the building department, the development authority, the planning commission, the zoning commission, the fire marshal, the fire department, and the public health department for citations on your target. If you find any, document them and make sure your target gets the slumlord reputation he deserves.

FINDING HIDDEN OWNERS

Belle Boyd, the lady who used to check on land sales for my paper down in Appalachia, used to take a lot of unfair guff from people who harassed her for printing information about land sales. (Belle Boyd, by the way, is not the woman's real name. The real Belle Boyd was a young Shenandoah Valley lady whose spying and vamping for the Rebels during the Civil War made her a beloved and notorious figure.) Belle, in her ladylike but straightforward hill-country way, told people she was only trying to keep things honest and on the up-and-up. And besides, she added, people could find out the market value for property by reading her column. They would be less prone to get rooked in real estate deals this way.

Belle was right. Keeping things honest and on the up-and-up benefits us all, especially those of us who are honest! But why did people try to hide land sales from her? And why do many people all over the country do likewise?

People hide property ownership for a number of reasons. Men might want to hide assets from ex-wives looking for fatter divorce settlements. People might want to hide assets from creditors or tax officials. People might want to hide their real worth so when they buy other property the sellers won't try to milk them for more because they're wealthy enough to afford to pay more. Company officials might try to keep the wraps on a project they are working on. And in smalltown America, some people want to shield their affairs from the prying eyes and jealous hearts of others. Some of these reasons are legitimate; others are questionable.

On a more sinister level, landowners hide land ownership to cover conflicts of interest or to make money in other illegal ways. The scam a landowner will use is having a "straw" (an employee or friend or relative) buy the land using his (the landowner's) money, then turn the land over to him. The landowner makes out two titles for the land. The title with the straw's name is registered at the courthouse, while the title in which the straw transfers interest in the land to him is kept hidden.

The U.S. Department of Housing and Urban Development Inspector General's reports to Congress contain lots of tidbits on such illegal activity. The agents report that speculators pay straws to qualify for low-interest loans; the straws then buy the properties, and turn the properties over to the speculators so they can sell the properties at profit based on the loan differentials. And if speculators default on the loans, HUD has to cover the loans when the lenders foreclose on the properties. In the reports, the agents name those whom they prosecute for illegal strawbuying.

I know of a woman who stiffed a friend of mine, whom I'll call "The Godfather," for a number of bills she owed his business. The Godfather didn't buy her pleas of poverty, and resorted to the means he saw fit to make her pay her debts. A couple of years later, this same woman, now the mistress of a Mob figure, was able to buy the whole city block across the street from The Godfather's establishment. Obviously, the little moll was a straw for her Mob man's real estate dealings.

Louis Rose, an investigative reporter with the St. Louis *Post-Dispatch*, has made a career out of investigating dirty land dealings. In his book *How to Investigate Your Friends and Enemies*, he gave the following advice on figuring out who truly owns a piece of property:

- Check to see if the straw has the same mailing address as a business or some other property owned by another person. The business owner or other property's owner could be the true owner.
- Check the straw for other property deals. If in the past he's shown a tendency to deal with the same people, he could be holding the property in question for them.
- Check on the straw's background. A straw who

lives in a low-rent area, drives a beat-up car, and holds a low-paying job could be serving as a straw (possibly for an employer or a relative or a friend).

- Check the tax rolls for the property in question. Sometimes the real owner doesn't trust the straw's ability to remember to pay the property taxes for him, so he does it himself. If the local tax collector mails the property tax bill to someone other than the person the deed says owns the property, it could be that the person getting the tax bill is the real owner.
- In some areas, the fire marshal or the county recorder keeps a list of straws for arson investigation purposes. Check this list.
- Get a realtor friend of yours to find out. There are times they know about the straw and who he fronts for.

Louis Rose is a high-powered journalist. But he probably didn't learn these kinds of relentless investigation techniques in a journalism school. And he probably didn't learn too much from other journalists. Odds are he is so stubborn and so nosy that he built himself into a power-digger. The moral of his professionalism is this: With some drive and some common sense, you should be able to make progress using land records to do your own excavating.

END NOTES

1. The information on indicted Hamilton County auditor Joe DeCourcy comes from articles in the Cincinnati *Post* on July 2, 1991.
2. The information on how Cincinnati Public School officials overcharged the taxpayers $2.5 million for passing a school levy comes from a May 10, 1988 article in the Cincinnati *Enquirer*.
3. The article on property owners who challenge incorrect tax bills was in the October 14, 1991 issue of *U.S. News*.
4. My article on the school board official who was one of his county's biggest property tax deadbeats appeared in the Kingsport (Tennessee) *Times-News* on September 13, 1986.
5. The information on the health code-violating public health official comes from a June 4, 1991 article in the Cincinnati *Enquirer*.

Organized Digging on Organizations

I've already covered checking on the wrongdoing of a couple of kinds of organizations. I spent two whole chapters discussing how to dig dirt on businesses and part of another chapter on digging dirt on labor unions. However, it wasn't enough. This chapter will show you how to check for an organization's purpose, its leaders' records, who and what they support and oppose, and how they handle money.

Political parties, political action committees, cause groups, professional and business associations, cults and scams posing as religions, and many other organizations are operating with a harmful agenda or a commitment to a fast buck. These groups can be as structured as United Way or as loose as the Manson Family, but any one of them has the potential to cause just as much or more harm to the public as any business or union.

Just think of what people consider some of the most vicious evils and injustices in our society today. Racism. Bigotry. Widespread pollution and land-raping. Government officials. AIDS-infected people infecting others without restraint. Abortion on demand. Insane greed. Tax breaks of all kinds for those who don't deserve them. Drugs. Runaway children being exploited. Exploitation of migrant workers and the working poor. Pornography. Child molesters. Other sexual perverts. Piracy in the medical, legal, banking, insurance, and real estate fields. Megapiracy by China, Japan, Britain, OPEC, oil companies, and other multinationals which cost our workers jobs and our businessmen money. Crippling taxation. Violent criminals. White collar criminals. Crooked televangelists. Cult leaders who prey on the yoyos who follow them.

Believe it or not, all of these evils and injustices have one or more organizations in favor of them. And all of these organizations need at least one or more citizen investigators like yourself digging up dirt on them to expose them and bring down on them the punishment they so richly deserve.

On the other hand, you might want to be kinder and gentler, and check out some "point of light" nonprofit group before you give your money or your time to it. You can use this chapter to prove groups are decent as well as prove they are slimy. The tone of this chapter is negative and accusing (so what else is new?), but if your target organization is untarnished in your eyes after you get through looking into it, then you're probably dealing with ethical folks. Either way, using the techniques of this chapter will enable you to check on all kinds of public, private, and nonprofit organizations.

FINDING OUT A GROUP'S BASIC INFO

In many instances, if you're investigating a group, you already know what it stands for. However, there will be times when you need to check a group and you're not exactly sure what its agenda is. At other times, you're reasonably sure of what the group is involved in, but you want black-and-white proof.

The best source of this information is the group itself. Call the group's publicist or one of its leaders and ask for literature about the group. Tell her or him you're a student doing a term paper or a freelance writer doing an article on a topic that concerns the target group. Say you would appreciate getting some literature from the group on the topic, and some general literature on the group itself—literature that discusses the group's goals (its agenda), its programs, its membership, and other relevant information.

After you get the initial bunch of information, analyze it, then call the group's publicist or leader back and say thanks for the info. Then ask her or him follow-up questions you might have thought of (see other items in this chapter for hints). Ask who the group's supporters are, in and out of public office. Ask who the group's enemies are—in and out of public office, and for what reasons. If you're asked why you need this information, reply in sincerity that your research project requires you to have this information. After all, any good college prof or editor would hold students or writers to this standard of research.

Once you have this information, you can contact the group's enemies for dirt, contact the group's friends for info and leads, or plunge right into the task of digging up dirt on the group via the public records which I've discussed elsewhere. I favor the approach of looking up public record info first, then contacting the group's enemies, then contacting the group's friends, then going back into the public records to do any follow-up work I need to do as the result of getting previous leads. So that's how the next couple of sections of this chapter will go.

FOLLOWING YOUR TARGET GROUP'S PAPER TRAIL

By now, you should know who the target group's officers are, and what the group's agenda is. But you've just scratched the surface. Using public documents, you're going to be able to find out a lot about the activities of the group and its officers. Some instructions on the best documents to check follow.

Corporate Paperwork. Even though I've already covered corporation registration at length, I'll say a little bit more about it here. Virtually all groups, whether or not they run a for-profit business, will incorporate to protect their leaders from lawsuits, to cover their assets at tax time, to make it easier to solicit for contributions or raise money, and to show other people they mean business. No matter what kind of group you're checking, get the group's incorporation paperwork per instructions in the first chapter on the private sector so you'll know who the group's principals are and other basic information. While you're at it, don't forget to pick up the group's annual reports or any other documents your state makes organizations file. These should be in the custody of the secretary of state in your state capital.

Business And Labor Paperwork. If your target group is a business, do the kinds of checking I recommended in the two chapters on the private sector. If your target group is a labor union, do the kinds of checking I recommended in the chapter on labor.

Political Paperwork. If your target group is a political action committee or a lobbying group, check with the Federal Election Commission in Washington. The FEC can supply you with a list of candidates who any group's political action committee or similar pressure group financed, and how much money they gave to each of them. FEC agents make a number of other records available to the public besides the campaign finance statements. You should be able to get reports these organizations have to file, and correspondence between the FEC and these organizations' key people. (It's illegal, by the way, for a company or a labor union to donate directly to a campaign, but it is legal for company officials or union officials to form a political action committee and solicit or arm-twist people to get donations.)

Some states have similar systems. In some counties, it is possible to go to the county election board and view a list of all PACs doing business with politicians in the county. In such counties, each PAC

has to file a donor report with the clerks at the election board. This report is a public record, and you can check on who's giving money to help the PACs support or buy your local politicians. At any rate, check with your state's secretary of state and your county election officials for information on what rules organizations have to play by. Get copies of contribution reports and other reports available to you under your state's freedom of information law.

Check each of the target group's favorite politicians' financial disclosure records for evidence each one has some sort of financial ties to officers in your target group, or ties to the group itself. See which politicians your target group supports or owns or rents. See if there's evidence any politician is a board member of the group, or if any key member of the group is a board member with any politician for another organization or business. This way, you can tell if the relationship between the group and any politician is more personal than just the group having a call on his votes in exchange for campaign contributions.

Tax Returns. If you know or suspect the group is a nonprofit corporation, call the freedom of information officer at the nearest Internal Revenue Service office. Ask the officer to check if the group is a nonprofit group. If the group is a nonprofit group, ask the IRS officer to tell you the procedure for filing for the last five years of the group's Return Of Organizations Exempt from Income Tax (Form 990) tax returns.

These tax returns, which nonprofit organizations have to file to avoid paying taxes, are public records and will contain all kinds of good information. Info on the group's leaders, the group's board of directors, the group's leading donors, the group's income sources, the group's "nonprofit" activities, the group's business activities, the group's lobbying activities, the group's assets and investments and accounts, the salaries and names of the group's key staffers, and the group's spending practices will appear on these returns.

If your target group does not have nonprofit status, check local tax records to make sure the group is paying all its taxes correctly. (Sometimes, groups "forget.") And even if the group is above-board on paying taxes, the tax records will show some useful information on its assets and activities.

Criminal And Civil Cases. Check for criminal cases and lawsuits involving the group and its leaders. Usually businessmen and labor leaders come to mind when criminal cases and lawsuits are mentioned, but other groups and their key people get involved in these cases as well.

For example, members of the National Organization for Women saw two of their people accused in the early 1980s of murder and bribery. Ginny Foat, an official of the feminist organization, was tried in 1983 for helping her ex-husband rob and murder an Argentine businessman in a case that went back to her days as a barmaid in a New Orleans nightclub. It was alleged Ms. Foat lured the Argentine into a car that her then-hubby was hiding in, then when they drove into a deserted area, he emerged and he and Ms. Foat beat the man to death and took $1400 from his wallet. The feminist escaped conviction.

Wanda Brandstetter did not. This NOW operative was accused in 1980 of trying to bribe an Illinois legislator to get him to vote to ratify the Equal Rights Amendment. The feminist was convicted of bribery later that year, and the conviction stood despite numerous appeals on her part. Ms. Wanda proved women can be just as corrupt as men.

Lawsuits are great places to find information on the group's officers, affiliate groups and subsidiary groups and parent groups, and other organizational and financial information. So are real estate records. Check these carefully for such information and evidence. Also, if you see in the paperwork any other named group or individual with the same address as the group, suspect an affiliation of some sort.

Likewise, regulatory agencies may have filed lawsuits or criminal cases or may have taken administrative actions against your target group. Check in with agency enforcement officials and freedom of information officers to find out what dirt they have on your target group.

Government Contracts And Grants. Government contracts and grants for your target group will yield further information on what the group is up to. Check the chapter on contracts and grants for more detailed information on this kind of dirt-digging.

Postal Records. If your target group sends any publications, mailings, or ads through the mails, you can get a rough estimate of how many people your target group is reaching by calling the U.S. Postal Service and finding out how to obtain a copy of the group's mailing permit. A second-class mailing permit for a newsletter, formally known as a Statement of Ownership, Management, and Circulation (Postal Service Form 3526), is a form group leaders have to file if they hope to get postage breaks for their publication. It's a public record. The form will contain the names of the publisher, the editor, the managing editor, and all persons or groups with more than a one-percent financial interest in the group. The form will also list how many copies of each issue the group publishes and sends out. A copy of this form should be available for your viewing at the post office from which your target group mails the newsletter.

A third-class mailing permit for advertising, formally known as the Application to Mail at Special Bulk Third Class Rates (Postal Service Form 3624), is a form group leaders have to file to get price breaks for flooding your house with junk mail. It's also a public record. The form will contain as appendixes documents that contain info on the organization's stated primary purpose, its articles of incorporation or constitution, and proof the organization operated as claimed for the previous six months (such as meeting minutes, financial statements, or bulletins). A related form (PS Form 3602-N or 3602-R) will show how many pieces of mail the group sends out in bulk mailings. A copy of these forms (with appendixes) should be available for your viewing at the post office from which your target group sends its mailouts.

If you review these postal records and find they contradict what you know and can prove about the group's purpose, membership, or status, your target group might be getting postal breaks illegally. Turn your info over to the postal inspectors. A visit from them will be less enjoyable for your target group's key people than a maildrop of a ton of junk mail!

Library And Media Sources. Two resources investigators often overlook are libraries and media outfits. Both sources contain a lot of good information you can use. See the chapter *Tap Other Information Sources* for more details.

Personal Info. There's always the old standby of digging into the group leaders' personal lives for dirt. Check out the chapter on checking into targets' personal lives. Check your target group's leaders' criminal records, lawsuit records, real estate records, divorce records, and other personal records for evidence of wrongdoing or shady behavior.

Even past lowlife behavior before a well-publicized "conversion" can cause some people problems. Some supporters of homeless activist Mitch Snyder no doubt were upset to find out that this servant of humanity had abandoned his own wife and children years earlier. How much this evidence of apparent hypocrisy hurt Mitch's cause or donation tally is hard to measure. Even though Mitch "changed" and became a caring person to street people later on, I don't recall any of Snyder's defenders publicly saying before or after his 1990 suicide that Mitch was making child support payments for the upbringing of his own two little children. If he was doing right by his children, his publicists and his friends should have said so louder to protect him from wearing the horns of a wife-and-children deserter.

DOCUMENTING CORRUPTION AND OTHER MONEY PROBLEMS

The old adage, "Follow the money trail," always applies to suspected corruption. If you're motivated enough to dig dirt on a group, some of the best dirt to dig is evidence of a group's corruption. You then can trash the group's reputation to the public at large, and make many within the group hate the group leaders.

Documents that could contain evidence of nepotism, cronyism, and other possible corruption problems include the group's incorporation papers and annual reports, its Form 990 tax returns, other reports it has to file with the government accounting for income and expenses and staffers and officials, lawsuits, and government grants and contracts. KNOWING WHERE A GROUP GETS ITS MONEY IS IMPORTANT, BECAUSE THIS IS WHERE YOU WOULD LOOK TO FIND THE POTENTIAL FOR CORRUPTION AND THE EVIDENCE OF CORRUPTION.

In his book *The Muckraker's Manual*, M. Harry tells researchers to alert when they see evidence of a lot of people with the same last name on the payroll. Why? Because when people hire relatives, corruption often follows. (The same holds true for an organization in which friends hire friends.) Harry also said some groups do extensive business with one or two vendors, and he suggested that investigators find out the owners of the vendor companies. His reasoning is that the group may be taking money from its own members and enriching one of its leaders (or a leader's cronies) by doing business with a company he (or the crony) owns.

Check on real estate deals involving group leaders or the group for evidence they paid too much for a piece of property they bought from a buddy or sold property for much too little to a buddy. Maybe kickbacks or favoritism are involved in such irregular-looking deals.

Check the group's banks, too, for evidence someone at the bank has ties to leaders of the group. It could be that the group isn't getting a full return on its money because of some sort of sweetheart deal between the higher-ups of the bank and the group. Another item to check on, especially in case of a labor union or a nonprofit group, is the report or return that shows employee expenses. The leaders may be paying employees or key staffers excessive wages for what they actually do, and then might be taking kickbacks from some of them. Or they may have ghost employees on the payroll.

Related to corruption is misuse of group funds. Jim and Tammy Bakker, for example, misused their PTL followers' money to live extravagantly. Jim and other PTL leaders also reportedly misused money by paying off Jessica Hahn, the church secretary-turned-bimbo (or shall we say "love offering?"), to keep quiet about Jim's sexual dalliances with her. (This charge gave rise to the joke that PTL stood for Pay The Lady.)

On the other side of the coin, dissident members of an Ohio group with a semifeminist bent sued their own trustees for misusing grant money. They said the trustees collected money that was earmarked for specific projects, then looted the donations and stashed the money in a general expense account.

Other misuses of group money include donations to politicians and other causes. Generally, it's good business for group members to donate to politicians who will vote their way on issues they care about. But the leaders still have to live by group rules in deciding who to contribute to. Sometimes they back a politician who may not give a group a good return on its investment (or whose personal traits might infuriate the rank-and-file despite his willingness to help the group). Likewise, group leaders have to follow some sort of authorization procedure before they can spend the group's money on other outside causes.

Again, the places to look for evidence of misuse of funds include the group's incorporation papers and annual reports, its Form 990 tax returns, other reports it has to file with the government to account for income and expenses and staffers and officials, lawsuits, and government grants and contracts. Check for exorbitant spending on salaries, perks, overhead, and other administrative costs (like expensive office furniture and vehicles, for example). Check for evidence of donations to politicians, accounting of contract and grant money, and other items that indicate the group's leaders aren't taking good care of the group's money.

USA FOR AFRICA—THE CASE HISTORY

The group United Support of Artists for Africa, an entertainment industry group started in the wake of news coverage of the Ethiopian famine, is well-known for the 1985 song *We Are The World* and the 1986 *Hands Across America* event. The group has done a lot of good for many people. However, people might be surprised to see how group officials spent the money they raised.

Records I got from the California attorney general's office for 1986 indicate the following things about the group:

- In 1986, they raised $26 million from individual donors, $7 million from corporate donors, and $11 million from royalties connected with the song *We Are The World* and other products. The group collected $46 million for the year; the other $2 million came from interest and other sources.

- In 1986, they spent $14.2 million on projects in Africa, $5.1 million on projects in America, $1.6 million on "public education", and $10.6 million on the *Hands Across America* event. They spent another $6.9 million on administration. The remaining money—$7.6 million—they saved. Donations for African and U.S. projects were extensively documented.

- Minutes of the group's board meetings indicate the board members thought the *Hands Across America* stunt would raise much more money than it evidently did. They also estimated the event would cost $17 million to stage. It's hard to tell from the documents how much money donors contributed to the group as a result of the event. On paper the event may have lost money for the day, but in the long run it probably stimulated many donations.

- Key staffers received generous salaries. For example, the medical director got $100,000 that year, the executive director got $82,000, the purchaser got $57,000, the donor administrator got $51,000, and two PR types got $59,000 and $42,000, respectively. On the other hand, three clerical workers probably got little more than $15,000 each.

- The group spent $165,000 on accounting services, $376,000 on lawyer services (one of the board members was a lawyer with the firm that provided the services), and $911,000 on travel.

I am not implying criticism of the group by writing about it here. Since the group was in the news, I spot-checked it as an exercise. But those who did criticize the group for self-promotion, and those who donated to the group would have done well to see how wisely the group leaders spent the money they got.

DIGGING WITH THE ENEMY

Sometimes, in a world where it's hard to find real friends, it's comforting to know that people, especially those in your target group, can have real enemies. These real enemies might be more than willing to share dirt with you if they think you will make trouble for their enemies in your target group.

There are two kinds of enemies. One kind includes those in the same group as the target. The other kind includes those outside of the group. An inside enemy will probably have more and uglier dirt on a target— especially when it comes to providing evidence of corruption. However, an internal enemy who loves his group but hates others in his group will be hard to deal

with compared with an enemy outside a target's group who hates the target and his group.

Let's start by discussing a target's enemies outside his group. Since you already know what your target group's agenda is, you should be able to figure out easily which kinds of groups will oppose your target group. For example, Republicans and Democrats oppose each other (except when politician pay hikes are at stake), labor unions and business interests fight each other (but they join forces to oppose tree-hugging ecofreaks who threaten union jobs and business profits), radical feminists and homosexuals clash with Catholics and evangelical Protestants, the NAACP and the Ku Klux Klan have little in common, skinheads and the Jewish Defense League aren't pals, and so on. Also, law-enforcement types tend to hold grudges against groups they've gone after, or groups who have accused them of misconduct.

Once you've identified your target group's outside enemies, contact their information people. Tell them you're doing some sort of research project on a group and need negative as well as positive information to do a thorough job. Don't fully tip your hand even if the enemy sounds only too willing to dump his dirt truck wherever you want the pile. He may be suckering you, or you may fall victim to the excesses of your own enthusiasm and reveal yourself as an amateur instead of a rational investigator. If you come off as a professional, the enemy is more prone to trust you, take you seriously, and give you as much help as he can.

By all means let the enemy group's information people know you'll be grateful to use any information they can give you or any documents they can send you. Likewise, if you have to visit your target's enemy, look and act professional. Sell the enemy on your willingness to listen to what he has to say about your target, and on your ability to create problems for the target if the enemy co-operates with you.

You already know it, but I'll say it anyway. CONSIDER THE SOURCE. The enemy has an ax to grind. Treat enemies of the target group with friendly skepticism (accent on friendly). Approach enemies with the "I believe you but I've got to show some proof to *MY* bosses" routine. Documents and verbal information that can be verified are the best types of information. Some enemies are flakes, some are so angry they can't focus, some are out-and-out liars, and some appear to have their ducks in line. The best source I ever had as a reporter made no secret of his hatred toward local officials. But this man, a former union executive and also a successful businessman, could always document his accusations against the officials, or at least could always point me toward evidence that would confirm them.

Now let's talk about the enemies of a target within his group. If you've done some homework on your group through the public record, you should know who some of the enemies are. For example, a union official who's lost a bitter election or a politician in a faction of his party who lost out on an important issue could make a good internal enemy. So could a businessman or bureaucrat who got passed over for a promotion because of your target. People in a group with different goals or methods than your target might be willing to open up a little about your target. Reformers within an organization will only be too happy to talk about the leaders' flaws.

Contact these enemies, and tell them you're doing some sort of research project or article on an issue of interest to the group. Tell them you need to cover some negative points as well as the positive points of the issue (and the groups involved with the issue) to do a thorough research or reporting job. Say also that you heard he or she would be an excellent source of information about the group and also a credible source of information about particular people (i.e., your target(s)) within the group.

Again, don't fully tip your hand even if the internal enemy sounds only too willing to help you destroy the target. Also, remember to CONSIDER THE SOURCE, and treat the enemy with friendly (accent on friendly) skepticism. If you come off as a professional, the enemy is more prone to trust you, take you seriously, and give you as much help as he can.

Another word of caution about dealing with enemies of your target who are in the same group or cause as your target is ... don't tell them what your real reason is for digging dirt on the target. The enemy and the target probably have a different viewpoint from you. For example, as a labor union operative, you wouldn't tell a man's enemy in his business organization you want dirt on him so you can make trouble for the organization they both belong to. The enemy and the target might hate each other, but they probably hate your type much more.

By all means let the internal enemy know you'll be grateful to use any information he can give you or any documents he can send you. Likewise, if you have to visit your target's enemy, look and act professional. Sell the enemy on your honesty in doing research, and on your willingness to listen to what he has to say about the group and your target. Again, don't give him the idea you want to nail the whole group (if that's what you're up to).

The rewards of getting dirt from an internal enemy

are worth the hassles and risks. Why? Because the people inside a group have the easiest access to the group's *REALLY* dirty laundry. They know the group's internal workings. They know how their leaders can conceal things from the public, the government, and their own rank and file. And an enemy within a group will disclose dirt about his or her group in the process of disclosing dirt about people in the group he or she doesn't like. Sometimes, it's intentional; sometimes it's not. But remember the old adage, "No news is good news," and consider anything truthful that you find out about the group will be no good for it.

Just consider some of the great dirt organizational infighting has produced over the past few years. Former Attorney General Ed Meese had to resign in disgrace after his own underlings in the U.S. Justice Department called him a sleaze because they knew about his involvement in the Wedtech scandal. Michael Dukakis' campaign workers leaked damaging true information about fellow Democrat Joe "Copycat" Biden when both were running for the 1988 presidential nomination. One of Ginny Foat's feline rivals in NOW let the cat out of the bag about her suspected involvement in killing an Argentine businessman; Ms. Foat's murder trial hurt her NOW career. Watergate era weasel John Dean certainly contributed his share to the demise of his fellow dirtbags in the Nixon administration by turning into a stool pigeon. Union officials and mobsters sometimes tip off federal investigators on what no-good their rivals in their organizations are up to.

My dad, who was with Mayor Daley's Kennedy delegation at the 1960 Democratic convention, said his favorite incident of intramural bloodletting took place in 1972. Hubert Humphrey and George McGovern, in competing for the presidential nomination of the Democratic Party, crisscrossed the country making speeches about what a bum the other guy was. McGovern was saying Humphrey was to old and tired and was tied to too many special interests. Humphrey was saying McGovern would sell our country down the river at the first opportunity he got. Dad laughed and said, "These two scumbags are at least telling the truth about each other."

WITH FRIENDS LIKE THESE, WHO NEEDS ENEMIES?

Whether they want to or not, friends of most groups just can't help but hurt the group when they talk about it. Why? Because sooner or later, they'll drop information that can be used against the group. Even you, talking about your friends to people at work, may say something about a friend that doesn't seem harmful to you, but a co-worker may consider it proof your friend is a lowlife.

And so it is with friends of your target group. Once you've identified friends of a target group, contact them. Tell them you're doing some sort of research or article on the group and need some information from sources to do a thorough job. Of course, don't tell the friend about your malicious intent. Would it surprise you to find out you'll get less help if you do?

The approach I suggest in talking with the group's friends is a basically a sympathetic approach. Tell the friend you've found out a lot of good things about the group, but get him or her to elaborate further on the programs and goals of the group. See if you can get some good background information on group leaders from the friend. See if he or she will tell you what he or she knows about the group's past efforts and its strategies for the future. See if he or she knows about other allies of the group and other information sources on the group.

Then hit up the friend for the dirt, but do it smoothly. Say almost apologetically that you've come across some negative information on the group in your research, and ask the friend to comment on it or rebut it. The friend will do what he can to defend the group, but in many cases he will mention items of interest when he talks.

He may try to "explain away" a group's bad points, and in doing so, could reveal some information you were unaware of. Or, in responding to your open-ended question, he won't know what you know or don't know about the group. In order to avoid making you think he's covering up for the group, he might tell you about a problem that you were totally unaware of because he thought you *DID* know about it! Either way, you'll be less ignorant about the group after talking with its friends.

FOLLOW-UP WORK

Now that you've got solid input from enemies and friends, it's back to the public records sources for you. Follow up on all the leads the enemies and friends have given you. Get new documents and recheck old documents to see if you can verify or disprove some sort of misconduct is going on in your target group.

MAPPING OUT PATTERNS OF GROUP BEHAVIOR

A good detective studies a subject's patterns of behavior when he investigates him for involvement in crime. He will know the subject's background, his strengths and weaknesses, his means of support, his daily routine, and the ways in which the criminal commits his crimes. Almost every criminal has a repetitious M.O. (mode of operation) for his crimes. An unsophisticated criminal uses the same simple M.O. because it has worked for him in the past. Or the criminal might be committing complex white-collar crimes that require a specific set of actions for him to get his payoffs. In either case, the criminal will have a pattern of activity that the detective will spot.

The situation is the same for your target group, only more so. Since most organization leaders operate more openly than the average criminal, there is much more info available on your target organization. This will allow you to determine the target organization's pattern of activity. It will also make it easier for you to figure out what the group will try to do—legally or illegally—to get money, punish enemies, reward friends, or influence policy. If you're fighting this organization, it goes without saying that such knowledge will be helpful.

Since you've done your homework, you already know what your group's agenda is and what its tactics are. You also know which politicians they support and oppose, and who they consider to be their friends and their enemies. Further, you know who their leaders are, how they get their money, and how they spend it. And you may know through criminal or civil cases what unethical behavior they engage in. The group's literature, the help of enemies and friends, articles in publications, and documents in government agencies all have helped you build a file on your target group.

Having this information gives you something to go by. For example, if an entrepreneur has tried hostile takeovers, if a business leader has used bankruptcy to get out of labor contracts and other obligations, if a union has used sabotage and strikes, if a special-interest group has used certain types of political pressure to stampede legislators into voting their way, or if a group has used certain tactics to raise money or put out its propaganda, you should plan for the target to use this approach again. You should also plan on organization leaders who haven't used really drastic tactics to consider them if kinder and gentler tactics aren't getting the job done for them.

NONPROFIT ORGANIZATIONS PROFIT WHEN YOU'RE KEPT IN THE DARK

Many nonprofit organizations are very wonderful organizations. Religions and charity groups are nonprofit organizations. However, there are some nonprofit groups who are money-grubbing maggots that give off enough stench for the whole nonprofit field.

Basically, people establish their groups as nonprofit organizations to avoid taxation. After all, a religious denomination or a charity group exists to help people, not to serve as a money source for the government leeches. Since they can help people more efficiently than the government can, they deserve the tax relief.

But some groups' people use loopholes in the law to make a lot of money for themselves while not paying corporate taxes on it. What they do is establish a nonprofit corporation, then pay themselves huge salaries and run up corporate expenses right up to the limit of their revenue sources. This way, they can show they are "nonprofit", because the corporation doesn't have the stated purpose of turning a profit.

For example, Reproductive Health Services, the St. Louis abortion facility involved in the 1989 Webster case before the Supreme Court, is a nonprofit corporation. And yet records show its operators were able to pay Dr. Robert Crist $415,000 for performing abortions on a part-time basis in 1984 and 1985. Malpractice records show Crist was also performing abortions in Kansas City and/or Houston during that time. (As an aside, malpractice records also show the mother of Diane Boyd—a retarded teenager who was raped and made pregnant in a Missouri state mental hospital—sued Crist and Reproductive Health Services when Diane died after undergoing an abortion at the facility in October 1981.)

Earlier in the chapter we mentioned finding out info on a nonprofit group by obtaining its Form 990s from the IRS. These documents will contain info on the group's leaders, board of directors, leading corporate and private donors, income sources, "nonprofit" activities, business activities, lobbying activities, assets and investments and accounts, the salaries of the group's key staffers, and the group's spending practices. Check also with the secretary of state or the state treasurer or the state attorney general to see what other kinds of regulations apply to nonprofit groups in your state. Then file for all the paperwork you can on your target group with every agency that makes the group file paperwork for its activities.

Right away, you can see an opportunity to make trouble. If you don't like a particular nonprofit group, you can interfere with its money supply by getting people to boycott corporations which give it money. (To be on the safe side, confirm the corporate gift by phoning the corporation's PR person and asking which charities the firm funds.)

Another way to find out info on nonprofit organizations is to check copies of the *Non-Profit Times*, a New Jersey trade magazine that covers nonprofit corporations. The journalists of this magazine can provide you with data on many nonprofit corporations. Also, the editors of this magazine publish a report called "NPT 100." This report shows how much money the largest nonprofit groups took in, and how much they spent on programs, fundraising and administration. You can see how well these outfits use your money to help people, or see how well they use it to help themselves.

For example, the "NPT 100" report for 1990 shows officers of the American Cancer Society (a group with a 1989 income of $358 million) spent 6.8 percent of the money on administration. By comparison, Planned Parenthood officials (a group with a 1989 income of $332 million) spent 14 percent of the money on administration, more than double the percentage the American Cancer Society officers spent. NPT 100 editors noted Planned Parenthood was one of the worst major nonprofit groups of 1989 in terms of having high administrative costs. Two religious charities of comparable financial size—United Jewish Appeal and Catholic Relief Services—spent 0.74 percent and 1.83 percent of 1989 income, respectively, on administration.

Planned Parenthood officials could claim in response that they didn't spend a great amount on fundraising. NPT 100 figures show they spent 4.46 percent of their 1989 income on fundraising, compared with the American Cancer Society's 14.91 percent, the United Jewish Appeal's 5.22 percent, and the Catholic Relief Services' 6.62 percent. However, an analysis of how each group raised its money shows Planned Parenthood has some more explaining to do. For the American Cancer Society, the United Jewish Appeal, and the Catholic Relief Services got no dues or income money in 1989. And of these three charities, only the Catholic Relief Services got any government money—$180,000 to be exact. By comparison, Planned Parenthood made $120 million from providing abortions and birth control services, and they soaked the taxpayers for another $118 million in government funding.

For "military" or "civilian" purposes, it's always a good idea to contact the nonprofit group as a potential donor and ask for information on the group's programs, fundraising, and spending. The honest outfits will tend to give you legit information and keep their overhead low. After all, they're quite aware of all the hucksters out there and they don't want people like you thinking they run with the thieves.

Unfortunately, some organizations which are clean might give you a hard time when you ask for such information. This will tend to make you confuse them with the huckster groups, which will also tend not to release honest or accurate information so donors can get a valid picture of what they're really up to.

HOW THE BIG BOYS DO IT—A CASE STUDY IN GROUP WARFARE

In 1991, *Time* magazine higher-ups decided to depart from form and actually get their hands dirty with a little old-fashioned muckraking. They decided to run an exposé on the Church of Scientology. Scientology, to its followers, is at least a belief system. Scientology, to its detractors, is a cult at best and a scam at worst.

Scientology gets its money from group members by selling them all sorts of parapsychological treatments. The group generates favorable publicity for itself through the testimony of actors, singers, and other celebrities whom they pamper. (One celebrity who was once reportedly into Scientology but whose testimony is probably not welcome by the group is Charles Manson.) They also get some good ink by publishing best-selling books (which others allege they buy back from book sellers to goose them onto the best-seller list), by buying lots of favorable advertising, and by occasionally releasing dirt on government and industry activities.

Time staffers did a heap of dirt-digging on Scientology. Of course they interviewed enemies like former staffers, former members who say the group ripped them off, and the parents of a young man who said the group drove him so crazy with demands for money that he committed suicide. They also interviewed law-enforcement officials and lawyers who have fought Scientology in court. And they looked at a lot of court records—lawsuits, tax cases, and criminal cases.

Scientology leaders refused to grant interviews for the article, *Time* people said. So they must have known something unfriendly was in the air. But the *Time* article was uglier than even the Scientology people must have suspected from such a tame publication. For starters, the cover for the May 6, 1991 issue of the magazine showed a volcano with octopus tentacles and the caption read, "Scientology: The Cult of Greed." The eight-page article itself was major-league ugly. Writer Richard Behar made these major accusations against Scientology in the article:

Many people have sued Scientology for a number of reasons. Former group members and family members have accused the group of bleeding them for money like leeches. Key members of the group have drawn prison terms for wiretapping, infiltration, and burglary. Key members of the group have also been accused of stock manipulation, of running scams to suck in health care professionals, and of other financial wrongdoing.

Scientology is in court against the IRS on scores of cases. The group has also been accused of physically and mentally abusing former members, filing nuisance lawsuits against its enemies, paying detectives to tail and snoop on and harass enemies, and making defamatory accusations.

Behar couldn't have written that article without doing a full-blown excavation of every major dirt source he could find. The magazine's lawyers wouldn't have let the article run (you would presume) unless Behar had the paperwork and the notes and the tapes to prove people had made those allegations.

Scientology officials slung back a little mud of their own. The group ran an ad in major newspapers which focused on *Time's* credibility. In the ad, they slammed the publication because former *Time* staffers had been easy on Hitler during the 1930s. They repeated this tactic with a similar ad accusing the Internal Revenue Service of police-state terror tactics against average people. Scientology's leaders would have had to have at least some basis of truth to run these ads, unless they are *TOTALLY* unconcerned with libel suits.

THE LIVESTOCK REPORT

Maybe animal rights activists have a point. Some people and animals do act alike. We all know snakes in the grass, jackals, jackasses, weasels, slugs, sloths, and many other creatures in human bodies. Groups are the same way. Birds of a feather really do flock together. Too many group members and too many in society are sheep. The leaders of some of these groups are like dogs—individually, they're not too bad, but when they roam around with other dogs, they rediscover their pack instincts and prey on others.

Using the info you can find per this chapter's instructions, you can be a dogcatcher for the group leaders and a stockman for the group's lost sheep. After all, the alternative for many is rabies or hoof-and-mouth disease.

Also, groups, like animals, have natural enemies. Using the dirt you've dug on your target group as a carnivore lure, you can get government agents and other predators out of their lairs so they can sink their teeth into group leaders' hides. If you don't control the group this way, its members will overgraze your area and foul your nest.

END NOTES

1. Information on the murder case of NOW leader Ginny Foat comes from articles in the January 24, 1983 issues of *Time*

and *Newsweek*, the November 21, 1983 issue of *Newsweek*, and the November 28, 1983 issue of *Time*. Information on how Ms. Font's NOW rival Shelly Mandel caused Louisiana authorities to have here arrested comes from the article in the November 21, 1983 issue of *Newsweek*.

2. Information on the bribery case of NOW activist Wanda Brandstetter comes from an article in the June 2, 1980 issue of *Newsweek* and from articles in the Springfield (Illinois) *State Journal-Register* on November 6, 7, and 8, 1980, January 11 and 12, 1982, May 29, 1982, and November 8 and 9, 1982.

3. Information on Mitch Snyder comes from articles in the July 16, 1990 issue of *Newsweek* and the July 23, 1990 issue of *People*.

4. Information on the misdeeds of PTL higher-ups comes from articles in the April 6, 1987 and December 19, 1988 issues of *Newsweek* and from the November 6, 1989 issue of *Time*.

5. Information on the group whose dissidents sued their own trustees for reportedly misusing grant money comes from Case A8500586 in Hamilton County (Cincinnati), Ohio Common Pleas Court.

6. Information on USA for Africa comes from paperwork the group's leaders filed with the California Attorney General's Registry of Charitable Trusts bureau.

7. Information on Ed Meese's troubles with his own subordinates in the U.S. Justice Department comes from Marilyn Thompson's book *Feeding The Beast*.

8. Information on how Dukakis staffers leaked info about Joe Biden comes from an article in the September 12, 1988 issue of *Time*.

9. Information on how John Dean squealed on other Nixon Administration characters comes from Victor Lasky's book *It Didn't Start With Watergate*.

10. My satirical remarks on Humphrey and McGovern are based on accounts of the 1972 campaign in Victor Lasky's book *It Didn't Start With Watergate* and in Theodore White's book *The Making of the President—1972*.

11. Information on Reproductive Health Services 1984 and 1985 payments to Robert Crist comes from the Form 990s the abortion facility's people filed with the IRS.

12. Information on the abortion-related death of Diane Boyd comes from St. Louis City Circuit Court case 812-11077.

13. Information on Planned Parenthood, American Cancer Society, United Jewish Appeal, and Catholic Relief Services comes from the *Non Profit Times* and report "NPT 100—America's Biggest Charities". The figures are for 1989.

14. Information on the feud between Scientology and *Time* comes from Richard Behar's article on the group in the May 6, 1991 issue of *Time* and in an article in the June 10, 1991 issue of *Newsweek*.

15. Information on Charles Manson's reported involvement with Scientology comes from Vincent Bugliosi's and Curtis Gentry's book *Helter Skelter*.

Tap Other Information Sources

When I was a little boy, I saw a movie about two guys in the Army. They had ticked off their sergeant, and he stuck them on KP duty peeling potatoes. They peeled several bushels of potatoes, emptied the potato bin, and thought they would be done. But as they were getting ready to escape, a veritable boxcar load of spuds came cascading down the chute and into the bin. The two Sad Sacks gave out moans of dismay, and went back to their peeling.

This chapter is like the chute. You've already worked through a pile full of information in following the advice of this book. And now I'm going to throw a few more stacks of paper on the pile.

GOVERNMENT SOURCES

Your taxes, besides supporting armies of dopers, do-gooders, derelicts, and deadbeats, have also helped pay for a collection of paperwork that's probably large enough to reach to the moon and back. The next few paragraphs will tell you how to gain access to some of the most interesting portions of it.

Government Accounting Office. The U.S. Government Accounting Office in Washington does a lot of investigating and auditing work on all kinds of targets. The agents of this agency do so much dirt-digging they have to print a periodic *CATALOG* of reports they file on fraud, waste, incompetence, and other forms of wrongdoing. You can get this catalog and its updates from the GAO or review it at many college libraries. How good is their dirt? A lot of so-called "investigative journalists", especially on the TV networks, lift many GAO reports and use them as if they'd done the legwork themselves. For example, the information I gave you about Stanford's white-collar wrongdoers came directly from a GAO report. Also, the GAO's people made public the "Rubbergate" scandal—they noted congressmen were bouncing checks on the House Bank.

Government Printing Office. Another source of information is the U.S. Government Printing Office in Washington. This agency puts out a periodic catalog of all government publications. You can subscribe to the catalog or contact a public library or college library on the subscription list. Skim through the catalog and order any document that might contain dirt on your target.

Congressional Record. The Congressional Record, the daily journal of the U.S. Congress, contains a lot of slams by congressmen at businesses, government agencies, other congressmen, and other people in the public eye. The Congressional Record provides transcripts of debates, speeches, and other floor proceedings of the House of Representatives and the Senate. It also contains documents and speeches placed "on the record" by congressmen. Also, it contains texts of bills, presidential messages, treaties, and other important documents.

Congressmen's remarks (congressmen like Jim Trafficante and Bob Dornan are very quotable) and staffers' reports that contain a lot of negative references on people are in the Congressional Record. Some of the old-timers from past congresses have publicly accused people of everything from Mafia membership to Communist Party affiliations to Klan and Nazi activism to drug trafficking to pimping to massive fraud upon the public.

The Congressional Record is available at many public and college libraries. See if your target has been mentioned in the Congressional Record. And then check it to see what dirt some Congressman has tarred him with.

Congressional Hearings. Another good source of information is the record of a congressional hearing. Again, congressmen and their staffers load up the hearings with a lot of juicy information. And since congressmen can routinely grill people who no other court of inquiry in America can touch, their committee hearing records might contain information available nowhere else.

Contact your congressman's office and get his staffers to help you locate info you need on your target that appears on the record of a committee hearing. You could also contact the Government Printing Office in Washington for help in finding such hearing records; the people of this agency should have an index of committee hearing records they've printed. Further, you could contact the Congressional Information Service; the people in this group can get you such reports.

One feature of congressional dirt sources that is

really nice is that they'll keep you out of legal trouble even if the information turns out later to be false. Why? A representative or a senator is protected from slander or libel—even if he lies his ass off—when speaking on the floor of either the House or the Senate or adding "extension of remarks" to the Congressional Record. So you can't be sued successfully for defamation, libel, or slander by a target if you quote accurately the congressman's ravings about the target in the Congressional Record or in a committee hearing.

Library of Congress. While we're talking about Congress, let's mention the Library of Congress. The staffers routinely prepare highly professional reports for congressmen at their request. However, these are hard for the average citizen to get. One relatively painless way to get your hands on such reports is to ask your congressman's staffers to get them for you.

Congressional Information Service. Another excellent source of information is the Congressional Information Service. The people of this group can get you info on presidents' executive orders and congressional committee hearings. They can also get you info on congressional committee prints (reports), laws, resolutions, Justice Department documents (like indictments, affidavits, depositions, plea-bargains, other court data, and press releases), and a lot of other documents.

Your Congressman. Your own congressman—or any congressman who crusades for the same causes as you do—can get you dirt on targets if you ask him to. As a Congressman, he can get damn near any record he wants even from the most fascist or lazy or obtuse government employees. Also, his staffers tend to know what dirt is available on certain targets. So they can help you in many ways.

Federal Information Centers. Federal Information Centers, located in the largest cities of the nation, contain many other types of information that may help you. Check under the U.S. Government listings in your phone book to find the one nearest you. If none are listed, call your congressman's office and ask the staffers where the closest one to you is.

Consumer Resources Handbook. The Consumer's Resources Handbook, put out by the U.S. Office of Consumer Affairs in Washington, contains addresses and phone numbers and names of people in hundreds of the nation's biggest corporations. It also contains addresses and phone numbers of industry arbitration associations, consumer protection agencies, commissions on the aging, weights and measures offices, selected federal agencies as they relate to citizen assistance, state vocational and rehabilitation agencies, and "Better Business Bureaus."

Other Government Sources. Even though I've mentioned these sources all over this book, I'll do so again here. Check the government agencies' Office of Inspector General semiannual reports, the agencies' annual reports, the records of the agencies' offices of grants and contracts, and records of the agencies' general counsels. Also, check in with the freedom of information officers, the public affairs officers, or the information officers of the agencies to see how they can help you.

PRIVATE SOURCES

Although businessmen don't kill as many trees needlessly as the bureaucrats and the gossip tabloid publishers (unless you count their junk mail), they still generate their fair share of documents. And while the records of corporate America are nowhere near as public as those of the government, plenty of useful information is still available on private sector documents that you can obtain. Likewise, there is a lot of useful information available on labor unions, other organizations, and individuals that is available through non-government channels. The next few paragraphs will cover tapping these sources.

Organization Journals and Newsletters. These publications contain lots of good information on an organization itself. After all, the group's leaders use the publication to get their message out to their followers or employees; you can use these publications to figure out what the leaders are up to. Also, these publications contain good information on groups' enemies. After all, part of a leader's job is mobilizing followers to fight opponents. For example, the story I told you about a coal miner's death at a nonunion mine—and the possible attempts to "paper over" his death—came from the United Mine Workers Journal.

Trade and Business Journals. These publications contain a lot of good information about trades and businesses. For example, the story I told you about the Cleveland *Plain Dealer*'s antitrust problems came from articles I got from a newspaper trade journal. I'm not alone in using such journals. Corporate types spy on other corporations using leads provided in the stories of trade publications. For example, the reporters of *Aviation Week* (fondly known as "Aviation Leak" by aerospace professionals) evidently have sources in many aerospace outfits who feed them many bits of "hush-hush" information. Corporate spies and foreign spies have reportedly used this magazine to figure out the score on a number of civilian and military aviation projects.

Professional Journals. Doctors' groups, lawyers' groups, engineers' groups, and many other professional groups put out a number of publications aimed at people in their professions. These journals contain information on trends in the profession, government actions affecting the profession, and other items of interest. Sometimes they contain dirt on those in their own profession. For example, Ann Saltenberger, a New Jersey writer, used stories from medical journals to document cases of abortion-related malpractice, complications, and deaths for her cult classic exposé *Every Woman Has A Right To Know The Dangers Of Legal Abortion.*

Organization PR People. These good folks get paid to put out propaganda for their groups. Sometimes they slip and reveal the truth. In either case, they're usually willing to get information on their group for writers (and for sly investigators who say they're writers).

Corporation Annual Reports. These documents, published by corporations for stockholders and potential investors, contain a good deal of information on the corporations which publish them. The U.S. Securities and Exchange Commission has many of these available to the public. Also, you can probably get one direct from a company if you call its PR people and say you're interested in investing in the company or in doing business with the company.

Other Corporate Sources. If you're interested in finding out more about a company, you could check with a stockbroker, or consult an industry information service such as Moody's or Standard and Poor's. Your local library will have several industry guides, such as the *Thomas Register,* which can give you basic information on a company, such as its size, its executives, and its major products and services.

Corporate publicists are also good sources of information for writers and investigators posing as writers. And there's the old activist's standby of buying a single share in a company he wishes to target, then using his status as a shareholder to get company information that is available only to shareholders.

Professional Societies. These groups have certain amounts of background info on its members that they make available to the public. Generally, they only release certain types of general personal data on members, but occasionally, they will give out info on complaints on one of their members.

Libraries. Librarians can show you how to figure out what trade, business, and professional journals exist and how to find copies. They can also tell you which libraries have government publications such as the Government Printing Office catalog or the Congressional Record. Further, they can show you how to use the *Reader's Guide to Periodical Literature* to find out if any articles on your targets have appeared in magazines. Likewise, they can show you how to use other library resources to see what other easy-to-get information is available on your targets.

Newspapers. Newspapers are good sources of dirt on people and groups in their local areas. Remember this—newspaper people are often rude to the public but kind to other writers (and sly investigators who say they're writers). Newspaper staffers treat kindly those out-of-town callers who say they're writers; do what you have to do to get these folks to lend you a helping hand. (If your local paper's staffers won't help you, but make you go to the local library for copies of old newspaper articles, do what you have to do to get newspaper article copies. Then at the editor's next public forum, raise hell about your paper's police-state attempts to keep their files inaccessible!)

Cause Groups. Cause group members do a lot of research on topics related to their causes. Cause group members can give you plenty of dirt on their enemies, and can give you plenty of fluff on their friends. They can also point you toward specialized sources of information regarding your target's activities in areas of concern to them. Bear in mind you'll be dealing with biased and sometimes fanatical people, but I guarantee you they can quickly come up with documents and other info on people that no one else seems to have.

DIRT-DIGGERS' TEXTBOOKS

I have quoted Louis Rose's *How to Investigate Your Friends and Enemies* in several chapters. This is an excellent source book for investigating real estate, public finances, and business. Rose is considered a heavyweight muckraker by many in the business, including me.

The Muckraker's Manual, by M. Harry, is also a good source. I've quoted this miserable little gem in several places for ideas on gaining access to government, organization, and personal information. This book also contains a good deal of information on how to do interviews, if you want to add this dimension to your muckraking skills.

Instant Information, by Joel Makower and Alan Green, contains the addresses and phone numbers of close to 10,000 government agencies, trade associations, think tanks, pressure groups, and other sources of information. The book also contains a brief blurb on each group's function.

The National Directory of Addresses and Telephone Numbers, printed by General Information, Inc., contains addresses and phone numbers of tens of thousands of entities such as accounting firms, advertising firms, associations and organizations, business services, colleges, computer services, finance institutions, federal and state and local government agencies, industrial corporations, lawyers, libraries, and media. It costs more than $50, which seems like piracy compared to the $10 I paid for it when Bantam published it several years ago, but it's still a bargain if you do a lot of interstate calling.

Consumer Revenge by Chris Gilson, Linda Cawley, and Rick Schmidt, contains quite a bit of useful information on how to create trouble for businesses and white-collar professionals. Since two of the three authors are lawyers, they have a fixation (or maybe a vested interest) in recommending you go to court on almost everything.

Street Law, by Georgetown law profs Edward McMahon, Lee Arbetman, and Edward O'Brien, gives some good basic information on criminal law and civil law.

The Investigator's Handbook by Arthur Liebers and Capt. Carl Vollmer (NYPD). This book contains some excellent info on public records research and other tools of the private investigator's trade.

Other books I found helpful in writing this book include the following:

Death at Chappaquiddick by Richard and Thomas Tedrow. The Tedrows, a father and son tag team, hammered Teddy Kennedy for the death of Mary Jo Kopechne. They wrote this book largely on public records research. Reading the public records they included in the book, and just reading about how they went after such evidence is an education in muckraking all by itself.

Feeding the Beast by Marilyn Thompson. Ms. Marilyn, a reporter with a New York newspaper, was able to uncover evidence of Wedtech officials' crookedness by reviewing public records on Wedtech. The furor her articles caused helped lead to investigations and criminal prosecutions which brought down two congressmen, an attorney general, and a number of other prominent folks. Her book is another example of the rewards of records research.

Seeds of Treason by Ralph De Toledano. De Toledano, in telling the story of how Communist agent Alger Hiss was exposed and convicted, showed how valuable information on the public record was in helping send the pin-striped quisling to a well-deserved prison stay. Hiss and his wife, in lying about their ties to the man who exposed him as a traitor, made statements which contradicted public records, and helped destroy their own credibility in the process.

The Sting Man by Robert Greene. This book on the Abscam scandal showed not only the criminal greed of congressmen, but also the bickering between lawmen in pursuing the case and taking credit for the results. Greene also noted how some prosecutors may have obstructed justice by failing to prosecute certain defendants vigorously. Further, he noted how the media and other politicians hypocritically criticized the FBI undercover men who nailed the politicians instead of criticizing the politicians for taking the bribes.

Greylord: Justice Chicago Style by James Tuohy and Robert Warden. If you had any faith in lawyers and judges, you won't after reading this account on the FBI sting on Chicago judges. Some of the judges the authors wrote about are so crooked that when they die, the undertakers will have to screw their corpses into the ground!

It Didn't Start With Watergate by Victor Lasky. This classic exposé is must reading for everyone. It will open the eyes of the trusting and confirm the skepticism of the knowledgeable with its presentation of all the crooked crap presidents from FDR to Tricky Dick pulled.

Helter Skelter by Vincent Bugliosi and Curtis Gentry. This book on the Manson Family, co-written by the prosecutor who sent many of them to prison, contains many shocking examples of police bungling and lawyer misconduct. The police and lawyers in question made bringing these killers to justice much more difficult than it had to be.

Two of a Kind by Darcy O'Brien. This book on the Hillside Strangler case shows the ruses that rapist/murderer cousins Angelo Buono and Kenneth Bianchi used to lure girls and young women into their clutches. It also showed how L.A. County prosecutors were willing to let Buono go free for perceived political and/or career advantage.

Challenger: The Final Voyage by Richard Lewis. Though not a muckraking book per se, Lewis' account of business pressures, government pressures, and the misconduct of NASA and Morton Thiokol officials which led to the *Challenger* disaster is eye-opening.

The Search For Amelia Earhart by Fred Goerner. This riveting account of a newsman's search for the truth about the death of the brave aviatrix shows how hard the reporter worked, the public info he used in the investigation, the interviews he sought, and the massive U.S. government cover-up he ran into. (The Japanese haven't said much about Amelia's death either.) It will fascinate you and make your blood boil at the same time.

Criminology by Robert Bonn. This textbook provides some good insights on police, courts, and criminals. It also contains a number of thumbnail sketches on some of the most notorious crimes and court cases of the 1900s.

And now I'll mention some other books that will give you some further insights:

Crime and Its Victims by Daniel Van Ness. This book advocates victim's rights, more understanding for certain types of criminals, and the use of some of the victim-helping punishments of Old Testament Israel. Van Ness presents these ideas as a startling departure from the mindset of the typical plea-bargaining prosecutor and the "bust 'em and let the courts sort it out" policeman. I've held for a long time it's more worthwhile to make most offenders (petty crooks, bullies, vandals, druggies, and other nickel-and-dime criminals) pay restitution, submit to regular beatings, perform work projects, endure house arrest or take Antabuse than to lock them up with the criminal elite in our nation's pens. It's cheaper to send a kid to an Ivy League school (even with price-fixing) than it is to send an offender to prison. And why should the taxpayers be forced to foot the bill when the offender could be productive? Also, imprisonment of petty offenders doesn't help the victim or help the offender square himself away or make our society much safer. Judges and prosecutors should concentrate on locking up the violent career criminals and the sex offenders, and getting money or some other form of payback out of the other offenders. Fewer prisoners means the judges and prison officials could really crack down on the vicious murderers and thugs, the scumbag rapists and molesters, and the most predatory career thieves.

What Cops Know by Connie Fletcher. This book—basically a series of interviews with Chicago policemen about the streets, drugs, sex crimes, violent crimes, property crimes and organized crimes—will really open your eyes if you're not streetwise. I like to think I know it all, but I learned a few things from the cops who explained to Connie the facts of life about criminal tactics and police practices.

The Child Abuse Industry by Mary Pride. This woman's account of how government agents break up families and allow child abusers to operate is ugly and hateful ...and sadly enough, true. When you get done with this book, you'll want to mug child welfare agents.

The Case Against Pornography by Donald Wildmon. Although I don't agree with a lot of what Wildmon says in this book, the experts he quotes on pornography's effects provide useful ammunition to anyone—churchgoer or feminist—who is fighting the acts of degradation committed by the sexploitation industry. This book also has some useful information on child molesters, and on spotting real and potential victims of these vermin.

Diseasing of America by Stanton Peele. This guy slams the whole "I drink/do drugs/cheat/rape/steal/overspend/overeat/gamble, etc. because I'm sick, not evil or weak" excuse-making mindset. He says this attitude is fostered by those who devise profit-making "treatment programs" for these "sicknesses." Although I don't agree with Peele on many points, I think his book by and large is a public service. Why? Because he says people have these problems for the most part because they don't have the guts or the desire to stop their misconduct.

War on Waste by J. Peter Grace. This book, basically a report that business leaders prepared to show how federal leaders could save the taxpayers money, contains some excellent ideas. Also, the book is worth having because it identifies a lot of agencies and government spending practices most of us have never heard of!

Street Smart by Curtis Sliwa and Murray Schwartz. This is basically a Guardian Angels handbook showing people how to protect themselves and others. Curtis "the Archangel" and Murray explain a number of street scams and security guard scams. They also stress that people in ghettos, barrios, and suburbs, instead of hoping unrealistically that the undermanned police will solve all their problems, must work together with the community spirit needed to make life unsafe for the bullies.

I'm Mad As Hell by Howard Jarvis. Crusty old Howard, the father of California's 1978 Proposition 13 tax revolt, was an old newspaper man himself. So he did a lot of records checking to identify areas of wasteful spending. He laid this all out in the book. I saw Jarvis speak one night, and I interviewed him after his talk. He was probably the best public speaker I've ever covered.

Joan of Arc by Mark Twain. Mark Twain/Sam Clemens wrote this historical novel about the saintly and heroic Maid of Orleans with the help of one of the most sinister public records of all time...the official court record of her infamous Great Trial in 1431. This record, known as "Le Proces d' Jeanne d' Arc" was available for Clemens in the National Archives of France. This record proved how the English and their French lackeys connived to burn Christendom's most heroic lady at the stake for merely trying to free her homeland from English oppression. Clemens wrote this sad and stirring book about Joan of Arc near the end of his life, and he considered it worth all his other books put together. Saint Joan (along with Saint Patrick and the Maccabees) is a favorite of mine, too!

A FINAL NOTE

Of all the federal government sources I contacted in doing research for this book, I found the people of the Labor Department and the Federal Trade Commission were the most helpful. Also, many individual agents at many federal and state agencies were as good as gold when it came to getting me documents and offering me sound research advice.

The Justice Department folks I dealt with were good people or were jerks. Antitrust agents were very helpful. FBI people were reasonably helpful. But Immigration and Naturalization Service people I dealt with were lazy, rude, and eager to withhold information. I also witnessed (and lashed out at) INS pukes who treated immigrants rudely and callously; maybe they treat foreigners this way because they know foreigners have to kowtow to them to stay in this country.

And the most unhelpful government people? In my experience, they camp out at the State Department. These bureaucrats denied (or failed to respond to) every request for information I sent them.

But then, the State Department people have plenty to be unproud of. The Pearl Harbor sneak attack, the Communist enslavement of Eastern Europe, the criminal waste of fighting men's lives in Korea and Vietnam, the POW/MIA issue, the Bay of Pigs fiasco in Cuba, anti-Israel anti-Semitism, collaboration with OPEC states, failure to protect American workers' jobs from foreign piracy, complicity in British oppression of the Irish, ignoring the people of Latin America and Africa except to overthrow leaders and target the people for population control, slamming the door shut on desperate Haitians (whose ancestors helped us fight the British for our liberty), and being asleep at the switch when Iran and Iraq went sour on us are just some of the "achievements" of the striped-pants set over the last two generations.

Fight Crimes of Dishonesty

Throughout this book, I've showed you how to find evidence of wrongful behavior others have uncovered. This chapter will cover how YOU can uncover evidence of your target's criminal activity and other wrongdoing using your own observations and public records. Specifically, this chapter will cover how to find evidence your target is breaking laws in the fields he operates in, how to find evidence of white-collar crime, how to find evidence of bribery, and how to document instances of parole violation, perjury, and tax evasion. This chapter will also point you toward presenting your evidence to people who can really make some trouble for your target.

KNOW THE LAW, KNOW HOW YOUR TARGET CAN BREAK IT, AND KNOW HOW TO PROVE HE BREAKS IT

Gathering evidence on crime comes from knowing what is legal and what is illegal, and from knowing how your target can commit illegal acts. Knowing specific laws is important, but even the person armed with no more than good old common sense can usually figure out what kinds of behavior can get people into trouble. My own rules of thumb are:

- For actions involving theft or moneygrabbing of some sort, unethical behavior is also usually illegal. However, a lot of cheating in business is either perfectly legal or normally tolerated.
- For actions involving violent behavior such as killing, assault and battery, and rape, wrongful behavior is almost always illegal.
- For any action involving a license, a credential, or a tax break, operating outside of what the code says is illegal.
- For any action involving discrimination based on age, race, sex, handicap, religion, or ethnic group, wrongful behavior is illegal.
- For any action involving immoral social behavior, there is no good hard and fast rule. It depends on the community and the judge.

If you have a sense of what is legal and what is illegal, you can help fight crime. The best places to look for information that might show your target is engaged in illegal activity are the fields he operates in. If he's a businessman, for example, he may violate labor laws, pollution laws, product-safety laws or antitrust laws to make money. He might ignore miscellaneous regulators to avoid hassle and money loss. He might also breach contracts with the intent of making unethical profits.

If your target is a politician, he might have questionable financial ties and he might misuse his authority to benefit or harm others. If your target is a health-care professional, he might be misusing his access to narcotics to sell junkie-value drugs to pushers, or he might be misusing his access to insurance programs and government medical programs to overbill for services. And the list goes on and on... other chapters of this book cover many of the sleazy details. There are acres of lawbooks that contain laws which regulate people's activities. Sooner or later, you'll be able to find evidence your target has violated one of them, if he or she is as rotten as you think he or she is.

Once you know what is legal and illegal in your target's field(s), determine how you can prove the target is breaking the law. Documentary evidence on the public files can do it; taking photos or securing other physical evidence when it's safe for you to do so can do it; tips from those in the know can do it. Then figure out which government agency enforces the laws your target is breaking. Be a good citizen; present accurate evidence of the target's wrongdoing to the agency's agents and let them take it from there.

THE CASE OF THE CROOKED FRIDGE DEALER

I'll illustrate my advice—know the law, know how your target can break it, and know how to prove it—with a case from my file that involves a businessmen who tried to cheat me on a refrigerator deal. My knowing the laws regulating warranties, sales tax collection, and business licensing laws not only cost him a defeat in court, but several ugly experiences with state, local, and federal tax authorities, and a few negative encounters with the local police. I'll explain the laws which applied to the case (which he broke), then tell you how I was able to nail him.

Most people know about express warranties— warranties that cover certain kinds of product problems for given time periods. But few people know products also carry implied warranties of merchantability. This means the product is supposed to be suited for its designed use. In other words, appliances have to operate, clothes have to be wearable, food has to be edible, and so forth, when you buy any of these things. If the product doesn't perform, you can revoke acceptance—take it back and demand an exchange or demand your money back.

Sales tax burial is one of the oldest scams in the country. It works like this: A businessman will tell you if you pay him cash for an item, he won't charge you sales tax for the item. Of course, he doesn't report the sale on his business ledger, either, and he gives himself massive tax breaks. It's not a good idea to do business with this kind of guy, because he'll probably try to cheat you on the product warranty also. But if you know your target does this kind of thing, you can fix him good by reporting him to the state agency in charge of sales tax collecting.

In some areas, big-ticket merchants like car dealers and appliance sellers need police permits to sell used merchandise. The reason for this is to limit the amount of stolen property a crook can unload through his own "front" business or through the business of an "uninvolved" businessman who doesn't question the crook over how he can come up with cars or appliances so cheaply. Check with your local police or sheriff's department to see if such a law applies in your area. Then get them to check whether your target business has such a license.

Now for the story. The crook, a businessman who owned an appliance store, sold me a used refrigerator with a six-month warranty, after he offered to "bury" the sales tax if I paid him cash. I declined the cash sale offer, and I wrote him a check instead. This helped me in a number of ways later on.

First, he had to give me a receipt with the terms of the warranty. So when the fridge crapped out a couple of weeks later and he couldn't fix it, I told him to honor the warranty, remove the piece of junk from my house, and give me my money back. He refused to do so unless I gave him 20 percent of the purchase price of the now-room temperature fridge. I told him to stick his offer where the sun didn't shine, and I sued him in small claims court.

Since I had the check and the warranty-containing receipt, I won judgment in court, but the crook appealed. In the meantime, I reported his offer to "bury" the sales tax to the appropriate sales tax agents. And since a sales tax cheat is also an income tax cheat, I thought the state and federal income tax agents in my area might be interested in this guy. They were.

I also did two other things to the jerk. I asked the police in our city if he had a license to sell used appliances. He didn't, they said, so I reported he was selling used appliances without the proper license. The next day, the cops showed up at his store and pinched him. Also, since I had paid for the fridge with a check, I knew where he banked, because he cashed the check at his bank. I phoned the bank VP and suggested that the official freeze the jerk's business credit because he had just lost a money judgment involving his business. The VP also came through.

By this time, the shady salesman was highly upset with me. And he wasn't smart enough to surrender. We went to court on his appeal, and I won again. And this time, the judge awarded me court costs as well as the cost of the fridge. So the crook sent me a check for the amount of the original purchase. But since I was also entitled to court costs, I refused payment. Instead, I went to the county sheriff's office, filed against his business for the higher dollar amount that the judge had awarded me, and laughed when lawmen went out to his store a few days later and sat by his cash register. Some would-be customers were scared off. What he made from other customers went into my pocket.

But that was the least of his problems. The fraudulent fridge salesman had to suffer a credit freeze, undergo investigation from three separate tax authorities, and answer charges of selling appliances without a permit. This is the kind of punishment you can apply to a target if you know the law, know how he can break it, and know how to prove he breaks it.

PUTTING THE RING ON WHITE-COLLAR CRIME

Americans, when they think about crimes, think of people like killers and bank robbers. However, most willful killings are performed by doctors who perform abortions and medical facility staffers who mistreat or withhold treatment from weak and dying patients; most of these willful killings are not illegal. Jesse James, the Dalton Gang, Bonnie and Clyde, Pretty Boy Floyd, John Dillinger, and Willie Sutton put together stole far less money than a typical white-collar criminal who makes a bank collapse.

People in all walks of life follow behavior patterns from the time they know right from wrong until the day they die. Criminals are the same way. Once a bully, always a bully. Once a sex offender, always a sex offender. And once a thief, always a thief. White-collar criminals, being thieves, follow behavior patterns like other thieves. Their crime's success revolves around having a reason to steal, having the chance to get their hands on the money, and having a way to conceal the theft. Criminologists like Robert Bonn call these elements offenders, targets, and absence of capable guardians, while muckraker M. Harry calls them motive, opportunity, and cover.

Reason. The usual motive for white-collar crime is greed. But pressures such as addiction, blackmail, domestic problems, and legitimate financial trouble brought on by a family matter can also cause a person to think about stealing.

Chance And Concealment. The opportunity for white-collar crime involves control over money itself or control over business decisions that generate money. And the cover for white-collar crime involves the white-collar criminal committing the theft or helping it take place by performing his job crookedly. For example, a business owner might steal money by overcharging customers, or by failing to pay what he owes in taxes. Or several businessmen, like Ivy League officials, could work together in an illegal conspiracy to keep services like college educations artificially expensive.

Or local tax officials could undercharge businessmen on their local taxes, and get payoffs or campaign contributions as a result. Or corporate officials could leak company information to stockbrokers who make fabulously profitable stock deals based on the information. (This crime is known as insider trading.) The officials then get payoffs for the information they leaked.

White-collar crime writer William Moran, quoting a U.S. Justice Department agent named Robert O'Neill, noted, "All white-collar crimes involve to some extent the manipulation of everyday business processes." For example, real estate criminals manipulate the terms of property sales. Banking criminals manipulate the terms of loans. Industrial criminals manipulate product quality, worker pay and conditions, and waste disposal. The key to discovering white-collar crime is to figure out how the criminal has manipulated the process to produce a payoff for himself. Or, as a cast of thousands have said over the years, "Follow the money trail."

Evidence Of White-Collar Crime. There are a number of things people do that could indicate they are committing white-collar crimes. Your target may be a white-collar criminal if you can prove he or she is engaged in the following behavior:

■ Living a lifestyle above his or her declared means. Other chapters in this book tell you how to look into a person's private life and his land and business holdings. Divorce records are solid info on what money and property people have. So are photos you take of their property. The local paper's gossip column, ex-lovers, neighbors, and enemies are potential sources of dirt on your target's lifestyle. If your target says he holds a low-paying job, and yet owns a couple of Mercedeses and a mansion, or hangs out at all the right country clubs and fancy watering holes, odds are he got his money illegally.

■ Acquiring lots of property on a low budget. Dog-lovers whined about LBJ because he pulled his mutts' ears. Watchdogs hounded LBJ during his political life because he entered politics when nearly broke, yet was a millionaire when he was president—after spending virtually all his adult life on the government payroll. Likewise, your target may have acquired a lot of property by investing shrewdly, by inheriting, or by winning the lottery. Then again, perhaps he thieved to get it.

■ Failure to comply with laws. A businessman who shows a pattern of pollution citations, labor law violations, health code violations, and/or violations of building and zoning codes is probably breaking the law deliberately to save money and generate more profit. If, by using instructions in other chapters of this book, you can document a pattern of your target's outlaw activity, tie it all together in an easy-to-read report. Then present the report to an interested government agent. If he's looking for justice or some good PR, he might have your target prosecuted.

■ Many lawsuits. A person who gets sued a lot is often a liar and a cheat. If, by checking lawsuits, you can document on your target a pattern of breaching contracts, failing to do what a contract requires, overbilling, fraud, or other dishonest or unethical activity, tie it all together in an easy-to-read report and present it to an interested government agent. Again, if he has the right motivation, he might take action against your target.

■ Contract violations. Government contracts are public records. So are private contracts, once an attorney files one as evidence in a court action involving your target. Check for evidence of contract violations like adding excessive costs to a low-bid contract award, failing to deliver the promised goods and services, overbilling the client on time spent or on supplies used, and providing obviously substandard goods and services. Check for evidence your target overbilled government clients in comparison with their private customers. (Sadly, even though such wrongdoing is often easy to prove, the government agents often don't sue the wrongdoers unless pressure of some sort is applied to the government agency.)

- Billing Fraud. To demonstrate this activity, I'll use health care providers as examples. Every now and then, medical lab operators and doctors break the law by charging patients or insurance companies or the government for services not rendered. Medical records, and medical billings can show if your target health-care type pulls this kind of fraud. Likewise, any other businessman whose records you can obtain could be vulnerable to your snooping. Victims, criminal case files, lawsuit files, and government agencies might have such records for you to check.

- Tax evasion. This subject is covered in depth later in this chapter. We'll say here there are a number of state, local, and federal agencies which levy taxes, and your target may have "forgotten" to check in with them. Give yourself a little tax relief by getting the courts to make your target cough up the money he hasn't paid.

- Dealings on a consistent basis with shady characters. Birds of a feather really do flock together. If your target is doing business with shady bankers, crooked vendors, dishonest buyers, and sleazy partners, odds are he's part of their club. Ditto if his political connections and personal associations are tainted. Honest people usually avoid crooks; crooks often do business together, and they work to rip off the public.

- Hiring friends and relatives, and doing business with firms controlled by cronies. Where these behaviors take place, corruption often follows. Check all available records on your target's employees, vendors, buyers, and partners. If you find widespread evidence of cronyism, suspect corruption of some sort.

- Strawbuying. See the chapter on real estate special projects for a detailed discussion about strawbuying. A common scam is for a dishonest operator to give a low-income "straw" money to buy property under the terms of a program designed to help low-income people, then have the "straw" turn around and secretly transfer the property deed to him. This means he gets a good deal on property illegally.

- Evidence of favoritism and/or bribery. A person who can routinely buy property at way below market value or sell it at way above market value is either a Napoleon of real estate or is a crook benefiting from illegal or unethical behavior. Likewise, a person with an unrealistically low tax assessment on his property is probably the commercial friend of the tax assessor (or a friend of someone who can lean on the tax assessor).

- Any important contradiction between public records. Newswoman Marilyn Thompson was able to uncover evidence of wrongdoing by the operators of Wedtech because what they told the Small Business Administration about their company wasn't what they told the Securities and Exchange Commission. Reviewing Wedtech's records at both agencies, Marilyn discovered evidence the company had a large number of employees, and it was not minority-controlled. These were serious finds, because they showed Wedtech's operators may have improperly gotten a lot of business via a government program designed to help small businesses owned by disadvantaged minority people. Eventually, Wedtech's operators went to prison and took a number of government officials with them.

- Any other violation or evidence of wrongdoing you've found on your target. Using the techniques throughout the book, put together a report summarizing his sleazy conduct. Individual episodes by themselves may not look like much, but the track record from several agencies over a long period of time can show a pattern of your target's white-collar criminal behavior.

This list is by no means complete. But by compiling it, I'm trying to point you, as a citizen investigator, in a direction that might lead you to uncover evidence of wrongdoing.

A FEW WORDS OF CAUTION

I'll give you a few words of caution in digging dirt on white-collar crime. Try to find out a little about the business norms and lingo of the field your target is in. An excellent way to find out is to check with a friend who is in the same kind of business as your target. Or study about the business, or call a business operator (preferably one who doesn't know your target) and glean some of this knowledge from him by posing as a college student or a freelance writer.

The reasons for doing this are obvious. One reason for knowing such information is that it will allow you to check records and leads more quickly, and you won't sound so much like a dumb outsider when you ask questions. The second reason for knowing such information is it will tell you what kind of behavior in a business field is legal and what isn't. For example, few outside of the mining industry know of the rock-pile of regulations mine operators have to abide by; your knowledge of the business may point you toward possible white-collar crimes on the part of a mine operator. On the other hand, seemingly grossly un-ethical behavior may be perfectly legal. Opponents of Congressional perks point to some of the shaky but legal grubbing of our elected officials as key examples of this concept.

I avoided embarrassment as a reporter by finding out it was legal in the state I worked in for a county prosecutor to conduct personal business with private clients in the courthouse if the county was small enough. I'd seen our local prosecutor conducting such business, and I was considering exposing this activity until I said to myself, "The prosecutor knows me and he does this while I'm waiting outside his office to interview him. If he's breaking the law, then why isn't he hiding it?" After doing some research, I found out the prosecutor's practice was legal. The county he served paid him only a few thousand dollars a year because he had very few cases to prosecute. But since the county needed a prosecutor, the state allowed lawyers like him to retain their private practices as long as no conflict of interest got in the way.

CRIME LORDS AND BUSINESS IN FLORIDA

Saying the Miami area is notorious for druglord activities is like saying Washington is notorious for government waste, corruption, and boneheadedness. It's understood. What isn't understood all that well was how druglords and other major-league criminals have been using their immorally-gotten money to buy up South Florida, costing the people of that state millions and millions of dollars in the process.

Economist Charles Kimball, using public records, showed just what a drain these criminals really are. Kimball's observations, which Joel Garreau wrote about at length in his book *The Nine Nations of North America*, revealed the mind of an incredibly able dirt digger. Using real estate records in Dade (Miami) County and Broward (Fort Lauderdale) County, Kimball said $7 billion worth of housing units and $5 billion worth of commercial property changed hands in 1979. Sampling only those real estate deals in the last quarter of 1979 worth $300,000 or more, Kimball said 42 percent of these deals involved foreign-con-trolled entities buying property. Of these foreign land-buys, he said, 54 percent of them involved anonymous offshore corporations. These corporations' paper-work is not available to the American public (or even to American government officials). And in many cases, they don't pay U.S. taxes because U.S. officials assume they're paying taxes in their home country.

Kimball said most of the anonymous offshore cor-porations he knew about were involved in drug deal-ing, international swindling, tax evasion, and other forms of corruption. He said these major criminals then would use their criminally-obtained money to outbid legitimate buyers for property, thus driving up the cost of real estate. "If the doctor has to pay more for his office," Garreau wrote of Kimball's con-clusions, "or a warehouse where brooms are kept in has to have higher rent, because of this type of infla-tion, you can begin to see the impact on every citizen. And in some areas we see virtually all shopping centers in large metropolitan areas, virtually all office buildings, going into the hands of foreign investors."

Related to Kimball's observations are Garreau's on South Florida banks. For years, many have known that crimelords have bought legitimate businesses to launder their racketeering and drug money. In other words, they route crime-profit money through the business accounts to the bank so the bankers won't report them to the government agents who use bank info to track down illegal activity. Garreau said some crimelords have bought Florida *BANKS* and have installed puppets on the board of directors to cover their money. He wrote, "A standard parlor game among Miami journalists is figuring out which banks are knowingly operating illegally and which are simp-ly being used without their knowledge."

The moral of this section is that public records can give you clues on potential white-collar criminal ac-tivity. Information on bank ownership and board of directors is public record. So is information on busi-ness ownership and property transfers. If you see shady names, then you might have found indicators of trouble. As for the anonymous offshore corpora-tions—would you *REALLY* think such an entity is above-board if you stumbled across one while check-ing land and business records?

BATTLING BRIBERY

Bribery is much like other forms of white-collar crime. Bribery contains a reason for giving or taking bribes (usually greed), a chance to steal (bribing someone to break the law himself or look the other way while the briber breaks the law), and concealment (the briber gets the bribe-taker to perform the illegal act in the course of his work).

Looking for evidence of bribery is much like look-ing for evidence of other forms of white-collar crime. Your target may be a bribe-taker if you can show he or she is engaged in the following behavior:

- Living a lifestyle above his or her apparent means. To do this, you have to figure out what the person should be making at his or her job. If the person is a government official or employee, some personnel or financial officer or public affairs person connected to the agency which employs him or her will have his or her job title, pay grade or position at hand. Since government employees' salaries are public record, you can find out how much a public servant makes by checking his agency's budget or by asking his agency's personnel office or public information office what an employee of his position or pay grade and length of service can expect to make. (If the person works with a private company, the personnel people in the company will know the salary. What you'll have to do is ask them what a person of your target's position can expect to make if the company hires him and he works the same amount of time as your target. If the person works with a labor union, a nonprofit group, or one of certain other groups, his or her salary may show up on a public record the group has to file with Uncle Sam.)

Then you'll check the public record (financial disclosure statements, divorce cases, car records, land records, corporate records, and so on) to figure out what the target owns. Document his land, car, and other major property holdings. Take photos of his property. Use the local paper's gossip column, ex-lovers, neighbors, and enemies as potential sources of dirt on your target's lifestyle. If his or her lifestyle far exceeds what his or her salary and business investments could pay for, odds are he or she is getting money illegally.

- Getting property or business interests at below-market value. If the person is a government employee, look to see if the person giving him such a good deal may have benefited earlier from the bureaucrat's actions while performing his job. Likewise, check for any evidence a labor union target or a private sector target or a target working in a nonprofit group or some other kind of group got such a bargain from a person who may have benefited earlier from the target's actions.
- Financial entanglement. For political figures, the financial disclosure statements and the campaign contribution statements reveal who does business with him and who helps him out at election time. Check for any evidence he helped people who do business with him or who contribute to him for non-ideological reasons. For non-politicians, see likewise if public records and other sources will reveal evidence of close personal or business contact between the target and those who benefit from his decisions.
- Making odd-looking decisions. If, for example, a

judge decides a case in an unorthodox way, many people in the know will think he's fixable. Likewise, a business executive or any other organization official who makes oddball decisions that might hurt the legitimate interests of his organization might be taking bribes. This is especially true if a labor leader "sells out" his people to the company at contract time. But then, as Mike Royko would say, the person in question might be honest but just dumb.

This list of potential evidence on bribe-taking is not all-inclusive. But it serves as a guide for you and should stimulate you to think of other ways to prove your target is a bribe-taker.

Your target may be a bribe-giver if you can show he or she is engaged in the following behavior:

- Failure to comply with laws. Government contract violations. Tax evasion. All these activities are evidence the target is either a blatantly obvious criminal or he is confident the officials he's bribed are taking care of business for him.
- Sudden financial gain or other good fortune. Sometimes people get lucky because Lady Luck smiles on them. Sometimes they get lucky because their hard work and foresight put them in a position to benefit from the present situation. And sometimes people benefit because they engage in insider trading, shady government contracting, or other forms of unethical behavior based on bribery. Try to find out *WHY* someone or some company had a string of good luck. If the lucky break was the result of the target "sensing" a change in the business world before it happened, or if it was the result of some government action that definitely benefited the target (and/or crippled his rivals), suspect the target bribed people to help him.
- Participating in sweetheart "sellout" deals. Giving away or selling land, business assets, and other valuables at ridiculously low prices. These behaviors may be the result of bad business judgment. Or they may be the payoffs in bribery scams. After all, a bribe-taker must get something of value from the bribe-giver in order to clout for him.
- Taking out tax-deductible ads in trade journals and political convention programs, and doing other types of questionable advertising. This sort of activity may be considered nothing more than good sound business, because the ad-buyer wants to land contracts and/or obtain favorable legislation. On the other hand, bribe-givers and bribe-takers know the score. Victor Lasky wrote that

Democrats solicited such ad-buying from the captains of industry for their 1964 convention program so the private sector bigwigs (at $15,000 a page) could demonstrate their appreciation to LBJ and his party.

William Moran, citing a U.S. Justice Department agent named Richard Condon, wrote that experienced bribers also pull stunts like these:

- Crimelords (and other bribers) make large deposits in some banks. The bankers then make loans to borrowers recommended by the crimelords (and other bribers). The borrowers never pay back the loans and the bankers let them slide.
- Bribers hire people with ties to the bribed, then have low performance expectations of the people. In other words, the people hired get good money (and sometimes even expense accounts) to goof off or otherwise do little useful work on the briber's payroll.
- Bribers extend favors to the bribed such as use of company cars, hotel suites, and other perks. They might also do something wild and crazy, like setting up a gambling account at a casino for someone in their pocket to use. The briber then makes good on any losses of the bribe-taker.

This list of potential evidence on bribe-giving is not all-inclusive. But it serves as a guide for you and should stimulate you to think of other ways to prove your target is a bribe-giver.

PAROLE VIOLATION—THE PERFECT REPORTABLE CRIME

If you know your target has a criminal conviction and is on parole for the conviction, you can make his life miserable. Something as routine as crossing a state line can send a paroled criminal back to prison for parole violation. If you ever read *The Grapes of Wrath*, you'll remember how Tom Joad's mother worried about the police questioning him. Tom was on parole, and he had illegally left Oklahoma with his family when the greedy bankers drove them from their land.

You can contact local law enforcement authorities for a summary of laws covering parole violations. And when your target violates one of the conditions of his parole, contact his parole officer. The parole officer's name might be in your target's criminal case file. The local parole officers in the county where your target was convicted should be able to tell you which of their brother parole officers has to baby-sit him. Parole officers are always glad to get tips about their criminals' misbehavior.

PERJURY IS ANOTHER PERFECT CRIME TO PUNISH

What if your target is a liar who manipulates the legal system by making false police reports? Women going through divorces often lie about their exes being child molesters, for example. Related to this is the act of "hotlining"— in which the liar calls a child abuse hotline and claims a person she or he holds a grudge against is a child abuser or a child molester. She or he could then discredit the target if the authorities make any arrest or take any other kind of action against the target of the false complaint.

There are other ways to make false police reports to make money or trouble. For example, jerks who pick fights, then lose, falsely accuse the winners of felony assault. The scam here is that the jerk hopes the fight winner will get scared of going to prison and will accept a plea-bargain to a lower misdemeanor assault and battery charge from the oily local prosecutor. This leaves the fight winner open to a big-money lawsuit because the misdemeanor criminal conviction is now on his record.

A similar scam is for hired goons who guard crooked businessmen's properties from picketers to con policemen into arresting demonstrators. The businessmen then might be able to get money from the protesters in a lawsuit. The goon's interest is in impressing the businessmen so he'll keep getting business from the businessmen and maybe win a little bonus money.

To punish these liars, obtain copies of their reports from the public files. Then obtain other document evidence (such as their later testimony or the testimony of others) to show they lied. You can file charges against these liars for their statements, and the penalties can be quite severe for them. Or you can get the victims of the liar's slander to sue for defamation.

The only time I ever named an alleged rape victim in a crime story was to punish her for lying about the alleged rape. I had written a story about a man (whom we'll call Tom Katt) who was charged with raping a woman. Friends of Tom Katt rang my phone off the hook complaining about the story. They told me a woman was having a fight with her boyfriend—a locally-prominent businessman—and decided to spite him by dating their friend Tom.

Her scheme worked too well. The boyfriend got jealous, and he ambushed Tom in an all-night convenience store. The jealous boyfriend beat up Tom with an ax handle, and Tom filed a criminal complaint. Possibly, the jealous boyfriend threatened the woman with harm, and several days after her date with Tom, she reported him for rape.

Well, I'll say this for Tom Katt—his friends were right as well as true-blue. I checked the court records, and found Tom's complaint against the boyfriend. He had filed it almost as soon as the beating took place. The woman's rape complaint noted Tom tried to rape her at her apartment (which was eight miles away from the spot where the boyfriend beat up Tom), and she listed the exact same time as Tom did on his complaint. So either the woman was a stone liar or Tom Katt had an incredibly long item of male plumbing! (Tom could have been lying, but there was evidence that he received a beating at about the time he said he received it.)

I checked further into the court records. I found out the woman had accused her jealous boyfriend a couple of months earlier of putting her in restraints, spanking her, and calling her a whore. She had later dropped her charges.

So I ran an article on Tom's upcoming court hearing, and I noted he had reported his beating almost as soon as it had happened. I also implied there were problems with the woman's story. My article caught the judge's attention, as well as the attention of the boyfriend and the woman.

The judge questioned the woman at length about the contradictions in her report. The woman was publicly shamed into dropping her false charges, and the boyfriend paid Tom Katt a substantial amount of money for the beating he dished out. I printed the lying bitch's name in a story I wrote on the court hearing (and in the article I included her previous accusation that her boyfriend had restrained her and spanked her) to humiliate her and punish her for her lying. All's well that ends well.

HELP THE TAXMAN PUNISH YOUR TARGET

I've mentioned the story of Al Capone in other parts of this book, but his story bears repeating one more time. The goons of this master criminal, who put together a syndicate to organize crime in Chicago during the Roaring 'Twenties, killed large numbers of rival gangsters and innocent people. Fearless Eliot Ness and the Untouchables—a group of U.S. Justice Department agents—raided Capone's breweries and distilleries and forced the mobster to "import" booze and beer from outside of Chicago. This strategy cost Capone big money, but Ness' team of G-men couldn't prove Capone did anything more serious than conspire to violate the Volstead Act—the law pushed by feminists and other bozos to impose the stupid Prohibition Era on a thirsty America.

Instead, it was IRS agent Frank Wilson who sent Scarface to The Rock. Wilson knew Capone hadn't filed income tax returns. Wilson and his men, after doing painstaking research on Capone's property holdings, cars, belongings, and other evidence of wealth, figured out the millionaire ganglord owed hundreds of thousands to millions of dollars in taxes. Wilson's men also found a ledger confiscated from a casino raid that tied the casino's illegal profits to Capone. They then studied handwriting samples to figure out who made the entries, concluded Capone's former bookkeeper made them, and tracked him down and arrested him in Florida. After giving the bookkeeper "the third degree," the agents got him to talk. Wilson's men got Capone indicted by a federal grand jury for income tax evasion in June 1931. A federal jury found Capone guilty of the charges in October 1931, and he drew an 11-year prison term.

Ness had secured a 5000-count Prohibition violations indictment for Capone and his cronies in case Al beat the tax evasion charges. But the Feds never brought Capone to trial on the booze-running charges the Untouchables had documented. After all, damn near everyone in the country was violating the worthless antibooze law. Ness did have the pleasure of escorting Scarface to the train that took him to prison in May 1932.

Capone, who reportedly feared needles, refused treatment for syphilis he had contracted before his imprisonment. The disease trashed his mind so thoroughly that the Feds released him early in 1939, and he died a near-vegetable on his Florida estate a few years later.

Eliot Ness went on to become Cleveland's director of public safety, and he cleaned up a corrupt police force. Sadly, however, Ness turned into a neo-Nazi. He ordered his cops to beat up on striking union workers. He also ordered his cops to burn down a hobo shanty town when they couldn't find a dismemberment-style killer in the "hobo jungle." Ness eventually had to resign in 1942 after police proved he left the scene of an accident—supposedly while driving drunk. Ness fell dead of a heart attack in 1957.

At any rate, the moral of the Capone story is the IRS can get crooks no one else can. In fact, federal prosecutors still use the Capone strategy to imprison dangerous mobsters and thieving businessmen when it looks like it will be too tough for them to prove their more serious offenses to the satisfaction of a jury. Sorry I took so long in getting to the point, but who could pass up the Capone and Ness story?

In fact, you can be like Frank Wilson and find evidence your target is cheating on his taxes, too. And then, of course, you'll be a good citizen and share your dirt with the IRS, the state treasurer's people, the local treasurer's people, and anyone else with an interest in collecting what is Caesar's.

There are a number of things people do that could indicate they are committing tax evasion crimes. Your target may be a tax cheat if you can prove he or she is engaged in the following behavior:

- Burying sales tax in purchases if buyers pay cash. This is, as I said before, one of the oldest tax evasion tricks in the books. A related trick is for businessmen to empty cash drawers and ditch tapes to avoid paying sales tax or any other kinds of tax on money they took in. If they're sloppy enough about it, you might catch them doing it in front of you.

- Operating a business without a license or proper registry. From the humblest flea market vendor to General Motors, business operators require vendor licenses to charge (and then forward to the state) sales tax money. Depending on your area, your local government's treasurer may also require business operators to obtain other licenses or register their businesses for tax purposes. Your local and state treasury people can tell you what the law requires for any taxing situation. A businessman who operates without the proper licenses is either ignorant of the law (and is begging to get pinched) or is a deliberate tax evader.

- Underpaying or failing to pay property taxes, personal property taxes, or other taxes the state or local treasurer collects. Check the first chapter on the private sector for details on how to check such tax records. You can personally see some business' inventories by walking through the business establishments. You can check whether your target is paying a whole lot lower property taxes than those who own comparable property (size, zoning, use, location, age and value of structures, etc.) elsewhere in the local tax district. You can see potential evidence of tax evasion by checking and estimating the value of the target's residence and other properties, his vehicles, his business interests, and his other holdings.

- Failure to have needed credentials or licenses for certain professions or businesses. People who don't abide by the laws regulating the professions they operate in (like a realty owner who isn't retaining anyone with a broker's license or a "doctor" who doesn't have a medical license) are probably hiding taxable income. Why? Admitting the extent of what they make would alert authorities to their illegal businesses. (Even if the

lawbreaker is paying the taxes he owes, you may still want to report his failure to have the proper license or credential. You may be saving the public from harm.)

These are warning signs, and this list is not complete. However, I listed them to give you an idea of what kind of evidence to look for. You may come up with some good ideas on your own.

In the interests of citizenship, report the information you have to the IRS and state and local taxing authorities. Tell the agents you want to help the public and tell them the facts as you know them. Tax agents are very good at following up on leads. And if their past performance is any predictor, your target will be in for a long inquisition and prosecution.

A VANDALISM WHODUNIT

In the spring of 1991, several people became suspects because an abortion facility they picketed regularly reportedly had been the target of vandals who wreaked thousands of dollars of damage on the place. However, a service buddy of mine who goes by the street name of "Ugly" said he knew the people and he said they were too mousy to do anything major-league like a six-figure trash job.

Ugly then said, "Kev, the guy who owns the mill— he's in debt up to his ass. Dollars to donuts *HE'S* the culprit!" (This was Ugly's way of saying he knew a businessman in debt can often raise money from his insurance company by staging a fire or some other destructive activity at his place of business.) Ugly then proceeded to use the public records to check the doctor's situation.

Ugly did a job worthy of his name. Ugly found the abortion provider had been sued for malpractice 13 times from 1983 to 1991. He also found out one of the doctor's staffers had evidently copulated her way to the manager's job at his facility, only to find herself out in the street when she reportedly stopped putting out for the doctor. Ugly found out she reported the doctor to state authorities for sexual harassment. Ugly also dug up some dirt on the guy from a radical feminist tabloid whose writers and readers accused him of abusing women and cheating them out of money— and of performing slipshod and unsanitary abortions.

Ugly's topper was finding out through the lawsuit records that businesspeople and the doctor's own landlord were suing him for tens of thousands of dollars of bills he evidently wasn't paying. Ugly had the evidence he needed to show maybe the doctor ought to find a place on the suspects list himself. Ugly turned in the dirt to the authorities. The investigation is ongoing as this book goes to print.

DICK TRACY AND YOU

In the Dick Tracy comic strip is a little feature called *Crimestopper's Handbook*. It gives people tips to use to fight crime. Out of respect to the lawman in the yellow raincoat, I'll finish this chapter with a few such pointers of my own.

- There are a zillion different laws, and a zillion different ways for your target to break them to steal money, thwart the will of the people, or otherwise harm the public. Sooner or later, he'll do something wrong if he's as bad as you think he is.
- Keep as familiar as you can with the laws and agencies which govern your target's key activities. If he falls, odds are he'll trip over one of these.
- Follow the advice of this chapter in determining illegal activity. Document it.
- Gather all evidence of illegal activity, and put it into a readable and usable report. See the chapter on using the info you find for more detailed instructions.
- Contact people who can make trouble for your target and present them with proof of your target's illegal activities. Such people include:
  - IRS agents, and state and local tax authorities.
  - The inspector general or the enforcement chief or other law-enforcement agents of regulatory agencies whose laws he's broken.
  - FBI and state and local police detectives.
  - Politicians who have an ax to grind against people like your target.
  - Media people.
  - Parole officers.

For more details, see the chapter on using the info you find.

Even if the cops and the agents and the prosecutors and the judges were all honest and efficient, they wouldn't be able to punish all the bad people out there for the most serious crimes they've committed. The most dedicated of these people appreciate citizen help. They *NEED* the help, and they like to know there are a few decent people out there who *DO* care!

When you approach government agents with evidence, remain a total professional in your actions. They're used to hearing from nut cases and liars, and they'll be naturally skeptical toward you for a while. Also, they are frustrated about their relative impotence, so some of them may take it out on you because you as a "vigilante" have used your time and your smarts to do what they couldn't do.

NEVER LIE OR EXAGGERATE. If you lie about someone just to get him in trouble, you're probably no better than he is. Punishers need to work on truth to believe you and to find a valid reason to punish your target. Besides, if your target is as big a scumbag as you think he is, you won't *HAVE* to lie to get him in trouble. Just report the truth about what scum he is!

Well, that about wraps it up. If you use the public records and your own gray matter wisely, you may be able to make your target sadly think, "CRIME DOESN'T PAY."

END NOTES

1. Quotes and ideas used by William Moran come from his book *Investigative Methods for White Collar Crime*.
2. Information on LBJ's finances comes from Victor Lasky's book *It Didn't Start With Watergate*. Apparently, Lasky reported, a lot of Johnson's money came from the radio station and TV station he and Lady Bird owned. Lasky said Johnson's TV station was the only one in the Austin, Texas area, and friendly Federal Communications Commission agents may have protected his monopoly of the area's airwaves.
3. Information on the Wedtech scandal comes from Marilyn Thompson's book *Feeding The Beast*.
4. The observations of Charles Kimball and Joel Garreau on questionable land and bank deals in Florida come from Garreau's book *The Nine Nations of North America*.
5. Information on industry ad-buying for the 1964 Democrat convention program comes from Victor Lasky's book *It Didn't Start With Watergate*.
6. The information on Al Capone and Eliot Ness comes from Steven Nickel's article "The Real Eliot Ness". This article appeared in the October 1987 issue of *American History Illustrated*.

Fight Sex Offenders

Rapist. Sex offender. Child molester. Just hearing these words makes your stomach turn and your trigger finger itch.

Sex offenders are the lowest form of life.

Why someone would commit rape is beyond me. Guys, it just ain't worth it, even if the lady is a tease. When you rape, you prove you aren't enough of a man to be secure in a love relationship with a woman. You also prove you're a worthless scumbag who treats women like they have no humanity. What if someone tougher than you got the idea you were put on the earth for *him* to exploit?

I feel the same about homosexual rapists. Homosexuality is no excuse for exploitation of another. On top of that, some of the homosexual rapists are also killing their victims by putting AIDS-laced semen into them.

And child molesters? These people make rapists look like solid citizens. Other criminals in prison will punish child molesters because these vermin have committed acts of evil against defenseless little children. Even felons have some moral outrage!

I'd execute all child molesters by gutting them with a shovel or burning them alive if I could. Since almost every child molester commits multiple molestations, killing them all is the only "therapy" for them that will protect our nation's children. Critics might claim my proposed penalty is cruel, but if we carried it out often enough, it wouldn't be unusual any more!

I'm not concerned about being politically correct. My only concern is that my words don't adequately cover how much I hate sex offenders.

This chapter gives instructions on dirt-digging of the most serious kind—determining who in your neighborhood, in your community, and in the lives of your children are the kinds of vermin who would rape the helpless or molest the innocent. This chapter also contains instructions on how to expose government agencies for failure to protect women and children from sexual abuse. It also contains instructions on how to fight sexploitative businessmen if they decide to fester in your neighborhood.

Unlike most chapters, this chapter will challenge you to do a little more detective work. It will also challenge you to pay more attention than normal to people's behavior—behavior that could tip you off to whether someone you know is a sex offender or a sexual abuse victim. Meeting the challenge will be worth it if you can expose a sex offender and keep him away from more victims.

A word of caution before we go any further: DO NOT MAKE SUCH A CHARGE LIGHTLY. You could trash an innocent person's reputation for life, and you could leave yourself open for ugly retaliation or prison time. Also, you won't help the victims if you falsely cry "Wolf" about someone being a sex offender. Jerks who have falsely accused others of sex offenses have made it harder for the authorities to take seriously reports of real sex offenses.

But when you do have the evidence, don't hold it back, either. A sex offender will almost always commit repeated sexual assaults. The quicker you provide legitimate evidence to the authorities about a sex offender, or about an agency's ridiculously inept screening of people who want access to children, the quicker someone with power will crack down.

Before we really get into this chapter, I'm going to tell you too many government people who are supposed to be protecting women and children from sexual exploitation have not been doing their jobs properly. In fact, it's truly frightening that people in the legal system and other alleged professionals abuse victims of sex crimes even more by the miserable way they treat them.

The procedure for removing a rapist's sperm and pubic hairs from a woman's vagina for evidence is greatly humiliating to the woman in itself. To add insult to injury, bumbling cops and lab people lose such pieces of physical evidence much more often than they want us to believe. If the rapist has VD, odds are the victim will be infected. Ditto for AIDS!!

At trial, the defense attorney figuratively rapes the woman all over again. He tries to make it sound like she's been pounding the streets in relentless search for a roll in the hay with a dirtbag like his client. Her whole sexual history will be put on trial. Children who have been molested suffer abuse in court from aggressive attorneys who badger them and make them feel like they've been bad children to be in a spot like this.

And prosecutors botch the cases. Yeah. Worthless prosecutors botch sex crimes cases by doing substandard work. As a result of the prosecutor's laziness or incompetence, the rapist or molester gets off free. Or the wrong man goes to prison for the crime, while the real sex offender continues to roam free and prey upon others because the prosecutor was too lazy to figure out the truth behind the facts in his case and conned the jury into convicting the wrong man.

THE McMARTIN PRESCHOOL CASE

A prime example of the outrages that molesters—and lawyers—commit against children is the McMartin Preschool case. I know I mentioned this case in the chapter on prosecutors, but this case is so hateful, it bears repeating. According to published accounts of the case, this is what happened:

Police investigators determined 369 children who attended this big-name facility in Manhattan Beach, California, had suffered sexual abuse in the early 1980s. In 1984, Los Angeles County prosecutors charged Peggy McMartin Buckey, her son Raymond Buckey, and five other staffers at the school with multiple counts of child molestation.

Bizarre stories of sexual abuse came out of the case. The children said staffers sexually molested them. The children also said adults made them play a game called "Naked Movie Star", in which they would have to take off their clothes and the adults would take pictures or movies of them. Further, they said, they were taken on "field trips" to houses where strangers molested them. This raised the ugly specter that someone was pimping the little children and using them for kiddie porn.

The children said the staffers forced them to watch as they killed little bunnies and ducklings. The children also said the staffers told them they would kill them likewise if they told anyone about being molested. IF YOU DON'T FEEL LIKE KILLING THE PERPETRATORS BY NOW, THERE'S PROBABLY SOMETHING WRONG WITH YOU.

But the Los Angeles County district attorney's case against the school's staffers started to unravel. First, Judge Aviva Bobb allowed defense lawyers to emotionally wear down 13 child witnesses at the staffers' pretrial hearings. The little children cracked under this abuse. Instead of fighting Bobb's ruling that denied children the protection of testifying on closed-circuit TV (even though the children's parents had gotten the law changed in California to allow it), or getting her removed from the case, the prosecutors decided not to have any more children testify. Bobb

then dismissed roughly 200 charges against the defendants.

The case unraveled even more. It was alleged that the social worker who interviewed the hundreds of children for the D.A.'s office was browbeating them into making up stories of sex abuse and animal killing to strengthen the prosecution's case. Ira Reiner, the new district attorney (Reiner had briefly been a defense attorney in the Manson Family trial), dropped charges against five staffers in early 1986.

Later that year, a prosecutor named Glenn Stevens resigned from the case under pressure after the discovery of leaks from the prosecutor's office to the press. Stevens turned around and said the defendants were innocent *AFTER* he signed a book and movie deal about the case. Stevens said the case went on only because of political pressures; he also claimed there was no medical evidence to confirm the molestations.

Many parents irately refuted him. After all, they had to pay the doctor bills for the vaginal and rectal damage and infections their children had suffered. They had to deal with their children's bedwetting and nightmares and erratic behavior. One parent said, "Our child is just another piece of evidence and no one's looking out for her interests."

Eventually, Peggy McMartin Buckey was acquitted in early 1990. Her son Raymond survived two trials; each ended in a hung jury. As the jurors put it, the evidence proved the little children had been molested, but the prosecutors couldn't prove who had done the molesting. Prosecutors decided to drop the case after the second trial ended in mid-1990. The case cost the taxpayers $13.5 million.

Whether the Buckeys committed the crimes or not, SOMEONE did. And since no one was convicted of these terrible crimes against children, that means only one thing. THE REAL MOLESTERS ARE FREE TO MOLEST MORE LITTLE CHILDREN.

CATCHING THE CHILD MOLESTERS

Little children are trusting. And the vermin who molest little children take advantage of their trusting natures. Once a child is molested, his or her childhood is basically over. He or she now can't trust any adult; he or she will suffer nightmares, guilt, and a feeling of worthlessness over the molestation. They will blame themselves because creeps sexually used them.

In Connie Fletcher's book *What Cops Know*, Chicago policemen recall their hatred for child molesters. They also say what I've said for years; it's the teacher, clergyman, youth group leader, coach, or someone else in a position of authority over kids who is the most likely to molest them. Why? A lot of scumbags get into these jobs so they can get at little children! One cop said he and his partner in one year arrested six teachers who were producing child pornography. Two were doing it in their CLASS-ROOMS!

Crime usually has physical evidence. I've said for years there are certain things you can look for in children to sense whether or not someone is molesting them, and policemen agree with me. And a medical researcher a few years ago also confirmed my opinion. Dr. Ann Burgess, who headed a research team studying sexual abuse of children, said parents can and should monitor the adults in their children's lives for possible child molestation. This is what she recommends:

- Be alert to adults who spend an undue amount of time in the company of children. As an example, she said, a man who goes to a lot of children's birthday parties is someone to watch.

- Be suspicious of unusual variation in a normal routine. She cited one case in which a teacher asked some children to come to school long before others.

- Watch for such telling things in children as extreme anxiety around a specific adult, declining grades, and withdrawal from playmates. "They think about it (the sexual abuse) a lot," says Dr. Burgess. "They can't do their school work and they can't play with friends." (I'd also add to look out for certain types of nightmares and certain types of morbid or sexual questions coming from a child. Bear in mind a father of one of the McMartin Preschool children said his daughter cried and cried when he dropped her off at the facility. He felt guilty for missing this behavior sign.)

- Pay attention to physical symptoms. She said headaches, loss of appetite, vomiting, genital soreness and sleep disorders were all warning signs. (I'd add looking for damage to and infections of the child's genitals and rear end, and looking for symptoms of VD. Further, I'd add heavier-than-normal bedwetting to the list. Bear in mind many of the children in the McMartin Preschool case suffered anal and/or genital damage and infections.)

- Be aware of a precocious sexuality in language, dress, or behavior. (After all, kids don't pick up descriptions of copulation, oral sex, or sodomy from watching Bugs Bunny or the Flintstones.)

As for a child molester's mode of operation, I've had my own ideas for years on how the scumbags most likely do it. Again, policemen I've talked with tend to agree with me. Kenneth Wooden, an advocate of child victims, interviewed molested children and imprisoned child molesters to come up with these conclusions on molesters' methods of operation:

- Children 10-12 years old are the most likely victims because they are close to puberty and have the most sexual turn-on potential.

- Most abductions take place between the end of school and dinner time. The easiest prey are kids who take shortcuts from school, kids who are loners on the playground or in the neighborhood, and kids who seem depressed.

- Most child molesters (almost 80 percent) are white males 20-40 years old.

- The lure child molesters most often use on children is to ask for help such as finding directions, finding a lost dog, or carrying packages or groceries.

The Chicago police who Connie Fletcher interviewed added these observations:

- Many child molesters seek out single women with children. They date or become friendly with the women, then molest their children. "Stepfathers and live-in boyfriends are common child molesters," one cop said.

- Almost all child molesters gain access to children through their professions, volunteer work, or family contact. "Some of these people (one cop said)...they're there because they're pedophiles."

- Some child molesters will target children with home problems, behavior problems, credibility problems or low self-worth. "He's not gonna hit on the kid that has two solid parents and a home or the kid that he knows is gonna run home and tell on him," one cop explained.

Now you've heard from a couple of people in the know. USE YOUR POWERS OF OBSERVATION TO LOOK FOR SITUATIONS AND EVIDENCE OF CHILD MOLESTING. I'll go a step farther. I say all concerned adults should watch for such signs in the children they come in contact with on a regular basis. As a reminder, check any suspect molester's criminal record. Since child molesters molest many children, maybe one or more children came forward against him in the past. If any did, the record will show it. Also, look for other crimes on the suspect's record, like contributing to the delinquency of minors or drug offenses or exposure offenses. Often, these are plea-bargained convictions of offenses that once had been molestation or drug sales to minors charges.

Another set of records to probe is the set the court clerks keep in the juvenile and domestic portion of the courthouse. Clerks will try to deny you access to these records, and for most juvenile cases, they're right. But you should have the right to look at the docket and the court index to see if your target is among the ADULTS who have had to appear in this court. The court clerks might falsely tell you an adult's record or case is confidential. They're wrong. An adult's criminal case is a public record, and they will have to let you see it. (You may need the help of a friendly pol or a lawsuit to get it done.) Once you get your hands on such a case, treat it like any other criminal case you would check.

You can check out the adults who run a school or a children's hospital or a youth group if you want to. WHEN YOU FIND EVIDENCE FROM PHYSICAL OBSERVATION AND/OR FROM THE COURT RECORDS, GO STRAIGHT TO THE POLICE WITH IT. IF THE POLICE DON'T ACT, GO TO THE MEDIA!

Why be concerned? Because there are lots of child molesters out there, and some of these creeps have even formed groups (like the Rene Guyon Society in California and the North American Man/Boy Love Association in the East and the Midwest) to fight age-of-consent laws so they can get their hands on little children for sex! Maybe we should start a group to work for the repeal of all laws against vigilantes and parents executing child molesters.

Follow these instructions listed above, and you'll be doing your bit to protect children from these child-molesting scumbags. Don't feel guilty about it, either. It is up to you to protect defenseless children. Using your powers of observation, your skills as a public records researcher, and your relentless effort, you'll be able to spot the child molester, and stop him before he molests more young children.

TRAPPING MOLESTERS OF TEENAGERS

Teens are at risk for rape much more now than in previous years. They are not as defenseless as young children, but they have other vulnerabilities that sex offenders exploit. Teenage girls, for example, don't mind being able to get clothes and fashion items cheaply. And teenage boys appreciate the chance of buying contraband, like booze or fireworks, from "cool" adults.

Sex abusers use other lures to trap teens. Runaways need work and a place to stay, and molesters often prey upon these desperate kids. Your local newspaper is full of stories of the wretched ends of these young people's lives.

Teenage girls can undergo abortions and certain birth control treatments without parental consent. They are prime targets for sex abuse at the hands of abortion facility staffers and sex clinic staffers. For example, published reports indicate a 15-year-old girl accused a Planned Parenthood staffer in downstate Illinois of sexual assault in 1991.

Knowing that a sex offender has many victims, Illinois state child protection agents demanded Planned Parenthood officials turn over a list of the 50 or so teenage girls the doctor had seen in a two-month period so they could question the girls about any sexual abuse the doctor could have inflicted on them.

Believe it or not, Planned Parenthood officials refused to turn over the names of the girls. They had the gall to claim the state's sex crimes probe (which agents intended to do confidentially) would violate the girls' confidentiality! (Some Planned Parenthood staffers evidently violate teenage girls' privacy by sending collection letters for as little as $12 to their parents' addresses. Naturally the parents find out about the allegedly confidential abortions. So who's kidding whom?)

As this book goes to print, Planned Parenthood officials, according to a published report, worked out a deal with the state's top dogs in which they promised to contact the girls themselves. Does this deal smell like a scam, or what? This reported deal allows Planned Parenthood, as the employer (and eventual possible co-defendant in a criminal case or a civil case) of an accused sex offender to have the chance to scare off witnesses without the state agents finding out. How? They'll have the opportunity to tell these girls their visits to the facility could be exposed if they go to the authorities with evidence against the doctor.

Youths looking for after-school jobs fall into the webs of those who pose as would-be employers. Chicago area homosexual rapist/mass murderer John Wayne Gacy used this tactic to lure teen boys to his house. If the boy showed up alone, Gacy would con the kid into getting handcuffed for a magic trick he would attempt. The teen would often consent, thinking it would help his chance at getting a job. Instead, it would get him raped and murdered.

Teens hanging out after hours naturally draw police attention. Teens expect a certain amount of hassle from the men in blue, so they don't usually suspect any foul play from them. Rapists who know this can pose as policemen, order kids into cars, and then abduct them. John Wayne Gacy posed as an undercover cop to kidnap, rape, and murder teen boys.

Meanwhile, out in L.A., cousins Angelo Buono and Kenneth Bianchi—the Hillside Stranglers—decided in November 1977 to take a brief break from raping and killing young women. They decided to prey upon two young girls instead. The two murderous cousins—posing as policemen—spotted schoolgirls Sonja Johnson and Dolores Cepeda at a bus stop on November 13, 1977. They ordered the girls to come along with them. Sonja, 14, and Dolores, 12, were afraid and felt guilty— they had just shoplifted a couple of pieces of costume jewelry. The murderous cousins took the two girls to Buono's house, then raped and sodomized them. They took the 80-pound Sonja in a bedroom, strangled her, then came for Dolores. When the young girl—dazed and degraded—asked pitiably for her little friend, they told her not to worry, then murdered her. They dumped the girls' bodies in a trash pile near Dodger Stadium. It was a nine-year-old Hispanic boy's sad job to find them and report their deaths.

To protect teens, be prepared to make the following observations:

- Be aware of adults who make themselves readily available to teens, especially if they do it at unusual times. (For example, suspect a youth group leader who often has youths at his house late in the evening.) Be aware of the teen coming up with hard-to-get possessions or contraband. The teen might be getting it from an adult planning to rape him or her. (Or some other adult lowlife is selling contraband or hot (stolen) goods to him or her, which isn't any good, either.)
- Check if the teen starts suffering health problems or displays the signs of some form of VD. Sometimes kids choose promiscuity, and that's not good. But sometimes the kids are victims of an infected rapist. Also, monitor the teen's other symptoms, such as loss of appetite, headaches, and sleep disorders for possible changes.
- The average rapist of teens is much like the average child molester. He's a white male between 20 and 40 who is often clean-cut and well-thought of. A single man or woman who is a teacher, a cleric, a counselor, a coach, or a youth group leader fits the profile of teen molester a lot better than the stereotyped creep who lurks in our minds.
- Be aware of weird behavior on the part of your suspect or youths who come in contact with him. Black neighbors of Jeffrey Dahmer, for example, told police they heard a buzz saw running at all hours of the night and smelled a smell much like rotting flesh coming out of his apartment. However, Milwaukee police ignored these tips. Dahmer, a convicted child molester, was able to continue raping, murdering, dismembering, and eating the flesh of his victims.

- Be aware of the presence of teens (especially girls) around a man or a woman, especially if they don't seem related to the adult or tied to the adult in any other way. Be suspicious if there are a lot of comings and goings of these teens. They could be working as prostitutes for this person. Or they could be trading sex for food and shelter. (Or they could be committing street crimes for him, which is also undesirable.)
- Be suspicious if a teen's performance in school (and at work) drops, if he or she becomes moody or withdrawn, or if he or she engages in bizarre behavior (something different from good behavior or normal teen "junior lowlife" rebellious or obnoxious behavior). Teen girls especially tend to become depressed or suicidal when subjected to rape and incest.

A classic example of teen depression tipping off sex abuse to a responsible adult took place when a 13-year-old Baltimore girl wrote on the bottom of a history test, "I hate life. I hate school. I hate people. I hope to die. Soon!!!" Her teacher saw this clue and reported it. A frightful case of a father who, with his wife's help, repeatedly raped his 13-year-old daughter and her two older sisters over a nine-year period was uncovered within hours.

The sordid details are these: The woman would bring her own daughters to their father, so he could rape them in their big bed. Each girl would scream and try futilely to fight off her swine of a father before he overcame her and raped her, while her sullen whore of mother would roll over and pretend to go to sleep.

The three girls together got pregnant by their scumbag father 10 different times, and each time, their worthless mother would take them to an abortion provider so he could kill the evidence of their sexual enslavement to their debased father. No abortion provider ever reported these girls' cases to the authorities; they were too busy raking in the cash the mother was paying them to wonder why her girls were constantly getting pregnant at such young ages. In late 1990, the parents were tried for their crimes. The father received a 30-year prison term, and the mother received a 15-year term. They got off far too lightly.

Don't forget...check any suspect molester's criminal record. Since rapists of teens rape many, many teens, maybe one or more teens came forward in the past. If any did, the record will show it. Also, look for other offenses on the suspect's record, like contributing to the delinquency of minors, indecent exposure, or drug offenses. Often, these are plea-bargained down convictions for offenses that once had been rape or drug sales to minors charges.

Another set of records to probe is the set the court clerks keep in the juvenile and domestic portion of the courthouse. Check these per instructions in the section on child molesters.

Don't buy the crap that you're inhibiting the teens' choices by checking on their behavior. These young people may be the victims of a seriously debased form of sexual exploitation. If your suspicions are wrong, so what? It's better to err on the side of the teens. If people like you don't ignore the bleeding-heart idiots and step forward to protect these young people, they'll go down like Kitty Genovese.

Kitty, for those of you too young to remember, was assaulted and stabbed to death in New York City in 1964. What made her case so disturbing—and such a national story—is that 40 people watched from their apartments as Kitty, screaming in agony, was stabbed repeatly for a half hour before dying. Not one of these subhuman morons went to save her from death. AND NONE OF THEM EVEN CALLED THE COPS!!

DIGGING DIRT ON THE SYSTEM

Many children, teens, and women in this country are getting molested and raped as you read this book because of government employees and officials. Inadequate screening of foster and adoptive parents, substandard screening of teachers and day care workers and health care workers and police, and light sentences for child molesters and rapists are to blame. In this section, I'm going to show you how to dig up the dirt on the government's failures to protect these victims from their rapists. Armed with this info, maybe you can get the laws changed and make the government actually protect women, teens, and children from sexual abuse.

Check Child Welfare Agencies For Foster And Adoptive Parent Screening. I first became heavily interested in the child protection issue when I was investigating the case of a professed bisexual who wanted to become a foster parent. Since I suspected he wanted to use the foster parent ruse to gain access to young boys, I ran checks on him. I found out the deviate had been a suspect in at least two attempts to molest children, and I found proof he had plea-bargained a fairly serious drug charge (manufacturing marijuana) down to a lesser charge. I reported these facts in an article. Later, the switch-hitter was shut out by county child welfare agents.

In the process of investigating this maggot, I discovered the ugly truth about how slipshod the government really is in screening potential foster parents and adoptive parents. I interviewed child welfare agents in several states to find out how they checked on these

people to protect children. One state's official told me his agency had no access to the police computer network or to any centralized file of people with records of child abuse, child molestation, or child neglect. He said his agents were reduced to doing local background checks on prospective foster and adoptive parents.

Another state's official bragged her state had a centralized crimes-against-children file for her agents to use. Then the smirk went out of her voice as I started giving her "the third degree." She admitted she did not cross-check the number of checks her people were running against the number of applicants. Such a check, she conceded, would verify whether her people were doing their jobs. Also, she admitted, her state did not give child welfare agents access to the police computer network so they could double-check the applicants for crimes they may have committed in the state—and for crimes they may have committed in other states.

There is nothing keeping you from doing a similar exposé on your state's child welfare people. Call the child welfare agency in your state capital and ask them their procedure for screening potential adoptive and foster parents. As a minimum, they should be able to check a central "crimes against children" file, and they should have access to the police computer network. (I'll go a step or so further. I say we must pressure all states' child welfare officials into maintaining a "crimes against children" file, pressure them to share the data with other states, and make it—as well as police computer data—open to the public.)

Then ask the officials how they check on their agents to make sure they're doing the proper screening. A long silence, a garble of gibberish, or a multi-syllable backpedaling answer should cue you to the fact that you've probably caught your state's child protection people asleep at the switch. As a final touch, ask for a summary of the state's child welfare laws and a copy of the procedures the agents have to use in screening adults who want kids. If the bureaucrats stonewall you, go to your local elected officials and the local media. Politicians and reporters can't resist generating headlines about fighting bureaucrats who are slow to protect children. If the information is out there, gather it and use it. As long as Big Brother is out there, we might as well make him do some useful work for the people.

Check On Screening Processes For Those Who Have Access To The Vulnerable. By now, you're well aware of how to check for criminal records of targets. Your digging job now is to find out if your government officials know how to check on those who have access to women or teens or children, or if they're too lazy to do it. As a minimum, the officials should be checking on the police computer network, on the state "crimes against children" file, and on any leads which the person's background may reveal.

Policemen and policewomen, by their police powers, have access to suspects, runaways, and children in general. So do prison guards and jail guards. Some cops and guards have molested children and raped women. Some dykes in blue have also raped women and teenage girls. Interrogate local law enforcement officials and state law enforcement officials on what kind of background checks they perform on officers. (They can't be doing too good a job in many places, especially in places where cops and deputies are poorly-paid.)

Get them to turn over copies of the state and the local code for checking on officers. Also, get them to give you copies of their internal procedure for checking on officer backgrounds. Ask also for what kind of work they do to verify the checks are being made. If the police officials "take the Fifth" or refuse you any such records, put a bug about it in your local elected official's and investigative reporter's ears. Point out any weaknesses in the law or in the administrative procedure to the media and to your elected officials.

Teachers have semi-custodial control over children and teens, and teachers have quite a bit of influence over kids. Occasionally, some teachers decide to teach children about the birds and bees by way of practical exercise whether the children like it or not. Demand an explanation from school officials what kinds of background checks they perform on teachers to weed out the sex offenders. Again, ask for copies of the code regarding checking teachers' backgrounds, and ask for copies of the procedures background checkers actually use. Also ask how they verify the agents are doing their homework on these checks. If the school officials do unsatisfactory work on this issue, flunk them and let your local elected officials and media people know about the "F" you gave them. Point out any weaknesses in the law or in the administrative procedure to the media and to your elected officials.

Likewise, day-care center operators and staffers have semi-custodial control over small children. Find out who regulates day-care centers in your state. Then get on the phone with them to ask for what kinds of background checks they perform on day-care operators and staffers. Ask for copies of the codes which require these checks and copies of the procedures the agents are supposed to use. Ask how the bosses are making sure their agents are actually making the checks. Let the press and your elected officials know about any shortcomings; also let parents of kids in day-care centers know. They'll generate heat and light for you.

Doctors and other health-care workers have private access to women, teens, and children. Often, the patients are scantily-clothed or nude, and many times they're drugged or anesthetized. Some doctors take advantage of them. Remember the case of Laurence Reich. This abortion provider was fondling women and reportedly forced a woman to perform oral sex on him. (In a plea-bargain, Reich pleaded no contest to two counts of battery and paid a small fine.)

Check with your state medical professions licensing agents to see what checking they do on doctors, nurses, and other health care workers. Again, get copies of the state code which spells out what checks they have to do on these people, and get copies of the procedures they actually use to run the checks. Ask how they know their staffers are actually running the checks they should be running. Again, share any negative diagnosis with local elected officials and media people. Also, spread the word to religious groups, women's groups, and child-protection groups so they can make trouble on their own.

Mental hospital staffers have custodial control over people that in some cases is greater than prison guards' control over inmates. After all, most prisoners are sane, while most mental hospital patients are not. Further, many patients may be drugged into some sort of compliant-behavior fog. Recall the story of how New Jersey state senator Richard Codey, using the name of a sex offender, got a job at a state mental hospital without a background check. Recall also how he said other staffers bragged to him about abusing patients and sexually assaulting the pretty women patients. Who's to say the staffers aren't doing likewise in your state?

Again, contact state health officials and demand information on how they screen potential staffers. Get copies of the state laws which require these checks, and get copies of the procedures the agents actually use. Ask the officials what verification they do to ensure their staffers are doing the checking. Report the officials if they're not getting the job done. Point out any weaknesses in the law or in the administrative procedure to the media and to your elected officials.

While you're at it, don't overlook blue-collar and pink-collar workers at the various institutions. They are just as capable of committing sex crimes as the white-collar staffers. Demand the same kinds of checking procedure data on them as you would on the degreed staffers.

Bear in mind something else: In many states, doctors, teachers, policemen, and other such professionals in a position to know are required to report evidence of statutory rape (children having sex below the age of consent) to public health agents or police authorities. The purpose for this law is to allow state agents to find incidents of incest, child molestation, or other instances of sexual assault committed on children. They can then punish the guilty sex offenders, and protect children from sexual abuse.

Dr. Ben Graber, a Florida abortion provider and state representative, found out the hard way he should have paid closer attention to this law in his state. Graber came under fire because in 1987 he performed an abortion on a 10-year-old girl whose mother reportedly said neighborhood teens had had sex with her; he didn't report the statutory rape of the girl to authorities. In late 1988, according to newspaper accounts, the girl's father was arrested for molesting her and his other four daughters after hospital workers reported they had to treat her for injuries stemming from a sexual assault she suffered. In other words, the girl suffered almost two more years of sexual abuse from her father, in part because Graber didn't report her case. Graber, who reportedly admitted he knew the girl was only 10 years old, was probed for misconduct. But the state representative was never prosecuted for his failure to report.

JUDGING COURT PERFORMANCE

Since sex offenders are the hard-core criminals most likely to commit more such crimes, you'd think judges and prosecutors would get wise and have them kept in prison a little longer. But they don't. Too many judges are politicians who turn into little Hitlers. Too many prosecutors are basically bureaucrats who aren't good enough to cut it in private law practice. The result? Sex offenders who are released too soon rape and molest thousands more women and children every year.

For detailed instructions on figuring out whether a target judge is too soft on sex offenders, check the chapter on how government officials use power. The best types of evidence will be a low conviction rate in his court relative to other courts, a low punishment rate relative to other judges, and evidence from sex offenders' trial paperwork that shows he allows defense lawyers to trash victims and he suppresses solid prosecutor evidence.

Check the chapter on prosecutors for detailed instructions on figuring out if your local prosecutor is a lazy stooge who shuffles papers instead of a defender of the people who prosecutes the real criminals. If he's too willing to plea-bargain down serious sex charges to get easy convictions, if he loses cases because he does a poor job of preparing them and arguing them in court, and if his peers say he's a shyster, odds are he's a threat to women and children just by holding a job as a prosecutor.

Any dirt you can find on soft judges and incompetent prosecutors will help the public. Why? Because the media does a poor job of covering the job performance of judges and prosecutors. As a result, most voters get little or no information on most judges and prosecutors. When election time rolls around, the voters are without guidance. As a digger, you can publicize dirt on judges and prosecutors. This could knock bad judges and prosecutors out of office. Maybe other shysters will take their places, but at least you will have verified for the public those judges and prosecutors who deserve to be EX-government officials!

Remember the story I told you about convicted child molester Carson Payne. I published the names of the judge, the prosecutor, and the defense attorney involved in the case who agreed to give this multiple child rapist probation with no prison time. I also published the molester's name and address so his neighbors knew to keep their children away from him.

I got fired for doing this, because it wasn't my paper's policy to print the names of child molesters, and I had deliberately violated this policy a number of times. (My editor's whining argument was that people who knew a child molester would suspect he molested his own children if he had any. So what? Children need to be protected from these monsters, so I identified them.)

Also there was fallout between me and the paper's higher-ups over my coverage of the bisexual drug producer (and possible child molester) who wanted to become a foster parent. They claimed I was too hard on the deviate and they softened an article I wrote on him. And they were upset because I cursed out a senior copy editor who castrated an article I wrote about flaws in the process for screening potential foster parents and adoptive parents.

I'm not sorry I did what I did. People need to know about those who pose a threat to their children. In the absence of capital punishment and life without parole, judges need to make sex offenders wear tattoos on their foreheads and mark their houses and cars with warnings that they are threats to rape and molest. And the public must pressure media people into exposing sex offenders instead of covering up for them.

As for the culprits? All I'll say is this—my former bosses who tried to keep child molester crimes against children hidden had better pray to God none of their kids is molested by the scum they protected.

INVASION OF THE CHILD-SNATCHERS

A growing problem in America is the intrusion of government into the family. "Big Mother"—the social welfare people—has developed a new game to harass people. It's called snatching kids away from parents because the parents have committed the sin of poverty, religious fervor, sound discipline with a certain amount of corporal punishment, or weakness (asking for protection from an abusive situation). Big Mother's agents swarm down on the children like the Wicked Witch of the West's winged monkeys, and carry them off to foster homes or county "shelters" or jails. In these places of confinement, children often suffer in unsanitary conditions, and all too often suffer beatings, rapes, and even death at the hands of strangers.

Why? Because the administrators of these government agencies make big bucks and need to justify their existence. They have to point (often incorrectly) to an out-of-control American family to justify needing money and staffers for more and more programs. And they claim the situation is getting even worse. (This might be a left-handed admission their programs don't work.)

The best interests of children are often totally ignored because some fuzzy-headed bureaucrats in these administrators' kingdom say there's a problem. They threaten parents with never being able to see their children again, and parents have to spend small fortunes in court costs to fight the bureaucrats and get their children back home. Obviously, such a lousy system discriminates most against minorities, because their family norms and income levels aren't familiar to the middle-class white college kids who become social workers in these agencies.

If you never considered serial-killing government agents, lawyers, judges and policemen for their crimes, Mary Pride's book *The Child Abuse Industry* might make you think otherwise. Her book lays out the truth, and it will make you sick. In one case, she reported, social workers were pimping girls out of a government-run group home. In some instances, the johns were seen taking showers in the group home after having sex with the girls! In another case, a Florida doctor said she stuck her fingers in little girls' vaginas as part of sexual abuse investigations to find out how deep the penetrations were. In short, she was re-molesting these little girls as part of her state job. (Was she screened for sexual preference???) Then there were the accounts of some teachers who "hot-lined" (reported for child abuse) every parent of every child in their classes for spite. These scumbag teachers caused scores of families untold anguish.

How do you check on this kind of state-sanctioned child abuse? You'll have to find out which agencies in your state can yank kids out of homes. Then find out all cases in juvenile and domestic courts and in upper-level courts which involve these agencies. Look for names and addresses of parents so you can contact them. Review each agency's budget to see how much money they spend on foster care in government institutions and in foster homes.

File freedom of information requests for documents pertaining to various child programs so you can see what the agency is up to. File freedom of information requests for summaries and case numbers of all children the agents remove from their homes, for what reason they remove each child, and the resolution of each case. The agents will probably stonewall you on confidentiality grounds. In that case, you will probably have to get a public official interested enough in the cause to help you gain access to the records.

Then, there's another approach. Investigate the agency like you'd investigate a police force for brutality. If you can get names of parents, you'll be able to contact them and get further information if they'll talk. Level with the parents, tell them what you're up to and offer proof of your intentions. This will make it easier for them to trust you and help you get even for them.

State-sponsored child abuse, like other crimes, has physical, documentary, and/or circumstantial evidence. Children who suffer sexual or physical abuse severe enough to require medical attention will have medical records. Government agencies have to maintain accounts to pay for medical care of these children. These should be public records. If you push hard enough, you should be able to make the responsible agency come up with records showing how much money was spent on medical care for these children, which facilities and doctors received the money, and how many children were involved. The paperwork might also indicate where the sexual assaults or injuries took place, who reported them, and who may have been responsible for them.

Likewise, the reported cases of children who are raped in state or foster custody (but don't receive medical treatment) are kept by some bureaucrat. Find him and demand copies of agency data relating to children being raped while in state or foster custody. Find out how many rapes were reported, how many suspected rapists were identified, and how many of these were prosecuted. Press for the identities of the defendants; press for info on cases in which the suspect wasn't prosecuted.

Another way to get this information is to check dockets and indexes at the juvenile and domestic court in your county courthouse. As you check the list, key in on any adult named as a criminal defendant in a juvenile case. Then ask to see the court paperwork. The clerks may refuse you. If you have to, use heavy persuasion or the aid of local officials to gain access to the records; the criminal records of adults are public records. As needed, threaten to call the media about the bureaucrats' stonewalling.

And finally, though I hate to say it, there is a standard record for children who suffer the ultimate abuse in state or foster custody. It's called a death certificate.

KEEPING SEXPLOITATION OUT OF YOUR NEIGHBORHOOD

Like most American males, I have looked at the pictures in *Playboy*, *Penthouse*, *Hustler*, and other such magazines. I've seen my share of pornographic movies and have been in my share of strip joints and other low dives. Many people can testify I have an R- to X-rated vocabulary at times—even when I'm not angry. So I'm not necessarily coming at the sexploitation issue from a religious zealot point of view.

However, let's say you're an upright person who takes the word of God seriously enough to run sexploiters out of business. Or let's say you're a woman who doesn't like to see the woman-as-sex-toy message that most pornography (except fag pornography and women's "beefcake" pornography) spreads. This section is for the both of you.

Many folks question why you'd want to fight pornography. Most of these people have the mindset I used to have—"It's basically harmless and might help couples overcome their inhibitions." Most men (and lesbians) like to see pictures of good-looking women without any clothes on. Many women (and homosexuals) like to see pictures of handsome men without any clothes on. But let's say you believe those who still want smut can always buy it by mail so it isn't displayed in the faces of children or teen girls or women clerks who need jobs at convenience stores.

Let's say you're opposed to the people out there who want more than just the magazines—those who want scumbag sexploitation businesses such as porno shops, movie houses, strip joints, and massage parlors. They don't care if these businesses operate in your neighborhood. Many of these pro-scum types are civil libertarians who may be prudish enough not to be caught dead with a Bible in their houses. Many

more of these pro-sexploitation types fit into more sinister or stupid categories. These include:

- "Adult" losers who aren't man enough to attract and satisfy women. Some of these yoyos actually buy into the fantasy that they've got a shot at some casual sex with the Miss Aprils of their world.
- Sexually immature little suckers, like college kids and other young punks who we hope won't turn into "adult" losers when they get older.
- Sex offenders like child molesters, rapists, and other sexual scum. Police say they rarely arrest a sex offender who doesn't have pornography at his place. Child molesters will show kiddie porn to children to lower their inhibitions. They point to the children performing sex acts and tell their little victims, "*THAT* little girl (or boy) is doing it."
- Racketeers who make money off of the sexual degradation of women. Some of these dirtbags pay little, if any, attention to age of consent laws; some of their hottest little starlets are underage girls. Some of these vermin sink even lower; they produce kiddie porn. (Unfortunately, we're not an advanced enough society to execute those who sexually exploit children. I'm normally against euthanasia, but I'll make an exception for the bedwetters out there who support kiddie porn on "freedom of expression" grounds or for any other trivial excuse.)
- Hypocritical jerks who call pornography "freedom of expression" but would choke if someone put a picture of Moses or Christ in front of them. (However, some of them would probably get excited staring at the naked statue of King David.)
- Hypocritical jerks who want the action, but not in their neighborhood. This way, they can enjoy the fun and still hide from people who know them, avoid violent sexual types, keep runaways and horny losers out of their neighborhood, and avoid having to keep picking up empty beer cans and wet panties and used condoms off their lawns.

To those of you who claim prostitution is a victim- less crime, I've got a wake-up call for you. As a man who has lived where prostitution is legal (and in another area where it is winked at), I'll say the pros- titute herself is a victim. She is debased, beaten, and exploited by her johns and her pimp. Also, the in- nocent girls and women in the neighborhood are vic- tims. They have to suffer sexist treatment, abuse, and propositioning from a bunch of lowlifes.

If you want to fight scumbag sexploitation busi- nesses, use the other chapters of this book to dig dirt on the owners. Find out who operates the business from the chapter on businesses. Find out who owns the property the business is on from the land records chapter. Check zoning records for possible violations and check building inspection and fire code records for possible violations; instructions for these checks are in the first real estate records chapter.

But don't stop there. Check the owners of the scumbag business and the owners of the property for any past criminal convictions or lawsuits per the chapters on these topics. Many in this business have criminal or negative civil records. To see if the business is a public nuisance, get the definition from the city attorney or a lawyer friend on what constitutes a public nuisance in your town. Then check with your local police public affairs officer for reported incidents at or outside of the business in which the police had to get involved. As needed, file a freedom of information request or get a friendly politician's help to make the cops turn over the records. Videotape patron behavior in parking lots and streets outside of the business. Videotape any vandalism and littering.

Don't stop there. If the sexploitation business seems to be a magnet for runaway girls, maybe the police should know about it after you've done your share of videotaping of these girls. If the business is using females that look young and fresh-faced, it could be that the little ladies are underage; this is a serious felony for anyone employing them. This is *NOT* a "shot in the dark!" Traci Lords, one of the hottest starlets in the pornographic movie business, was underage when she starred in her earliest skin flicks. Gonzo journalist Hunter S. Thompson implied in a column Traci Lords was a runaway with a fake ID. Therefore, all the porno movies she was in before she turned 18 are illegal. Those who made bucks off of her movies should have been punished, but I don't believe any were.

There is another tactic you can use with your dirt. Find out where the owner of the sexploitation business lives per instructions in the personal records chapter, and picket his house. Some of his neighbors will become angry a scumbag like him is polluting their neighborhood. None of his neighbors will appreciate the fact he's a magnet for demonstrators who trash the calm of their neighborhood. (You can do the same to the owner of the property the business operates on.)

To get even with those who defend these scumbag businesses but don't want them in their neighborhoods, use similar tactics. Find out who the ringleaders are, then picket their homes. Pick up some of the unmentionable trash from around the business and dump it in their front yards as a visual reminder of what goes on in your neighborhood due to their hypocrisy. (Likewise, show the stuff to the media types who show up to cover your picketing.) Find out where they work and spread the message outside of their places of business. Very few bosses would enjoy having one of their employees generate such negative attention for the company. Of course, many co-workers would backstab him or shun him. If the pro-sexploitation target owns his own business, your picketing his establishment sure won't help it any.

Since most sexploiters dump their businesses in lower-income neighborhoods, accuse the pro-sexploiter types of discrimination and bigotry. Let the media know that lower-income people have rights, too...including the right to a decent neighborhood without the crime and other forms of lowlife behavior that many sexploitation businesses attract. Make the pro-sexploitation bozos' class bigotry an issue to discredit their alleged commitment to First Amendment rights. (As an aside, I think Hugh Hefner is a hypocritical scumbag because he tries to clothe *Playboy* with a G-string and pasties made from the pages of the Constitution. *Hustler* publisher Larry Flynt may be a scumbag, but at least he's not a hypocrite about his pornography.)

Should you feel guilty about trashing your targets if they have it coming? Hell, no! If you are a woman, just remember the sexploitation business operators are basically treating other women like naked meat. If you are a religious person, just remember these scumbags and their apologists in the media have slammed your belief system and your people for decades. As the Bible says, "An eye for an eye."

BRANDING THE SEX OFFENDERS

Sources of mine in the Vatican tell me that a long-dead relative of mine, Father Paul Sherlock, was in the early 1600s the first Christian to write a Biblical commentary on the Song of Solomon. This book is easily the raciest book in the Bible, unless you count some of the miscellaneous acts of adultery, fornication, rape, and incest that appear elsewhere in the Good Book. What's my point? Sherlocks will tackle topics others are afraid to even touch.

If some of you were offended by the blunt tone of this chapter, I won't apologize to you. Sex offenders are some of the most vicious enemies our people—especially our most helpless people—will ever face. It takes blunt talk and harsh action to deal with these vermin. Some judges recognize this and make sex offenders mark their cars and houses with "CONVICTED SEX OFFENDER" signs if the law allows their release from prison. If you have to personally alert a sex offender's neighbors, co-workers, and other social contacts to his crimes, DO IT. Your actions will protect others.

Until the day comes when sex offenders are non-existent— which might be never, because we are not advanced enough to kill them—the public's best defense is vigilance. I hope you will use the information in this chapter to become alert to potential and actual situations of sex abuse. I hope you will use the instructions in this chapter to remorselessly dig dirt on sex offenders—and on the government agents who unwittingly or deliberately cover for them.

The bottom line of this chapter is simple. Use the dirt you dig to castrate sex offenders before they can rape any more of the innocent.

END NOTES

1. Information on the McMartin Preschool case comes from an article in the April 9, 1984 issue of *Newsweek*, an article in the June 24, 1985 issue of *Newsweek*, an article in the July 8, 1985 issue of *People*, an article in the December 15, 1986 issue of *Newsweek*, an article in the January 29, 1990 issue of *Time*, and an article in the August 6, 1990 issue of *Time*.

2. Information on Ira Reiner's role in the Manson Family case (the Tate-La Bianca killings in which the defendants were Charles Manson, Susan Atkins, Patricia Krenwinkel, and Leslie Van Houten) comes from Vincent Bugliosi's book *Helter Skelter*. Bugliosi, who prosecuted the case, said Reiner solicited Manson about representing "Family" members in court. He also said Reiner represented Leslie Van Houten of the "Family" until she dismissed him from the case.

3. Observations of Chicago policemen come from Connie Fletcher's book *What Cops Know*.

4. Dr. Ann Burgess' recommendations on monitoring for possible child molestation were carried in Donald Wildmon's book *The Case Against Pornography*.

5. Kenneth Wooden's conclusions on the methods of child molesters were carried in Donald Wildmon's book *The Case Against Pornography*.

6. I first became aware of the two child molester advocacy groups known as the Rene Guyon Society and the North American Man/Boy Love Association from an article I read in a magazine years ago. Further information on these two groups comes from Donald Wildmon's book *The Case Against Pornography*.

7. Information on Planned Parenthood's apparent cover-up for their reported sex offender doctor comes from an article in the June 2, 1991 issue of the Chicago *Tribune* and from articles which appeared in the Arlington Heights (Illinois) *Daily Herald* on May 24, June 6, and June 12, 1991.

8. The case in which Planned Parenthood officials reportedly violated a girl's confidentiality and told her parents about her abortion to collect $12 more from her is Case No. 90-09090. It was filed in Hennepin County (Minneapolis) District Court in Minnesota in 1990. Likewise, a Michigan girl sued Planned Parenthood for violation of confidentiality because an off-site lab staffer reportedly sent a pregnancy test billing to her home and her mother discovered she had undergone an abortion. Her case is Case No. 89-38135; it was filed in Washtenaw (Ann Arbor) County Circuit Court in Michigan in 1989.

9. Information on John Wayne Gacy comes from articles in the January 8, 1979 issues of *Newsweek* and *Time*.

10. Details of the rapes and murders of Sonja Johnson and Dolores Cepeda which the Hillside Stranglers committed come from Darcy O'Brien's book *Two of a Kind*.

11. Information on the Jeffrey Dahmer case comes from an article in the August 18, 1991 issue of *Our Sunday Visitor* and from articles in the August 5, 1991 issues of *Newsweek* and *Time*.

12. Information on the man who raped his three daughters with his wife's help comes from an Associated Press story which appeared in the New Orleans *Times-Picayune* on December 8, 1990.

13. Information on the professed bisexual who wanted to be a foster father comes from my article which appeared in the Kingsport (Tennessee) *Times-News* on August 10, 1986. My follow-up article on inadequacies in screening foster parents and adoptive parents appeared in the *Times-News* on September 26, 1986.

14. Abortion provider Laurence Reich's sex offenses case is M107591, Santa Monica (California) Municipal Court.

15. Information on New Jersey official Richard Codey's exposure of his state's mental hospitals comes from articles which appeared in the Newark *Star-Ledger* on March 1, 1987, March 10, 1987, April 10, 1987, and October 18, 1987.

16. Information on Florida politician/abortion provider Ben Graber comes from articles that appeared in the Coral Springs *News* on December 14, 1988, the *Sun Sentinel Times* on December 6, 1988, the South Florida *Forum* on December 15, 1988, and the *Miami Herald* on November 2, 1990.

17. My article on child molester Carson Payne appeared in the Kingsport (Tennessee) *Times-News* on October 24, 1986. Payne's case is A-0959-01, filed in Lee County (Virginia) Circuit Court.

18. Information on child welfare agency abuses comes from Mary Pride's book *The Child Abuse Industry*.

19. Hunter Thompson's column which mentioned porno starlet Traci Lords, was named "Sex, Drugs, and Rock 'n' Roll" and was dated July 21, 1986. The column is in Thompson's cult classic book *Generation of Swine*.

20. Confirmation of Thompson's remark about Traci Lords comes from Craig Hosoda's book *The Bare Facts*. He wrote this book for the sizeable number of bozos out there who want to know what movies and magazines in which their favorite celebrities appeared nude so they can find them. I found a use for this book that its author might not have envisioned; I used it to check on how many feminist actresses allowed themselves to appear nude or partially nude to make money and/or further their careers. This book lists nude or semi-nude scenes and "photo opportunities" of Jane Fonda, Amy Madigan, Morgan Fairchild, Ali MacGraw, Cybill Shepherd, Shirley MacLaine, Vanessa Redgrave, Susan Sarandon, and Vanessa Williams, among others. It even lists Melissa Gilbert, who slid from *Little House on the Prairie* straight into some pretty sleazy pictures where she showed more than just her smile. All these ladies who rail against sexual exploitation and viewing women as mere sex objects have some explaining to do.

Spread The Dirt

Those of you who have been using this book for "civilian" purposes are welcome to tag along, but this chapter is really for all you muckrakers and troublemakers out there who want to bomb the bad people in your lives back to the Stone Age. We're going to discuss how to use the dirt you've dug up to really bury your targets.

Up to now, I trust you've been doing a fine job digging up the dirt on your target. Now you have one more job to do. SPREAD IT LIKE MANURE.

This is the final and most important job of a muckraker—making sure all the good damaging info on his target gets into the hands of people who can hurt his target. And the best places for dirt on your target are in the hands of your elected officials, the agents who regulate the field he's in, cause groups which oppose his activities, the media, his customers if he's in business, and his neighbors if he does anything that is an affront to common decency. Don't let such info gather dust in a corner of your home!

The purpose of this chapter is to show you how you can use the dirt you have gathered on your target to damage him in the eyes of all the people mentioned above. It will show you how to organize the information you've found, how to prepare an "expose" flyer and an in-depth report, and how to get the right kind of info to the people who can cause your target the most trouble. It will also give you some specific tried-and-true ideas for causing your target maximum damage.

THE WILLIE HORTON CASE

Democrats criticize George Bush for using the Willie Horton case to make Massachusetts governor Michael Dukakis look like a soft-on-crime wimp during the 1988 presidential election. Dukakis had led Bush by whopping public-opinion poll margins. Then Bush's people started cranking out hard-hitting negative ads about the killer who committed rape and felony assault while away from his Massachusetts prison on a Dukakis-supported furlough. Eventually, Bush won the election, and media types called him a dirty campaigner. Bush and his fat cat buddies shrugged their shoulders and poured champagne at their victory parties. Meanwhile, Kitty Dukakis

presumably started pouring herself some good belts of booze and rubbing alcohol.

Bush might never have been able to celebrate if some Massachusetts women hadn't acted on their own to kill the furlough program after politicians couldn't get the job done. According to an article in a national publication, this is how it went down:

Police arrested Willie Horton and two other thugs in 1974 for knifing teenage gas station attendant Joey Fournier to death after robbing him of $300. Despite being convicted of first-degree murder and receiving a life sentence in 1975 (just weeks earlier, Dukakis had vetoed a death penalty bill), Horton was getting unescorted 48-hour passes several years after his conviction. On one of these passes, Willie Horton left the state for Maryland, and celebrated his 1987 weekend in the Crab State by slashing a man 22 times with a knife, and raping his fiancee twice.

A young reporter, puzzled by how Horton could get furloughs, tried to get information on prisoners in the furlough program from Massachusetts prison officials. They stonewalled her. She wrote articles about Horton's case and the furlough program. As a result, two state legislators tried to get the furlough program ended. Meanwhile, the reporter's editor got other editors to put heat on state officials to release Horton's prison records. Later, it would surface that close to 80 prisoners—some of them murderers and rapists—had walked away from prison during furloughs and other poorly-supervised prison programs...and vanished!

Dukakis supported the prisoner furlough program. Dukakis' allies stalled the anti-furlough bill in committee, and eventually killed it in the state senate. Meanwhile, three women who supported the bill (two of the three had lost loved ones to murderers) confronted Dukakis in a police station. He told them he would not change his mind on the furlough program, and gave them the politician's stock condescending line, "If you don't like the system, you can change it."

The women decided to do just that. They put together a grass-roots group, and started a petition drive to let Massachusetts voters kill the furlough program. They recruited other murder victims' loved ones. Using prison records, testimony of victims at public hearings, and prison officials' own inane statements in favor of the furlough program, they fashioned a successful petition drive. They ensured voters would have the chance to kill the furlough program in November 1988.

But the furlough program ended even earlier. Because of the success of the women's efforts, the legislators re-introduced a bill to kill the furlough program. The bill passed both houses of the state legislature. Dukakis, by now locked in the presidential primary season and under increasing justifiable political pressure, said he wouldn't veto the bill. It became law in April 1988, and the furlough program was history.

Bush's people didn't invent Willie Horton. Nor did they invent the women's anger at Dukakis for allowing guys like Horton the liberty to victimize others. All they did was know a good thing when they saw it, and get their man to run with it. Likewise, the women didn't invent Horton or guys like him; they just used the facts they found on guys like Horton to get others in the Red Sox State to see things their way.

Are you ready to do likewise? Then let's get started.

ORGANIZE THE INFORMATION

The first thing you must do with the dirt you've found is put it into logical order. The best way to do this is to put all criminal cases together, all civil cases together, all agency citations together, all other negative data together by type, and all personal data together.

Next, write a short summary of each set of documents. For example:

- You would list each lawsuit by name of plaintiff and the case number, then write a paragraph or so on each case. This paragraph would include, as a minimum, what the plaintiff accused your target of doing, a sentence on the outcome of the case (or a note it is still active), and a list of documents you are using as evidence. You might also include a sentence on your target's defense, and a sentence summing up any bizarre, shocking, or disgusting information that would tend to make your target look bad.
- You would handle criminal cases in much the same way as the lawsuits. List each case by name and case number, then include info on charges against your target, his defense (if any), any plea-bargaining, the outcome of the case, any other reputation-harming info, and a list of documents you are using as evidence.
- On other forms of wrongdoing, summarize each instance in much the same way as above. Like old-fashioned reporters, include WHO, WHAT, WHEN, WHERE, and WHY. Also include info on any penalty your target received. Organize

instances of wrongdoing by type, and by citing agency.
- On political contributions, land records, corporation affiliation, or on any other set of info that shows ties or financial interest, summarize the sets of records in outline or paragraph form. For instance, note a target's land deals by each parcel of land (how he got it, how he disposed of it, who put liens on it, etc.) Or note a target's business dealings by type and summarize each venture.
- For politicians, list their major contributors, gifts they received, and other financial goodies that came their way (like junkets). List times in which they voted business to people who were political contributors or buddies in other senses. Also, list their holdings. And list votes in which they might seem beholden to special interests. (Bear in mind, though, that often special interests reward politicians who think their way anyway. There's nothing illegal about it.) Further, list contributions or votes that might prove embarrassing.
- For businesses which deal with government, list contracts and grants by amounts and by services provided. For governments, list contracts and grants awarded by the receiving businesses and amounts. Write brief paragraphs on deals which seem shady or stupid.

Two last bits of advice—take the time to file your documents in some semblance of order, and make a duplicate file. On the first point, you save time and trouble in having your documents organized for easy access. On the second point, making a duplicate file and giving it to a friend or your lawyer ensures you won't have to hunt up dirt again in case your working file documents are lost, damaged, or destroyed.

WRITE A SCANDAL SHEET

Now that your info is organized, you can turn your attention toward writing a one-page flyer or "scandal sheet." You want it to be short and hard-hitting, so it can properly emphasize the most negative aspects of your target. The "scandal sheet" will have many "military" uses. For example, you can hand out this flyer to a target's neighbors or customers to disgust them or drive them off. Or you can use it to leaflet parking lots or neighborhoods to trash his reputation. Or you can use it as a handout at public meetings to call attention to what a scumbag he is.

This project will be easy and fun! Just find the most hateful and/or sleazy things your target has done, use good action words and short sentences to describe these things, and get the text to fit on a single 8½ by 11-inch page (with enough room left over for a mean headline). Make the thing read like something out of *True Detective*.

Of course, doing this could get you sued for libel, slander, or defamation. Libel is writing and distributing something *that is untrue* and defamatory with malicious intent. Slander is saying something *that is untrue* and defamatory with malicious intent. Defamation is saying, writing, or distributing something *that is untrue* and defamatory with malicious intent. However, if you write the flyer truthfully, and back every statement with documentation, you will win in or out of court, and you might be able to force your target to disclose his private records in the course of his suit against you. Also, you could countersue *HIM* for abuse of process or malicious prosecution or defamation! DON'T FEAR LAWSUITS. JUST MAKE SURE YOU CAN WIN THEM BY WRITING THE FLYER CORRECTLY.

Here's some advice on how to write the flyer to keep out of trouble:

- TRUTH IS ALWAYS YOUR BEST DEFENSE AGAINST DEFAMATION, LIBEL, AND SLANDER. The whole idea behind muckraking is to expose wrongdoing, so all you have to do is write the truth! NEVER WRITE ANYTHING YOU CAN'T PROVE. Besides, if your target is as bad as you think he is, you won't have to use untrue statements to tar him. Use sleazy, hateful, TRUE details on him from the public record!

- Use qualifiers such as "allegedly", "apparently", "evidently", "reportedly", "accused", "asserted", "alleged", "charged," "claimed", and the like if you want to write about items that did not lead to a set-in-stone conviction, judgment, or citation on your target. Let the reader draw the proper conclusion!

  (For example, you may not be able to prove beyond the shadow of a doubt that a doctor damaged a woman with surgery. But you can easily prove a woman who sued the doctor claimed he damaged her. After all, she'll say so in the lawsuit! List enough of these cases on your flyer, and make sure you say it like "the woman sued Dr. Butcher, claiming he damaged her uterus" instead of saying "Dr. Butcher damaged her uterus"; the average person will conclude Dr. Butcher is a hack artist. In short, you're not *SAYING* the doctor is a butcher, but you *ARE* saying someone has accused him of hacking. On reading what you've written, many people will look past the qualifiers and will conclude Dr. Butcher *IS* a butcher!)

- If you can't prove a statement, or rewrite it with

the proper qualifier to make it a correct statement, then DON'T USE IT. You could lose a lawsuit if you violate this rule. Besides, you should have so much verifiable reputation-damaging dirt on your target anyway, you shouldn't have to use anything even remotely questionable.

If you're still a bit worried about defamation, libel, and slander, run your flyer past a lawyer friend who is sympathetic to your cause. Give him documentation, and a footnoted copy to make it easy for him to review the flyer. In general, follow his advice on how to reword things. But don't let him castrate the flyer. Remind him you're not worried about being SUED; you're worried about being WRONG. Remember, if you do get sued by a miserable target and his shyster, you can sue him for abuse of process or malicious prosecution or defamation and collect money. Or you can demand all kinds of records from his private collection in motions, depositions, and interrogatories if he sues you.

WRITE A REPORT

A report takes longer to write than a flyer, and is aimed at a different audience. A report is designed to get law enforcement people and other kinds of professional people to take action against your target. It's also designed to get media people interested in your target. And since many of these folks might not share your agenda, you'll have to write the report in a toned-down, matter-of-fact style. You'll have to convince them your target is an unethical operator who gets sued all the time, a proven lawbreaker who gets cited or arrested constantly, a thief who steals tax money or the people's after-tax money, or a menace to the public in some other way.

However, a report doesn't entail quite the defamation risks that a flyer does. And a good report in the right hands can lead powerful people to do ugly things to your target. And besides, a report sometimes becomes part of the public record, even if it doesn't lead to any immediate action against your target.

A few bits of advice follow:

- In the first paragraph of the report, tell the receiver the purpose of the report. In the rest of the report, maintain as dispassionate tone as you can without making the wrongdoing seem unimportant. Remember, your report's receivers may not share your agenda!

- For non-law enforcement receivers, you want to inform them of your target's overall misconduct. Include general information as well as specific instances that would apply to certain narrow kinds of misconduct.

222 / HOW TO BE YOUR OWN DETECTIVE

- For law-enforcement receivers (this includes government agents, prosecutors, executive officials, legislators, and judges), you want to show them WHY they should take action against your target, and on what grounds. Focus in on the part of the law your target has violated that your receiver enforces or influences. Throw in other types of dirt as background information.
- The rules of libel, slander, and defamation that apply to a flyer also apply to a report. TRUTH IS ALWAYS A DEFENSE. USE QUALIFYING WORDS; LET THE RECEIVER DO THE JUDGING. IF YOU CAN'T PROVE IT, DON'T USE IT.
- Use toned-down, matter-of-fact language when you write the report. Write it like a term paper that needs good writing skills and plenty of footnotes to prove you know what you're talking about. Include copies of documentation as needed. Make your documentation as easy as possible for your receiver to check.
- Watch the correctness and the tone of your report. YOU DON'T WANT A REPUTATION AS A PERSON WHO DEALS IN INCORRECT INFO, OR A PERSON WHO'S JUST A LUNATIC FRINGIE.

Double-check your work for references and mistakes before you send it. You may want a lawyer friend or some other professional with good judgment to check your work.

If you find out you've made a mistake after you send in a report, send a correction. Explain your mistake, and point out you want to maintain your credibility. If you can, include new dirt in the correction, so it can attack as well as defend.

ANITA HILL'S PEAKS AND VALLEY

The old saying, "Look before you leap," applies to making charges of misconduct as well as to taking most other actions. I've said throughout this book that you should NEVER make a charge of misconduct unless you can back it up with facts. And I've said throughout this book that acts of wrongdoing generally have evidence and that most people follow typical patterns of behavior. The Anita Hill/Clarence Thomas fiasco proves why these are good adages to remember.

Opponents of Clarence Thomas' nomination to the Supreme Court thought they were going to get a last-minute chance to stop him. Oklahoma University law professor Anita Hill had come forward (allegedly after much behind-the-scenes prodding) to accuse Thomas of sexual harassment on the job. Many of them believed Thomas would not accept the nomina-

tion, or that the charges and their pressure would scare enough senators into voting against putting him on the Supreme Court.

But Thomas' opponents forgot the American people have much more common sense than the members of the Senate. Average men and women found it hard to swallow Ms. Anita's claims that Clarence Thomas sexually harassed her while they worked together at the Department of Education's Office of Civil Rights. Why? Because the details of her tale flew in the face of normal patterns of human behavior.

People know that a sexual harasser doesn't hit on only one woman; he hits on many. Many women who worked with Clarence Thomas came forward to defend his character. The feminists and other doubters of Thomas couldn't produce anyone else besides Anita Hill to make the charge of sexual harassment against Thomas under oath. Ms. Hill made the charge a decade after the incidents allegedly took place. Meanwhile, many women who worked under Thomas came forward to vouch for his decency and chivalry.

Anita Hill admitted to following Thomas to the Equal Employment Opportunity Commission. She also admitted to keeping in touch with Thomas over the years even after she stopped working with him. Most women are not weak enough or stupid enough to do such things with men who have sexually harassed them. Why would someone supposedly as strong-willed and brilliant as Anita Hill stoop to such lapdog behavior?

Anita Hill's brilliance and strong will hurt her credibility in another way. Since she was working as a lawyer to fight sexism and discrimination, it would seem logical for her to go to work "wired for sound" to catch Thomas making sexual advances to her if he was doing so. It would also seem logical that she at least would keep a log of incidents of sexual harassment that Thomas allegedly committed against her over the years, and include dates, times, and specifics in the log. And it would seem logical for her to at least file a complaint against Thomas for such demeaning behavior. Yet she produced no tapes, she produced no log, and she produced no formal complaint to back up her story. In short, this Yale Law School graduate produced no evidence. A high-school dropout with a low IQ might be excused for such oversights, but not a lawyer who was being paid to fight sexual harassment!

Anita's lawyer friends did her no help when they testified. They basically claimed they only listened to Anita. None of them suggested to Ms. Hill that she quit, and no account I saw or heard noted any of them advised Ms. Hill to gather evidence against Thomas to build a case against him. To many, it seemed Anita Hill's friends were either wimpy for not giving her better advice or were lying through their teeth. Folks know that their friends stick up for them and support them better than Ms. Anita's allegedly did. Considering her witnesses were lawyers, they at the very best came off as a weak-kneed bunch.

Those in the know are also aware of a tactic some feminists use—they make false accusations of male sexual misconduct. For example, Dallas waitress Norma McCorvey, using the pseudonym Jane Roe, sued Texas officials in 1970 to get an abortion. She claimed she wanted the abortion because she got pregnant after men gang-raped her. Her lawsuit went as far as the Supreme Court—and in 1973, the justices used her case (Roe vs. Wade) to make abortion on demand legal throughout the land. In 1987, Ms. Norma, now a Dallas businesswoman, admitted in an interview to columnist Carl Rowan that she lied about being raped and admitted her boyfriend had fathered her child.

Interestingly, the Jane Roe approach seemed to show up again. Ms. Hill accused Thomas, a black man with a white wife, of bragging about his sexual prowess and penis size. Klan literature couldn't have insulted black men any better. This insult made Thomas stop behaving like a lawyer and start behaving like a real man in fighting for his honor and the honor of other black men.

People by a large margin believed Thomas and his friends instead of Ms. Hill and her friends. Why? Because Ms. Hill and her lawyer friends gave accounts that most normal people found hard to believe. Many people also decided Thomas and his friends acted like normal people would react when confronted with false accusations. (Although if it was me, I'd have watched Anita Hill's testimony instead of ignoring it like Thomas said he did.) The late-hour revelation that Anita Hill's accusations of Thomas mentioning porno film actor Long Dong Silver read suspiciously like an EEOC complaint filed in Kansas a couple of years earlier was like the final nail in the coffin as far as Ms. Anita's credibility with many Americans was concerned.

What's the moral here? No charge, no matter how ugly, can stick if the facts don't back it up (and the accused has some decent legal help). Bear that in mind as you prepare to release negative information on your target. And remember one last adage popular in the blue-collar world, "Measure twice, cut once." In other words, have the dirt you need on hand to measure your target's rottenness before you cut on his reputation. Give any negative information you send out a good double-check and one last check before you deliver it to someone else. If you slash wildly and inaccurately at your target, you may find out he's a better knife-fighter than you.

DUMP DIRT IN THE LAPS OF THE RIGHT PEOPLE

As I said earlier, there are several groups of people who, if they knew a fraction of what you know about your target, could shoot holes in your target. These people include politicians, government agents, special-interest group leaders, and journalists, for starters. Some of these people may already have it in for people like your target. Others should be natural allies of your target, but the right amount of dirt might convince them to make trouble for him, or drop their support of him.

Some pieces of advice follow:

- The views of politicians on various issues are a matter of public record, and are often well-known. Pick a politician whose views on your target or his activities are similar to your own. If you can't find a politician like this to help you, then try one of the politicians who is not publicly against you. To find out where he stands, call his office and talk to him or one of his staffers about his position on the issue in question. If the person asks why, say, "I want to know," or "The topic came up during a gab session at my workplace, bar, bowling alley, barber shop, beauty parlor, diner, church, union hall, etc." DON'T TELL YOUR VIEWS TO THE POL OR HIS PEOPLE. This way, they won't be able to tell you what they think you want to hear.

- Work with a friendly politician's staffers. Provide them with your well-organized dirt and a report. This way, they can plow through the dirt quickly, and spot-check it for accuracy. Make it easy for them to use your work to look into and move against your target. Work with them on keeping publicity to a minimum until they do their homework on your package, if they ask for this from you.

- Work with government agents who monitor your target as part of their jobs. First, figure out which agencies are supposed to regulate the various facets of your target's activities. Then, for each agency, provide the agent with evidence your target has apparently violated any laws or engaged in any unethical conduct related to his type of law enforcement powers.

You can also provide the agent with other forms of dirt on your target; it reinforces the fact that your target is scum, and it makes the agent's job easier. After all, many agents are overworked, and it's easier to verify well-documented dirt than it is to dig it up in the first place. And besides, your report on your target's activities can serve as the string the agent will use to tie together the various aspects of your target's wrongdoing.

Government agents have told me they pay close attention to competent citizen sources. They have also admitted to me that government agents often fail to cross-check with other agencies as to what other negative information might exist on a subject they are investigating.

(The best way to get advice on how to get a government agency to take any action against your target is to call the proper agent and ask for advice! Double-check his advice with another agent at another time, then follow up on it to start some trouble. Don't let the agents know who you're after or what your views are; just make it a general, broad conversation. Otherwise, agents friendly to your target or hostile to your cause might not give you good info.)

- Work with a friendly special-interest group's staffers. Just like the politicians, the special-interest group leaders have agendas. If your dirt fits their plans, they'll use it to sully your target publicly. Treat them much like you would a friendly politician's staffers.

- Show a judge your information if he's set to hear any case involving your target. It's said you can't unring a bell, and a judge who hears credible negative information about your target can't put it out of his mind, either. One time, I set an appointment with a judge, and I showed him damaging evidence about the sexual misconduct of a man whose case he was going to hear a few days later. He didn't forget, either. He ruled against the man with a fury he rarely showed to others who appeared before his bench.

- Show reporters your information. Find out which reporters logically cover the beats your target shows up in. Figure out their views by reading what they write, or by contacting groups with an interest in issues involving your target or with an interest in your target himself. Aim for the friendliest reporters first. Give the reporters your dirt, let them verify the items you offer as proof your target is scum, and sit back and laugh as they report on your target. Even if THEY get the glory, you've accomplished your goal of getting your target trashed publicly.

- Show your target's enemies your information.

You may not like these people, but if they can help you make trouble for your target, it's worth your while to deal with them or manipulate them.

One last piece of advice: Don't take it personally if these people view your work with skepticism at first. After all, the world is full of liars, and from time to time, they try to give politicians, special-interest group leaders, and journalists bad info. Consider all the screwball conspiracy stories surrounding JFK, Martin Luther King, Marilyn Monroe, and Elvis Presley. Or you may be dealing with a journalist who heard about how the top people of the Washington *Post* in the 1950s were suckered into preparing a series of negative articles on Wisconsin senator Joe McCarthy. The articles were based on some faked background interviews and a stack of phony documents a con man sold to some prominent liberals for thousands of dollars. These people wanted to sting McCarthy so badly that they got stung themselves.

CONCRETE EXAMPLES OF CONSTRUCTIVE DIRT-SPREADING

There is more than one way to skin a cat. (Sorry, pet owners.) Likewise, there is more than one way to make trouble for a bad person. I have seen, heard of, taken part in, or masterminded all of the incidents which I list below; believe me, they work. In each instance, the tactic listed allowed the hero to cause the villain (his target) the pain he deserved. And in no case did the hero get in trouble for using the tactic, because in each case, it was legal. Without further ado, I present these tactics to you for your education. Use these as you see fit.

HOME IS WHERE THE HURT IS

- Leaflet your target's neighborhood to let his neighbors know just what kind of a louse he really is. People can deliver a "scandal sheet" by night or by day to each residence in the target's neighborhood. Imagine your target's discomfort and disgrace when he finds out his neighbors have been given a fact sheet that shows he's lower than pond scum.

- Picket your target's house. Can you imagine the public shame you'll put someone through if people who oppose him demonstrate in the street outside his home and call him all sorts of ugly names? Besides having chanting demonstrators with signs calling your target everything but a paid-up member of the human race, you'd naturally have teams of people running wild in the streets leafleting the neighborhood to alert the target's neighbors to his lousehood.

And of course, you'd plan this action for a Saturday or Sunday, when a great percentage of your target's neighbors will be home to take this all in, and the media won't have anything better to cover than your protest. Of course, you'll call the media, especially TV and radio reporters, so they'll have something to report on an otherwise slow news day. They'll spread your message even farther!

What would the neighbors think? A lot of them will be angry at your target, even if they don't have anything personal against him, because he's the reason the neighborhood's calm is being disrupted. Something he did, they'll reason, caused the sudden disruption of calm, the shouting, the parking problems and congestion, the police presence, the inevitable littering and lawn trampling, and the other negative effects the neighborhood is suffering because of your group's presence.

Some of your target's neighbors will defend him and try to confront you, but if there's enough of you, they'll probably avoid you. Or you all can brush them off like horses brush off flies.

NEGATIVE ADVERTISING

- Leaflet the parking lot and areas surrounding a shopping center, office building, industrial park, or other commercial area containing the business your target owns or works at. This is the commercial equivalent of leafleting his neighborhood.
- Take a hint from union members and picket the lowlife's business. Pick a time when you can generate maximum media coverage and maximum inconvenience to your target. Such picketing is a good approach for tenants who want to expose a slumlord and pro-lifers who want to expose an abortion provider. I'm sure you've seen news reports in which tenants show pictures of their rented hovels and wave copies of building code violations or news reports in which abortion opponents show pictures of aborted babies and wave copies of the abortion provider's malpractice cases.

Some of your target's clients or customers will stay away from his business because you've made them think there's something wrong with him. Either your presence will alert them to your target's specific acts of misconduct, or they'll just think he's got a problem simply because he's being picketed. After all, how many other businessmen get picketed? Not many! Many people will stay away because they agree with you; others will stay away just to avoid trouble. If your target is an employee of a business in a commercial building, or is a business owner who is a tenant in a commercial building, the picketing might force him to work or do business elsewhere.

TAKE A BITE OUT OF CRIME

- Report your target to the agencies which regulate your target's business or organization. Believe it or not, a lot of agents who routinely make trouble for your target on one front are unaware of his other problems. The ignorance of agents may be due to turf wars with other agencies, the reluctance of other agencies to press cases, agent overloading and overworking, and simple foul-ups in co-ordination.

For example, the agents which cite your target for labor law violations may be unaware other agents have cited him for environmental violations, and vice-versa. Both agencies' people may be unaware many people have sued the target for damage his business has caused them. And they may be unaware the local prosecutor or a federal prosecutor has filed criminal fraud or tax evasion or antitrust charges against your target. And they may be unaware of the link, contributionwise or businesswise, between your target and politicians.

You as a responsible citizen can fill the information gaps and inform all the agencies of what dirt the other agencies have on your target. This is bound to provoke at least one of the agents to take further actions against your target. Evidence of license abuse, building or zoning code violations, labor law violations, environmental violations, tax evasion, misuse of government money, unhealthy treatment of people, and criminal activity or civil activity which points to lawbreaking all are types of evidence your friendly agents will be only too happy to use.

- Report your target to the Inspector General of any agency which regulates your target's business or organization if the regular agents of the agency's enforcement group seem too slow in getting the job done. Other eager law enforcement types you can inform of your target's wrongdoing include the FBI (any crime or activity which might involve interstate commerce or racketeering), your state attorney general's office, your county prosecutor, and the dreaded IRS secret police. Remember, it took an IRS agent to send Al Capone to prison. Guys like him can make a tax evasion case out of almost any instance of improper behavior. After all, most criminals (including, probably, your target) operate on the greed motive. They "forget" to tell the tax man about all their gains.

MAKE A NOT-SO-FEDERAL CASE OUT OF YOUR TARGET'S MISCONDUCT

If you believe your target has caused you or your community any kind of damage at all, file a small claims court action against your target. It will cost you only a few bucks. Then load up your legal briefs with evidence of your target's verminlike behavior. (Get a lawyer friend to recommend a case you can file that won't let your target countersue you for big bucks.) As needed, subpoena your target's records on grounds you need them to prove your case. All you'll have to do is show up in court, present your case, and wait on a verdict. You could win some money from your target. But even if you lose the case, you've put dirt on the public record once again. Friends of yours in the cause can point government types, media types, and others to the case as proof of your target's rottenness.

HELP G-MEN, POLITICIANS, AND LOBBY LEADERS LOOK COOL

- Show evidence of your target's misbehavior to politicians and special-interest group leaders who don't like him or the activities he's involved in. They will naturally take credit for nailing his scalp to a tree, if it's done. So what if you miss out on some ego gratification (shrinkese for "bragging rights")? All you're interested in is seeing the scalp nailed there in the first place.
- Show the same kinds of evidence to government agents.

I helped one agency by getting criminal and civil records against a target's business to go along with its agents' citations and investigations. The agent who was handling his agency's case against the target didn't have the time to round up this extra dirt, and the courthouse folks and the prosecutor's people were political enemies of the agent, so they wouldn't help him.

I presented the agent with nearly 2000 neatly-bound pages of evidence on the target's court appearances for civil and criminal matters, summary sheets to help him plow through all that dirt easily, and a professionally-written report he could borrow from almost verbatim to make his case. When he used my dirt, he looked mighty professional in court against the target; this thorough preparation on his part sure didn't hurt his reputation. From time to time, he would call me for more dirt, and I was only too happy to oblige him.

- Get your friends and allies to contact the public official's office. Have them say they are aware of your target's abuses and wish the pol would do

something to stop him. Most public officials have at least some sensitivity to the expressed will of the people. This approach can bolster a friendly politician's confidence, it can strengthen the resolve of a politician on your side who's wavering, it can convince fence-sitters to jump to your side of the fence, and it might even convince some hostile politicians to take the proper action or at least stay out of the way.

PUBLIC JEERING

- Show up with dirt on your target at a public hearing or public meeting. Enter it into the record during public comment time, and make sure a copy of your dirt gets to any government official at the public hearing who is or may be sympathetic to your concerns.
- Public hearings and public meetings are good times to release dirt concerning programs you want to block, government spending you want to question, government taxing you want to stop, conflicts of interest, and any number of other concerns you want to voice. Reporters like little goodies like these, and they'll often follow up on them if the person who presents them seems like a rational person. Some officials at the hearings or meetings will pick up on your disclosures, as will others in the audience. Some reporters can get your message into the late newscast or the morning paper if you look and sound credible and interesting—and if what you have to say stirs up controversy.

POLITICAL ASSASSINATION

- Release dirt on a politician concerning his voting record, his financial interests, his campaign contributors, any conflicts of interest, lawsuits or citations involving his business interests, or any other wrongdoing. The book is chock full of such examples; follow any of them or come up with your own approach.

Media types, government agents, and the politician's enemies are all likely recipients of such information. You can turn it over to them quietly and let them raise hell with it. Or you can use an event such as a public meeting, a public hearing, or your group's staged media event to release the info.

- Release dirt on a judge's track record, and on his finances, his possible conflicts of interest in cases, lawsuits or citations involving his business interests, or any other wrongdoing. Check rulings for evidence of bias or danger to society.
- Treat the politician or judge like any other

lawbreaker. Turn over evidence of his wrongdoing to the appropriate law enforcement officials. (See the section in this chapter labeled "Take A Bite Out of Crime.")

- Treat the politician or judge like any other deadbeat or lowlife. Sue him in small claims court. (See the section in this chapter labeled "Make A Not-So-Federal Case.") A novel approach is to sue him if his ineptness or some other mistake or action on his part cost money; sue him for the amount your own taxes will be affected (which will be a small claims court figure).

GOOSE THE GOVERNMENT

Release information on instances in which a target government agency isn't doing its job. Such instances include failure to perform programs properly, sloppy handling and spending of taxpayer money, failure to cite serious lawbreakers or political allies or big corporations, and persecution of people who are not in the wrong.

You can release this information quietly to the media, rival government officials, government agency higher-ups, local or federal prosecutors, politicians and judges who have been critical of the agency, and to special-interest group leaders who are critical of the agency. Or you could release the info loudly and noisily yourself at your group's media event. Or attack them at THEIR public event! Marshal your facts about how poorly your target bureaucrats or politicians perform, then hit 'em when there are a bunch of witnesses who can watch 'em squirm.

JOIN THE GOVERNMENT WITNESS PROGRAM

Get a friendly politician or government agent to call you into a government proceeding as an "expert witness." As needed, you could appear as a witness at a public hearing, at an administrative hearing, in a meeting with key government officials, or in some other setting where you can help effect some change or bring down some punishment with the info you've gathered. As an invited witness, you'll be dealing from a position of strength, and you'll often be able to get the officials to give your info a fair hearing.

One bit of advice—rehearse your testimony and get friends to ask you negative devil's-advocate questions. This way, you'll be prepared to handle most of what any government official can throw at you. You've worked too hard for an opportunity like this to throw it away with a poor appearance.

MEET THE PRESS

- Show reporters your information. Find out which reporters cover the beats your target shows up in. Figure out their views by reading what they write, or by contacting groups with an interest in issues involving your target or with an interest in your target himself. Aim for the friendliest reporters first. Give the reporters your dirt, let them verify the items you offer as proof your target is scum, and sit back and laugh as they report on your target, and publicly trash him.
- Consent to an interview. Treat this like you would a government witness opportunity, and pretend you're running a fire drill in the process. Radio and TV reporters only have a little time to work in your interview, so develop a pitch where EVERY sentence is short and strong. PRACTICE so you'll be ready if called to do an interview. During an interview, don't ramble; get to the point. Get your point across even if you have to interrupt the interviewer. If he tries to distract you or fake you out with a red herring question, ignore it and concentrate on trashing your target. If you handle it right, your attack on your target is what people will remember, not the newsperson's attempt to distract you.

If the interview is with a print media reporter, take more time, have your documents available, and answer the interviewer's legitimate questions thoroughly. Brush off the red herring questions that the reporter throws at you in his attempt to trip you up. Again, it's not a bad idea to prepare for interviews by having friends question you and try to trip you up. (And for any interview, it's not a bad idea to run a tape recorder of your own to make an accurate recording of the session. Use the tape to critique your performance, or for evidence in case you need it.)

PERSONAL VENGEANCE

Public officials, especially judges, police chiefs, and prosecutors, enjoy almost total shielding from the effects of their wrongdoing. To a lesser extent, so do elected officials, bureaucrats, wealthy businessmen, education types, and "politically correct" group leaders. Also, celebrities are all too often isolated from reality and the consequences of their actions. There is one way to get even with these people—make their addresses and phone numbers a matter of public knowledge.

Find out where your target lives by checking his voter registration record. Or, you can check his residence using real estate records (home ownership) or lawsuit records. Other specialized records, such as attorney registration records with the state's highest court, medical board records, and other records pertaining to professions should indicate where the target lives. Sometimes his phone number is available on these records, too.

Then make up a flyer showing the target's name, picture, and address, and post it all over town. Odds are there's at least one criminal or hoodlum out there who would make life miserable for a target if only he knew where the target, his wife, and his kids lived. Other people—especially in groups which oppose the target—might not get so ugly physically toward the target, but they certainly could disrupt his suburban squire's calm by picketing his home and vandalizing his property. Even if neighbors support him, they're sure to dislike the trouble his presence is attracting.

A word of caution—pull this stunt only if you can handle the consequences of putting up the flyers. The public official or businessman or celebrity who doesn't crack under this kind of pressure will probably survive the problem you've caused him and will try to make life miserable for you and your loved ones in return. Release a target's home address and phone number only in an emergency or in case you have a relentless desire to bring this scumbag to justice.

WRAPUP

The above list of uses for the dirt you've dug is not complete. I'm sure you'll think of some other excellent ideas on how to use the information you've found to effect change or punish your target.

I'll leave you with three pieces of advice.

The first one is USE COMMON SENSE. Don't do anything stupid when you fight your target. Don't come off like a nutcase and discredit your cause and yourself. Make sure you can back up anything negative you say about him. Be sure you can withstand his counterattacks. Be wary and keep your guard up, but don't let fear paralyze you. After all, your target is vulnerable, and *YOUR* action might be what it takes to start wounding him!

The second one is BE FAIR. Don't do anything that is unethical or anything that would undermine your credibility. After all, you're trying to punish bad behavior, not engage in it yourself! Besides, you don't want to get into trouble you'd deserve for falsely defaming someone. And further, you don't want to destroy your value as a source of valid information on your target's wrongdoing. Stick to the truth; it will protect your credibility, your backside, and your soul.

The third one is DISH OUT WHAT'S FAIR. If your target is no more than a nuisance, get him pinched, not nuked. But if he's a major threat to people, hit him hard. Killers, sex offenders, and others who cruelly exploit others deserve no quarter, so give them none! Even God's own prophets verbally slashed bad kings and other powerful people when they had it coming. Sometimes these men of God killed the wrongdoers! Likewise, women of God like Joan of Arc showed the enemies of their people no quarter to punish them for their crimes.

Good luck in your efforts. Remember, it takes people like you to make the changes that will benefit us all.

END NOTES

1. Information for the Willie Horton/Mike Dukakis fiasco comes from Robert Bidinotto's article "Getting Away With Murder" in the July 1988 issue of *Reader's Digest*.
2. Information that served as the basis for the sarcastic remark about Kitty Dukakis' drinking problem comes from an article in the November 20, 1989 issue of *Newsweek*. The article noted she had been drinking to excess after her husband's trashing at the hands of the American people in the 1988 election. And it noted a year after his drubbing she was hospitalized for drinking rubbing alcohol.
3. Information on the Anita Hill/Clarence Thomas fiasco comes from articles in the October 21, 1991 and October 28, 1991 issues of *Time, Newsweek* and *U.S. News*, and from articles in the October 14, 1991 issues of the Cincinnati *Post* and Cincinnati *Enquirer*. One bit of information comes from an article in the Cincinnati *Post* on October 11, 1991.
4. Information on the false gang rape charges of Norma McCorvey (Jane Roe) comes from an article in the September 9, 1987 Cincinnati *Enquirer*.
5. Information on the con artist who sold fake documents on Joe McCarthy to prominent liberals comes from Victor Lasky's book *It Didn't Start With Watergate*.

Conclusion

Summary And Dedications

Now that you've gotten through a book that has angered you, entertained you, and informed you, you may feel a little bit guilty over using this book to punish bad people. Or you may feel like a malcontent because it's not a socially acceptable thing to make waves, and yet this book might have tempted you to do so.

My response is, "Can the guilt. America was founded by malcontents, liberated by malcontents, populated by malcontents, and improved by malcontents."

Muckraking malcontents who harness their anger to force change are as American as baseball, hot dogs, apple pie, corn whiskey, and the music of Elvis Presley, Ray Charles, Johnny Cash, and the *American Graffiti* soundtrack. Leo Durocher of Brooklyn Dodger fame put it another way: "Nice guys finish last." "Timid defensive thinking will get you killed every time." (Leo died in late 1991, and quite a bit of Americana died with him. Rest in peace, Leo, rest in peace.)

So do what you've got to do knowing you're living up to an American tradition. Remember, no one held a gun to bad people's heads to make them act like scum. And these enemies of the people already know about the dirt on them, because their misbehavior generated it. It's up to you to perform a public service and make the dirt on your targets public knowledge.

And even Christ Himself had something to say about being too kind to people who don't deserve it. He said, "Don't cast pearls to the swine."

Remember the advice I gave you in this book. In the very earliest chapter of this book, I stressed the mindset you need to have to search out the truth. Suspect everyone is no good until you can prove otherwise, but don't make up your mind until you've got all the facts. Know what is legal and illegal, be patient, develop street smarts, and harness your anger to be effective. Also, remember how to behave in the presence of government employees and others who maintain records you want; be polite, composed, tight-lipped, and fully protective of your rights.

The body of this book covered the "meat" of citizen research and investigation. I covered how to check people's criminal and lawsuit records, their property ownership, and their personal affairs.

Likewise, I showed you how to figure out who's running corporations and other groups, and what no-good they're up to. Further, I talked about tracking down how politicians exercise power, spend your money, and get other people to bankroll them.

I showed you how to check on people in the public service and safety area like educators, law-enforcement types, and health care professionals. I then told you how to use research and investigation skills to fight crimes of dishonesty and fight sex offenders. In each instance, I stressed what records were public, the best ways for you to gain access to them, and what to do with them once you got them. I also stressed observing people for evidence. The last part of this book covered the good stuff—how to use the sordid truth about bad people to make life miserable for them.

And I'll add two last instructions here. The first is DON'T LET THE PERFECT BE THE ENEMY OF THE GOOD. The second is DON'T LOSE YOUR SENSE OF HUMOR.

What do I mean by the first thought? Simply this: Don't get so hung up on every piddling detail of a research project that you never get off the ground; or if you do get underway, don't miss deadlines and waste effort. You can't get everything letter-perfect, so just concentrate on getting the important things taken care of first, and get the rest later. Do what you can; it's better than doing nothing.

And on the second thought, loosen up every now and then; it will improve your attitude, and boost the morale of those around you. Don't let lack of immediate results sap you of your drive. Sooner or later, you will break through against your targets; as Joe Louis used to say, "They can run, but they can't hide." So laugh, take a little time for yourself, and share problems and good humor with your friends and loved ones. It will keep you fresh for the digging that lies ahead.

You may think because of the sarcastic tone of this book that I have it in for this nation and its people. I don't; I only hate those who abuse the freedoms they enjoy in our nation to victimize other people. And sadly, many of these scum happen to be public officials, as well as the rich and powerful. They abuse the system of democracy that the people of this nation have paid for with their blood and their labor.

America isn't a people; it's an ideology. It's our beliefs and our support of our way of life that makes us a nation of many peoples but one goal: the goal of free people building a free nation where they can live free and worship free, where they can work for themselves, and work for the common good. I hope we all aspire to America at its best—a land whose people's senses of fairness, hard work, neighborliness, and commitment reflect their belief in one God who demands moral conduct from His children. When I see our ideals attacked and our people abused by scum unethically seeking money or power, my blood boils.

Much of this book is based on my own experiences, which made the book easy to write, but also sad and bad in many ways. A lot of things I remember were very depressing to witness or find out about, and I felt bad in recalling them. Other incidents still make me angry even now. These kinds of heart-rending and blood-boiling incidents continue to happen all over the country today. They could be happening in your community right now. Only the names and the details will be different.

I hope by sharing my anger and my methods with you in this book, you will internalize my punish-the-bad message and start punishing. The realist in me knows that normally, only a few people act, but the optimist in me hopes more of you will get involved to force ethical change in our country. Get away from the TV and other worthless distractions. Take control of your future and the future of your kids away from those who want to exploit all of you for their own purposes.

Just before I completed the rough draft of this book, Boris Yeltsin had led the men of Russia to protect their loved ones' rights and hopes for the future from Communist scum. Yeltsin, in an act of raw courage, leapt onto a tank and stared down the soldiers of the coup plotters that day in August 1991. Yeltsin's act rallied the men to come to the aid of the people, stop the coup, and give him the authority he needed to kill the Soviet Communist Party soon afterward. I hope Yeltsin is for real...and I hope he turns the respect he commands into a blueprint for a Russia whose leaders and people believe in freedom, fairness, and morality. Russia and the other republics are going through some hard times as this book goes to print, and Yeltsin might, God forbid, fail to deliver the people lasting democracy. But even if he does fail, no one can deny that he and the men who stood with him were real heroes who showed moral and physical courage. They were prepared to die to protect their loved ones and the Russian people.

People have a need for heroes to inspire them to do great things. There is always a need for brave men who treat people right so little kids can look up to them, teens can learn from them, and women can appreciate and respect them. There is always a need for good women who better society with their talents and hold the menfolk and kids to acceptable standards of behavior.

It's good to have examples of heroic manhood like Abraham Lincoln, Teddy Roosevelt, Martin Luther King, Al Smith, Chief Joseph, and Benito Juarez as role models for boys and men. Likewise, it's good to have examples of heroic womanhood like Joan of Arc, Harriet Tubman, Mania Sklodowska (better known as Madame Curie), Amelia Earhart, Clara Barton, and Mother Theresa to show women and girls what they can achieve.

Even in sports, some are real heroes instead of just gifted athletes. I point to Jackie Robinson, who broke baseball's color line, doggedly carried the cross of discrimination with dignity, and played the game with such a vengeance that it seemed as if he thought his efforts would somehow punish racists. I point to Lou Gehrig, who handled his crippling disease, the loss of his career, and his impending death with true grit so touching that "The Pride of The Yankees" made 50,000 crazy New Yorkers cry that fateful day in 1939 and has made countless thousands cloud up ever since.

I point to Roberto Clemente, who—while others partied on New Year's Eve 1972—died in a plane crash while on an errand of mercy flying supplies to disaster victims. And I point to Knute Rockne and the Notre Dame Fighting Irish, the team whose players crushed other kids from more "socially acceptable" backgrounds on nearly every Saturday. These players, with their aggressively unpronounceable ethnic names, their hard-driving, charismatic immigrant coach, and their adrenalin-jolting fight song, helped many ethnic Americans stop feeling inferior over where they or their people came from.

Starting somewhere in the 1960s, the screwball intellectuals, whiners, wanna-bes and other losers in this country have conspired to attack the heroes because of their own inadequacies. The Establishment's respectability freaks helped them with their own bungling on the Bay of Pigs, Vietnam, Watergate, the Iran hostage crisis, the Iran-Contra fiasco, and many, many other situations. Many thought the losers would succeed in wearing down the American people's love of country and its heroes, because their kind dominate college campuses, the media, the entertainment industry, Congress, and other areas of American opinion shaping.

American victory in Operation Desert Storm changed all that. Our troops' efforts and successes started making Americans feel good about the country once again. And they were so starved for heroes in the tough competent mold that they gave wild acclaim to Norman Schwartzkopf, a career officer who simply did his job in having his troops execute the draftees of a tyrant. America needs heroes, and once again, our people aren't ashamed to show it.

In order to muckrake, punish bad people, and maybe improve things in your community and your country, you don't have to be a hero, just someone like General Schwartzkopf who competently does what needs doing. Your ancestors—whose lives were infinitely more difficult than yours—survived the hardships and made changes. So can you.

But even if people don't need to be heroes to do the right thing, they still need encouragement. The child in the school recital, the teen in the garage band, the athlete in the arena, the man or woman taking on harder duties at work, the politician or bureaucrat preparing to take an unpopular stand, and the soldier going into battle will always do better with encouragement.

This reminds me of a story I heard about Shirley Temple. It was the last year or so of World War II, and the cute little child star was blossoming into an attractive young lady. Shirley was doing her bit for the war effort, making appearances and visiting the wounded in hospitals.

One day, as Shirley was visiting men in a hospital ward, a young GI asked her to be present when the doctors were to amputate one of his limbs. After the innocent young woman recovered from her shock and queasiness, she asked the young man why he wanted her to witness such a terrible surgery. He responded simply, "I'm afraid right now. If you are there, I'll have a reason to be brave."

Need I say that the young GI touched Shirley's heart to its innermost recesses? She was there with him during the awful surgery, and he WAS brave!

If you're working on a project with others, encourage each other, especially your point people, so they (and you) don't use up emotional reserves and burn out. Give each other a reason to be brave.

And now come the dedications. And there are several. So bear with me as I dedicate this book to the following folks:

To my Dad, a combat veteran of World War II, whose common-sense outlook brings a lot of complex problems into focus. Dad says, "The fruits, nuts, and flakes in this country will get too bold and try to do more stupid things too quickly. This will anger most people bad enough to thrash them good and proper." Dad in his prime was a muscular stud who was well-equipped to protect Mom and us kids, work like a one-man gang, lead or at least impose his will on others, and shoulder his responsibilities. After Dad turned 60, he could still work as a construction boss on a public housing project; he still has what it takes to command the respect of the construction workers and harass the hoodlums who try to prey on the project's residents.

To my Mom, who inspired the term "tough love" as it applies to child rearing. She was easily the toughest mother in our neighborhood. She also served as a yard mother at my Catholic school; she would break up any fight I was winning, but she'd let any fight I was losing go to the bitter end. When I asked Mom about her double standard (I was a precocious little tyke), she replied, "Do you want the other kids to call you a sissy because your MOMMY had to save you?" On the flip side, Mom is a woman of great charity. She has spent her adult life helping the young, and aiding disaster victims, inner-city kids, unwed mothers, and many other needy people. Mom and Dad raised us kids with plenty of discipline, but also with plenty of humor and love.

To my brothers and sister, who all urged me to write this book. Their faith in my abilities and their support for my efforts has lifted me over a number of obstacles. And to my other sister who died many years ago. I hope she is watching with approval from the gates of Heaven.

To family members, friends, and associates who read and critiqued my manuscript. They caught errors and made suggestions that helped make this a better book. I DON'T know it all, and they made me painfully aware of this. In my listing (which reads like a Dick Tracy cast because most of these people are in sensitive positions and need aliases for honorable mention here), I include Elaine Spillane, "Gravedigger" Sexton, "Naughty" Marian Ireland, Jimmy "The Wire" Callender, Conan Higdon, Cathy "Tough Cookie" Jersey, Karen "Kindheart" Sabina, and Darrell the Baptist.

To those who sent me articles and other documents for this book, especially Carol Nova and "Murf the Surf." They helped make this book more interesting and hard-hitting.

To Lisa Lydic and Troy Dobosiewicz, my Slavic editors. These talented young writers checked my manuscript to make sure the book would be factual and readable. They corrected my mistakes. And they made a number of suggestions that would have made the book less vicious and more grammatical...but I ignored most of them.

To Eli and José Flores, my Hispanic publishers. These men had the guts and the vision to see the merits of this book and sink money into publishing it. I hope this book brings their publishing house more money and notoriety. Also, thanks to the folks at J. Flores Publications for turning my manuscript into a finished product.

To Shirley Cleaver, the mother of Maria Barker Tanner. I interviewed Shirley after her son-in-law beheaded her daughter in 1990 and beat criminal charges. She was VERY frightened and VERY hurt, but still very brave. She cursed Raymond Tanner as he came toward her in court, then vowed publicly to get the insanity law in Ohio changed to keep killers like him from getting away with murder. Shirley has done legal research, appeared on talk shows, and contacted public officials in an effort to get the law changed so she can keep her vow to her daughter.

To Kim Bergalis, an innocent victim of the deviates who spread AIDS and the jerks who cover for them. Like a modern-day Joan of Arc, Kim fought against the scum in the medical and political establishment who put their bankrolls and their agendas ahead of the good of the people. Like the Maid of Orleans, Kim in 1991 died a martyr's death. At least she will be able to face her Maker and say she died with her boots on.

To all the fighting heroes of America, from the famous to the unknown. We all owe these men a debt of gratitude for the blood sacrifices they made at Bunker Hill, New Orleans, Gettysburg, Iwo Jima, Normandy, and a thousand other battlefields too numerous to name here. Recall blacks who fought for our freedom in our wars even when they were denied full citizenship. Recall the Irish, the Hispanics, the ethnic Europeans, and the Asians fought against our nation's enemies while having to overcome prejudice concerning their religions, their skin color, the sounds of their last names, their brogues and accents, and questions about their patriotism.

Recall the Johnny Rebs and the Indian braves who may have lost their causes in fighting against the Billy Yanks, but never lost their honor. Recall the average white guys with no ethnic or racial thing to deal with, but who fought for the country because they knew it was the right thing to do. And especially recall the guys whose names are on the Vietnam "Wall" ...men who died in vain, and men who may still exist in wretched captivity. And let's not forget the widows, the orphans, and the sweethearts whom all our fighting men left behind...women and children who would grieve for the rest of their lives. We have it too good in this land. Are we really worthy of the sacrifices the heroes have made for us?

And to you, the people of the United States. Despite the growing selfishness of too many of us, we are still the nation with the biggest heart in the world. And despite the poor job many of our educators are doing, we the people still have more know-how and common sense than we're given credit for. Governor Al Smith, one of my heroes, used to say, "When I have a problem as a politician, when there's something I don't understand, I always give it back to the people. Their collective judgment is better than the collective judgment of the legislature or the governor."

As a reporter, I tried to give my readers the plain truth in down-to-earth and entertaining prose so their hearts and minds could do the rest. This book has the same purpose. I hope you found the book informative and fun to read. And I hope the book made you angry enough to get involved in making the changes our nation needs. NEVER APOLOGIZE FOR MORAL BEHAVIOR, NEVER APOLOGIZE FOR DEFENDING YOUR LOVED ONES AND YOUR-SELVES, AND NEVER APOLOGIZE FOR EX-POSING EVIL. May God bless you all, and may all the important news in your life from this day forward be GOOD news!

—KEVIN SHERLOCK

Index

Bibliography

How To Investigate Your Friends and Enemies by Louis Rose

The Muckraker's Manual by M. Harry

Instant Information by Joel Makower and Alan Green

The National Directory of Addresses and Telephone Numbers

Consumer Revenge by Chris Gilson, Linda Cawley and Rick Schmidt

Street Law by Edward McMahon, Lee Arbetman and Edward O'Brien

The Investigator's Handbook by Arthur Liebers and Capt Carl Vollmer

Death at Chappaquiddick by Richard and Thomas Tedrow

Feeding the Beast by Marilyn Thompson

Seeds of Treason by Ralph De Toledano

The Sting Man by Robert Greene

Greylord: Justice Chicago Style by James Tuohy and Robert Warden

It Didn't Start With Watergate by Victor Lasky

Helter Skelter by Vincent Bugliosi and Curtis Gentry

Two of a Kind by Darcy O'Brien

Challenger: The Final Voyage by Richard Lewis

The Search for Amerlia Earhart by Fred Goerner

Criminology by Robert Bonn

Crime and Its Victims by Daniel Van Ness

What Cops Know by Connie Fletcher

The Child Abuse Industry by Mary Pride

The Case Against Pornography by Donald Wildmon

Diseasing of America by Stanton Peele

War on Waste by J. Peter Grace

Street Smart by Curtis Sliwa and Murray Schwartz

I'm Mad As Hell by Howard Jarvis

Joan of Arc by Mark Twain

About The Author

People who know Kevin Sherlock say he was meant to write a book like *How To Be Your Own Detective*. For Sherlock, a "digger" and "agitator" by blood, has spent more than a decade doing investigation and research work.

As an Army officer, Sherlock helped investigate suspects on charges ranging from felony assault to drug dealing to black marketeering to attempted rape. He helped get criminals punished and wrongfully-accused soldiers cleared. He also investigated civilians for discrimination against minority-group soldiers.

As a newspaper reporter, Sherlock uncovered and wrote on many incidents of politician finagling, corporate wrongdoing, child exploitation, court system breakdown, school system failure, and government waste and stupidity. Readers who liked him wrote in and compared him to the great muckrakers; officials who didn't like him called his bosses and compared him to the Inquisition. (Sherlock, a Catholic, felt complimented.)

As an independent investigator and researcher, Sherlock has found and documented police and prosecutor shortcomings, social worker and judge neglect of duty involving crimes against children, large-scale doctor malpractice involving treatment of women, government mistreatment of immigrants, cases of wrongful death, and incidents of white-collar misconduct.

Sherlock is the descendant of Irish and Slavic immigrants; many of his forebears fought for freedom in their homelands. Some became labor leaders or political leaders in America. One of his grandfathers was a Chicago police detective. One of his grandmothers was savvy enough to help locate and rescue a stolen child.

Sherlock, who operates a technical publishing and research business, says, "I wrote this book to make money, of course. But more importantly, I wrote it to help the average person find out things about government, corporations, and individuals. Short of the intervention of God, an informed public is our best defense against abuse."